Report writing
for business

Report writing for business

Raymond V. Lesikar, Ph.D.

Professor and Head
Department of Management
North Texas State University

Sixth Edition 1981

RICHARD D. IRWIN, INC.
Homewood, Illinois   60430

Irwin-Dorsey Limited
Georgetown, Ontario   L7G 4B3

ISBN 0-256-02479-0

Library of Congress Catalog Card No. 80-84708

Printed in the United States of America

1 2 3 4 5 6 7 8 9 0 MP 8 7 6 5 4 3 2 1

Preface

Because of the success of the preceding editions, I did little to change the general pattern and content of this sixth edition. Most significant of the changes I made was the addition of a second introductory chapter (Chapter 2). The plan of Chapter 2 is to build a base for the report writing principles and techniques presented in following chapters. Specifically, Chapter 2 shows how reports are written, how they fit into the communication needs of business, and why current techniques developed. Because of this new content, I found it necessary to shift some of the information in the writing chapters. As you will see, the Gunning Fog Index is now Appendix F.

In addition to these organization changes, I revised wherever I could. As with the preceding editions, I worked very hard to remove all traces of sexist bias in the writing. I truly hope these efforts were successful. I wrote new report problems —more than ever before. I revised many of the illustrations. And wherever necessary, I updated content. I sincerely feel that my efforts have produced an improved book.

Just as did the earlier editions, this sixth edition has the primary goal of preparing students to write the reports they must write in business. That this goal is essential in preparing one for business was logical speculation at the time the first edition appeared. With the appearance of following editions, the necessity of this goal became more apparent. Today as we view the ever-increasing needs for communication in our rapidly developing technological world of business, the need for report writing proficiency is unmistakably clear. Without question, today's business students must learn to write reports if they are to meet the needs of today's business world. I hope this book will help them to achieve this goal.

As preferred by most report writing teachers, the text places major emphasis on organizing and writing reports. In addition to covering this traditional material, it strives to meet the demands of the forthcoming research-minded business world by placing adequate stress on the research methodology which precedes report preparation. And it strives to meet the ever-increasing demand for higher educational standards by challenging the student with realistic, mind-stimulating problems.

The text fully recognizes the fact that reports differ widely by organization and company. To overcome this problem, it approaches the subject of report preparation from a general viewpoint. It follows the assumption that although reports may differ, the principles of their construction (writing, organizing, and such) are universal. Thus, the general teachings of the book may be adapted easily to the specific report requirements of any organization. At the same time, however, the text contains sufficient specific instruction to enable one to construct the conventional reports.

In writing this sixth edition, I received valuable inputs from adopters of the preceding editions. I was especially helped by those who reviewed the last edition: Robert S. Rudolph, University of Toledo; Thomas A. Burdick, California State Polytechnic University; Ross F. Figgins, California State Polytechnic University; and H. Lon Addams, Northern Illinois University. I can report that their work was especially well done. As one would expect, however, they did not agree on all matters. Thus I could implement only some of their suggestions. Even so, virtually all of the organization and content improvements in this edition must be credited to them.

In addition to the reviewers, I am indebted to Mary Ann Heinricks, University of Toledo. The improved decimal outline system she suggested made sense; so I adopted it. Then there are·the many reviewers from past years whose contributions continue to appear in the book. Add to this group the friends and colleagues who over the years have given advice and suggestion. For all the contributions made by all these people, I am truly grateful.

And last, but far from least, I acknowledge the contributions of my dear wife. Without her patience, love, and understanding, this book would not exist.

Raymond V. Lesikar

Contents

The nature of oral reports: *A definition of oral reports. Differences between oral and written reports.* General aspects of oral reporting: *Planning the oral report. Consideration of personal aspects. Audience analysis.* Presentation of the oral report: *Language style and the conversational mode. Bodily actions. Use of voice.* Use of visual aids: *Proper use of design. Forms of visual aids to consider. Techniques in using visuals.*

The need for correctness. Standards for clarity through punctuation. Standards for correctness in grammar. Standards for the use of numbers. Other common errors.

1

Orientation to business reports

As the business student begins the study of a business subject, two questions logically come to mind: What is it I am about to study? How will it benefit me in my career? It is appropriate to answer these questions as a first step in the study of business report writing.

THE WHAT AND WHY OF REPORT WRITING

What are reports?

On first thought the answer to the question of what is report writing appears to be elementary. Certainly reports are commonplace in the 20th-century business world. Virtually all organizations use them—businesses, government agencies, civic groups. And most use them extensively. In fact, it is unlikely that any modern-day organization of size could function without using reports. But in spite of the fact that reports are so commonplace there is disagreement in defining them.

Definitions in current use range from one extreme to the other. By the broadest definition, reports are all presentations of information ranging from the extremely formal to the highly informal. Narrower definitions limit reports to the more formalized presentations of information. For the student of business reports, a definition approaching the narrower ones is best. Such a definition is the following: A business report is an orderly and objective communication of factual information which serves some business purpose.

Careful inspection of this definition reveals the identifying characteristics of the business report. As an *orderly* communication, a report is given some care in preparation. And care in preparation distinguishes a report from the casual, routine exchanges of information that continually occur in business. This is not to say that all reports are carefully prepared, but it does mean that at least something above minimum care is given in their preparation. Everyday, oral exchanges of information, for example, do not classify as reports. Nor do the most casual handwritten notes.

1

The *objective* quality of a report is its unbiased approach to the facts presented. The report seeks truth, regardless of its consequences. Because few people can be thoroughly objective, perhaps report writers seldom achieve true objectivity. Nevertheless, they must work for it. Certainly, some papers disguised as reports are heavily persuasive, but they represent a specialized form of administrative writing. They are not true reports.

The word *communication* is broad by definition, concerning all ways of transmitting meaning (speaking, writing, drawing, gesturing, and such). For all practical purposes, however, business reports are either written or oral. And for reasons that will be given shortly, in today's complex business operations the more significant reports are written.

The basic ingredient of the report is *factual* information—events, records, and the various forms of data that are communicated in the conduct of business. In no way is the content fictional. Nor is there major stress on opinions, except in those rare cases when in the absence of facts authoritative opinions are the best information available. This statement does not mean that interpretations, recommendations, and conclusions (which may border on opinions) may not be included. They can and should be a part of most reports. But it does mean that they should be either supported by fact or clearly labeled as opinion. As far as possible, the emphasis should be on fact.

Not all reports are business reports. Research scientists, medical doctors, ministers, students, and many others write reports. Thus, the need for the final phrase of the definition is obvious. To be classified as a business report, a report must *serve* some *business purpose*.

This purpose may be to solve a problem: Should X Company diversify its line? How can Y Company increase sales in the Northeast district? How can Z Company profitably use an electronic computer? The purpose may be to present information needed in the conduct of business: a weekly report of a salesperson's activities, a summary of the day's production, an explanation of expenditures on a particular project, a description of the condition of a piece of equipment. In general, the purpose could concern the thousand and one areas of information a business needs in its operation.

Even though this definition of a business report is specific enough to be meaningful, it is broad enough to take into account the variations to be found in reports. For example, some reports do nothing more than present facts. Others go a step further by including interpretations. Still others proceed to conclusions and recommendations. There are reports formally dressed both in writing style and in physical appearance. And there are reports that evidence a high degree of informality. The definition given permits all these variations.

Why study business report writing?

The question, "Why study business report writing?" may be answered from two standpoints. One is the standpoint of the companies for which the student will work some day. The other is the personal standpoint of the student. Convincing argument supports both positions.

From a business standpoint.   In answering the question from the organization's position, one needs only to note the communication that is required in business. It is well known that today's complex, technological business organizations literally feed on information. In every phase of business work, people send and receive information. For example, salespeople send in orders and weekly summaries of their activities; and they receive instructions and sales information from the home office. Production supervisors receive work orders; and they submit summaries of their production. Research specialists receive problems; later they communicate their findings to those who need the information. It is like this in every niche of the organization. Everywhere workers are receiving and sending information in the conduct of their work.

This information flow involves many forms of communication. Obviously oral communication makes up a large part of it. In addition, there are all the various types of forms and records that are kept and exchanged. There are the storage and retrieval facilities that electronic computers now provide. And, of course, there are the various forms of written communication. Among the written forms of business communication, reports play a very major role.

That reports are vital in today's business operations is hardly a debatable point. Universally business executives recognize the importance of reports. Executives know that they must have information in order to make decisions; and they know that they get much of their information from reports. They know how important it is that the reports they receive be orderly and clear, for they need to get the information quickly and easily. The pressures for their time in business make quick and easy communication necessary. These general comments about the importance of reports, however, may not be convincing to traditionally wary students. They want, and have a right to expect, more concrete data. Fortunately such data are not hard to find.

The most convincing evidence of the importance of writing for business comes from research conducted over the past 30 years at a number of American universities. Originating at such prestigious schools as Michigan State University, Ohio University, the University of Texas, the University of Washington, the University of California at Los Angeles, Louisiana State University, and Florida State University, this research consists of surveys to determine the business subjects considered most important by business people. Without exception, these studies found business writing, especially report writing, at or near the top. A more current study conducted by the American Assembly of Collegiate Schools of Business (AACSB) supports this conclusion. These words from the AACSB report express the conclusion of this study: "The most significant item which the respondents list under the open-ended question is Communication. The total time units it received is . . . eight times more than the next most frequently mentioned item. . . ."[1] These respondents clearly placed major emphasis on written communication—especially reports, memos, and letters.

It is a sad commentary on our educational system that in spite of the clear

---

[1] "Accreditation Research Project, Report on Phase I," *AACSB Bulletin,* vol. 15, no. 2 (Winter 1980), p. 21.

evidence of the importance of writing, little has been done to emphasize it. In fact, a deemphasis appears to have occurred. Supporting this observation are the SAT (Student Aptitude Test) scores over recent years. The scores have declined steadily. In 1963 the national average on the verbal portion of the test was 478 (out of a possible 800). The 1980 average was 424.

Our colleges also have failed to heed the evidence. A 1979 study by Andrews and Koester found that 48 percent of the executives in CPA firms considered recent accounting graduates to be "ineffective" or "highly ineffective" in written communication.[2] Perhaps explaining this finding are these words from the AACSB study cited previously: "The heavy emphasis which respondents give to Communication indicates that this subject might not be receiving the attention some feel it deserves in the required curriculum."[3]

From a personal point of view. Convincing as the foregoing facts tend to be, it is from the personal advantage standpoint that the strongest argument for the study of business writing can be made. That is, if the individual student can be shown how one, personally, stands to profit through improving writing ability, the argument is won.

Proof of personal gain is easily made from a logical interpretation of fact. The fact is that writing is important to business. Thus, those employees with writing skills are apt to be rewarded personally. This conclusion, however, is more convincing when made through another line of reasoning.

This reasoning also begins with a simple statement of fact: The promotions employees receive are determined largely by the impressions they make on their superiors. They impress their superiors in many ways, but mainly by their personal characteristics, appearance, job performance, and intellectual capacity for work. It is in this last-named area, intellectual capacity for work, that the writing skills come in.

Satisfactory performance of the work assigned usually is enough to communicate intellectual capacity for promotions to rank-and-file positions. For promotions to high-level assignments, however, employees must impress their superiors with their intellectual capacity for these assignments. Such impressions are made largely through the employee's ability to communicate to others. And in business, this communicating often must be done in writing. Thus, the ability to write good reports and other business papers is a requisite for business advancement. Employees without this ability are likely to be doomed to mediocre roles in business. This is true even if the employees happen to be capable intellectually in their fields, for all are judged mainly by the intellectual capacities they are able to communicate. What they cannot communicate is known only to them. The old adage, "Who is to say what the deaf-mute knows?" could be appropriately adapted to this situation.

---

[2] Douglas Andrews and Robert J. Koester, "Communication Difficulties as Perceived by the Accounting Profession and Professors of Accounting," *Proceedings of the 1978 Southwest ABCA Spring Conference*, p. 57.

[3] "Accreditation Research Project," p. 21.

Proof of the value of writing in business could go on and on, for there is no shortage of supporting evidence. To the student, however, the foregoing presentation of fact and reason should be sufficiently convincing. Certainly there can be no denial that good writing is needed in business. Nor should there be doubt that writing skills can lead to personal gain. Possibly these observations will serve as incentives as the student progresses through the chapters that follow.

A REVIEW OF REPORT CLASSIFICATION

Since the first organized efforts to study the subject, scholars of report writing have advanced many classifications of reports. Each of these classification plans proposes to divide all reports written into distinct categories. A review of these classifications provides an appropriate introduction to the study of report writing. Such a review is appropriate for two main reasons.

First, discussion of the ways of classifying reports illustrates the variation in approaches to the subject. Reports are far from standardized. With tens of thousands of companies writing them and unknown scores of authorities determining their construction, they could not be otherwise. A knowledge of report classification gives some insight into this complex picture.

A second benefit derived from reviewing report classification is that the various classification terms are used in discussing report writing. As with most subjects, report writing has its own specialized terms—the technical language of the field, so to speak. Logically students of report writing should be acquainted with the vernacular of their subject. The terms used in classifying reports comprise much of this vernacular.

Subject matter as a basis for classification

Possibly the simplest of all report classifications used is one by subject matter. Obviously all reports concern some subject. It is equally obvious that reports can be classified on the basis of some logical grouping of subjects.

The possibilities of grouping by subjects are almost limitless, being bound only by the infinite differences among report topics. Subject classifications, therefore, could be based on minute differences in content, or they could follow broader and more general lines. For example, in the field of accounting, distinctions in subject matter could provide classifications such as *cost, audit, tax,* and *finance.* But such divisions generally are not practical. A more practical and more widely used subject classification is one that follows broader lines—for example, one based on broad subject fields such as *accounting, management, economics, finance, engineering,* and *marketing.*

Classification by time interval

One often-used means of classifying reports is by the frequency of their occurrence. Some reports are written regularly—daily, weekly, monthly, or annually.

These may be referred to as *periodic* reports. Examples of this type are the routine weekly and monthly reports made by salespeople, the periodic summaries of progress in any large-scale operation, and the corporation's typical annual report of operations. Completing this classification are the *special* reports—reports prepared for a special assignment. By special assignment is meant an assignment that is not likely to be repeated with any degree of regularity.

Functional classification of reports

Possibly the most popular classification in use is that based on the function of reports. By this plan, reports are classified by what they do. On this functional basis, it is practical to classify reports into three groups—*informational, examination,* and *analytical.*[4]

As the term implies, the *informational* report is a presentation of facts on the subject. It contains only the facts. It has no analyses and no conclusions.

The *examination* report carries the problem one step further than does the informational report. In the examination report, in addition to presenting the facts about the problem, the writer analyzes and interprets the data. But the writer's assistance stops here. There is no effort to follow the analysis to the point of concluding or of recommending. Any possible conclusion or recommendation to be derived from the information must be made by the reader, but doubtless the reader will be guided in these efforts by the writer's presentation of fact.

Like the examination report, the *analytical* report presents and analyzes data. But it goes a step further. It also draws conclusions from the data. And when the problem warrants, it may even make recommendations. It is the most complete of all reports, covering all phases of a particular problem. It presents a problem in its entirety. It begins with an orientation and description of the problem; it presents the information gathered; and it analyzes and examines the information. And from these analyses and examinations, it derives a solution or conclusion to the problem. Typically an analytical report is written by one with good knowledge of the subject matter—one whose analyses are respected. These analyses are likely to form significant inputs in the decision-making process of the executives who read them.

Formality as a division criterion

Still another area of variation that leads to classification is the formality of the report. It is easy to see that the same degree of formality is not required in all report situations. A study addressed to an august body such as the U.S. Senate logically would be strictly formal in its makeup. On the other hand, a report written by one employee for the use of another employee of equal rank might be extremely informal. The differences between these two reports is sufficient to serve as a basis for classification. Two groups are commonly represented in this

---

[4] Sometimes referred to as problem-solving reports.

classification—*formal* and *informal*. By this classification, the term *formal* applies to all those reports that are dressed up physically and are appropriately worded to fit the requirements of a formal occasion. The term *informal* includes all reports with the makeup and wording requirements of an informal occasion. Obviously there is a hazy and indefinite dividing line between the two types.

Division of reports by physical factors

The physical makeup of reports provides a simple and logical basis for grouping. It may be noted, however, that physical makeup is largely influenced by the formality of the situation and the length of the report. These two factors should be kept in mind as the following classification is reviewed.

At the bottom of the formality and length scale is the *memorandum* report. Generally it concerns a routine matter that must be transmitted within an organization. In the typical business situation, memorandum reports are written on specially prepared forms. Most common of these forms is one that begins with the headings "To; From; Subject;" and has space provided below for informal presentation of the subject. Other variations resemble questionnaires, providing space for routine presentation of specific information.

Short topics with some need for formal or semiformal presentation are frequently submitted in the form of a *letter* report. From all outward appearances, they are letters, with all the physical properties of a typical business letter. They are classified as reports principally because of the nature of their content.

Topics that are of medium or moderate length and have no great need for formal presentation usually are submitted in a form classified as a *short* report. Although there is no one set makeup of the short report, usually it is one that is minus much of the prefatory pages (contents pages, epitome, title fly, and such) associated with more formal works.

At the top of this classification scale in formality and length is the *long* report. Long reports, as the term implies, concern presentations of relatively large problems. As a rule, such topics have some need for formal presentation. The typical long report is well supplemented with prefatory parts. Its contents are carefully organized and marked with captions. It may even require such supplementary parts as an appendix, bibliography, or index.

Writer–reader relationship as a basis for grouping

Classification arrangements have also been constructed on the basis of the relation between reader and writer. Although there is wide variation in the terms used in this division, possibly the most common are *administrative*,[5] *professional,* and *independent*.[6] *Administrative* reports are those reports officially written within a business organization to facilitate operations. *Professional* reports are

---

[5] Administrative reports are also known as *internal* reports.

[6] Professional and independent reports are sometimes referred to as *external* reports.

submitted to an organization by outside specialists. For example, an outside management consultant may be called in to study a particular problem of a company. The consultant's findings, when presented in written form, would constitute a professional report. *Independent* reports are written for no particular group or person. Frequently nonprofit research organizations publish such reports as a service to the public.

Classifications by status of authorship

A commonly used classification is one that distinguishes reports by the employment status of their authors. Reports written by those engaged in private business are logically referred to as *private* reports. Reports that originate through employees of public institutions (government groups, professional societies, colleges, and such) are known as *public* reports. Completing this classification is the *independent* report—one written by an individual without the authorization of any public or private group. For example, research scholars working on their own authority would present the findings in an independent report.

Miscellaneous report types

In addition to the terms used in the preceding classifications, scholars use numerous other terms to describe specific report types. Many in this group are known only within the narrow confines of a particular field, industry, or business. A few in this group, however, are so widely used as to warrant special review.

The *progress* report is one of the best-known types used in industry. Actually it is strictly an informational type of report. The information it presents is limited to the progress of some undertaking such as the construction of a bridge, an advertising campaign, or the operation of production machinery.

In recent years the term *justification* report has become popular. It is a type of report that presents a decision to a particular problem—usually a short one. Its text contains a logical review of the points that affect the decision. This review, of course, justifies the author's decision.

Frequently in report-writing discussion there is reference to the *recommendation* report. A recommendation report is nothing more than a variety of the analytical report referred to previously. Specifically it is an analytical report that concludes with a recommendation. Another name for this type is the *improvement* report, although some authorities draw minor distinctions between the two terms.

The role of classification in studying reports

As noted previously, the conventional classifications are useful in describing reports. And they show something of the wide variations that exist in approaches to the subject. It would not be logical, however, to study reports by types, as perhaps these classifications suggest.

In truth, there is little difference in the basic principles used in any good report.

With small exceptions, the basic writing principles, the rules of logical organization, techniques of writing style and tone, and so on remain the same in all reports. Thus, any plan to study the subject by report types would be plagued with needless repetition. A more workable approach to the subject is one that treats all reports as being integrally related. Such an approach is followed in this book.

QUESTIONS

1. Critically review the definition of reports given in the text. Bring out the key words in this definition, and discuss their significance in the study of report writing.
2. Does a person who conducts a one-person business need to know how to write a report for business purposes? A ten-person business? Fifty? One hundred?
3. Why is it important to you to be able to write good reports?
4. How do you interpret the survey findings presented in this chapter?
5. Assume that you have in your hands the following reports. Classify them on the basis of each of the classification schemes discussed in this chapter.
   a. An independent public accountant performs an annual audit of your business. A 20-page report is submitted on the results of the examination.
   b. Salespeople out on the road submit a weekly report of their activities to the sales manager. These reports are submitted on printed forms which provide for all the information required (number of calls, number of sales, travel mileage, and so on).
   c. The controller of a corporation prepares a yearly review of activities (production, marketing, finance, and such) for the stockholders, employees, and the public at large.
6. Inspect the reports in Appendix D and classify them by each of the classification schemes discussed in the chapter.
7. Why should the report student be concerned with report classification?

2

Development of report-writing methods

The structure and techniques of report writing presented in the chapters ahead are the products of years of development. From the earliest days of report writing, business people have worked to develop the most practical and effective ways of communicating through reports. Their efforts have been influenced by two general needs. One is the information needs of business. The other is the needs of the communication process. Understanding these needs and how they have influenced report-writing methods is basic to a study of the subject.

INFORMATION NEEDS OF BUSINESS

As we noted in Chapter 1, businesses need information in order to function. Every worker, every supervisor, every staff employee must have information in doing his or her job. In fact, there simply could be no organized productive effort without information.

At the lower levels, the need for information is relatively light. Assembly-line workers, for example, may require little more information than their work assignments. The same is true for janitors, gardeners, cooks, and others with routine assignments.

On the other hand, more involved work assignments are likely to require more information. Especially is this so for those assignments with administrative duties. Take, for example, the job of supervisor of a production department. The department's major goal, of course, is to produce—to make things. The supervisor's job is to guide the department toward this goal.

In guiding the department toward its goal, the supervisor must have a wide assortment of information. Of major importance is information on production needs—primarily production schedules, quotas, and the like. Also vital is information which tells of the progress of production—information such as data on output and quality of production. In addition, the supervisor needs information on the condition of the production equipment and of the workplace. He or she also needs information on the quality of the work done by each worker and of inventories of raw materials and supplies. From other departments the supervisor needs production and planning information in order to coordinate the department's efforts with the efforts of the total business. Also, the supervisor is likely to need all sorts of other information—information on the competition, new production techniques, new equipment, industry happenings, to name a few. We could continue the list indefinitely. The fact is plain and simple: this person needs a lot of information in order to do the job.

We could describe the information needs of other workers and supervisors; and the effect would be the same. The obvious conclusion is that all members of all business organizations need information in order to do their jobs. There is no question about it. The need for information in business is great.

A jungle of information

Because a business must have information if it is to function, supplying information is a major part of business activity. Certainly, much time is devoted to the task, and typically great quantities of information are the result. In fact, all too often so much information is supplied that a jungle of information exists. The situation resembles a jungle because the information supplied is dense and disorganized. Some of the information, of course, is precisely what is needed. But much of it is not needed; and some that is needed is not available. As a result often business people must search through this jungle for what they need. And as we know, the typically heavy work load of business people leaves little time for searching.

Effects on report writing

Perhaps it is evident that business has needs for information. But what is the relationship of these needs to report writing? More precisely, how have the needs affected the development of report writing? Two answers are apparent. First, writers have responded to the need to clear the jungle of information often found in business. As a result, modern-day report-writing instruction stresses including in the report only the information needed and leaving out information not needed. It stresses organizing the information for logic as well as for quick and easy understanding. For example, it stresses placing major facts, analyses, and conclusions in positions of emphasis. It stresses using summaries at places which help readers to collect their thoughts. Current instruction also stresses using introductory and connecting parts to permit readers to begin reading a long report at any place and quickly get a bearing. In general, current report-writing methods stress the needs of reports to communicate the information needed for the work done in business.

Second, the development of report structure has been influenced by the information needs of business. As will be discussed in Chapters 8 and 9, the design of reports actually helps readers to get the information they need. For some examples, the text of a report may include headings (captions) placed at the beginnings of sections to help organize the information in the reader's mind and to guide the reader's thoughts through the information. Reports may have beginning summaries to give a quick review of highlights for readers too busy to look at all the details. They may include tables of contents which provide guides to contents and enable readers to find information quickly and easily. When the goal is to aid in decision making, the report's structure may emphasize recommendations by placing them at the beginning where they stand out. Report writers may use forms of graphic presentation (charts, diagrams, pictures, maps, and such) to supplement the written word and to communicate quickly and effectively. They may use forward and backward references in the writing to tie together the parts of the report, thereby relating the report parts and ensuring the reader's quick understanding. The list could go on and on.

In summary, we can say that the report structure that has developed over the past makes information easy to find. It permits busy readers to go quickly to the facts needed and to ignore the information not needed. It enables them to find the minor, supporting details when these details appear to be useful. In general, it permits readers to get the information they need in the shortest time possible.

THE NEED TO COMMUNICATE

Much of the report-writing instruction presented in following chapters developed from the need to communicate. Reports, of course, are specialized forms of communication. And just as any other form of communication, they involve the communication process. It is not surprising, therefore, that writing techniques developed to make the communication process more effective in reports. In order to understand these developments, it is helpful first to understand the communication process.

The communication process

In describing the communication process, we shall use a situation involving two people. One is a man named Jones; the other is a woman named Smith. The sitaution described involves communication in general (not necessarily written reports). But as reports can be both written or oral, this general description is useful.

Sensory receptors and the sensory world.   We may begin the description of the communication process with one of the two people (say, Jones) communicating something to the other. The message sent may be any of a number of forms—gestures, facial expressions, drawings, or, more likely, written or spoken words. The message sent enters the sensory world of Smith.

The sensory world of Smith consists of all things around her as her sensory receptors detect them. The sensory receptors, of course, are those parts of the anatomy (eyes, ears, nose) that record impressions from reality. Thus, the sensory world of Smith contains all that she feels, sees, hears, or smells. From this sensory world, Smith's receptors pick up impressions and send them to her brain.

It should be noted, however, that Smith's receptors cannot detect all that exists in the world about her. Just how much they can detect depends on a number of factors.

One determining factor is the ability of her individual sensory receptors to receive impressions. Not all receptors are equally sensitive. All ears do not hear equally well. Likewise, eyesights differ. So do abilities to smell. And so do the other senses vary from person to person.

Another determinant is Smith's mental alertness. There are times, for example, when her mind is keenly alert to all that its senses can detect. There are other times when it is dull—in a stupor, a daydream, or the like.

Still another determinant is the will of Smith's mind. In varying degrees, the mind has the ability to tune in or tune out the events in the world of reality. In a noisy room full of people at a party, for example, one can select the conversation of a single person and keep out the surrounding noises.

When Smith's sensory receptors record something from Smith's sensory world, they relay the information to her brain. The message sent by Jones probably would be recorded in this way, but it could be joined by other impressions, such as outside noises, detection of movements, facial expressions, and such. In fact, Smith's brain receives these impressions in a continuous flow—a flow that may contract or expand, go fast or go slow, become strong or become weak.

The preverbal stage. This flow of stimulations into Smith's mind begins the preverbal stage of communication. At this stage, the stream of sensory perceptions produces reactions in her mind—reactions that will be given meaning and may trigger a communication response.

It is at this preverbal stage that the most complex part of the communication process occurs. The sensory perceptions pass through the filter of Smith's mind, and they are given meaning. Smith's filter is made of all that has ever passed through her mind. Specifically it is made up of all her experience, knowledge, bias, emotions—in fact, all that she is and has been. Obviously no two people have precisely identical filters, for no two people have precisely the same experience, knowledge, bias, and such.

Because people's filters differ, meanings they assign to comparable perceptions also differ. One person, for example, may smile pleasantly when his or her filter receives the word *liberal;* another with sharply differing background may react with violent anger at the same word. In one person's filter, the word *butterball* rings a jolly note; in the filter of one who has long been troubled with weight problems a negative connotation may occur. Even a salesperson's cheery "good morning" may produce sharply varying reactions. In a filter surrounded with happiness, the full positive meaning is received. A filter of a burdened, emotionally upset mind, on the other hand, may react with annoyance at these words that break into the mind's unhappy state.

The symbolizing stage. Next in the communication process is the symbolizing stage. At this stage, Smith's mind reacts to the filtered information it has received.

If the filtered information produces a sufficiently strong reaction, her mind may elect to communicate some form of response by words, by gesture, by action, or by some other means.

When Smith's mind does elect to communicate, it next determines the general meaning the response will take. This process involves the innermost and most complex workings of the mind; and little is known about it. There is evidence, however, to indicate that one's ability here, and throughout the symbolizing stage, is related to one's mental capacities and to the extent to which one will permit the mind to react. Especially is one's ability to evaluate filtered information and formulate meaning related to one's ability with language. Apparently ability with language equips one with a variety of symbol forms (ways of expressing meaning), and the greater the number of symbol forms in the mind, the more discriminating one can be in selecting them.

Smith ends the symbolizing stage by encoding the meaning formed in her mind. That is, she converts her meanings into symbols, and she transmits the symbols. In most instances, her symbol form is words, either made as sounds or as marks on paper. She also may select gestures, movements, facial expressions, diagrams, and such.

The cycle repeated.   Transmittal of the encoded message ends the first cycle of the communication process. The transmitted signals next enter the sensory world that surrounds Jones, and then begins a second cycle, identical to the first. Now Jones picks up these symbols through his sensory receptors. They then travel through his nervous system to his brain. Here they are given meaning as they pass through his individual filter of knowledge, experience, bias, emotional makeup, and the like. The filtered meanings may also bring about a response, which Jones then formulates in his mind, puts in symbol form, and transmits. The process may continue indefinitely, cycle after cycle, as long as the participants want to communicate.

The model and written communication

Although the foregoing description of the communication process applies more specifically to face-to-face communication than to other forms, it generally describes written communication as well. But some significant differences exist.

Effects on creativity.   Perhaps the most significant difference between face-to-face and written communication is that written communication is more likely to be creative effort of the mind. The fact is that it is more likely to be thought out and less likely to be the spontaneous reaction to signs received by the receptors. More specifically, the message in a written communication is more likely to be a result of stimuli produced by the mind than of outside stimuli picked up by the sensory receptors.

In a report-writing situation, for example, before beginning work on the report, the writers have decided to communicate. Before they begin the task of communicating, they gather the information that will form the basis of their communication. Then through logical thought processes they encode the communication that will accomplish their communication objective. Thus, there is not likely to be an interchange of stimuli between communicants, nor is there likely to be any triggering of desires to communicate. The process is a creative and deliberative one.

On the other hand, a letter or memorandum situation can be an exception, at least to some extent. In a sense, this situation can be like a face-to-face situation in slow motion. Stimuli picked up by one person's receptors could produce a reaction that would bring about a communication response—in this case a written letter or memorandum. This message could, in turn, bring about a communication response in its reader's mind. Thus, a reply would be written. This reply could then bring about another reply. And the cycle could be repeated as long as each message brings about a communication response. Even so, letters and memorandums represent more deliberate and creative efforts than face-to-face communication.

The lag of time.   Most obvious of the differences in face-to-face and written communication processes is the time factor. In face-to-face communication, the encoded messages move instantaneously into the sensory environments of the participants. In written communication, however, some delay takes place. Just how long the delay will be is indeterminate. Priority administrative announcements or telegrams may be read minutes after they are written. Routine letters require a day or two to communicate their content. Research reports may take weeks in communicating their information to the intended readers. And all such written communications may be filed for possible reference in the indefinite future. They may continue to communicate for months or years.

The lag of time also makes a difference in the return information one gets from communicating. Return information, commonly called feedback, helps greatly in determining when clear meaning is being received. In face-to-face communication, feedback is easy to get. The participants are right there together. They can ask questions. They can observe facial expressions. They can repeat and simplify whenever it appears to be necessary. In written communication, feedback is slow at best. Often it does not occur at all.

Limited number of cycles.   A third significant difference between face-to-face and written communication is the number of cycles that typically occur in a communication event. As previously noted, face-to-face communication normally involves multiple exchanges of symbols; thus, many cycles take place. Written communication, on the other hand, usually involves a limited number of cycles. In fact, most written communication is one-cycle communication. A message is sent and received, but none is returned. Of course, there are exceptions, such as letters and memorandums, which lead to a succession of communication exchanges. But even the most involved of these would hardly match in cycle numbers a routine face-to-face conversation.

Some basic truths

Analysis of the communication process brings out three underlying truths, which are helpful to the understanding of communication.

Meanings sent are not always received. First, meanings transmitted are not necessarily the meanings received. No two minds have identical filters. No two minds have identical storehouses of words, gestures, facial expressions, or any of the other symbol forms; nor do any two minds attach exactly the same meanings to all the symbols they have in common. Because of these differences, errors in communication are bound to occur.

Meaning is in the mind. A second underlying truth is that meaning is in the mind and not in the words or other symbols used. How accurately meaning is conveyed in symbols depends on how skilled one is in choosing symbols and how accurately the person receiving the symbols is able to interpret the meaning intended. Thus, skilled communicators look beyond the symbols used. They consider the communication ability of those with whom they want to communicate. When they receive messages, they look not at the symbols alone but for the meaning intended by the person who used them.

Communication is imperfect. Third is the basic truth that communication is highly imperfect. One reason for this imperfection is that symbols, especially words, are limited and at best are crude substitutes for the real thing. The one word *man* can refer to any one of a few hundred million human males, no two precisely alike. The word *dog* stands for any one of a countless number of animals varying sharply in size, shape, color, and in every other visible aspect. *House* can refer equally well to a shanty, to a palatial mansion, and to the many different structures between these extremes. The verb *run* tells only the most general part of the action it describes; it ignores the countless variations in speed, grace, and style. These illustrations are not exceptions; they are the rule. Words simply cannot account for the infinite variations and complexities of reality.

Another reason for communication imperfection is that communicators vary in their abilities to convey their thoughts. Some find great difficulty in selecting symbols that express their simplest thoughts; others are highly capable. Variations in ability to communicate obviously lead to variations in the precision with which thoughts are expressed.

Although the foregoing comments bring to light the difficulties, complexities, and limitations of communications as a whole, human beings do a fairly good job of communicating with one another. Even so, incidents of miscommunication occur frequently. Those people who attach precise meanings to every word, who feel that meanings intended are meanings received, and who are not able to select symbols well are apt to experience more than their share of miscommunication.

Resulting emphasis on adaptation

How the communication process influenced the development of report-writing techniques is easily derived from the preceding review. This review shows that communication is a unique event. It shows also that every mind (filter) is unique in its content—different from every other mind. No two people know the same words; nor do they know equally much about all subjects. Obviously, these differences make communication difficult. Unless the symbols (mainly words) used have the same meanings in both minds, communication will suffer. Report writers of the past saw this problem. They developed the logical solution: adapt the message to the mind of the reader. Thus adaptation has become a fundamental principle of good report writing.

By adapting to the readers we mean using words and concepts that the readers understand. Adaptation involves first visualizing the readers—determining who they are, what they know about the subject, what are their educational levels, and how they think. Then, keeping this information in mind, it involves tailoring the writing to fit these readers. The subject is discussed in greater detail in Chapter 10.

Development of emphasis on readability

Emphasis on readability is a second major development resulting from report writers' efforts to improve the communication of reports. By readability we mean that quality in writing which results in quick and easy communication. Readable writing communicates precisely—and with a single reading.

The concept of readability developed from scientific studies conducted over past years. These studies show conclusively that different levels of readability exist. More specifically, they show that for each general level of education there is a level of writing easily read and understood. Writing that is readable to one educational level can be difficult for those below that level. To illustrate, the general level of writing that is easy reading for the college graduate is difficult for those below his or her educational level. A level that is easy reading for the high school senior is difficult for those with less education. Readability levels exist for each general level of education. These levels may be measured by various formulas also developed through the readability research. Perhaps the best known of these, the Gunning Fog Index, is described in Appendix F. This formula is a useful tool in determining the level of one's writing.

The concept of readability is well known to professional writers, who long have been writing for varying levels of readership. The currently popular magazines, for example, aim at varying levels of readability. The *New Yorker* aims at about the level of a high school graduate. Magazines like *Reader's Digest* and *Time* are easy reading for those of eighth- and tenth-grade level. And at the bottom and aiming at third- to fifth-grade level of readership are an assortment of celebrity gossip magazines. Report writers would do well to follow these professionals by adapting their messages to their readers.

Actually, writing readably for a given level of reader is a specialized form of adaptation. Thus, when we adapt we are also working for readability. As we will see in Chapter 10, the concepts of adaptation and readability form the foundations for the writing instructions in this book. It is comforting to know that they are based on authoritative research findings—that they are proven techniques for improving communication.

In conclusion

The preceding review of the development of the structure and techniques of report writing serve mainly to set the stage. The subjects introduced will be covered in greater depth in following chapters. For the moment the goal is to establish a point. The subject of report writing is not based on armchair theories or arbitrary rules and procedures. Rather it is based on logical developments over long years of experimentation—some scientific and some merely trial and error. One should keep this point in mind throughout the remainder of this book.

QUESTIONS

1. Discuss and illustrate the differences in information needs of various work assignments in the business organization. Use illustrations other than those in the book.
2. Can a business ever have too much information? Discuss.
3. Discuss the ways the structure of a report can help satisfy information needs.
4. Give some examples of words which will have sharply differing meanings in different minds because of filter differences. Explain the differences.
5. Two college professors were discussing a theory developed by a leading scholar in their field. Said one to the other, "You are wrong in your interpretation of this point. Look here on page 37 of his book. These are his exact words, and the dictionary definitions prove that my interpretation is right." Said the other, "But I studied under the man three years. I have heard him discuss this point many times." Discuss this situation.
6. Thirty students in a classroom all hear the same lecture and read the same assignment. No two are likely to learn precisely the same material. Explain.
7. In an effort to emphasize a key point of communication, a professor asked a student to come before the class. The professor gave the student a sheet of paper on which appeared a line drawing of a geometric design. Then he asked the student to describe the design in words so that the other students could duplicate it. After long minutes of fruitless effort, the student gave up. Explain his difficulty.
8. Near the end of a working day a supervisor walked through his shop. As he passed one of his machinists, he said, "I think you had better clean up around here." He said the same words to the next two machinists he passed. The first machinist immediately began tidying up his work area. The second man was embarrassed, but he agreed that he was overdue for a bath. The third man began to wonder how the boss found out that he had been telling dirty stories. Discuss from a communication point of view.
9. Trace the different meanings the following words could have under varying circumstances.

cat	pack	down	frame
stick	mark	drawl	hand
run	part	foot	head
club	chase	drive	key
bug	draft	form	

10. What is meant by "reader adaptation"?
11. What are "levels of readability"? What do they mean to the writer?

3

Determining the problem and planning the investigation

Before there can be a report, there must first be a problem. Then the investigators must determine precisely what the problem is. And next they must work out a plan for getting the information needed to solve the problem. Obviously these activities differ somewhat with each problem, for each problem is unique. Even so, problems are sufficiently similar to make feasible a general working procedure. Such a procedure is summarized in the following pages.

DETERMINATION OF NEED FOR A REPORT

Work on a business report logically begins when someone in a business organization recognizes a need for a report. Logically this someone is in a position of authority. Usually this someone is not the report writer. More than likely it is a person higher up the administrative ladder—one in a position to recognize the need and with authority to have something done about it. Typically it is an executive who needs information in order to make a business decision.

A subjective process

Recognizing needs is not a task for which there can be meaningful instruction. It is a highly subjective process, requiring an intimate knowledge of the subject. Authorities in every field know what topics need further investigation, whereas the novice does not know. Competent chemists, for example, know what areas of chemistry need further research. So it is with competent physicists, geologists, and psychologists. And so it is with competent business administrators. They know the boundaries of business knowledge and where these boundaries should be pushed back. They know their own business and the business' needs for information. They know their needs for information for their jobs, especially for the decisions they must make. On the basis of this knowledge they determine the needs for reports.

Two types of needs for reports

Needs for business reports generally are of two types. First, a company may have a special problem to be solved. For example, a company may face problems such as determining which of two machines to buy, why sales in certain districts have dropped, whether a change in inventory method should be made, or what is the root of labor unrest at X Plant. To solve such problems, someone would need to gather all pertinent information, analyze it, and from the analysis arrive at an answer.

A second need for business reports is that of supplying the information a business must have in order to function properly. As noted in Chapter 1, proper functioning of today's complex business organizations requires vast quantities of information—production records, sales statistics, activity descriptions, personnel reviews, and the like. Modern business needs such information to facilitate decision making, to regulate production, to measure progress, and generally to coordinate and control its multiphased operations. Without adequate transmittal of information, modern business could not function. Reports serve as a major medium in transmitting this vital information.

Three ways of assigning reports

Report writers may receive assignments in one of three basic ways. First, someone or some group may ask specifically for the information. In doing so, they may make the request in writing, usually in the form of a letter or an interoffice memorandum; or they may make it orally. Second, the report situation could be the result of a company's standard operating procedure. As noted previously, many companies require that reports be used to transmit certain types of information within the organization. Third, writers could originate the report on their own initiative. For example, an administrator may see a problem need, investigate the situation, collect information, analyze this information, and write a report. An employee may see a need for collecting and passing on information. Or an independent researcher may conduct an investigation on a topic of interest and record the findings for any who might be interested.

DETERMINING THE BASIC PROBLEM

After receiving the assignment, the researchers make certain that the problem clearly is in mind. In some situations, this is a simple and routine step, requiring little effort. The researchers may, for example, have worked on similar problems before; they may be intimately acquainted with the specific problem situation; or the problem may be a simple one. In other situations, the problem may be vaguely defined or complex. The more intricate and generally sophisticated such problems are the more likely the researchers are to misinterpret the objective. It is for problems such as these that the following suggestions for problem determination procedure are given.

Getting the problem clearly in mind

Researchers begin the task of getting the problem in mind by carefully reviewing the information available. If the problem was assigned in writing, they carefully study the written words for their most precise and likely meanings. In this effort the researchers may want to communicate further with those who originated the problem. If the problem was orally assigned, the researchers probe and question the authorizers until they are are certain of the authorizer's intent. If, perhaps, the problem was originated by the researchers, then they have the task of clearing their own thoughts.

The informal investigation

Problem determination is not always the task of merely interpreting words. Frequently researchers can make logical interpretations only by having a thorough knowledge of the subject. If they do not already have such knowledge, they must acquire it. Typically they acquire it through some form of preliminary informal research. They can conduct this informal investigation in any number of ways, for there is no one best course. In fact, whatever method will provide the basic facts in a given case will suffice.

Often the best course to read about the subjects from secondary sources—books, periodicals, brochures, or the like. Sometimes researchers can gain valuable background knowledge by searching through company records and documents. And there are times when they can learn what they need to know by discussing the problem with people who know something about it. They may, for example, talk it over with fellow workers, especially with those directly involved with the problem in their work situation. Or they may talk with authorities outside the company—private consultants, professors, government officials, and the like. If the problem is such that the opinions or practices of the general public are involved, they may just talk to people. In general, in their informal investigation researchers should use any source of information which will help them to understand the problem.

Clear statement of the problem

After researchers have the basic problem clearly in mind, they should put it in writing. Putting the problem in writing is good for many reasons. A written statement is permanently preserved; thus, it may be referred to time and again without danger of changes occurring in it. In addition, other people can review, approve, and evaluate a written statement, and their assistance may sometimes be valuable. Most important of all, putting the problem in writing forces researchers to do, and to do well, this basic initial task of getting the problem in mind. In this way, this requirement serves as a valuable form of self-discipline.

The problem statement normally takes one of three forms. One is the infinitive phrase. For example, a salesperson who must submit a summary of activities for the week might write the problem statement thus: *To present a summary of work activities for the week.* A researcher assigned the task of reviewing and analyzing data on three low-priced cars for the purpose of determining which is the best for a certain group could come up with this problem statement: *To determine whether Car A, Car B, or Car C is the best buy for middle-income families.*

The question is the second form of problem statement. For the sales activity report previously described, the problem statement might take this question form: *How did I spend my work time last week?* And for the automobile study it could be worded in this way: *Is Car A, Car B, or Car C the best buy for the middle-class family?*

A third and less popular form is the declarative statement. Although somewhat dull and not so goal-oriented as the other two, this form nevertheless gives a good indication of the problem. Using the two example situations previously described, these problem statements might be written: (1) *The company wants a summary of my work activities for last week,* and (2) *Cars A, B, and C will be compared in order to determine which one is the best buy for middle-income families.*

In all the preceding illustrations, the problem is unmistakably complete and clear. The researchers cannot help but be aware of what the report must do. Were the statements not so clearly worded, they could very easily lead the researchers to stray away from the goal. To illustrate the point, contrast the preceding statements on the automobile problem with this one: *To compare three cars as a guide to buying.* Obviously this one describes the objective loosely. Although it implies that a conclusion will be reached, it ignores the goal of the comparison—to determine the best buy for middle-income families. Certainly this factor makes a significant difference in the researchers' route to their objective.

DETERMINING THE FACTORS

From the problem statement, investigators turn to the mental task of determining the problem's needs. Within the framework of their logical imaginations, they look for the factors of the problem. That is, they look for the subject areas that must be investigated in order to satisfy the overall objective. Specifically these factors may be of three types. First, they may be merely subtopics of the broader topic about which the report is concerned. Second, they may be hypotheses that must be subjected to the test of investigation and objective review. Third, in problems that involve comparisons they may be the bases on which the comparisons are made.

Obviously this process is a mental one, involving the intricate workings of the mind. Thus, it may be described only in the most general way. The investigators begin the process by applying their best logic and comprehensive abilities to the problem. The same mental processes that helped them to comprehend the problem now should assist them in determining the structure of the solution.

Use of subtopics in information and some analytical reports

If the problem concerns a need for information (with or without analysis), researchers should determine the subareas of information needed. That is, they should look for the topical breakdowns of the problem. By topical breakdowns we mean the areas of information which must be covered—the subjects (topics) which the main problem involves. Perhaps this procedure is explained better by illustration.

The salesperson's report described in the foregoing example clearly is an informational type. It requires only a presentation of facts. Although there is no one best arrangement for these facts, they might well include such subareas as direct sales efforts, service expenses, promotion, prospect development, and competition activities. Thus, the analysis of the problem and its factors might take this form:

Problem statement: To present a summary of work activities for the week.
Factors:

1. Direct sales efforts.
2. Service.
3. Promotion.
4. Prospect development.
5. Expenses.
6. Competitors' activities.

Serving as another example of factor breakdown for an information report is the problem of reviewing for a certain company (say Company X) its activities for the past year. This also could be a routine informational type of problem. That is, it could require no analyses, conclusions, or recommendations. But it could be analytical. It could require that each of the information areas covered be analyzed. It could even require that the analyses lead to an evaluation of the overall quality of the operation. In all of these cases, the mental process of determining factors involves determining the subdivisions of the overall subject. After thinking through the possibilities, one may arrive at this problem statement and factor analysis:

Problem statement: To review the operations of Company X from January 1 through December 31.
Factors:

1. Production.
2. Sales and promotion.
3. Financial status.
4. Plant and equipment.
5. Product development.
6. Personnel.

Hypotheses for problems of solution

Some problems by their nature seek a solution. Typically such problems seek an explanation of a phenomenon or the correction of a condition. In analyzing such problems, researchers must seek possible explanations or solutions. Such explanations or solutions are termed *hypotheses.*

More precisely defined, hypotheses are tentative explanations of factual information. Researchers advance them based on the information available and their knowledge of the subject area. The process largely is mental and is a product of the researchers' intelligence. After they have formulated their hypotheses, researchers conduct systematic research designed to prove or disprove the hypotheses.

The process is much the same as that followed by medical doctors in their efforts to cure patients of ailments. First, medical doctors collect information by inspecting the patients and asking questions about the symptoms—a procedure that may be likened to the informal investigation. Then with this information and their knowledge of medicine, the doctors mentally derive possible explanations for the ailment. A doctor may, for example, hypothesize that a patient's illness may be due to stomach ulcers. A second possible explanation—that gallstones are to blame—may be advanced. A third explanation may be advanced or perhaps four or more. With these hypotheses in mind, the doctor next conducts medical tests (X rays, blood analyses, and such) to prove or disprove the hypotheses.

If the doctor's research findings support one of the hypotheses, the likely answer to the problem has been found. If they do not, the doctor must make additional hypotheses and conduct additional tests. The doctor continues advancing hypotheses and testing them until there is proof that one is correct. Then with the correct one identified, the doctor takes whatever action is necessary to cure the patient.

The procedure may be much the same in a business research situation. Illustrating this similarity is the case of a department store chain that seeks to learn why sales at one of its stores are dropping. In preparing this problem for investigation, researchers logically would begin by gathering information about the situation (the informal investigation). They would learn enough about the problem to enable them to work out a plan for solving it. They would begin the plan by making a clear statement, perhaps one like the following:

Problem statement: Why have sales declined at the Milltown Store?

Then, with this problem statement in mind, as well as the knowledge picked up through informal investigation of the problem, the researchers would look for possible explanations. Perhaps they have picked up information which suggests that competition in the area has become a major limiting factor. It could be that information can be found which supports the possibility that a change in the Milltown economy might be taking place, thus explaining the store's lost sales. Or it could be that the store's management is at fault—that there have been weak administration and merchandising. Thus, the researchers might state the three hypotheses in this way:

1. Increased activity of competition in the store's trade area has caused a loss in sales.
2. Declining economic activity in the trade area explains the loss in sales.
3. The loss in sales is a result of weak administration and merchandising practices.

Next, the researchers would design a research plan to test the three hypotheses. They may choose to test them one at a time; or they may choose to test them together. To get the information needed to test the hypothesis that competitors' increased activities have caused the sales decline, they might design a survey of consumers to determine changes in sources of supply, buying practices, attitudes, and such. To test the hypothesis that the sales decline is a result of a decrease in economic activity in the store's trade area, they might gather from government and industry sources all available data on the economic conditions. And to test the hypothesis that poor management is the cause of the decline, they might develop pertinent data through systematic observation of merchandising and administrative practices in the store.

After they have gathered these data, the researchers would apply them to the hypotheses, using good logic and appropriate statistical techniques. Their goal, of course, would be to test each hypothesis objectively, seeking with equal vigor to prove and disprove it.

Perhaps the researchers would find one or two or even three are valid. But it is also possible that they would find that all are false. Then they would have to advance additional hypotheses and test them. And they would continue until they found a hypothesis that proves to be valid.

Bases of comparison in evaluation studies

When the problem concerns evaluating something, either singularly or in comparison with others, researchers must determine the bases for the evaluations. More specifically, they must determine the characteristics that they will evaluate; and sometimes they must determine the criteria they will use in evaluating each characteristic.

The problem of a company seeking to determine in which of three cities it should locate its new factory illustrates this technique. In planning the work on this problem, researchers would, of course, begin by getting all the readily available information. They would learn from company officials what are the company's needs and requirements. And if they do not already have such knowledge, they would learn from books, journals, specialists in the field, and so on the requirements for locating a plant. With this information in mind, they would write the problem statement; then they would determine its factors.

Writing the problem statement would be an easy task, for the problem is a simple one. Something like this infinitive form would do the job:

Problem statement: To determine whether Y Company's new factory should be located in City A, City B, or City C.

Determining the factors would consist of identifying the bases for comparing the three cities. Obviously these bases would be the characteristics of cities which make some more desirable for plant location than others. Perhaps in this case, availability of skilled labor is an important consideration. And it may be that the plant will use bulky raw materials, thus making availability of raw materials important. Similarly the bulky nature of the manufactured product might require more than the usual transportation; thus, quality of transportation facilities might be of major concern in the location decision. These and other location considerations similarly derived would make up the factors for this comparison study. This researcher's final breakdown of factors might look like this:

1. Availability of labor.
2. Abundance of raw materials.
3. Tax structure.
4. Transportation facilities.
5. Nearness to markets.
6. Power supply.
7. Community attitude.

Also serving to illustrate this form of factor breakdown is the automobile selection problem described earlier. In selecting one of three automobiles as the best buy for middle-income families, the researcher would need to determine in advance the bases for the decision. In this case, overall costs most certainly would be a major determinant, for middle-income consumers must be frugal. Performance would be another, and so would safety, durability, and perhaps even riding comfort. Thus, the problem statement and its factors might well take this form:

Problem statement: To determine whether Car A, Car B, or Car C is the best buy for middle-income families.

Factors:

1. Cost.
2. Safety.
3. Performance.
4. Durability.
5. Riding comfort.

In either of the examples cited, the researchers would gather data for each item (city, car) to be compared on each of the factors. Then, using these data, comparisons could be made. On the bases of these comparisons they would develop their decisions.

Need for subbreakdown

Each of the factors selected for investigation may have factors of its own. For example, in the preceding illustration concerning location of a new factory, the comparison of transportation facilities in the three cities could be covered with this breakdown of factors:

1. Water.
2. Rail.
3. Truck.
4. Air.

Labor could be covered by these subfactors:

1. Skilled.
2. Unskilled.

And these subfactors in turn could have subfactors of their own. For example, skilled labor could be broken down by subfactors such as these:

1. Machinists.
2. Plumbers.
3. Pipe fitters.
4. Welders.
5. Electricians.

These breakdowns of factors and subfactors could go on and on. One should continue to make them as long as they appear to be helpful to an understanding of the subject matter.

The value of this step of finding the factors of the problem is obvious: It serves as a guide to the investigation that follows. In addition, it gives the problem the first semblance of order, and the value of order in any complex process cannot be questioned.

CONSTRUCTING THE RESEARCH PLAN

After deciding what information they need for the problem, investigators turn their energies to the task of planning the research. In the more routine problems their planning is likely to be quite simple. Research for a weekly sales report, for example, may require only collecting familiar data from personal records. Writers of such reports need hardly be conscious of a prescribed research procedure, for they are dealing with thoroughly familiar material.

In problems where the research needs are more complex, researchers are wise to construct a step-by-step research plan. For example, investigators seeking to learn consumer attitudes through a nationwide survey would need to chart a detailed course. The value of a detailed plan should be apparent. Certainly a plan serves to bring order to the investigation, and the larger, more complex investigations cannot be made without order. By thinking out a course of action, the investigators are likely to be aware of the possible errors and thus can avoid making them. A plan serves generally to clarify the investigators' thinking. In addition, it serves as a blueprint to be followed throughout the investigation.

In all but the simplest of investigations (such as those requiring only library research) investigators should write the plan. Not to write it would be to invite confusion, for most research plans are too involved for the mind to handle without help. Although the content and arrangement of the written plan need not follow any prescribed pattern, the plan usually follows the order in which the investigation progresses. The following checklist outline shows one acceptable arrangement.

A suggested arrangement of the working plan

1. *The problem*

   Statement of the problem; its scope and limitations.

   Factors (working hypotheses) or areas of information to be investigated.

   Background material.

   Limitations to the investigation (money, time, qualified people, and so on).

2. *Methodology*

   Complete yet concise description of how the research is to be conducted.

   If secondary research is to be employed: Would include description of basic sources to be consulted. May include a tentative bibliography.

   If primary research is to be used: Would consist of a how-to-do-it description that goes through the procedure step by step. Contains sufficient detail to permit one to follow. For a survey, for example, may include topics such as sample design, selecting and training of workers, conduct of investigation, plan for pilot study, controls and checks, and time schedule of work.

3. *Handling the findings*

   A description of how the findings will be prepared for application to the problem. Covers such activities as editing, classifying, tabulating, and verifying results.

4. *Reporting the results*

   Any preliminary thinking concerning the procedure to be used in giving meaning to the findings and applying them to the problem. May include a tentative outline and a discussion of approach for final report.

Important as the tentative working plan is to the analysis of a problem, it is unnecessary to discuss it further at this point. Logically investigators must be familiar with basic research techniques before they can wisely construct a plan for solving report problems. Chapters 4 and 5 summarize this material.

QUESTIONS

1. Discuss the needs for business reports. Give illustrations other than those in the text.
2. In what ways are problems assigned?
3. Write a clear statement of the problem and determine the factors involved in each of the following problem situations:
   a. A consumer research organization plans to test the three leading low-priced automobiles in an effort to determine which one is the best buy as a family car for the typical consumer.
   b. A national chain of dress shops wants to learn what qualities to seek in hiring sales personnel.

  c. A daily newspaper wants to know how well the various types of items in a typical issue are read.

  d. The sales division of a major national manufacturer compiles a semiannual report on its activities in all of its five sales districts.

  e. A major soap manufacturer wishes to determine how its leading bath soap compares with its competition in the minds of consumers.

  f. A distributor of a line of French perfumes is planning an advertising campaign. The company wants to know more about the people who are buying these perfumes. Such information will serve as a guide to slanting the distributor's advertising.

4. Select and analyze one problem each for hypothetical situations with factors that consist of (a) subtopics of information needed, (b) hypotheses, and (c) bases of comparison.

5. Defend the logic of writing a detailed research plan.

4

Collecting information: Library research

With the problem analyzed, investigators know the objective. They know, also, what information they will need to achieve the objective. Next, as pointed out in Chapter 3, they must make careful plans for collecting the information needed.

In this task investigators may use secondary research, or they may use a form of primary research. Secondary research is research through published material. It is research through material which someone else has uncovered—periodicals, brochures, and such. In most complex problems, it is the first form of research conducted (in the informal investigation) even though the bulk of the research may be by another method.

Primary research, as the term implies, is research which uncovers findings firsthand. It is originating research. That is, it brings about new findings—findings which were hitherto unknown. Logically one uses primary research when secondary information on a subject is not available.

Although there are times when report writers need only to be skilled in one or a limited number of research methods, often they must know the rudiments of all techniques. Thus, this and the following chapter summarize the whole area of business research: first, secondary research (Chapter 4); second, primary research (Chapter 5).

THE COMPLEXITY OF FINDING PRINTED INFORMATION

When the information needed to help solve a report problem is likely to exist in printed form, the researcher is wise to look for it. Almost always printed information is the least costly of research findings. And often it is the fastest to find.

Finding secondary data, however, is not always a quick, routine task. Often it is a complex and involved undertaking. In fact, often it involves long hours of fruitless effort. The reason for such unproductive results should be obvious.

Anyone who has seen the great bulk of printed information in a respectable library can easily understand why. The simple truth is that libraries are storehouses for millions upon millions of bits of information. And continually they add to their contents. Finding the precise bits of information one needs may indeed be compared to finding the proverbial needle in the haystack.

In order to perform this task efficiently and successfully, the researchers must know the general arrangement of a library; and they must know the aids to finding material in this arrangement. In general, they must know good secondary research procedure. One such procedure is summarized in the following pages.

LOCATION OF PUBLICATION COLLECTIONS

The first step in orderly research for printed information is to determine where the search should begin. The natural place to start looking for published material, of course, is a library, but libraries differ in their content. Although a choice of libraries is not always available, if there is a choice researchers should be familiar with the numerous types of libraries that exist and with specific differences in their content.

Foremost among the libraries available to most investigators are the *general* libraries. This group includes the best-known ones, consisting mainly of college and university libraries plus the great bulk of public libraries. These libraries are general to the extent that they contain data of all descriptions. Many in this group, however, have, in certain specialized areas, voluminous collections that are more complete than numerous so-called specialized libraries that are discussed in following paragraphs. As a rule, researchers have easy access to general libraries.

In addition to the easily accessible general libraries, researchers may use a number of lesser-known collections of a specialized nature. Unfortunately many of these *specialized* libraries are private collections generally not available to outside investigators. While many such libraries do not openly invite public use of their collections, frequently they are cooperative to investigators working on worthwhile projects.

Included in the specialized group are the libraries of private businesses. As a rule, these collections are especially designed to serve the sponsoring company; consequently, the collections provide excellent information in the specialized areas of the company's operations. Unfortunately company libraries are not so accessible as are other specialized types.

Frequently, specialized libraries are maintained by various types of associations —trade, professional, and technical groups; chambers of commerce; labor unions; and such. Like the company libraries, these collections may provide excellent coverage of highly specialized areas. And although they are founded principally for their memberships and occasionally research staffs, the association libraries frequently open their doors to those engaged in reputable research.

Libraries of a specialized nature are also kept by some public and private research organizations. Foremost in this group are the research divisions of big-city chambers of commerce and bureaus of business research of the major universities. To investigate some of the information sources from these types of organizations, the *Research Centers Directory* is available. Published by Gale Research Company, this directory lists nonprofit information centers. It is updated quarterly by *New Research Centers*. Many chambers of commerce and bureaus of business research maintain extensive collections of material covering statistics and general information for a local area. In many states, various state agencies maintain similar collections.

Specialized libraries are so numerous that the Special Libraries Association has found it desirable to publish guides to them. One of these guides, *Special Library Resources,* lists in four volumes the nation's best special libraries. It also lists some of the special collections in the general libraries. A second guide published by the association is the *Special Libraries Directory*. This publication is not so extensive in its description of the libraries as is *Special Library Resources*. Another useful guide is the *Directory of Special Libraries and Information Centers*. This Gale Research Company publication contains information about almost 14,000 special libraries, information centers, and documentation centers in the United States and Canada.

EMPLOYMENT OF DIRECT APPROACH WHEN PRACTICAL

After finding an appropriate library, investigators face the task of finding what they need from the great mass of information available. To untrained investigators, this task can be complex and confusing to an extreme degree. On the other hand, investigators who know the orderly arrangement of library material will find this task routine.

Experienced investigators follow two basic patterns in library research. In some instances, they proceed directly to the source of the information needed. More often, however, they take a more indirect and time-consuming approach.

In research situations where the information sought is of a quantitative or factual nature, investigators may be able to go directly to the source. The extent to which they will be able to move directly to the source will, of course, depend on their acquaintance with published material in the field of inquiry. While it would be impossible for good researchers to know all possible sources even within specialized fields, it is not only possible but also desirable that they be acquainted with certain basic sources.

Encyclopedias

Possibly the best-known sources of general information are the encyclopedias. Although encyclopedias provide an authoritative and wide coverage of factual information, frequently they are too scant and general for use on specialized topics. Particularly they are good for general background information and for the list of reading material they frequently present on the subject.

A number of good encyclopedias are in general use, but three may be singled out for special mention. These are the *Encyclopedia Americana, Encyclopædia*

Britannica, and the *New International Yearbook.* The *Encyclopedia Americana* is exceptionally good for American use, particularly with its coverage of statistical and technological material. All three are supplemented with yearbooks that summarize the happenings of each year and are designed generally to keep the series up-to-date. In addition to the more popular encyclopedias, some specialized types exist. Among this group are the *Encyclopedia of the Social Sciences, Accountant's Encyclopedia,* and the *Encyclopedia of Banking and Finance.*

Biographical directories

If it is biographical information about leading personalities of today or the past that is needed, a number of biographical directories may be consulted. Best known in this group are the currently popular *Who's Who in America* and *Who's Who in the World,* which summarize the lives of living people who have achieved some degree of prominence. Similar publications provide coverage by limited geographic regions. For information concerning prominent Americans of the past, the *Dictionary of American Biography* may be used. In addition to these general sources, biographical information on individuals in particular professions may be found in a number of specialized publications. *Who's Who in Commerce and Industry,* for example, gives wide coverage to prominent business people, as does *Poor's Register of Corporations, Directors and Executives,* although the Poor's publication is the more exclusive of the two. Other similar sources include *Who's Who in Insurance, Who's Who in Labor, Rand McNally Bankers Directory, Who's Who in Engineering, Who's Who in Commerce and Industry, Directory of American Scholars,* and on and on. Few areas of economic activity are not covered by some such directory.

Information on well-known personalities may also be found through the *Biography Index.* Published quarterly, this index is a guide to current biographical material in books and magazines. Its references are arranged alphabetically by the names of the personalities covered.

Almanacs

Needs for general, factual, and statistical information frequently can be met by publications known as almanacs. Perhaps the best known of all almanacs is the *World Almanac and Book of Facts,* an annual publication of the Newspaper Enterprise Association, Inc., of New York. It is without peer as a general source of factual and statistical information. Its general content, however, limits its usefulness in business research.

Trade directories

For information about specific businesses (their operations; the products they buy, sell, or manufacture; and other useful facts and statistics) numerous directories are available. So many of these directories exist, in fact, that guides to them have been published. One guide, *Trade Directories of the World,* is a loose-leaf service that keeps current lists of directories covering foreign as well as domestic companies. Another, *Guide to American Directories,* contains information on more than 5,200 U.S. and foreign directories covering 250 fields of endeavor. Especially valuable to the marketing person are two directories published by Dun & Bradstreet. The *Million Dollar Directory* identifies U.S. companies with a net worth of $1 million or more. Its companion publication, *Middle Market Directory,* identifies companies with a net worth of $500,000 to $1 million.

Government publications

A wide range of general statistical information is released by various departments, bureaus, and agencies of the federal government. Although these data are so numerous and complex as to require an indirect method of research in uncovering them, qualified investigators should be able to proceed directly to some of the more important sources. The importance of these sources obviously varies with the specific problems concerned and in the minds of the investigators. Nevertheless, the following review of the information made available by agencies of the federal government is presented as a summary of major government contributions to general research. The investigators should at least know that such data are available.

Possibly the most widely used of government-collected data are the censuses taken by the Bureau of the Census, a division of the Department of Commerce. Best known of the census series is the decennial count of population, which dates back to 1790. The results of this census are published in two parts, each of which is broken down by volumes. Lesser supplements and special reports are released from time to time. For example, *Current Population Reports* provide an annual updating for the years between census counts. Titles for the major publication necessarily vary to fit the period—for example, *United States Census of Population: 1980* and *United States Census of Housing: 1980.* The information is available by cities, counties, and states. A national summary also is presented.

In addition to the population and housing counts, the Bureau of the Census also conducts other censuses: *Census of Agriculture, Census of Manufacturers, Census of Transportation, Census of Mineral Industries,* and *Census of Governments.* It also publishes the widely used *Statistical Abstract of the United States.* Compiled in this work is a large portion of the statistics collected by the branches of the federal government. For selected data on cities and counties, the publication is supplemented by *The County and City Data Book.*

For current economic data, three government publications are especially useful. One is the *Survey of Current Business.* A monthly publication of the Department of Commerce, it contains information on income, expenditures, production, prices, and the like. The second publication is the *Federal Reserve Bulletin.* Although it includes some general economic information, its emphasis is on financial data. Third is the *Monthly Labor Review,* published by the Bureau of Labor Statistics. As its name implies, this journal presents data on employment, wages, price levels, and such.

Business services

Numerous business services supply a wide assortment of information to business people. Although most of these services are designed to meet the needs of business practitioners, especially investors, sometimes they are important to business researchers.

Perhaps the most widely known business services are those designed primarily to give investors the information they need in making their decisions. Moody's Investors Service is one of these organizations. Its *Moody's Manuals* summarizes financial data and operating facts for all major American companies. The manuals are broken down into five divisions of business: *Industrials, Banks and Finance, Public Utilities, Transportation,* and *Municipals and Governments.* They also include OTC (over-the-counter) Industrials. Another such service is furnished by Standard & Poor's Corporation. Their *Corporation Records* presents in loose-leaf form the latest financial and operating facts about the organizations covered. Both Moody's and Standard & Poor's provide a variety of additional services primarily of interest to investors.

Two other business service organizations about which business researchers should know are Predicasts, Inc., and Gale Research Company. Predicasts, Inc., provides ten separate business services, although it is best known for its publications featuring forecasts and market data by company, product, and country. (*Predicasts, World-Regional-Costs, World-Product-Costs, Expansion and Capacity Digest*). This organization's extensive indexing and digest service of business articles, studies, and the like can save business researchers valuable time in their research. Its *Source Directory,* compiled annually and supplemented quarterly, contains bibliographical information on worldwide information sources. Similarly, Gale Research Company provides a long list of services to business researchers. In addition to the directories mentioned previously, Gale publishes *Statistical Sources,* which is a useful guide to data on business, social, and financial topics. It also publishes *Encyclopedia of Business and Information Sources.* This publication lists business subjects with a record of source books, periodicals, or organizations, directories, bibliographies, and other sources of information on each. Among its additional publications are *Trade Names Directory, Encyclopedia of Associations, Consumer Sourcebook, Encyclopedia of Information Systems and Services,* and *Directory of Directories.*

MORE GENERAL USE OF INDIRECT METHODS

If researchers cannot move directly to the source of information needed (and this is the usual case), they must then find the data through indirect steps. Their first move in indirect research is to construct a bibliography—a list of publications likely to contain the information they need. After the bibliography is constructed, they gather the publications listed. Then they systematically check each publication for the information they need. Only the first of these steps— preparation of the bibliography—needs to be discussed. The last two steps are elementary.

Preliminary search for prepared bibliographies

Obviously the difficulty of the task would be lessened if the investigators could find already prepared bibliographies on their subjects. And, frequently, prepared lists of published material in specific areas do exist. Academic groups, associations, government agencies, and others continually contribute bibliographies in all major areas. Thus, in most areas of research, investigators are wise to search first for bibliographies on their topics.

In searching for prepared bibliographies, researchers typically look through the literature on the subject. Mainly they search through masters' and doctors' theses, research reports, journal articles, textbooks, and such. Many of these writings contain lists of publications on the specific topics involved.

Use of the card catalog

If search for bibliographies already prepared is fruitless, or if those found are inadequate, the investigators must then construct their own bibliographies. Their first step may well be to consult the card catalog.

Learning to use the card catalog is the key to the resources of the library and to the location of the books and periodicals it contains. The card catalog lists the books and all other sources one can find in the library. It lists the material by authors, titles, and subject matter. When the author's name is not known but the title is known, the card can serve as a guide to finding the book or other source desired. The title card is a duplicate of the author card but with the title typed in black above the author's name. Subject cards tell what sources are in the library on any certain subject. An example of an author card appears in Figure 4–1. An explanation of the author card is shown in Figure 4–2.

FIGURE 4–1

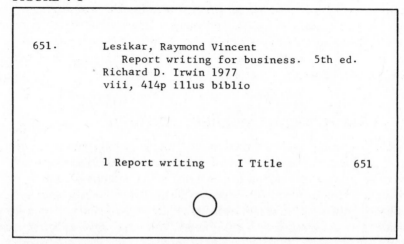

FIGURE 4–2

```
Cat. No.  Author's Name
Book No.    Title of book....Edition of book....
          Name of publisher...Date of publication
          Pages numbered with Roman numerals...
          Number of pages in text....Illustrations,
          diagrams....Bibliography

          Notes on book

          1 Subject entry  I Title entry    Catalog No.
                                             of book
```

The call number in the upper left-hand corner of the card is based on the Dewey Decimal System. This subject classification divides human knowledge in nine main classes, numbered one to nine. Encyclopedias, periodicals, and other sources of general information are marked zero and form a tenth class. Each class is similarly separated into nine divisions; general works belong to no division and have a zero in place of a division number.

These divisions are similarly divided into nine sections. This process is repeated as often as necessary. Thus 651 means Class 6 (Applied Science), Division 5 (Business Communication), Section 1 (Office Economy). All phases of office economy such as equipment, correspondence, and organization are numbered 651.

The following is a breakdown of the division of classes of the Dewey Decimal System.

000	General Works
100	Philosophy
200	Religion
300	Social Sciences
400	Philology
500	Pure Science
600	Useful Arts—Applied Science
700	Fine Arts
800	Literature
900	History

Although the Dewey system is quite adequate for some libraries, its use by the larger libraries is limited. In each division, class, or section, the number of division possibilities is restricted. Since this limitation creates rather complex indexing techniques for the larger libraries, many institutions of such character are presently adopting the Library of Congress System. And because business researchers should display skill in using all types of research facilities, an understanding of both systems is essential.

Whereas the Dewey system was initiated for use by all libraries, the Library of Congress method was developed for use only by the Library of Congress and for entries it had and expected to receive. Basically the plan combines an alphabetical series with a numbering pattern to provide potentially a more expansive classification system. However, its major advantage (expansiveness) is also a disadvantage. The system can be applied to a large collection of entries in many ways, and all may vary slightly.

Even though the specific adaption of the Library of Congress method may differ somewhat from library to library, the base of the system is consistent enough to allow business researchers to understand any particular variation. The following divisions, corresponding to letters of the alphabet, are the rudiments of the system.

A	General Works—Polography
B	Philosophy—Religion
C	History—Auxiliary Sciences
D	History and Topography (except America)
E,F	America
G	Geography—Anthropology
H	Social Sciences (includes commerce)
J	Political Science
K	Law
L	Education
M	Music
N	Fine Arts
P	Language and Literature
Q	Science
R	Medicine
S	Agriculture—Plant and Animal Industry
T	Technology
U	Military Science
V	Naval Science
Z	Bibliography and Library School

Divisions are made within each of these categories by additional letters and numbers. Thus, the book numbered 650–659 (Business) in the Dewey system would be replaced by the Library of Congress symbols HF (Commerce, General). Special works would be further indexed by additional numbers and letters. The letters not used (I, O, W, X, and Y) are being saved to permit expansion of the system.

Indexes as a guide to information

All too frequently, the card catalog is too general a guide to be of value for specific research topics. In such instances, researchers should use one or more appropriate indexes to published material. These indexes are numerous and are available for most general topics and many specialized ones as well. No research library of significance operates without at least some of them. A few of these indexes are so generally used as to deserve special mention.

Perhaps the most useful index in business research is the *Business Periodicals Index*. Issued monthly (except August) and cumulated yearly, this index serves as a guide to major periodicals in the business areas of accounting; advertising; banking and finance; general business; insurance, labor, and management; marketing and purchasing; office management; public administration, taxation; and specific businesses, industries and trades. Although the *Business Periodicals Index* began only in 1958, its predecessor, the *Industrial Arts Index,* goes back to 1913. Together these indexes cover the bulk of authoritative periodical writings in business for these years.

A good guide to the great volume of bulletins, pamphlets, special reports, and so on issued by governments, associations, businesses, and individuals is *The Public Affairs Information Service*. This service is kept timely with its weekly index. Although limited to the area of public affairs, the term is interpreted broadly and covers much of the field of commerce.

For business items that are newsworthy, researchers may consult *The Wall Street Journal Index*. For other newsworthy items they may use *The New York Times Index,* which goes back to 1913. And if the information sought is of international significance, they may consult *The Times* [London] *Official Index.*

If the information sought appears in book form, *The United States Catalog,* a 1928 compilation of all books in print in the United States may prove useful. For books appearing later than 1928, *The Cumulative Index* is a likely source. This monthly (except August) service is cumulated annually.

For research in more general periodicals, the appropriate basic indexes are useful. *The Readers Guide to Periodical Literature,* as its name implies, covers a general group of widely known periodicals from 1900 to the present. For periodical literature dating prior to 1900, researchers may consult *Poole's Index to Periodical Literature.* And for research in periodicals relating to the social sciences and humanities, researchers may use the *International Index.*

ORDER IN NOTE-TAKING

As researchers find the publications they seek, logically they look through them for the information they need. And when they locate such information, they take notes for future reference.

At first glance, note-taking may appear to be a simple chore that deserves little comment. It may appear to involve only the simple mechanics of writing down the information found, but the task really involves far more than this. It demands care in selecting that information likely to be usable. It requires careful determination of what parts should be recorded verbatim (word for word), what parts should be paraphrased (in the researchers' words), what parts should be recorded in detail, and what parts should be summarized. Most important of all, good note-taking entails order in recording this information.

Not to take notes in a predetermined, orderly plan is to invite chaos. Unfortunately too many researchers experience this kind of chaos. They may search through great numbers of sources and deligently write down an abundance of vital information. After exhaustive research, they may end up with reams of notepaper or thick stacks of note cards. Perhaps they have recorded in these voluminous notes all the information they need. But finding the information they want in these overample notes becomes a task of frustrating paper shuffling that resembles the proverbial search for a needle in a haystack. An orderly note-taking procedure would eliminate much of this confusion.

One such orderly procedure is presented in the following paragraphs. It is not presented as a one best plan, for doubtless there are others. For novice researchers who have not yet devised a plan of their own, this one should prove to be helpful. Its logic and value are apparent from its description.

This procedure uses two sets of note cards (or notepapers). One set is for the bibliography description; the other is for the information found in the sources.

Bibliography cards keyed with notes

For recording bibliography information, small cards are best (about 3 × 5). On separate cards, the researchers write the complete bibliography description (as described in Chapter 13). Then, they number each card consecutively (see Figure 4–3). As will be described later, these numbers serve as keyed references to the note cards.

FIGURE 4–3.　Illustration of bibliography cards keyed with note cards

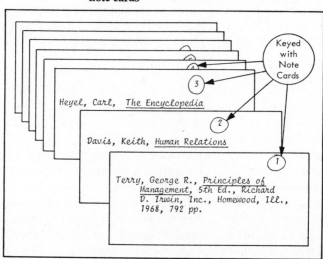

Note cards arranged by topics

The investigators use the second set of cards for recording the findings. For this set, they should use large cards (about 5 × 7). At the beginning of the research, they anticipate the topics and subdivisions of these topics on which they hope to find information. For each topic and subtopic, they set up a card, placing the topic and subtopic titles at the top (see Figure 4–4).

As they conduct the research, the investigators record each bit of pertinent information on the appropriate card. Should they find topics they did not anticipate, they set up cards for them. And when they fill up any one card, they start another card with the same topic heading and continue note-taking. At the end of their research efforts, they have all the findings on cards with all like information together.

FIGURE 4–4.   Illustration of note cards keyed with bibliography cards

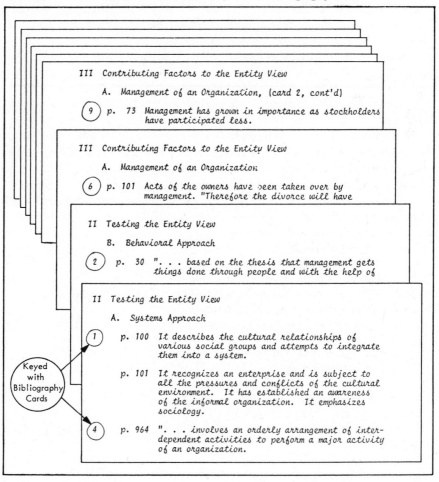

So that the source of each note can be easily determined, the investigators write by each entry on the cards the number they have given the source in the bibliography cards. Thus, they are spared the chore of writing a complete bibliography description each time they record information.

Two practical advantages of the system are apparent, and both are related to the fact that cards are easily arranged. First, the investigators can quickly and easily put the information collected into the order in which they will present it in their report. Second, they can prepare the bibliography for final typing simply by arranging the bibliography cards alphabetically by types of publications. Both advantages lead to significant reductions in costly, long hours of work time.

Use of photocopy services

With the widespread availability of photocopy equipment, researchers may find it more convenient to make copies of research findings than to summarize contents on notecards. The technique can be useful, especially when there is need to record verbatim much of the findings rather than to summarize or to extract highlights.

QUESTIONS

1. Suggest a hypothetical research problem that would make good use of a specialized library.
2. What specialized libraries are there in your community? What general libraries?
3. Under what general condition is it likely that investigators may be able to proceed directly to the printed source of the information sought?
4. Distinguish between the contents of encyclopedias and biographical directories.
5. Describe the contents and name the issuing branch of the following publications of the federal government.
   a. *1980 Census of the United States.*
   b. *Survey of Current Business.*
   c. *Monthly Labor Review.*
   d. *Statistical Abstract of the United States.*
6. Describe the contents of the following indexes to published material.
   a. *Readers' Guide to Periodical Literature.*
   b. *Poole's Index to Periodical Literature.*
   c. *Industrial Arts Index* and *Business Periodicals Index.*
   d. *Public Affairs Information Service.*
   e. *United States Catalog.*
   f. *New York Times Index.*
7. Discuss the major differences between the Dewey Decimal System and the new system of the Library of Congress.
8. In which of the indexes is one most likely to find information on the following subjects?
   a. Labor-management relations.
   b. Innovation in sales promotion.

    c.   Accident proneness among workers.

    d.   Safety engineering.

    e.   Trends in responsibility accounting.

    f.   Labor unrest in the 1800s.

    g.   Events leading to enactment of a certain tax measure in 1936.

    h.   Textbook treatment of business writing in the 1930s.

    i.   Viewpoints on the effect of deficit financing by governments.

    j.   New techniques in office management.

9. Select one of the topics listed above and set up for it a tentative note card arrangement and the beginning of a bibliography (at least five sources).

5
Collecting information: Primary research

When researchers are not able to find the information they need in secondary sources, they have no choice but to find their own. That is, they must get it firsthand. As was noted in the preceding chapter, this is primary research. It consists of four basic methods:

1. Search through company records.
2. Experimentation.
3. Observation.
4. Interrogation.

SEARCH THROUGH COMPANY RECORDS

The nature of the information needed for each problem will, of course, govern the research procedures employed. As many of today's problems concern various phases of company operations, frequently the information needed for presentation may be gleaned from the company's internal records. Production data, sales records, merchandising information, accounting records, and the like frequently are sources of report information.

Instruction on how to go about gathering and seeking information through company records, however, cannot logically be given. Company records vary much too widely to facilitate orderly discussion of the topic. But one simple standing rule should be kept in mind by those who engage in research through this type of information. Never should one attempt to conduct research through company records without the close cooperation of one thoroughly familiar with the records, except, of course, when the investigator is intimately acquainted with the information.

THE EXPERIMENT

The experiment is a research technique that is becoming more and more useful in the business areas. Originally a technique perfected in the sciences, the experiment is an orderly form of testing. In general, it is a form of research in which investigators systematically manipulate one variable factor of a problem while holding constant all the others. The investigators measure quantitatively or qualitatively any changes resulting from these manipulations. Then these findings are applied to the problem.

Illustrating the experiment is an investigation to determine whether a new package design would lead to more sales than the old. In such a case, investigators might first select two test cities. They would take care to select cities as nearly alike as possible on all characteristics that might affect the problem. First, they would secure information on sales in the two cities for a specified period of time before the experiment. Then in one city they would introduce the new package design. In the other city, they would continue to sell the product in the old package. For a second specified period of time, they would keep sales records for the two cities. During this time, they would take care to keep constant all other factors that might have some effect on the experiment. Specifically they would check to see whether advertising, economic conditions, competition, and such remained unchanged in the two cities. In the end, any differences they would find in sales in the two cities they could attribute to the package design.

The need for keeping constant all variables other than those that are the subject of the experiment cannot be overemphasized. All too frequently, this fundamental precept is unwittingly violated, thereby leading to false conclusions. There are times, too, when it is impossible to keep constant all the variables concerned. In such instances, investigators have no choice but to try in some logical way to compensate for the unwanted variations. At best, conclusions arrived at in such instances should be qualified with an explanation of any variations.

Design of the experiment

Each experiment should be designed individually to fit the requirements of the problem. Nevertheless, the general procedures one may use fall into a few basic designs. A review of the two basic experiment designs provides a workable framework for understanding and using this research technique.

The before-after design. The simplest form of the experiment is the before-after design. In this plan, investigators select a test group of subjects. Then they measure the variable in which they are interested. Next, they inject the experimental factor. After the experimental factor has had time to make its effects, the investigators again measure the variable in which they are interested. The investigators assume that the experiment is the cause of any differences in the first and second measurements. Perhaps Figure 5–1 more clearly explains the before-after design.

An experiment to determine the effect of point-of-sale advertising in a retail

FIGURE 5–1

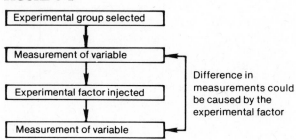

store illustrates this design. First, the researchers would select an experiment group. In this case, the selection is Y Brand of razor blades. Second, they would record sales of Y Blades for one week in which no point-of-sale advertising is used. Then they would inject the experimental variable—in this case the display of razor blades. Next, they would record sales of Y Blades for the week during which the point-of-sale advertising was used. Any increase in sales from the first to second week may be explained by the point-of-sale advertising. That is, if 500 packages are sold the first week and 600 the second, the researchers would attribute the increase to the advertising.

This conclusion points up a major shortcoming of this design. The assumption that the experimental factor explains all the difference in sales in the two periods simply is illogical. Sales could change for a number of other reasons—changes in weather, holiday and other seasonal influences on business activity, other advertising, and such. At best, one could conclude only that point-of-sale advertising *could* have some influence on sales.

Controlled before-after design. In order to account for influences other than the experimental factors, researchers use designs more complex than the before-after plan. These designs attempt to measure the other influences by means of some form of control. Simplest design of this group is the controlled before-after design.

In the controlled before-after design, the researchers select two groups rather than one. One is the experimental group; the other is the control group. Before they inject the experimental factor, the researchers measure the variable to be tested in both groups. Then they inject the experimental factor into the experimental group only. Next, they again measure the variable in both groups. The difference between the two measurements made in the experimental group is explained by two possible causes—the experimental factor and other influences. The difference between the two measurements made in the control group is explained only by other influences, for this group was not subjected to the experimental factor. Thus, comparisons of these findings give a measure of the influence of the experimental factor and the other influences. This design appears in Figure 5–2 in diagram form.

The point-of-sale advertising problem also serves to illustrate this design. First, the researchers must select two groups. One is Y Blades; the second is another

FIGURE 5–2

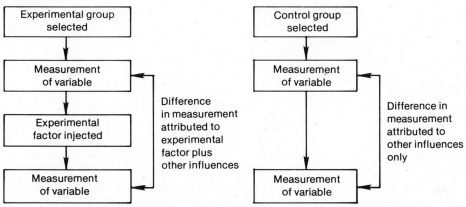

brand, X Blades. Then the researchers record sales of both blades for one week. Next, they use point-of-sale displays with Y Blades but not with X Blades. Finally, they record sales for the following week. Comparisons for the sales of the two groups over the two periods give a fair measure of the effects of the experimental factor as well as of outside influences. For example, if sales of X Blades were 400 packages during the first week and 450 packages during the second, the increase of 50 packages (12.5 percent) would be attributed to influences other than the experimental factor. If sales of Y Blades were 500 packages the first week and 600 the second, the increase of 100 would be attributed to other influences as well as the experimental factor. Other influences accounted for a 12.5 percent increase in X sales; so they can be assumed to have a similar influence on Y sales. An increase of 12.5 percent from 500 is 63. This leaves 37 additional sales, which are explained by the point-of-sale advertising.

High in accuracy but limited in use

The experiment is the most reliable and accurate of all research methods. Developed to a fine degree in the fields of the sciences, this technique greatly reduces the possibility of human error, the major source of all error. There is little wonder, therefore, that it is through this technique that almost all technological and scientific advancement has been made. As a technique in business research, however, the experiment is limited to problems concerned with the effects of change on a given set of conditions. Unfortunately most business research problems are not of this type.

Illustrations of business experimentation

Examples of the use of experiments in business serve to prove the value of the technique. For years, advertisers have experimented with copy and layout. In determining the best of two or more copy approaches, for example, advertisers may prepare advertisements that are identical in layout, size, artwork, and the like. Only the copy differs. Then they take great care to run the ads under identical conditions. Everything is done to make certain that the ads are read by comparable groups under comparable conditions. In short, the advertisers work hard to keep constant all variables other than copy, although complete success in this undertaking obviously is unlikely. Finally, the effects of the advertisements on sales is measured. It should be noted, however, that this description of procedure has been greatly simplified. Each of the foregoing steps involves numerous complex problems, some of which cannot be definitely solved.

As an additional example, a number of possible production techniques may also be tested through experimentation. Each technique can be tested under similar conditions and for a comparable time period. A measure of the effects of overall production then indicates the relative values of the production methods.

Similarly experiments may be made to determine the best location of departments or counters in a retail store. Each of the locations in question can be tested in actual practice. Great care is taken to make certain that each location is tested under comparable conditions. In this task, such variables as store traffic, the weather, and the season are considered. In addition to these illustrations, there are the numerous examples of experiments generally associated with the design and production end of a business, but most of these types are well out of the realm of business research.

OBSERVATION AS A RESEARCH TECHNIQUE

Like the experiment, observation is a form of originating research. Although it is not widely used in business, the potential value of observation as a research technique makes it worthy of careful study.

Recording observations of physical phenomena

Simply stated, observation is seeing with a purpose. It consists of watching certain phenomena involved in a problem and recording systematically what is seen. Observers watch the physical phenomena exactly as these phenomena occur. They make no attempt to manipulate the phenomena as they would do in an experiment.

This last point is made to clear some confusion that may exist in some minds. Because some experiments use observation in determining results, sometimes the two methods are confused. The distinguishing point to keep in mind is this: In the observation method, investigators make no attempt to manipulate phenomena; they observe the real situation. This is the whole procedure. In the experiment, investigators may use some form of watching to gather information, but this task is only a part of the whole procedure.

Practical use in business situations

Although observation is not widely used in business research, there is no shortage of illustrations of its possible uses. One good example is that of the shoe manufacturer who seeks to learn the shoe preferences of ladies. To get this information, the manufacturer can use observation to good advantage. Observers stationed at selected traffic centers can record on a simple tally sheet the shoe styles, colors, heel heights, and such as the wearers pass by. Or, possibly, observers can be stationed at points of sale to record actual purchases.

A research group that seeks to learn the canned vegetable brand preferences of different consumer groups may also use observation. Rather than use the conventional and somewhat biased system of asking homemakers what brands they buy, investigators can observe their purchases of canned vegetables at grocery stores. Or the investigators may go to the homes, get permission to check the canned vegetables stored in the pantry, and record the brands they see.

Plan of the observation

The procedure for planning an observation study is not easily summarized, for each problem presents its unique requirement. In general, however, the planning efforts involve two steps. First is the construction of a recording form. Second is the design of a systematic procedure for observing and recording the information.

Investigators design the observation recording form through the logical use of imagination, for the form may be any tabular arrangement that permits quick and easy recording of the information observed. Although observation forms are far from standardized, one commonly used arrangement (see Figure 5–3) provides a separate line for each observation. Captions at the top of the page mark the columns in which the observer will place the appropriate marks.

In designing the observation procedure, investigators determine whatever steps are necessary to record accurately the observations made. As few problems are likely to have anything in common, again the investigators must use their logical imagination. This work perhaps is best explained by illustration. In a problem of determining what style of clothing men wear in a certain city, the plan would have to produce a detailed schedule of observation for all appropriate parts of the city in proportion to the part's influence on the whole. It would specify times for the observations, with provisions made for weather and other complicating factors. It would include detailed observing instructions, telling each observer precisely what to do, and it would cover all possible complications the observer might encounter. It would be so thorough that it would not leave a major question of procedure unanswered.

Possibility of complexities

Although observation in general is a relatively simple technique, it can become complex by the occurrence of various limiting factors. For example, in the aforementioned study of shoe style preferences, observations made at a busy downtown street intersection might differ sharply from those made at a suburban shopping center or at a point across the tracks. Thus, care should be exercised in selecting the sites of observation.

FIGURE 5–3. Excerpt of a common type of observation recording form

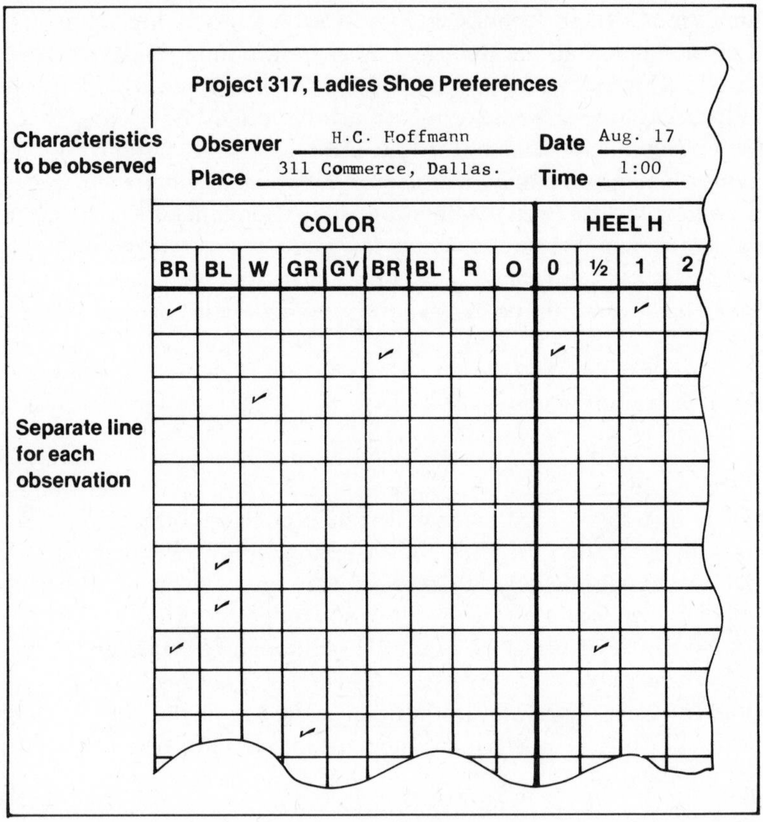

Project 317, Ladies Shoe Preferences

Characteristics to be observed

Observer ____H·C· Hoffmann____ Date _Aug. 17_

Place ___311 Commerce, Dallas.___ Time ___1:00___

Separate line for each observation

	COLOR									HEEL H			
	BR	BL	W	GR	GY	BR	BL	R	O	0	½	1	2
	✓											✓	
						✓				✓			
			✓										
		✓											
		✓											
	✓											✓	
			✓										

In addition, the actual recording of observations could become complex, particularly when the rate of traffic exceeds the speed of recording. Too, time would have to be reckoned with. Styles of wear differ with the hour of the day and with the season. The effects of the weather on shoe wear would add still further to the complex situation—and on, and on. There is no formula that can be used to overcome such problems. Only the foresight and logic of the investigators can be used to cope with the situation.

Merits and demerits of observation

Like the experiment, the observation method greatly reduces the possibility of human error. Thus, the chief advantage of the technique is its objectivity and accuracy. Although it may be claimed that observers are human and thereby subject to typical human shortcomings, they are likely to be individuals well trained in objective study and in the subject matter of the study. Also, a simple system of checks and controls can enhance the accuracy of their work.

The high objectivity and accuracy of observation are partially offset by two major limitations of the technique. First, observation is limited to only those physical phenomena that one can see. It is especially limited in studies of human behavior. It cannot pry into the human mind for information on attitudes, opinions, and the like. The technique is useful only for recording overt acts. But it may sometimes be possible to interpret the psychological significance of the overt acts. This practice, however, is highly dangerous, for seldom is there sufficient grounds to conclude that all overt actions have definite psychological explanations.

Second, the technique can be costly when compared with other methods. Its cost is largely set by frequency of occurrence of the phenomena to be observed. If the thing to be observed occurs frequently, cost of observing is low. For example, observing characteristics of ladies' shoes on a busy downtown street would keep the observer busy. Most subjects of observation, however, do not occur so rapidly. Some, in fact, occur so infrequently as to make costly any attempt to observe them. As an illustration, an observer stationed at a jewelry store to record actions concerning the sale of diamond rings would be likely to spend many idle and costly hours waiting.

RESEARCH THROUGH INTERVIEWING

Certain types of information may be gathered simply by asking questions. The techniques of interviewing (the name given to this method) vary greatly. In some instances, interviewing may comprise conversations with a few authorities. This type of research is a preliminary step in many research problems, but it could constitute the whole of the research work. More often, however, interviewing follows systematic and scientific procedure. The people interviewed are carefully determined through exacting statistical procedure, generally referred to as sampling. As a rule, interviews follow a uniform list of questions (the questionnaire). The questioning itself may be conducted through various means—personal interview, the telephone, and the mail being the most common.

Sampling theory as a basis for interrogation

The theory of sampling forms a basis for most research by interview. This commonly accepted theory should require little explanation, for already it is an accepted basis of logical procedure in many areas of work. Buyers of grain, for example, judge the quality of the grain by examining a small part of the whole. Buyers of cotton base their bids on the quality of a bit of cotton cut from each bale. Judges of jelly at a county fair base their decisions on the taste of a small portion of each entry. All these examples illustrate the theory of sampling. Behind each of the acts is the belief that the part inspected is representative of the whole. This belief, with some refinement, illustrates the theory of sampling.

The general law of sampling.   More specifically stated, the basis for the theory of sampling is the general law that a sufficiently large number of items taken at random from a larger number of items will have the characteristics of the larger group. One should note, however, that the law is applicable only when the whole comprises a large number of items. But it is only when the whole is large that there is real need for short cuts in determining overall characteristics. Small quantities can be analyzed item by item. From the remaining words of this general law, two fundamental principles are apparent.

Principle of sample reliability. First of these is the principle that samples taken must be sufficient in number to be reliable. Small samples are apt to contain chance errors. But as the number of items selected increases, these errors tend to offset. This tendency for the sample errors to level off is called stabilization. In all sampling studies as many items should be observed as are needed to produce stable results.

Researchers may use various methods to determine sample reliability. Each of these methods tests reliability of only one finding of the investigation at a time. That is, in a survey covering ten questions, one could use ten tests for sample reliability—one for each question. Although it is seldom necessary to test every question in such a study, investigators should test a sufficient number to assure a reasonable degree of reliability for the whole. At least, they should test the questions that require the most accuracy.

Among the methods available are some statistical as well as some less technical techniques. As the statistical techniques are beyond the scope of this book (the statistically inclined reader may want to consult Appendix B for a summary of this method), a review of one of the less technical ones is appropriate. This one is the cumulative frequency test.

Investigators begin the cumulative frequency tests by arranging the questionnaires in random order and dividing them into equal groups of 50, 100, or whatever number appears to be appropriate. Then they count for the first group the answers to the questions selected for the test and work out the percentage (or mean) for this group. They next count the answers for the second group, combine this count with the count for the first group, and compute the percentage (or mean) for the cumulative total. They do the same with the third group and with each succeeding group until all groups are included. Finally, they plot the cumulative percentages (or means) on a grid.

At first, the percentages are likely to plot in an erratic pattern. As the group totals are accumulated, however, the plot will tend to stabilize. When the plot line straightens out and begins to run parallel to the base line, one may assume that the answer is reliable.

To illustrate this technique, assume the case of a survey of 1,200 homemakers. The investigators feel that the one most significant question in their questionnaire is one asking whether the respondent prefers Product A to Product B. Obviously this is a question with a simple yes, no, and no opinion answer.

In applying the cumulative frequency test, the investigators decide to work with groups of 100, giving 12 test groups. And they decide to plot the yes answers. (They could just as easily apply the test to the no answer.) In the first group of 100 questionnaires, 74 yes answers, or 74 percent, are found. They plot this percentage on a grid. In the next group of 100, they find 56 yes answers. When this group total is added to the preceding group total, they have a cumulative total of 130 yes answers, or 65 percent. This percentage is then plotted on the grid. For the third group, 59 affirmative answers are counted. The cumulative total now becomes 189, for a percentage of 63, which is plotted on the grid. As shown in Figure 5–4 and Table 5–1 they continued to record, cumulate, and plot the

FIGURE 5–4. Cumulative frequencies plotted (illustrating tendency to flatten out as stability reached)

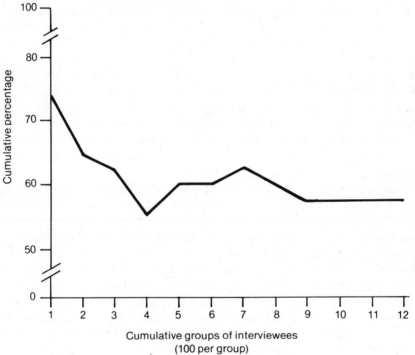

TABLE 5–1. Application of cumulative frequency test (12 groups of 100, yes answers to product preference question)

Group number	Yes answers in group	Cumulative yes answers	Cumulative percentage of yes answers
1	74	74	74
2	56	130	65
3	59	189	63
4	44	233	58
5	66	299	60
6	57	356	60
7	68	424	61
8	52	476	60
9	49	525	58
10	57	582	58
11	63	645	58
12	56	701	58

findings. As they cumulate the tenth total and plot the final cumulative percentage, they know from visual inspection of the plot that they have a reliable finding.

Principle of representativeness.　The second principle of sampling is that the sample must be representative of the universe (the group under study). Large numbers alone do not ensure representativeness. A basic error in selection favoring one segment of the universe is apt to continue, regardless of how many individuals are included in the sample. A sample selected from telephone directories, for example, would contain a disproportionately small number of very low-income families. And this disproportionate distribution would be present regardless of whether the sample selected includes 100, 1,000, or 10,000 families.

The techniques of sampling

In constructing a representative sample, investigators may select from a number of basic techniques. Each of these techniques has its advantages in certain situations and its limitations in others. The investigators' prime task in designing a sample is to select the one technique best suited for the problem and to adapt this technique to the special conditions of the case.

Random sampling.　Random sampling is the ideal and is the technique assumed in the general law of sampling. By definition, it is the sampling technique that gives every member of the universe an equal chance of being included. To assure equal chance, the investigators must first have the identity of every member of the universe. Usually this information is in the form of a list. Then through some chance method the investigators select the members of the sample.

For example, the researchers may record on individual slips of paper the names of every member of their universe. Next, the slips are placed in a container and mixed thoroughly. Then a chance drawing is made of a predetermined number of the slips. Since each slip in the container has an equal chance of being drawn, the resulting sample is random.

Stratified random sampling.　A special form of random sampling consists of dividing the universe into subgroups and making a random selection within these subgroups. Stratified random sampling, as this technique is called, ensures investigators that each subgroup is represented in the sample in whatever proportion is appropriate. Usually this desired proportion is the actual share of the universe the subgroups comprise. In some cases, however, investigators may choose to get a disproportionately large number from a small subgroup in order to get meaningful findings about the subgroup. In such instances, the investigators would take care to deflate this disproportionately large subgroup sample to its true portion of the universe when they are concerned with statistics on the whole group rather than the subgroup.

A problem of determining religious preferences of a group of workers illustrates this technique. In constructing a sample for this problem, the investigators might first divide their list of workers by religious affiliation—Catholic, Methodist, Baptist, Church of Christ, and so on. Then a random sample would be drawn from each of these denomination groups. Care would be taken that the number drawn from each subgroup was proportional to that subgroup's share of the whole. That is, if 31 percent of the universe was Catholic, 31 percent of the sample would be Catholic. If 22 percent of the universe was Baptist, 22 percent of the sample would be Baptist, and so on throughout the sample. Thus, the final sample would have the same makeup as the whole.

Systematic sampling.   Although not random in the strictest sense, systematic sampling is random for all practical purposes. It is the simple technique of taking selections at constant intervals (every *n*th unit) from a list of the universe. The interval used is, of course, a matter of the size of the list available and the sample size desired. For example, for a sample of 1,000 from a list of 10,000, the researchers select every tenth member of the list.

The technique approaches randomness if one makes the first selection purely a matter of chance. Thus, the investigators in the aforementioned problem may by some equal-chance process determine whether the sample will begin with number 1, 2, 3, and so on. If, for example, number 7 were selected, the sample would be made up of the 7th, 17th, 27th, 37th . . . 9,997th names on the list. And it could reasonably be assumed that all numbers had an equal chance of being selected.

Frequently systematic sampling and the other random techniques are difficult or impossible to use. Obviously one can use these techniques only when a list of all members of the universe is available. But in actual practice, such a list is not likely to exist. Even if complete lists were available for a particular group, the usefulness of the list would be short-lived. Because people are forever moving about and changing, lists quickly become obsolete. Thus, investigators frequently must find techniques that substitute for random ones.

Quota sampling.   A nonrandom technique that assures that a sample will have the same characteristics as the universe is quota sampling (or controlled sampling). One may use this technique whenever a proportionate makeup of characteristics of the universe is available. Knowing the proportionate makeup of the universe, one can design a sample so that it has the same makeup of characteristics as the universe. Specifically the investigators set quotas for each characteristic and make certain that each quota is met. Of course, the charateristic selected for determining proportionality should have some bearing on the problem.

For example, suppose investigators who want to survey a college student body of 4,000 decide to use a sample of 400. They may derive quotas for the sample, as in Table 5–2.

Area sampling.   One of the most widely used sampling techniques is area sampling. Area sampling consists of drawing the units for the sample in a series of stages. The units used normally are successively smaller divisions of geographic areas. For example, in drawing an area sample for a certain city, the investigators begin by dividing the city into homogeneous districts. (Census as well as *Sales Management* data provide very useful information for this division.) Next, through some random process some of these districts are selected for the sample. Then each of the districts is divided into subdistricts. (City blocks may be used for this division.) Next, a random selection technique is used to select some of the blocks

TABLE 5–2

	Number in universe	Percent of total	Number to be interviewed
Total student enrollment	4,000	100	400
Sex:			
Men students	2,400	60	240
Women students	1,600	40	160
Fraternity, sorority membership:			
Members	1,000	25	100
Nonmembers	3,000	75	300
Marital status:			
Married students	400	10	40
Single students	3,600	90	360
Class rank:			
Freshmen	1,600	40	160
Sophomores	1,000	25	100
Juniors	800	20	80
Seniors	400	10	40
Graduates	200	5	20

in each district. Finally, for each of the blocks drawn, the household units are listed, and again through a random process some of these households are selected. The households selected make up the sample.

A survey of the workers in an industry illustrates the flexibility of this technique. In constructing an area sample of this universe, the researchers could first get a list of the individual companies in the industry. Then for the first step in the selection process, they could randomly select some of them. Next, they could use the organization units (divisions, departments, sections, or such) of the companies selected as the bases for the next random selection and could randomly select some of them. Finally, in each of the divisions selected, they could randomly select specified numbers of workers. Those individuals selected would make up the sample.

Construction of the questionnaire

Most orderly interrogation follows a definite plan of inquiry. Usually this plan is worked out in a printed form called the questionnaire. The questionnaire is simply an orderly arrangement of the questions and information needed, with appropriate spaces provided for answers. But simple as the questionnaire may be in finished form, it is the subject of careful planning. It is, in a sense, the outline of the analysis of the problem. In addition, it must not violate certain fundamental rules. These rules are many, and sometimes they vary with the problem. The more general and by far the more important ones follow.

Avoid leading questions. An ever-present possibility of error in questionnaire construction is the leading question. A leading question is one that in some way suggests an answer. Violations of this rule range from the obvious and deliberate attempts to distort truth in the results to the subtle and innocent violations. An illustration of obvious attempts to lead the respondent are questions of the type,

"Is Ivory your favorite soap?" The quotation leads the respondent's mind toward favoring Ivory. Many people would answer yes, whereas, if they were asked simply, "What is your favorite brand of bath soap?" they would give another brand.

On the more subtle side are those leading questions that may not at first glance appear to be leading. Foremost in this group is the checklist—an arrangement for easy recording of answers by listing the most likely answers. Unless all likely answers have been included in the checklist, some bias will be present. The respondent's memory may be assisted by the list of possible answers, whereas if one were left entirely to one's own thoughts, an entirely different answer might be given. If a checklist is used, plenty of space should be left for other answers a respondent may want to fill in.

Subtle bias may also be brought into a questionnaire by any hint that may name or imply the group conducting the study. As a rule, people are inclined to be agreeable. Thus, they may tend to give the answers they believe the investigators would like to receive.

Make the questions easy to understand.   Questions not clearly understood by all respondents lead to error. In other words, respondents simply cannot supply information unless they know what information is wanted. Unfortunately it is difficult to determine in advance just when the respondent will not understand the question, for few writers can see the error in their own wording. Possibly the best means of detecting such errors in advance is through testing the questions before using them in the investigation. It is possible, however, to be on the alert for a few general sources of confusion.

Sometimes question confusion is the result of a general awkwardness and vagueness of expression. The ridiculous question, "How do you bank?" well illustrates this type of error. Who other than its author knows the question's meaning?

The use of words that the respondent does not understand may also cause confusion. Primarily this problem results from the use of technical words, unusual words with multiple meanings, and the like. A good illustration of this error is the question, "Do you read your house organ regularly?" The trouble here lies in the words used. The words "house organ" are technical, and those outside the publications field are not likely to understand them. "Regularly" is a word of multiple meanings. Some who answer the question may consider anything short of 100 percent as not regular; others may have in mind a proportion much smaller.

Sometimes researchers unintentionally combine two questions into one. Although the second question usually requires subtle detection, it nevertheless leads to error. In some instances, some respondents may see one question; some may see the other; and some may see both. To say the least, confusion would abound. An illustration is the question, "Why did you buy a Ford?" The answer may involve two questions: "What do you like about Fords?" and "What don't you like about the other makes of automobiles?"

Avoid questions that touch on personal prejudices or pride.   For reasons of pride or prejudices, people cannot be expected to answer accurately in certain areas of information. In these areas are such topics as age, income status, morals, and personal habits. How many people, for example, would answer no to the question, "Do you brush your teeth daily?" How many middle-aged people would give their ages correctly? How many solid citizens would admit to fudging a bit on their tax returns? The answers are obvious.

But one may ask, "What if such information is essential to the solution of the problem?" The answer is to use more devious means of inquiry. In determining age, for example, investigators could ask for dates of high school graduation, marriage, or the like. Then from this information they could approximate age. Or they could approximate through observation, although this procedure would be wise only if broad and general age approximations would be satisfactory. They could approximate income by first getting such harmless information as occupation, residential area, and standard of living and then using this information as a basis for approximating. Admittedly such techniques are sometimes awkward and difficult. But they can improve on the biased results that direct questioning would obtain.

Stick to facts as much as possible.   Although some studies must involve opinion, it is far safer to seek fact when possible. Human beings simply are not accurate reporters of their opinions. Oftentimes they are limited in their ability to express themselves. Frequently they report opinions erroneously simply because they have never before been conscious of having these opinions.

Usually, when opinions are needed, it is safer to record facts and from these facts judge the thoughts behind them. This technique, too, is hazardous, for it is only as good as the investgators' judgment. But a logical analysis of fact made by trained investigators is preferable to a spur-of-the-moment opinion.

One frequently occurring violation of this rule is made through the use of generalizations. Respondents are sometimes asked to generalize an answer from a large number of experiences over time. Although this fallacy touches on other rules, it nevertheless fits here. The question, "Which magazines do you read regularly?" serves as good illustration. Aside from the confusion that the word "regularly" would bring about, and the fact that the respondent's memory may be taxed, the question forces the reader to generalize. Would it not be better, for example, to phrase the question thus: "What magazines have you read this month?" The question could then be followed by an article-by-article check of the magazines to determine the extent of readership.

Ask only for information that can be remembered.   The memory of all humans is limited. So it is important that the questionnaire asks only for information that one can remember. In order to determine just what one can remember, a knowledge of certain fundamentals of memory should be understood.

Recency is the foremost fundamental. People remember insignificant events occurring within the past few hours. By the next day they will forget some of them. Possibly they will remember none of them a month later. One might well remember, for example, what one had for lunch on the day of the inquiry. Possibly one would remember what one had eaten a day, or two, or three previously. But one would be unlikely to know what one had eaten for lunch one year earlier.

Significant events may be remembered over long periods of time. This second fundamental of memory is easily illustrated. One may long remember the first day of school, the day of one's marriage, an automobile accident, a Christmas Day, and the like. In each of these examples there was an intense stimulus—a requisite for retention in memory.

Some fairly insignificant facts may also be remembered over long periods of time. Usually the mind retains such information through a third memory fundamental—association with something significant. Although one would not normally know what one had for lunch a year earlier, for example, one might remember such information if the date happened to be one's wedding day, Christmas Day, or the first day at college. Obviously it is not the meal itself that stimulates the memory. Rather it is the association of the meal with something more significant.

Plan the physical layout with foresight.   One should plan the overall design of the questionnaire to facilitate recording, analyzing, and tabulating the answers. Three major considerations are involved in this planning.

First, one should allow sufficient recording space for all answers. When practical, a system for checking answers may be set up. Such a system must always provide for all possible answers, including conditional answers. For example, a direct question may provide for three possible answers: Yes_____, No_____, and Don't know_____.

A second layout objective is to provide adequate space for identification and description of the respondent. Information such as the age, sex, and income bracket of the respondent is sometimes vital to the analysis of the problem and should be recorded. In other instances, little or no identification is necessary.

A third problem of design common to most questionnaires is that of determining the sequence of questions. Sometimes there may be psychological advantages for starting with a question of high interest value. In some instances, it may be best to follow some definite order of progression. Frequently some questions must precede others because they help to explain the others. Whatever the individual case requirements may be, however, one determines the best possible sequence only through careful and logical analysis.

Scaling techniques

Sometimes it is desirable to measure the intensity of the respondents' feelings about something (an idea, a product, a company, and so on). In such cases, usually some form of scaling is useful.

Of the various techniques of scaling, ranking and rating deserve special mention. These are the simpler techniques and, some believe, the more practical. They are not so sophisticated as some others;[1] but the more sophisticated techiques are beyond the scope of this book.

The ranking technique consists simply of giving the respondent a number of

---

[1] Equivalent interval techniques (developed by L. L. Thurstone), scalogram analysis (developed by Louis Guttman), and the semantic differential (developed by C. E. Osgood, G. J. Suchi, and P. H. Tannenbaum) are more complex techniques.

alternative answers to a question and asking him or her to rank these alternatives in the order of preference (1, 2, 3, and so on). For example, in a survey to determine consumer preferences for toothpaste, the consumer might be asked to rank toothpaste A, B, C, D, and E in order of preference. In this example, the alternatives could be compared on the number of preferences stated for each. Such a method of ranking and summarizing results obviously is simple; but it is a reliable technique in spite of its simplicity. There are various more complicated ranking plans (such as methods of paired comparison) as well as methods of recording results.

A rating scale graphically sets up the complete range of possible feelings on a matter and assigns a number value for the positions. The respondents then must indicate the positions on the scale which indicate their feelings. In a sense, the question is set up for graphic answers. That is, the scale is drawn graphically and shown to the respondents who then must indicate their positions on it. Typically the numeral positions are described by words, as the example in Figure 5–5 illustrates.

FIGURE 5–5

What is your opinion of current right-to-work legislation?

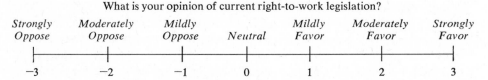

Because the technique deals with the subjective rather than the factual, sometimes it is desirable to use more than one question to cover the attitude being measured. Logically the average of a person's answers to such questions gives a more reliable answer than does any single answer.

Research by personal interview

Of the numerous techniques researchers use in interrogation, the most common one is the personal interview. Personal interviewing, as the terminology implies, consists simply of gathering information through formal oral questioning. Questions are asked of a group determined by the rules of sound sampling previously described. In large surveys, a carefully supervised field force of interviewers ask the questions, but in small studies a single investigator may do all of the work. Usually the interview follows the pattern of questions established in the questionnaire. In recent years, however, informal, conversational type questioning by skilled interviewers has been used, but this technique (depth interviewing) is in the field of the psychologist and is beyond the scope of this book.

Need for care in interviewing. Just as with any technique in orderly research, personal interviewing should not be conducted haphazardly. Instead, great care constantly needs to be exerted to assure accurate returns. And although the need for precautionary steps is not likely to be the same for any two problems, some common safety measures should be considered.

One of these safety measures concerns the need for extreme care in selecting the people to make interviews. Foremost of the requisites of the interviewers is the willingness to work, honesty, and general intelligence. In addition, interviewers should be well suited to meet the type of people concerned. A city dweller, for example, may not be able to get as much out of a farmer as a person who can talk the farmer's language. In selecting just the right individual for the task, frequently it is wise first to determine the job requirements in terms of characteristics such as age, physical appearance, social background, education, and sex. Each problem, of course, will differ in these requirements.

A second safety measure is to take great care in having all interviewers follow the same procedure. Variation in the opening introduction, the order and technique of questioning, explanations to the questions, and the like could affect the accuracy of the answers. Further, in instances when the interviewers are required to observe and interpret in addition to asking questions, lack of uniformity in procedure would be hazardous. Uniformity in procedure is accomplished best through the foresight and planning of the chief investigator. The chief investigator should consider all probable situations the interviewers may encounter and should work up instructions for covering them. The instructions must be easily understood by all those who use them. In most instances, the plan is put in writing as a detailed and simple instruction sheet distributed to all the investigators.

Even if investigators are selected carefully and clear instructions are prepared, the chances of major error are good. Investigators' errors are best controlled by a third safety measure—adequate supervision. Only in exceptional cases should investigators be allowed to work without supervision. In large research operations, the investigators are separated into teams, and a supervisor is selected for each group. It is the supervisor's task to teach the team the techniques of interviewing. Written instructions should be explained. Assignments to be made, advice to be given, and control of work standards are the supervisor's job. And, most important, the work of each interviewer should be checked at regular intervals. Were it not for such checks, a lazy or dishonest investigator could wreck the accuracy of the investigation.

Strong and weak points of the personal interview. Like all research techniques, personal interviewing is properly used only in certain instances. Just when conditions are right for its use is best determined by a review of its limitations and strong points.

Personal interviewing is best used when the group to be sampled is located in a compact geographic area. If interviewers lose much time traveling between interviews, the technique can become expensive. A sample taken from the entire population of a large city, for example, would be relatively inexpensive. A sample of the tree surgeons of the United States, on the other hand, would require much expensive travel between interviews.

The speed and expense with which interviews may be made is additionally controlled by the accessibility of the subjects. If interviewers can work at random on a busy street corner, costs will be low. But if they must work their ways into the busy offices of doctors, lawyers, or business executives, they will spend costly time waiting.

Only certain types of information can be gathered through the personal interview. Largely the technique is limited to factual data that one remembers. But opinion surveys and interpretive studies have also used personal interviewing. These two types of studies are criticized because they involve hazardous human interpretation. But usually one cannot gather such information by any other means.

Sometimes personal interviewing produces inaccurate information. Sometimes a few chronic jokers willfully distort their answers. Then there are those people who, for reasons of bias, give the answers that tend to elevate their positions, please the interviewers, or support their own prejudices. It is a general practice to eliminate these respondents from the sample when they are discovered. But the fact that there can be no certainty of detecting all such errors serves to limit the accuracy of the technique.

Possibly the greatest of all limitations of personal interviewing is the human factor. It is human to err; thus, when a human being asks questions of another human being, the possibilities of error are great. This deficiency is corrected, in part, because one of the human beings involved—the interviewer—may be well trained in objective and accurate reporting. There is little question that the limitations of the human factor vary with the quality of the interviewer.

The telephone as a research medium

Interviewing by telephone has become increasingly popular in recent years. Actually it is a form of personal interview. But the technique has distinct limitations and advantages that sharply distinguish it from personal interviewing.

Advantages of telephone interviewing. Telephone interviewing is particularly commendable for its speed. It can quickly reach large numbers of people, for it loses little time between interviews. And because of the possibility for speedy work, its cost per interview can be reduced. Unless the group being surveyed is located in compact geographic areas, however, cost is likely to rise. Obviously long-distance calls would not be advisable in most instances.

With telephone interviewing, a truly random sample becomes a possibility, provided that telephone subscribers make up all of the group being studied. When all of the group is known, it becomes a simple process to devise a representative sample of the whole. The exactness of procedure allowed in such instances is far higher than it is in instances when the group to be studied cannot be so clearly defined.

In reaching certain select groups, however, the telephone saves valuable time. With groups such as lawyers, doctors, and business executives, personal interviewers often spend long and costly hours working for appointments and waiting in outer offices. With the telephone, the same investigator may be able to make the interview in a fraction of the time.

Disadvantages of telephone interviewing. The technique is not all good, however. In fact, its limitations make its use prohibitive in many studies.

Foremost of the limitations is that the telephone subscribers are not truly representative of the whole of American society. Not all families have telephones. Although the condition is improving rapidly, the low-income group is not proportionately represented. Thus, any study of the whole of society could not use the telephone method effectively.

Telephone interviewing is limited in the amount of information that it can obtain. Only in rare instances is it likely that a long questionnaire can be used. The number of questions that one can ask by telephone, however, varies with the subject and the respondents.

In addition, the telephone method does not allow observation, which sometimes is necessary to determine economic conditions of the respondent or to judge sincerity. Similarly, explanations of questions are made much better when facial expressions and gestures can be seen.

Finally, widespread use of telephones for selling and promotion as well as for research has turned many people against such practices. It is easy for these people to hang up the receiver without answering questions.

Interview by mail

A third popular form of interview is through the mail questionnaire. In this technique, rather than ask questions personally or by telephone, investigators simply mail questionnaires to the respondents. They then hope that a good number of those receiving the questionnaires will write in the answers and mail back the questionnaires. Usually a letter explaining the purpose of the study and a stamped return envelope accompanies the questionnaire.

Mail survey advantages.   The mail questionnaire has two strong advantages: (1) wide geographic coverage is possible at (2) comparatively little cost. For these two reasons, the method is particularly good in reaching small and widely scattered groups. A widely scattered group such as U.S. tree surgeons, for example, could be reached for personal interviewing only with great loss of time and travel expense. Telephone interrogation likewise would be costly in reaching them. Chances are the mails would be the most economical method of the three.

There is some reason to believe that the mail questionnaire, by eliminating some of the human element, tends to eliminate some of the human error in research. Whereas the telephone and personal interview methods involve two human beings in each interrogation, the mail method involves only one. This one, however, is likely not to be skilled in objective and accurate reporting. Thus, a good possibility of human error remains.

Questionnaires that require care and time in answering may be answered more accurately by mail than by other methods. Particularly is this true if the topic of study is highly specialized and is high in the interest of the respondents. Too often, personal interviews are rushed by time conflicts of one kind or another. Mail questionnaires, on the other hand, may be answered at the leisure of the respondent.

Like the telephone, the mail questionnaire encounters little difficulty in entering doors not easily accessible to personal interviewers. But, of course, entry alone does not assure an answer.

A final advantage is that the mail questionnaire lends to sound sampling technique, provided that mailing lists available are representative to the group to be studied. As is pointed out in the following section, however, the selection of a sound sample for mailing does not assure a sound sample of returns.

Weaknesses of the mail questionnaire.   Offsetting these advantages are some significant weaknesses of the mail questionnaire. In many instances, these weaknesses are strong enough to make the method impractical.

One such disadvantage is the possibility of biased or nonrepresentative returns. Although it is true that questionnaires may be mailed to a representative sample scientifically drawn from the group under study, unfortunately not all of those who receive questionnaires will return them. As a rule, people who feel strongly in one way or another toward the topic of study are most likely to return questionnaires. Usually such people are not representative of the group under study. Thus, the representative quality of the original mailing list is likely to be lost.

The mail questionnaire, although inexpensive in problems requiring wide geographic coverage, can be quite costly. For example, assuming that the cost of each questionnaire mailed (including postage two ways, processing, handling, and cost of stationery) is a conservative 45 cents, a return of 10 percent (about average) would mean a cost of $4.50 per return. A return of 5 percent would raise the cost to $9.00. Such returns and even lower are not uncommon. On the other hand, with some select groups and with a problem in their fields of interest, much higher returns and a resulting lower cost may be expected.

Like the telephone method, the mail survey affords no opportunity for observation. And observation is sometimes essential in obtaining information like age, economic status, and nature of employment. Similarly the elimination of personal contact in turn eliminates the possibility of explaining and interpreting questions.

Still another disadvantage of the mail questionnaire is the possibility of its slowness. The mails do not work instantaneously. Nor do all respondents reply without delay. But even though the mail method may not be a quick means of finding an answer, it may be relatively fast in some instances. Certainly the mails would be a faster means of reaching a small and widely scattered group than would personal interviewing.

The panel survey

A special form of interviewing is the panel survey. This research method involves interviewing the same group of people more than once on the same subject. Frequently the panel is a continuing study with the same group serving an indefinite period of time.

As in conventional interviewing, the researchers in a panel survey assemble a group of people who can give information on the problem. The researchers may form the group in two general ways. First, if the problem is the usual type concerning the action, feelings, or reactions of a universe, the researchers may use conventional sampling techniques in forming the group. In a problem to determine consumer preferences for laundry detergents, for example, they may follow quota, random, area, or any other standard technique in constructing a sample of the consuming public. Second, in special cases when the investigators seek expert opinion rather than information from the public, the researchers may form the panel through careful and subjective selection. A national manufacturer, for example, may carefully select a panel of psychologists to help predetermine public reaction to advertising appeals, product designs, and sales techniques.

In practice, two general forms of the panel interview are used. One is in a sense a form of experiment. In it, the researchers interview the panel on the subject of concern. Then they make the phenomenon of the problem occur. Finally, they conduct another interview with the same group to detect any changes brought about by the phenomenon. To illustrate, a panel group might be interviewed on its feelings relative to the public image of a certain company. Next, the company might begin an intensive public relations campaign (the phenomenon). After sufficient elapsed time, the researchers could again interview the panel. Any changes in their answers from the first to the second contact might be explained by the public relations campaign.

The second and more popular form of panel is the continuing study. In this form, the participants serve as a sounding board or as a means of providing continuing consumer (or other) data. The Marketing Research Corporation of America, for example, gets information monthly from its standing panel of families on such topics as expenditures by product, by brand, and by geographic area.

Perhaps the most significant advantage of the panel is that it permits measurements of change over time. In addition, it can be a relatively inexpensive survey form, since usually it involves relatively small groups. Also, because the sample group remains available and willing for interviewing, information can be successfully gathered by this technique.

Of the disadvantages of the panel survey, two stand out. One is the tendency of the group selected to become nonrepresentative. The panel may be representative of the universe at the time it is selecte.d But its representativeness may change quickly. A panel made up of married couples representing all ages would be without young couples as time passed by. Of course, the problem is not so important in short-run studies. Also, this shortcoming can be offset by adding new members as the old drop off.

A second disadvantage of the panel is the artificial effect panel membership has on the members. Members are likely to become more self-conscious of the subject matter involved and thus become atypical. Or they tire of the questioning and become somewhat less accurate and comprehensive in their reporting.

QUESTIONS

1. What advice would you give an investigator who has been assigned a task involving analysis of internal records of several company departments?
2. Define experimentation. What does the technique of experimentation involve?
3. Explain the significance of keeping constant all factors other than the experimental variable of an experiment.

4. Give one example, each, of problems that can best be solved through (*a*) before-after designs, and (*b*) controlled before-after designs. Explain your choices.

5. Discuss the limitations in using experiments in business.

6. Define observation as a research technique.

7. Select an example of a business problem that can be solved best by observation. Explain your choice.

8. Using your imagination to supply any missing facts you may need, develop a plan for the experiment you would use in the following situations.

   a. The Golden Glow Baking Company has for many years manufactured and sold cookies packaged in attractive boxes. It is considering packaging the cookies in plastic bags and wants to conduct an experiment to determine consumer response to this change.

   b. The Miller Brush Company, manufacturers of a line of household goods, has for years sold its products on a house-to-house basis. It now wants to conduct an experiment to test the possibilities of selling through conventional retail outlets.

   c. A national chain for food stores wants to know whether it would profit by using trading stamps. It is willing to pay the cost of an experiment in its research for an answer.

   d. The True Time Watch Company is considering the use of automated sales displays ($9.50 each) instead of stationary displays ($4.50 each) in the 2,500 retail outlets that sell True Time watches. The company will conduct an experiment to determine the relative effects on sales of the two displays.

   e. The Marvel Soap Company has developed a new cleaning agent that is unlike current soaps and detergents. The product is well protected by patent. The company wants to determine the optimum price for the new product through experimentation.

   f. National Cereals, Inc., wants to determine the effectiveness of advertising to children. Until now, it has been aiming its appeal at the housewife. The company will support an experiment to learn the answer.

9. Using your imagination to supply any missing facts you may need, develop a plan for research by observation for these problems.

   a. A chain of department stores wants to know what causes differences in sales by departments within stores and by stores. Some of this information it hopes to get through research by observation.

   b. Your university wants to know the nature and extent of its automobile parking problem.

   c. The management of an insurance company wants to determine the efficiency and productivity of the workers in its typing pool.

   d. Owners of a shopping center want a study to determine shopping patterns of their customers. Specifically they want to know such things as what parts of town the customers come from, how they travel, how many stores they visit, and so on.

   e. The director of your library wants a detailed study of library use (what facilities are used, when, by whom, and so on).

   f. The management of a restaurant wants a study of its workers' efficiency in the kitchen.

10. Using your imagination to supply any missing facts you may need, develop a plan for research by survey for these problems.

    a. The American Restaurant Association wants information that will give its members a picture of its customers. The information will serve as a guide for a promotion campaign designed to promote restaurant eating. Specifically it will seek such information as who eats out, how often, where they go, how much they spend. Likewise, it will seek to determine who does not eat out and why.

    b. The editor of your local daily paper wants a readership study of his publication. That is, he wants to know just who reads what.

    c. An organization of tobacco companies wants to learn the current trend in tobacco use. They want to know such information as how many people are smoking, how many have stopped, how many new smokers there are, and so on.

    d. The American Association of Publishers wants a survey of reading habits of the American people. They want to know who reads what, how much, when, where, and so on.

11. Give examples of sampling problems that can make best use of random sampling. Do the same for quota and area sampling.

12. Construct three leading questions. Explain why they are leading.

13. Rewrite the questions in 12 above so that they do not lead the reader.

14. Assume that you need information on the following subjects, and that you have reason to believe the people in your sample will be reluctant to give it to you. How would you attempt to get this information?

    a. Family income.

    b. Age.

    c. Reading habits.

    d. Morals.

    e. Personal cleanliness.

15. Give an illustration of how a question asking for opinion could be substituted by one asking for fact.

16. What would be the effect of the laws of memory on questions concerning these matters?

    a. Articles read in a periodical.

    b. Expenditures for recreation.

    c. Clothing worn at one's wedding.

    d. Reasons for purchasing an automobile.

    e An automobile accident.

17. Discuss the pros and cons of using telephone, personal interview, and mail survey techniques for each of the problems listed in Question 10.

18. Point out violations of the rules of good questionnaire construction in the following questions. The questions do not come from the same questionnaire.

    a. How many days on the average do you wear a pair of socks before changing? _____

    b. (The first question in a survey conducted by Fortune cigarettes.) Have you ever smoked a Fortune cigarette?

c. Do you consider the ideal pay plan to be one based on straight commission? _____ Or straight salary? _____

d. What kind of gasoline did you purchase last time? _____

e. How much did you pay for clothing in the past 12 months? _____

f. Check the word below that best describes how often you eat dessert with your noon meal.

Always _____

Usually _____

Sometimes _____

Never _____

6
Arranging and interpreting
information

After researchers have gathered the information they need, the information may be in various states of order. If it has been collected through an orderly form of bibliographical research (as described in Chapter 4), it is arranged by like subjects and is likely to be ready for interpretation and application to the problem. Information collected through primary research, however, is likely to need classifying, editing, and tabulating before it can be applied.

CLASSIFYING DATA

Classifying data simply means grouping them by some logical basis, such as time, quantity, and place. In primary research problems, the plan for classifying usually precedes the work of editing and tabulating.

The technique of classifying information is best explained by example. A questionnaire survey of 1,000 people would have 1,000 different answers to the question of how many miles the family car was driven during the past years. To make this finding more meaningful, the investigators might arrange the answers by broad quantitative groups. Such a grouping might include these quantitative divisions: under 3,000, 3,000 to under 7,000, 7,000 to under 12,000, and 12,000 miles and over.

Another example is the case of an investigation to determine what homemakers like about a certain detergent. Of the many varied answers received, most could be classified into such categories as cleansing ability, mildness on hands, aroma, and sudsing quality.

In either instance, the information is brought together—or reduced so as to be more workable and understandable. Thus, the two chief reasons for grouping are apparent: (1) significant relationships of the data are brought to light; (2) the data are simplified, thereby aiding the mental process of interpretation.

The researchers may do the classifying and the correlate tasks of editing and tabulating while the research is going on or after all the information is collected. If the researchers elect to classify, edit, and tabulate as they collect the information, they must either predetermine the grouping plan for the information or base the groupings on early or incomplete information. With some problems, this early determination of the classification plan is easy. With others, however, it is difficult and may result in costly and time-consuming corrections.

EDITING AND TABULATING

After the researchers have determined the classifications to be used, logically they turn to the tasks of editing and tabulating. Editing generally involves inspecting all the data collected; looking for possible errors, inconsistencies, and omissions; making corrections whenever possible; and generally preparing the forms for tabulation. The process of interpreting the forms and looking for error is largely a subjective one and requires a thorough knowledge of the subject matter. Obviously such work is no better or worse than the quality of the editor.

Preparing questionnaires for tabulation can be a somewhat complex chore, depending on the tabulation system used. In most instances, it involves marking the classifications each answer falls into. For example, the answer $155 to a questionnaire question asking for weekly income might fall into an $150–$175 classification; thus an editor might write $150–$175 in a prominent position near the question. Perhaps the editor would use red or other colored pencil so that the proper answer could be clearly seen in the tabulating process.

If machine tabulation is being used, editing may also include writing a code number for each answer in the margin of the questionnaire. Machine tabulation requires that each likely answer to a question be given a number or letter designation. The editor then places the proper number or letter designations on the forms, usually in the margins near the answers. Later, when the information is punched on cards, the keypunch operator has only to read down the margin and punch the numbers and letters. Admittedly the foregoing description of coding for machine tabulation is general and scant. A more detailed explanation, however, is beyond the scope of this book.

Tabulation is the procedure of counting the answers recorded on questionnaires onto other forms. It is the procedure of reducing the findings to orderly and understandable form. At the conclusion of a survey, for example, the information collected may be on a few hundred questionnaires. In this form, the information is so voluminous as to be meaningless. To be meaningful, this information must be summarized. It is summarized through tabulation.

The task of tabulating may be done by machine, as mentioned previously. Machine tabulating involves recording the information collected on special cards and then counting the results by high-speed electronic machines. The machines and their operations are highly technical and need only to be mentioned at this time. It should be noted, however, that machine tabulating is economically practical only for large-scale surveys or when the tabulating plan is complex.

For less complex research projects, researchers can tabulate the results by hand. For this task they may use the old and familiar cross-five technique. Known to most children, this elementary technique involves counting by marks and making every fifth mark across the preceding four (**卌**).

AN APPROACH TO INTERPRETATION

When researchers have the information in logical order, they are ready to begin the task of interpreting the information in terms of applications to the problem. Obviously any review of so subjective a process as interpretation must be quite general. Interpretation is largely a mental process; and the human mind works in complex and diverse ways. Because of this complexity and diversity, the following discussion makes no effort to reduce interpretation to a formula or to a set of hard and fast rules. To do so would be folly, for no formula or set of rules could possibly fit all the varying human minds and all the varying interpretation situations.

Because interpretation is a mental process, the ability to interpret is closely correlated with one's mental capability. And like most mental functions, interpretation is improved with knowledge. Normally the analyst will gain interpretation knowledge through experience. But such knowledge may also be acquired from a review of the fundamentals of interpretation—fundamentals that ordinarily one would learn through experience. These fundamentals may logically be grouped into five areas.

1. Human frailties that lead to interpretation error.
2. Fallacious procedures in interpretation.
3. Attitudes and practices conducive to sound interpretation.
4. Statistical aids to interpretation.
5. Techniques in interpreting for the reader.

HUMAN FRAILTIES AND INTERPRETATION ERROR

Because interpretation is a product of the mind, it is affected by the limitations of the mind. It is common knowledge that the mind is subject to quirks of peculiarity, irrationality, and inconsistency. Certainly it would be impractical to review all such quirks, for such a review would encompass the field of psychology. It is possible, however, to list the major limitations to interpretation. Thus, the following review of the three major limitations is presented. Possibly by knowing the nature of human frailties one will be better prepared to guard against them.

Desire for the spectacular

Inside most human beings there is a love for the unusual—the spectacular. Sometimes this tendency is a result of wishful thinking. At other times, it is the result of a belief that true events usually are not sensational enough to kindle human interest. Whatever the cause, this tendency frequently reveals itself in everyday human living. The five-pound bass, for example, may gain to seven pounds between the time it is caught and the time the fisherman describes his catch to the boys downtown. A simple neighborhood tale will grow in intensity as it is relayed over backyard fences. Tales of athletic achievement tend to grow in incredibility each time they are told. We can also find examples in business. A production supervisor may add to the success record of a new machine. A department head may exaggerate information supporting the shortcomings of a subordinate. Or a salesperson may add to the qualities of a product.

Occasionally this tendency leads to exaggeration in the interpretation of report material, particularly in the reports of the less experienced analysts. For this, just as for most of the other human frailties, there is but one cure. One must continuously be aware of this possibility of error, and one must consciously work to avoid it.

Belief that conclusions are essential

Another cause of error in interpretation is a prevailing belief that there must be an answer to every question—that absolute finality and certainty is desirable in all cases. This belief is wrong. Few areas of information can be interpreted definitely. Even so, inexperienced analysts frequently make definite interpretations simply because they believe that not to do so would be evading a basic issue.

This form of error is well illustrated by the following example. In a consumer survey made for a soap company, 3 percent of the people interviewed voiced disapproval of the aroma of one of the company's toilet soaps. This information, however, was not asked for in the questionnaire used in the survey but was submitted voluntarily. Thus, not all those interviewed had an opportunity to express their opinions on this point. Yet, the writer of this report, probably feeling that a definite interpretation was necessary, concluded that the objection to the characteristic was negligible. A second survey, this one asking all respondents to comment on the soap's aroma, proved the analyst wrong.

Experienced analysts will recognize that oftentimes interpretation must be qualified with explanation. Sometimes more than one possible interpretation may be presented. Then there are occasions when analysts are incapable of interpreting some information. On such occasions, they should accept their incapability rather than make wild guesses simply because they believe not to interpret is an indicator of loose and illogical thinking.

Acceptance of lack of evidence as proof to contrary

Prevailing in the minds of many beginning analysts is a belief that when a proposition cannot be proved, the opposite must be true. Obviously this belief is fallacious. It is a rare case, indeed, when the lack of evidence to support one proposition can be used as evidence to support a contrary proposition. For example, the absence of data proving that a proposed advertising campaign will be successful does not prove that it will fail. Because there is no evidence available to prove that a person is a good credit risk does not make the person a bad risk.

Experienced analysts consciously work on the proposition that evidence must support every conclusion. They know that conclusions that cannot be supported cannot be made. They recognize the truth that evidence is not capable of being stretched or turned around. And they take great care to make certain that they use all evidence logically.

FALLACIOUS INTERPRETATION PROCEDURES

Interpretation errors may also be the result of fallacious interpretation procedures. Perhaps a review of some of the more common errors of this type will enable analysts to learn from the experiences of others rather than by the trial-and-error teachings of their own mistakes.

Bias in interpretation

Bias in interpretation may be unconscious or deliberate. In neither case is it excusable. Deliberate bias is unethical by any measure. Unconscious bias reflects on the mentality of the analysts. Of the two, however, unconscious bias is the more dangerous, for it is difficult to detect and to correct.

For example, consider the case in which two accountants were assigned identical tasks of determining the best inventory valuation method for use by a new company. The accountants began the problem with differing personal convictions that one particular method was best. The two accountants worked deligently and, so they thought, objectively in analyzing all the methods. They used the same supporting information. They came up with different decisions. Their decisions supported the convictions they held when they began the study; yet, neither was conscious of any bias in reporting.

Unconsicous bias is extremely difficult to detect and equally difficult to control. There is but one corrective measure that can be used against it, and that one is maintenance of constant mental alertness to detect bias. But this prescription is by no measure a panacea for bias. As in the case with many of today's wonder drugs, many people are allergic to such a prescription.

Comparison of noncomparable data

In most forms of reports, various comparisons of the collected information are made. As a rule, most such comparisons are logical and assist in developing a conclusion. Occasionally, however, the data compared are not really comparable. A recent journal article, for example, reported on the success of typical graduates of a number of American colleges. The data pointed to the fact that the earning power of graduates of one particular school was well above that of the graduates of any other school in the study. Without further explanation, however, this comparison is fallacious. In truth, the groups of graduates are not comparable. The school with the high-earning graduates is one traditionally attended by the children of the very wealthy. These people would be likely to have high earnings even if they never attended college.

Cause-effect confusion

Interpretation error sometimes is the result of a mistaken assumption that a cause-effect relationship exists between sets of data. This interpretation error is a result of a confusion of association with causation. Cause-effect relationships must be based on more than mere association. The association must also be clearly logical. But the problem is intensified because in some instances associations falsely appear to have a cause-effect relationship.

The almost classic illustration of this error concerns the series of data gathered on hourly traffic flow over the Brooklyn Bridge and the tide changes in the water below. Analysis of the two series shows a high correlation in traffic flow and the falling and rising tide. Yet, it would be foolish to contend that one caused the other.

Unreliable data

Unless the information collected is reliable, interpretations made from it are uncertain at best. Reliable data are statistically sound. They are collected through sound research methodology and by competent researchers. Usually they are facts—that is, they are verifiable truths as contrasted with opinions, which are attitudes of the mind.

Although it is not always possible to determine the reliability of information gathered, it is best to handle questionable information with extreme care. Only that information that is unquestionably reliable is worthy of interpretation. In no case are interpretations better than the data from which they are derived.

The first tests of the vaccine of poliomyelitis, for example, serve to illustrate the necessity for reliability of data. The medical researchers did not try the vaccine on a mere handful of children. Instead, they used tens of thousands. Had they included only a few in the preliminary tests, the data collected would have been highly unreliable. Most probably none in a small group would have acquired the disease. But who could say whether their good fortune was because of the vaccine or in spite of it?

Unrepresentative data

Oftentimes interpretations are based on data not representative of the subject of the interpretation. Too often, the analyst is guided by the numerical significance of the information rather than its representativeness. In reality, a small bit of representative data is far superior to great quantities of unrepresentative data.

Classic proof of this example are the election surveys of the 1936 presidential campaign. One survey made by the now defunct *Literary Digest* comprised a sample of 2,376,000 voters. The other, made by *Fortune,* comprised only 4,500 voters. The first survey, however, was not representative of the voting public, being weighted heavily with people in the upper income group. Its returns were in error 20 percent. The *Fortune* survey, small though it was, missed the actual outcome only 1.2 percent. Needless to say, it was a representative study.

Neglect of important factors

Errors in interpretation may stem from a review of only one factor in a complex problem of many factors. Few problems are so simple that they can be solved by analysis of a single area of information. The complex problem is the rule rather than the exception. The analysts, therefore, must take care to look for all possible factors that affect the problem and to give all of these factors their due weight in the analysis.

The principle is well illustrated by a survey of university students and their grades. The report on this study presented the startling conclusion that a direct correlation exists between high grades and the amount of money spent by the student. This conclusion contradicts the accepted belief that the hard-working poor student makes a better student than a frivolous classmate. But only grades and income were compared in the study. It is apparent that factors other than income determine grades. Isn't it likely that many of the poorer students' grades suffer because of the hours they must devote to outside work? Couldn't it be that the availability of study time has an effect on grades earned? Might it not be that the money spent is not a cause of high grades but merely associated with them— that the real cause may be that those with higher incomes have the advantage of higher cultural and academic backgrounds? Obviously the conclusion was based on only one factor of a complex problem.

ATTITUDES AND PRACTICES CONDUCIVE TO SOUND INTERPRETING

As noted previously, interpretation is the application of clear thinking to the information gathered. Clear thinking, of course, follows the rules of logic. But logic does not come to all people by nature. Nor can its method be reduced to a formula. Generally it is developed through experience and knowledge. Its development can be helped along, however, through the adoption of some attitudes and practices that characterize its use.

Cultivation of a critical point of view

The cultivation of a critical point of view is a requirement for all those who engage in research and reporting work. In report preparation, just as in two-party governments, criticism from an opposing standpoint tends to maintain a balance of reason. But usually in report preparation only one party is engaged in the work, so a dual role must be played. One must be both the critic and the advocate. The evidence for and against everything must be examined with equal objectivity.

Maintenance of the judicial attitude

The analysts would do well to assume the role of the judges. They should try to place themselves above the role of ordinary persons—without emotion, without prejudice, and with open minds. Their primary objective should be to uncover truth and to leave no stones unturned in the search for truth.

The judicial attitude, as described above, may appear idealistic and out of the reach of the investigators. Possibly it is. Yet, the investigators who honestly attempt to assume such an attitude cannot fail to succeed in part. There is some truth to the adage, "Those whose goal is the stars may never reach them, but they seldom fail to leave the ground."

Consultation with others

Even though the investigators may be well qualified in the field of inquiry, the chances of knowing all there is to know in the field are slim. Usually they may profit by talking over problems, appraisals, and interpretations with others in the field. They may profit, too, by submitting their ideas to an ardent critic. Then, armed with the critics's views, they are in a much better position to interpret opinions. It is a rare occasion, indeed, in which the work of one mind cannot be improved through the assistance of others. If it does nothing else, talking over the problem with someone helps to give the investigators courage in their convictions.

Testing of interpretations

Often it is not enough simply to look at all sides of an issue with an eye for criticism. The wise analysts may profit by extending their critical review to actual tests of their interpretations. Unfortunately few interpretations can be tested conclusively, for the means of testing are largely subjective. But the fact that the interpretations are tested at all should lend support to their logic. Two subjective tests may be given to any interpretation.

First is the test of experience. In interpretation, as in all scientific methods, the dominant method of testing is with the reason. In using this test, the analysts simply ponder on each interpretation, asking themselves the question, "Does this appear reasonable in the light of all that we know or have experienced?" This method may be explained best by example.

Numerous times in the primitive past the descent of plagues on villages and countries was interpreted by many a wise person of the day as a form of punishment for the sins of the people affected. It did not matter that their theory did not stand to reason. They were not moved by the failure of the plague to strike against all places of sin or all sinners. They took little cognizance of the fact that the plague struck against saint and sinner alike. Their appeal was to fear rather than to reason.

Their reasoning contrasts sharply with the testing by experience later used by scientists in finding the cause of the diseases. It was the scientists' approach to search through all experience for consistencies in the case patterns of the disease under study. With some diseases, they found that those stricken had drunk polluted water. Consistencies found in the case histories of other diseases led to tracing the causes to carriers such as flies, rats, and mosquitoes. In all cases, the scientists' conclusions were based on facts gathered through experience. Because their conclusions were based on consistencies of experience, they fulfilled the requirement of logic. Thus, their appeal was to the reason.

A second means of subjective examination of interpretation is the negative test. In a sense, it is a corollary to the interpretation fundamental of cultivating a critical point of view. The negative test consists of constructing an interpretation directly opposed to each interpretation made. Then the opposite interpretation is examined carefully in the light of all available evidence. The analysts may go as far as to build a case in its defense. Finally, the two opposite interpretations are compared with the stronger one retained. In other words, the pros and cons, the advantages and disadvantages, of each issue are examined.

Illustrating the negative test is an interpretation made of the findings of a survey of student reading habits at a certain state university. The supervisors of the survey hastily interpreted the findings to indicate that the quality of material read by students was high. They pointed to their collection of numerous facts and figures, which showed that most of the literature read by students was that considered good by literary standards. A critic of the study carefully pointed out that some of the data uncovered supported the opposite interpretation, for the data revealed that a sizable group of the students read low-quality literature. Further investigation proved the first conclusion not so clear-cut as was at first supposed. Had the supervisors applied the negative test they would have tried to support both interpretations. Then they would have favored the one best supported by fact.

Use of statistical aids to interpretation

Frequently the information the investigators gather is quantitative—that is, it is expressed in numbers. Usually such data in their raw form are voluminous, consisting of tens, hundreds, even thousands of individual figures. If investigators are to use these figures intelligently, they must first find ways of reducing these figures so that the human mind can grasp their general meaning. There is no shortage of such ways of giving meaning to vast quantities of data, as any student of statistics knows.

Obviously a review of the statistical techniques which investigators may use to present quantitative information is well beyond the scope of this book. Even so, report writers should know them, understand them, and use them.

Perhaps a quick mention of some of the more common methods is appropriate. Possibly of greatest use to the report writer are the various measures of central tendency—the mean, median, and mode. Such measures seek to find one value of a series that appropriately describes the whole. Then there are the measures of dispersion—measures which help to describe the spread of a series of data. Ratios (expressions of one quantity as a multiple of another) are useful in simplifying voluminous data. These and various other useful statistical techniques are described in any standard statistics textbook.

INTERPRETING FOR THE READER

After the analysts have thoroughly interpreted the problem, the interpretation chores are still not finished. The analysts must convey these interpretations to those who will read the written results. These efforts must be most thorough, for the readers are likely to be less informed on the topic than the analysts.

It is the analysts' duty to interpret the findings, not because the reader is incapable of interpreting raw data, for such usually is not the case. Rather, the analysts interpret for the reader because interpretation assists communication, and the communication of the findings is a major objective.

Communication is made easier if the reader's mind is not allowed to wander but is carefully guided every step of the way. There can be little reason for allowing the reader's mind to go over the same trial-and-error route that the analysts have painfully covered. The analysts have worked with the information, so chances are they know it better than anyone else. Their knowledge and experience are wasted unless the knowledge and experience are revealed in the interpretations.

ORDERLY PROCEDURE IN INTERPRETING

Even though there is no mechanical formula for the actual process of interpreting, it is possible that the interpretation efforts may follow a general order of steps. Such an order, however, should never be held definite and should be altered to meet the requirements of any problem. That a plan can be devised, however, should not be assumed to mean that interpretation is wholly an objective process. The subjective element can never be removed from interpretation.

Relate information to the problem

The researchers' first step in orderly interpretation is the simple task of relating the information collected to the phase of the problem it affects. Sometimes the researchers will find that one small bit of information may play a paramount role in the problem. In other instances, large quantities of information need to be combined in order to shed light on a single minor point. On other occasions, the researchers may find that a maze of comparisons and cross-comparisons is necessary.

Make all practical interpretations

Next, the researchers should make all plausible interpretations of the relationships of each bit of information to the phase of the problem it affects. They should ignore no interpretation with merit. In many instances, the researchers may advance a number of interpretations for one bit of information. In other instances, they may find only one interpretation deserving merit. The efforts here need to be orderly and thorough, for an error of omission at this point could very well affect the problem as a whole.

Reevaluate interpretations

In the third step, the investigators must carefully review all the interpretations they have advanced for the information collected. They should carefully evaluate each interpretation in the light of existing evidence. Possibly they can put the interpretations to the subjective tests previously discussed.

Select interpretations with most merit

A fourth step is for the researchers to select the interpretations that appear to have most merit. The decisions here rest on an evaluation of the test results of the preceding step. These interpretations that do not fare so well should be dropped or at least qualified by explanation.

Derive conclusions from the interpretations

Finally, from the interpretations retained, the solution (i.e., conclusions and recommendations) evolves.

This task of making conclusions and recommendations is yet another form of interpretation, except here the interpretations are based not on fact but on other interpretations. Thus, conclusions may be defined as interpretations of the information previously interpreted on the objective of the study. And recommendations are yet another step down this interpretation ladder, for in a sense they are interpretations drawn from the conclusions. They are the lines of action to which the conclusions logically point. They must be well supported by these conclusions, just as these conclusions must be supported by other interpretations, and these interpretations in turn must be supported by the information collected. As with any subjective process of this sort, there is no substitute for simple logic and knowledge of the field of the problem.

QUESTIONS

1. Assume that you have interviewed a representative group of the student body of your school on the subject of total out-of-pocket expenditures of students during the academic year. Making any logical assumptions, discuss the categories into which your findings might possibly be classified.

2. What should one consider in deciding between machine and hand tabulation of research data?

3. Discuss the need for interpretation in most report problems.

4. Discuss each of the major human frailties that produce interpretation error. Illustrate each with realistic examples different from those in the text.

5. Distinguish between unconscious and conscious bias. Comment on the effects of each on the interpretation of report information.

6. Explain the error of comparing noncomparable data. Illustrate with original examples.

7. In reply to criticisms of the living conditions of his troops in a foreign encampment, an army general replied with some interesting statistical comparisons. One of these comparisons showed that the annual death rate of his men was less than 17 per 1,000—about the same as that for the capital city of the homeland. Evaluate this comparison.

8. What is cause-effect error? Illustrate with original examples.

9. Explain how the reliability of data is related to their representativeness. Illustrate with original examples.

10. A survey of smoking habits among college students revealed that grades made by nonsmokers were generally higher than those made by heavy smokers. A conclusion that smoking caused low grades was reached. Do you agree? Explain your viewpoint.

11. In a report on living standards of production workers at an aircraft plant the following statement was made: "Of those employees in the $150- to $200-per-week group who employ maids, 50 percent are past 40 years of age." What is the interpretation fallacy that most likely occurred here?

12. A report on students in public elementary schools produced data showing that the health of the students was correlated with the grades they made. Grades of students with defective eyes, ears, and teeth were found generally to be lower than grades of children without these defects. Would it be logical to generalize that physical defects cause the retardation of students? Or are there other factors that might contribute to low grades?

13. Using company records covering a five-year period, a business executive concluded that most productive salespeople were in the 35-to-40-age bracket. Explain what the executive could do to test this interpretation.

14. Discuss the interpretation fallacies present in the following cases.
    a. A study produced data that showed U.S. college students to be far behind their comparable groups in European countries. The conclusion was made that the educational systems in these European countries are superior to that in the United States.
    b. A politician concluded that in his incumbent opponent's 20 years as mayor of a city, the city's expenditures had increased an exorbitant 280 percent.
    c. The editor of a leading magazine for business executives reported that unsolicited letters received from readers justified a conclusion that the public favored stronger government controls over unions.
    d. When questioned about their feelings concerning a certain personnel policy of the company, 14 percent of the employees interviewed strongly supported the policy, 62 percent showed little or no concern about it, and 24 percent

disapproved of it. A management report concluded that the policy should be continued, since 76 percent did not oppose it. The union objected to this conclusion.

e.   Records compiled at a certain university showed that students who had majored in engineering received an average of $80 per month more than business graduates. An analyst concluded that careers in engineering are more rewarding monetarily than are careers in business.

f.   A campus survey at a midwestern university showed that 92 percent of the students of Christian faith favored a certain issue, whereas only 33 percent of the Hindu students favored the matter. The conclusion reached was that Christians and Hindus were far apart on this matter.

g.   A top executive in a department store chain assembled statistics on sales by stores. The executive then concluded that those store managers who had achieved the best percentage gains were the best managers and should be so rewarded.

h.   A report writer found data showing that sales of soft drinks were correlated with vacation travel. It was concluded that soft drink sales were heavily affected by vacations.

7
Constructing the outline

After report writers give meaning to the information collected, their next logical step is to arrange the interpreted findings into an order appropriate for communicating them. Specifically they must construct the report outline.

The report outline, of course, is the plan for the writing task that follows. It is to the writer what the blueprint is to the construction engineer or what the pattern is to the dressmaker. In addition to serving as a guide, the outline compels the writer to think before writing. And when the writer thinks, the writing is likely to be clear.

Although this plan may be either written or mental, a written form should be used in all but the shortest of problems. In longer reports, where tables of contents are needed, the outline forms the basis of this table. Also, in most long reports, and even in some short ones, the outline topics may serve as guides to the reader when placed within the report text as captions (or heads) to the paragraphs of writing they cover.

PATTERNS OF REPORT ORGANIZATION

After they have made ready the information for outlining, and before they begin the task of outlining, skilled report writers decide on which writing sequence, or pattern, to use in the report. The possible sequences are many, but they fall into two basic patterns—*indirect* (also called logical and inductive) and *direct* (also called psychological and deductive). Some authorities suggest a third order, the *chronological* arrangement. Actually this order really is a special form adaptable to either the logical or psychological order. Although the emphasis at this stage of report preparation is on the selection of a sequence for the whole of the report, these patterns are useful guides to constructing any writing unit, be it a sentence, paragraph, major section, or the whole.

Indirect order

In the *indirect* arrangement, the findings are in inductive order—moving from the known to the unknown. Preceding the report findings are whatever introductory material is necessary to orient the reader to the problem. Then come the facts, possibly with their analyses. And from these facts and analyses, concluding or summary statements are derived. In some problems, a recommendation section may also be included. Thus, in report form this arrangement is typified by an introductory section, the report body (usually made up of a number of sections), and a summary, conclusion, or recommendation section.

An illustration of this plan is the following report of a short and rather simple problem concerning a personnel action on a subordinate. For reasons of space economy, the illustration presents only the key parts of the report.

Numerous incidents during the past two months appear to justify an investigation of the work record of Clifford A. Knudson, draftsman, tool design department. . . .

The investigation of his work record for the past two months reveals these points:

1. He has been late to work seven times.
2. He has been absent without acceptable excuse for seven days.
3. On two occasions he reported to work in a drunken and disorderly condition.
4. And so on.

The foregoing evidence leads to one conclusion: Clifford A. Knudson should be fired.

Direct order

Contrasting with the logical sequence is the *direct* arrangement. This sequence presents the subject matter in deductive fashion. Conclusions, summaries, or recommendations come first and are followed by the facts and analyses they are drawn from. A typical report following such an order would begin with a presentation of summary, conclusion, and recommendation material. The report findings and the analyses from which the beginning section derives comprise the following sections.

Clifford A. Knudson, draftsman, tool design department, should be fired. This conclusion is reached after a thorough investigation brought about by numerous incidents during the past two months. . . .

The recommended action is supported by this information from his work record for the past two months:

1. He has been late to work seven times.
2. He has been absent without acceptable excuse for seven days.
3. On two occasions he reported to work in a drunken and disorderly condition.
4. And so on.

Chronological order

In the *chronological* arrangement, the findings are in an order based on time. Obviously such an arrangement is limited to problems that are of an historical nature or in some other way have a relation to time. The time pattern followed may be from past to present, from present to past, from present to future, or from future to present. A report following an order of time may begin with an introductory section or with a conclusion, summary, or recommendation. In other words, the chronological order is generally combined with either of the two preceding orders. Therefore, it is the arrangement of the findings (the report body) to which the chronological sequence is usually applied.

> Clifford A. Knudson was hired in 1979 as a junior draftsman in the tool design department. For the first 18 months his work was exemplary, and he was given two pay increases and a promotion to senior draftsman. In January of 1981, he missed four days of work, reporting illness, which was later found to be untrue. Again, in February. . . .
>
> All of these facts lead to the obvious conclusion: Clifford A. Knudson should be fired.

SYSTEMS OF OUTLINE SYMBOLS

Various authorities have prescribed guides and procedures for outlining. The gist of most of this procedure is that the material to be presented should be divided into separate units of thought and that some system of arabic, roman, or alphabetical symbols should join the units. The most common system of outline symbols is the conventional form.

```
I.   First degree of division.
     A.   Second degree of division.
          1.   Third degree of division.
               a.   Fourth degree of division.
                    (1)   Fifth degree of division.
                          (a)   Sixth degree of division.
```

A second system of symbols is the numerical (sometimes called *decimal*) form. This system uses arabic numerals separated by decimals. The numerals show the order of division. The succession of decimals shows the steps in the division process. Illustration best explains the procedure.

```
1.   First degree of division.
     1.1   Second degree of division.
           1.1.1   Third degree of division.
                   1.1.1.1.   Fourth degree of division.
2.   First degree of division.
     2.1   Second degree of division.
           2.1.1   Third degree of division (first item).
           2.1.2   Third degree of division (second item).
                   2.1.2.1   Fourth degree of division (first item).
                   2.1.2.2   Fourth degree of division (second item).
```

THE NATURE AND EXTENT OF OUTLINING

In general, the outline builds around the objective of the investigation and the findings. With the objective and findings in mind, the writers build the structure of the report in imagination. In this process, the writers hold large areas of facts and ideas in mind, shifting them around until the most workable arrangement comes about. This workable arrangement is that order that will present the findings in their clearest and most meaningful form.

The extent of the outlining task will differ from problem to problem. In fact, in many instances investigators do much of the work long before they consciously begin the task of constructing an outline. The early steps of defining the problem and determining its subproblems may lay the groundwork for final organization. If a questionnaire or other form is used in gathering information, possibly its structure has given the problem some order. The preliminary analysis of the problem, the tasks of classifying and tabulating the findings, and possibly preliminary interpretations of the findings may have given the writers the general idea of the report story to be written. Thus, when the writers begin to construct the outline, the work to be done may be in varying degrees of progress. Obviously the task of outlining will never be the same for any two problems. Even so, a general and systematic procedure for outlining may prove helpful.

Organization by division

This procedure is based on the concept that outlining is a process of dividing. The subject of division is the whole of the information gathered. Thus, report writers begin the tasks of organizing by surveying this whole for some appropriate and logical means of dividing the information.

After the report writers have divided the whole of the information into comparable parts, they may further divide each of the parts. Then, they may further divide each of these subparts, and they may continue to divide as far as it is practical to do so (Figure 7–1). Thus, in the end the writers may have an outline of two, three, or more levels (or stages) of division. The report writers designate these levels of division in the finished outline by some system of letters or numbers, such as the two systems previously discussed.

Division by conventional relationships

In dividing the information into subparts, report writers have the objective of finding a means of division that will produce equal and comparable parts. Time, place, quantity, and factors are the general bases for these divisions.

Division by time periods.   Whenever the information assembled has some chronological aspect, organization by time is possible. In such an organization, the divisions of the whole are periods of time. Usually the periods follow a time sequence. Although a past-to-present and present-to-past sequence is the rule, variations are possible. The time periods selected need not be equal in length, but they should be comparable in importance. Determining comparability is, of course, a subjective process and is best based on the facts of the one situation.

FIGURE 7–1. Procedure for constructing an outline by process of division

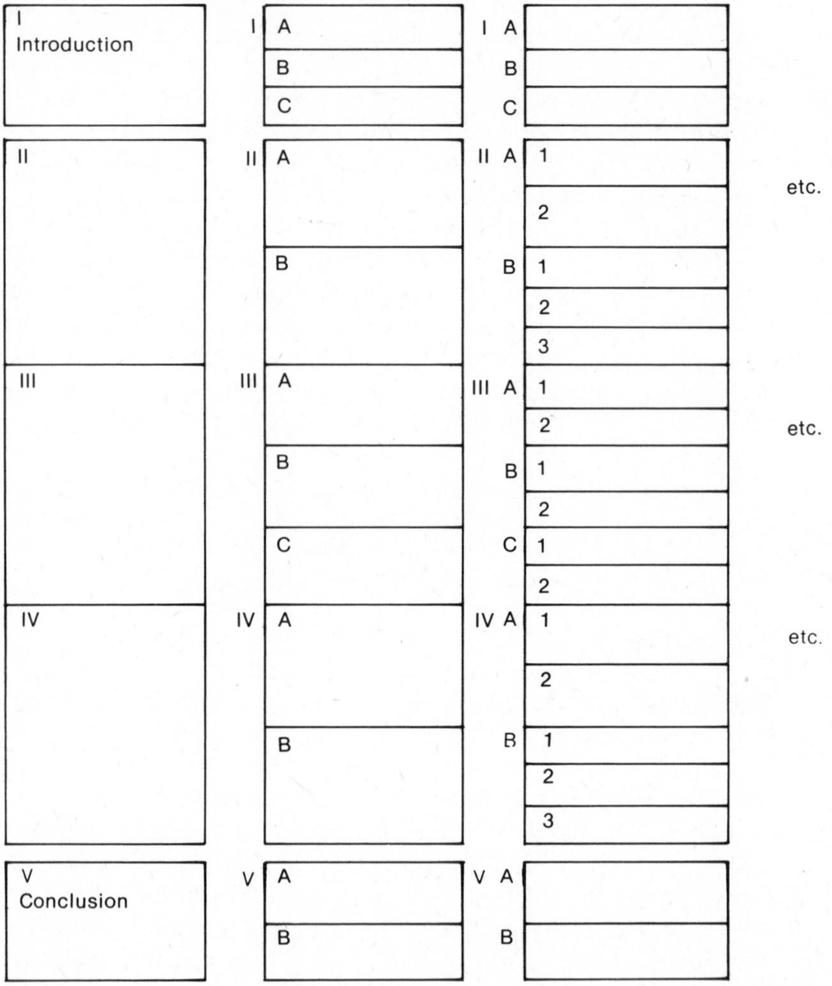

Step 1	Step 2	Step 3	etc.
I Introduction	I A B C	I A B C	
II	II A B	II A 1 2 B 1 2 3	etc.
III	III A B C	III A 1 2 B 1 2 C 1 2	etc.
IV	IV A B	IV A 1 2 B 1 2 3	etc.
V Conclusion	V A B	V A B	

Step 1	Step 2	Step 3	etc.
Divide the whole into comparable parts. This gives the roman numbered parts of the outline. Usually an introduction begins the outline. Some combination of summary, conclusion, recommendation ends it.	Divide each roman section. This gives the A, B, C headings.	Then divide each A, B, C heading. This gives the 1, 2, 3 headings.	Continue dividing as long as it is practical to do so.

A report on the progress of a research committee serves to illustrate this possibility. The time period covered by such a report may be broken down into the following comparable subperiods.

The period of orientation, May–July.
Planning the project, August.
Implementation of the research plan, September–November.

In addition to illustrating a time breakdown of a problem, this example shows a logical division of subject matter. Each of the three time periods contains logically related information (orientation, planning, implementation). Similarly the following breakdown of a report on the history of a company is made up of logical time periods. As in the preceding example, one may further subdivide each of these parts into smaller time units.

Struggle in the early years (1887–1901).
Growth to maturity (1902–29).
Depression and struggle (1930–39).
Wartime shifts in production (1940–45).
Postwar prosperity (1946–present).
The years ahead.

The happenings within each period may next be arranged in the order of their occurrence. Close inspection may reveal additional division possibilities.

Place as a basis for division.   If the information collected has some relation to geographic location, a place division is possible. Ideally the division would be such that like characteristics concerning the problem exist within each geographic area. Unfortunately place divisions are hampered in that political boundary lines and geographic differences in characteristics do not always coincide.

A report on the sales program of a national manufacturer illustrates a division by place. The information in this problem logically breaks down into these major geographic areas.

New England   Midwest
Atlantic Seaboard   Rocky Mountain
South   Pacific Coast
Southwest

Another illustration of organization by place is a report on the productivity of a company with a number of manufacturing plants. A major division of the report may be devoted to each of the company's plants. The information for each of the plants breaks down further by place—this time by sections, departments, divisions, or such.

The following outline excerpt illustrates one such possibility.

Millville Plant
    Production.
        Planning and Production Control.
        Production Department A.
        Production Department B.

Production Department C.
And so on.
Sales.
    Sales Office A.
    Sales Office B.
    Sales Office C.
    And so on.
Finance.
    Credit and Collection.
    Comptroller.
    And so on.
Personnel.
    Salary Administration.
    Employment.
    And so on.
Bell City Plant
    Production.
    And so on.

Division based on quantity.   Divisions by quantity are possible whenever the information involved has quantitative values. To illustrate, an analysis of the buying habits of a segment of the labor force could very well break down by income groups. Such a division might produce the following sections.

Under $5,000.
$5,000 to under $10,000.
$10,000 to under $15,000.
$15,000 to under $20,000.
$20,000 to under $25,000.
$25,000 and over.

Another example of division on a quantitative basis is a report of a survey of men's preferences for shoes. Because of variations in preferences by ages, an organization by age-groups appears logical. Perhaps a division such as the following would result:

Youths, under 18.
Young adult, 18–30.
Adult, 31–50.
Senior adult, 51–70.
Elderly adult, over 70.

Factors as a basis for organization.   Factor breakdowns are not so easily seen as the preceding three possibilities. Frequently problems have little or no time, place, or quantity aspects. Instead they require investigation of certain information areas in order to meet the objectives. Such information areas may consist of a number of questions that must be answered in solving a problem. Or they may consist of subjects that must be investigated and applied to the problem.

An example of a division by factors is a report that seeks to determine the best of three cities for the location of a new manufacturing plant. In arriving at this decision, one must compare the three cities on the basis of the factors that affect the plant location. Thus, the following organization of this problem is a logical possibility.

Worker availability.
Transportation facilities.
Public support and cooperation.
Availability of raw materials.
Taxation.
Sources of power.

Another illustration of organization by factors is a report advising a manufacturer whether to begin production of a new product. This problem has little time, place, or quantity considerations. The researchers will reach the decision on the basic question by careful consideration of the factors involved. Among the more likely factors are these.

Production feasibility.
Financial considerations.
Strength of competition.
Consumer demand.
Marketing considerations.

Combination and multiple division possibilities

Not all division possibilities are clearly time, place, quantity, or factor. In some instances, combinations of these bases of division are possible. In the case of a report on the progress of a sales organization, for example, one could arrange the information collected by a combination of quantity and place.

Areas of high sales activity.
Areas of moderate sales activity.
Areas of low sales activity.

Although not so logical, the following combination of time and quantity is also a possibility.

Periods of low sales.
Periods of moderate sales.
Periods of high sales.

The previously drawn illustration about determining the best of three towns for locating a new manufacturing plant shows that a problem may sometimes be divided by more than one characteristic. In this example, one could organize the information by towns—that is, each town could be discussed as a separate division of the report. This plan, however, is definitely inferior, for it physically separates the information to be compared. Even so, it serves to illustrate a problem with multiple organization possibilities. The presence of two characteristics is common. The possibility of finding three or even four characteristics by which the information may be grouped is not remote. As a rule, when multiple division possibilities exist, those not used as a basis for the major division may serve to form the second and third levels of division. In other words, the outline to this problem could take this logical order:

II. Worker availability.
  A. Town A.
  B. Town B.
  C. Town C.
III. Transportation facilities.
  A. Town A.
  B. Town B.
  C. Town C.
IV. Public support and cooperation.
  A. Town A.
  B. Town B.
  C. Town C.

Or it could take this inferior order:

II. Town A.
  A. Worker availability.
  B. Transportation facilities.
  C. Public support and cooperation.
  D. Availability of raw materials.
  E. Taxation.
  F. Sources of power.
III. Town B.
  A. Worker availability.
  B. Transportation facilities.
  C. Public support and cooperation.
  D. Availability of raw materials.
  E. Taxation.
  F. Sources of power.
IV. Town C.
  A. Worker availability.
  B. And so on.

The plan of organization selected should be the one that best presents the information gathered. Unfortunately the superiority of one plan over the others will not always be so clear as in the illustration above. Only a careful analysis of the information and possibly trial and error will lead to the plan most desirable for any one problem.

Introductory and concluding sections

To this point, the organized procedure discussed has concerned primarily the arrangement of the information gathered and analyzed. It is this portion of the report that comprises what is commonly referred to as the report body. To this report body may be appended two additional major sections.

At the beginning of a major report may be an introduction to the presentation (the reason the examples above begin with II rather than I), although some forms of today's reports eliminate this conventional section. Appended to each major report may be a final major section, in which the objective is brought to head. Such a section may be little more than a summary in a report when the objective is simply to present information. In other instances, it may be the section in which the major findings or analyses are drawn together to form a final conclusion. Or possibly it may lead to a recommended line of action based on the foregoing analysis of information.

WORDING OF THE OUTLINE

As the outline in its finished form is the report's table of contents and may also serve as caption guides to the paragraphs throughout the written text, one should take care in constructing its final wording. In this regard, a number of conventional principles of construction may be reviewed. Adherence to these principles will produce a logical and meaningful outline of the report.

Topic or talking caption?

In selecting the wording for the captions, the writers have a choice of two general forms—the topic and the talking caption. Topic captions are short constructions, frequently one or two words in length, which do nothing more than identify the topic of discussion. The following segment of a topic caption outline is typical of its type.

    II.   Present armor unit.
           A.   Description and output.
           B.   Cost.
           C.   Deficiencies.
    III.   Replacement effects.
           A.   Space.
           B.   Boiler setting.
           C.   Additional accessories.
           D.   Fuel.

Like the topic caption, the talking caption (or popular caption, as it is sometimes called) identifies the subject matter covered. But it goes a step further. It also indicates what is said about the subject. In other words, the talking captions summarize, or tell the story of, the material they cover, as in the following illustration of a segment of a talking outline.

    II.   Operation analyses of armor unit.
           A.   Recent lag in overall output.
           B.   Increase in cost of operation.
           C.   Inability to deliver necessary steam.
    III.   Consideration of replacement effects.
           A.   Greater space requirements.

B. Need for higher boiler setting.
C. Efficiency possibilities of accessories.
D. Practicability of firing two fuels.

Further illustrating the difference between topic and talking captions are the following two outlines.

A Report Outline of Captions That Talk

I. Orientation to the problem.
    A. Authorization by board action.
    B. Problem of locating a woolen mill.
    C. Use of miscellaneous government data.
    D. Logical plan of solution.
II. Community attitudes toward the woolen industry.
    A. Favorable reaction of all cities to new mill.
    B. Mixed attitudes of all toward labor policy.
III. Labor supply and prevailing wage rates.
    A. Lead of San Marcos in unskilled labor.
    B. Concentration of skilled workers in San Marcos.
    C. Generally confused pattern of wage rates.
IV. Nearness to the raw wool supply.
    A. Location of Ballinger, Coleman, and San Marcos in the wool area.
    B. Relatively low production near Big Spring and Littlefield.
V. Availability of utilities.
    A. Inadequate water supply for all but San Marcos.
    B. Unlimited supply of natural gas for all towns.
    C. Electric rate advantage of San Marcos and Coleman.
    D. General adequacy of all for waste disposal.
VI. Adequacy of existing transportation systems.
    A. Surface transportation advantages of San Marcos and Ballinger.
    B. General equality of airway connections.
VII. A final weighting of the factors.
    A. Selection of San Marcos as first choice.
    B. Recommendation of Ballinger as second choice.
    C. Lack of advantages in Big Spring, Coleman, and Littlefield.

A Report Outline of Topic Captions

I. Introduction.
    A. Authorization.
    B. Purpose.
    C. Sources.
    D. Preview.
II. Community attitudes.
    A. Plant location.
    B. Labor policy.
III. Factors of labor.
    A. Unskilled workers.
    B. Skilled workers.
    C. Wage rates.

 IV. Raw wool supply.
  A. Adequate areas.
  B. Inadequate areas.
 V. Utilities.
  A. Water.
  B. Natural gas.
  C. Electricity.
  D. Waste disposal.
 VI. Transportation.
  A. Surface.
  B. Air.
 VII. Conclusions.
  A. First choice.
  B. Alternative choice.
  C. Other possibilities.

The choice between topic and talking captions usually is the writer's, although some companies have specific requirements for their reports. Topic captions are the conventional form. Because they have the support of convention, they are most often used in industry, especially in the more formal papers. Talking captions, on the other hand, are relatively new, but they are gaining rapidly in popularity. Because they emphasize the main points in the report, they help the readers to get the messages quickly. Thus they help to save time. They are recommended as the superior form, but either is correct.

Parallelism of construction

Because of the many choices available, report writers are likely to construct outlines that have a mixture of grammatical forms. Some report writers believe that such a mixture of forms is acceptable and that each caption should be judged primarily by how well it describes the material it covers. The more precise and scholarly writers disagree, saying that mixing caption types is a violation of a fundamental concept of balance.

This concept of balance they express in a simple rule—the rule of parallel construction: all coordinate captions should be of the same grammatical construction. That is, if the caption for one of the major report parts (say part II) is a noun phrase, all equal-level captions (parts III, IV, V, and so on) must be noun phrases. And if the first subdivision under a major section (say part A of II) is a sentence, the captions coordinate with it (B, C, D, and so on) must be sentences.

The following segment of an outline illustrates violations of the principle of parallel construction.

 A. Machine output is lagging (sentence).
 B. Increase in cost of operation (noun phrase).
 C. Unable to deliver necessary steam (decapitated sentence).

One could correct this parallelism error in any one of three ways, by making the captions all sentences, all noun phrases, or all decapitated sentences. If all noun phrases are desired, such captions as these could be constructed.

   A. Lag in machine output.
   B. Increase in cost of operations.
   C. Inability to deliver necessary steam.

Or as all sentences, they could appear like this.

   A. Machine output is lagging.
   B. Cost of operations increases.
   C. Boiler cannot deliver necessary steam.

Another violation of parallelism is apparent in the following example.

   A. Rising level of income (participial phrase).
   B. Income distribution becoming uniform (decapitated sentence).
   C. Rapid advance in taxes (noun phrase).
   D. Annual earnings rise steadily (sentence).

Again, one could correct the error by selecting any one of the captions and revising the others to conform with it. As participial phrases, they would appear like this.

   A. Rising level of income.
   B. Uniformly increasing income distribution.
   C. Rapidly advancing taxes.
   D. Steadily rising annual earnings.

When revised as noun phrases, they would take this form.

   A. Rise in level of income.
   B. Uniform increase in income distribution.
   C. Rapid advance in taxes.
   D. Steady rise in annual earnings.

As decapitated sentences, they would read this way.

   A. Income level rising.
   B. Income distribution becoming uniform.
   C. Taxes advancing rapidly.
   D. Annual earnings rising steadily.

As a general rule, the talking caption should be the shortest possible word arrangement that also meets the talking requirement. Although the following captions talk well, their excessive lengths obviously affect their roles in communicating the report information:

   Appearance is the most desirable feature that steady college users of cigarette lighters look for.
   The two drawbacks of lighters mentioned most often by smokers who use matches are that lighters get out of order easily and frequently are out of fluid.
   More dependability and the ability to hold more lighter fluid are the improvements most suggested by both users and nonusers of cigarette lighters.

Obviously the captions contain too much information. Just what should be left out, however, is not easily determined. Much depends on the analysis the writers have given the material and what they have determined to be most significant. One analysis, for example, would support these revised captions.

Appearance most desirable feature.
Dependability primary criticism.
Fuel capacity most often suggested improvement.

Variety in expression

In the outline, as in all forms of writing, report writers should use a variety of expression. They should not overwork words and expressions, for too-frequent repetitions tend to be monotonous. And monotonous writing is not pleasing to the discriminating reader. The following outline excerpt well illustrates this point.

A.   Chemical production in Texas.
B.   Chemical production in California.
C.   Chemical production in Louisiana.

As a rule, if the captions talk well, there is little chance for occurrence of such monotonous repetition, for it is unlikely that successive sections would be presenting similar or identical information. That is, captions that are really descriptive of the material they cover are not likely to use the same words. As an illustration of this point, one could improve the outline topics in the foregoing example simply through making the captions talk.

A.   Texas leads in chemical production.
B.   California holds runner-up position.
C.   Rapidly gaining Louisiana ranks third.

QUESTIONS

1.   Explain the relationship of the report outline to the finished report.
2.   What are the basic patterns of report organization? Can you see advantages and shortcomings in these patterns? Discuss.
3.   Describe the two conventional systems of symbols used in outlining the report. Illustrate each to the sixth level of subdivision.
4.   Discuss the concept of outlining as a process of division.
5.   By what four relationships may the information on a subject be divided? Illustrate each.
6.   Select a problem (different from the text illustrations) that has at least two division possibilities. Evaluate each of the possibilities.
7.   Assume that you are working on a report on the history of manufacturing in the northeastern section of the United States. What division possibilities would you consider in organizing this problem? Discuss the merits of each.
8.   What are talking captions? Topic captions? Illustrate each by example (different from those in the text).

9. Point out any violations of grammatical parallelism in the following subheads of a major division of a report.
    a. Sporting goods shows market increase.
    b. Modest increase in hardware volume.
    c. Automotive parts remains unchanged.
    d. Plumbing supplies records slight decline.

10. The following subheads of a major division of a report are not all parallel in grammatical construction. Correct them.
    a. Predominance of cotton farming in southern counties.
    b. Livestock paces farm income in the western region.
    c. Wheat crop dominant in the north region.
    d. Truck farming leads in central and eastern section.

11. Correct another set of captions:
    a. High rate of sales in district III.
    b. District II ranks second.
    c. District IV reports losses.
    d. District I at the bottom.

12. Correct yet another set of captions:
    a. Need for improved communication.
    b. Alternative plans considered.
    c. Complicating factor of qualified personnel.
    d. Selection of education plan.

13. Elaborate on the need for variety of expression on the outline headings. Back up your presentation with illustrations.

14. Mark the point of error in the following portion of a report outline. Explain the error.
    a. Initial costs differ little.
    b. Brand B has best trade-in value.
        1. Brand A is a close second.
    c. Composite costs favor brand B.

15. Assume that you are writing a report on the expenditures of students at your college. Work up a tentative outline for this problem.

Constructing the formal report

W hen the outline is in finished form, orderly report writers next turn to the task of planning the makeup of the report. This task is complicated by the fact that reports are far from standardized in regard to physical arrangement. The variations among reports are countless. In fact, report types in use are so numerous as to almost defy meaningful classification. Even so, if report writers are to determine the best makeup of each report, they must be generally acquainted with the possibilities of choice available. Thus, report writers should be acquainted with some workable approach to the structure of all reports.

AN APPROACH TO REPORT MAKEUP

The following paragraphs present such an approach. It should be pointed out, though, that the concept of this approach is quite general. It does not account for all possible reports nor the countless variations in report makeup. But it does serve to help one grasp the relationship of all reports.

Structural relationships of all reports

To understand this relationship, one may view the whole of reports as resembling a stairway, as illustrated in Figure 8–1. At the top of this stairway is the formal, full-dress report. (See also an illustration of the long, formal report in Appendix D–1.) This is the form used when the problem is long and the problem situation is formal. In addition to the report text (usually introduction through conclusion), this formal report has a number of parts. They appear before the report text in the same way the prefatory parts appear before the text material of this or almost any other book. Such pages are included primarily for reasons of length and formality. Although there is no standardized set of prefatory ingredi-

98

FIGURE 8–1. Progression of change in report makeup as formality requirements and length of the problem decrease

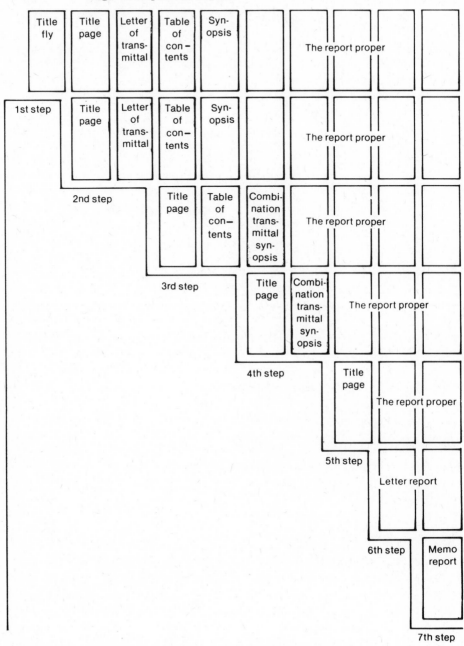

ents, these parts are traditional to the typical long, formal report: title fly, title page, letters or transmittal and authorization, table of contents, and synopsis. Detailed descriptions of the content and form of these papers appear elsewhere in this book.

As the need for formality decreases and the problem becomes smaller, the makeup of the report also changes. Although these changes are far from standardized, they follow a general order. First, the somewhat useless title fly drops out. This page contains nothing other than the title, and the title information appears on the next page. Obviously the page is used strictly for reasons of formality. Next in the progression, the synopsis (summary) combines with the transmittal letter. When this stage is reached, the report problem usually is short enough to permit its summary in relatively short space. A third step down, the table of contents drops out. The table of contents is a guide to the report text, and such a guide serves little value in a short report. Certainly a guide to a 100-page report is necessary, and a guide to a 1-page report is illogical. Somewhere between these extremes a dividing point exists. The report writers should follow the general guide of including a table of contents whenever it appears to be of some value to the reader.

Another step down as formality and length requirements continue to decrease, the combined letter of transmittal and synopsis drops out. Thus, the report now has only a title page and report text. The title page remains to the last because it serves as a useful cover page. In addition, it contains the most important of the identifying information. Below this short-report form is a report that reinstates the letter of transmittal and summary and presents the entire report in the form of a letter—thus, the letter report. And, finally, for short problems of even more informality the memorandum (informal letter) form is used. These steps are illustrated in Appendix D–2, 3, and 4.

As previously mentioned, this analysis of report change is at best general, and perhaps it oversimplifies changes in report structure. Few of the reports actually written coincide exactly with its steps. Most of them, however, fit generally within the framework of the diagram. Knowledge of this relationship of length and formality should be helpful to investigators as they begin to plan the report for their problem.

Ingredients of the formal report

In a sense, the report writers' task of designing a report is much like the task of the architect. Both have a number of possible ingredients with which to work. Both seek to select and arrange the ingredients to meet the requirements of a given situation. And in order to do their respective tasks skillfully, both must know well the ingredients at their disposal.

For report writers, these ingredients are the report parts. Because the traditional long, formal report contains the most common of these parts, it is described in the following pages. In addition, one such report is illustrated in Appendix D–1, and the mechanics of some of the parts are illustrated in Chapter 12. Less formal and shorter reports are described in Chapter 9. The following outline of the parts of a traditional long, formal report serves as a preview to the discussion that follows. For convenience, the parts are arranged by groups. First are the prefatory parts— those that are most related to the formality and length of the report. Then comes the report proper, which, of course, is the meat of all reports. It is the report story. The final group consists of appended parts. These contain supplementary materials. As a rule, these materials are not essential to the report presentation. They are included largely to serve any special interests the readers may have in the problem or to help the readers in their use of the report.

 Prefatory parts:
  Title fly.
  Title page.
  Letter of authorization.
  Letter of transmittal, preface, or foreword.
  Table of contents and table of illustrations.
  Synopsis.
 The report proper.
  Introduction.
  The report findings (usually presented in two or more major divisions).
  Conclusions, recommendations, or summaries.
 Appended parts.
  Bibliography.
  Appendix.
  Index.

CONSTRUCTION OF THE PREFATORY PARTS

In constructing the prefatory parts of a report, one should keep in mind that these parts make significant contributions. They give vital identification information. They contribute to the formality of the report situation. And they aid in communicating the report information. The following review shows the specific contributions of each.

Title fly

First among the possible prefatory report pages is the title fly. As a rule, it contains only the report title (see Appendix D–1). The wording of the title should be so carefully selected that it tells at a glance what is covered in the report. That is, it should fit the report like a glove, snugly covering all the report information— no more, no less.

For completeness of coverage, report writers may build titles around the five Ws of the journalist: *who, what, where, when, why*. Sometimes *how* may be added to this list. In some problems, however, not all of the Ws are essential to complete identification; nevertheless, they serve as a good checklist for completeness. For example, a title of a report analyzing the Lane Company 198— advertising campaigns might be construed as follows:

Who: Lane Company.
What: Analysis of advertising campaigns.
Where: (not essential).
When: 198—.
Why: (implied).

Thus, the title emerges: "Analysis of the Lane Company's 198— Advertising Campaigns."

Obviously one cannot write a completely descriptive title in a few words— certainly not in a word or two. Extremely short titles are usually vague. They cover everything; they touch nothing. Yet, it is the objective of writers to achieve conciseness in addition to completeness; so they must also seek the most economical word pattern consistent with completeness. Occasionally, in the attempt to achieve conciseness and completeness at once, it is advisable to use subtitles.

Title page

Like the title fly, the title page presents the report title. But, in addition, it displays other information essential to the identification of the report (see Appendix D–1). Usually it presents the complete identification of the writer and authorizer or recipient of the report. Normally such identification includes titles (or roles), companies and/or departments, street and city addresses. It may include the date of writing, particularly if the time identification is not in the report title. As was pointed out earlier, it is the last of the prefatory parts to drop out as the report changes form. It remains to the last because the part contains some vital identification material. The page is mechanically constructed and may take any of a number of forms. Two such forms are illustrated in Chapter 12.

Letter of authorization

As discussed in Chapter 3, a report may be authorized orally or in writing. If the authorization is written, a copy of this document (usually a letter or memorandum) may be inserted after the title page. If the authorization is oral, the letter of transmittal and/or the introductory section of the report may review the authorization information.

Letter of transmittal

Most formal reports contain some form of personal communication from writer to reader. In most business cases, the letter of transmittal makes this contact (see Appendix D–1). In some formal cases, particularly when the report is written for a group of readers, a foreword or preface performs this function.

The letter of transmittal, as its name implies, is a letter that transmits the report to the intended reader. Since this message is essentially positive, the letter is preferably written in direct style. That is, the letter beginning transmits the report directly, without explanation or other delaying information. Thus, the opening words say, in effect, "Here is the report." Tied to or following this statement of transmittal usually comes a brief identification of the subject matter of the study and possibly an incidental summary reference to the authorization information (who assigned the report, when, and so on).

If the letter is combined with the synopsis, as may be done in some forms of reports, a quick review of report highlights may follow the opening transmittal and identification, much in the manner described in the following discussion of the synopsis. But whether the letter of transmittal does or does not contain a synopsis of the report text, generally report writers use the letter to make helpful and informative comments about the report. They may, for example, suggest how the report information may be used. They may suggest follow-up studies, point out special limitations or mention side issues of the problem. In fact, they may include anything that helps the reader to understand or appreciate the report.

Except in very formal instances, the letter affords the writer an opportunity to more or less chat with the reader. Such letters might well reflect the warmth and vigor of the writer's personality. Generally, good use of first and second person pronouns (*you, I, we,* and so on) is made. A warm note of appreciation for the assignment or a willingness and desire to pursue the project further traditionally marks the letter close.

Minor distinctions sometimes are drawn between forewords and prefaces, but for all practical purposes they are the same. Both are preliminary messages from writer to reader. Although usually they do not formally transmit the report, forewords and prefaces do many of the other things done by letters of transmittal. Like the letters of transmittal, they seek to help the reader appreciate and understand the report. They may, for example, include helpful comments about the report—its use, interpretation, follow-up, and such. In addition, prefaces and forewords frequently contain expressions of indebtedness to those helpful in the research. Like the letters of transmittal, they usually are written in first person, but seldom are they as informal as some letters. Arrangement of the contents of prefaces and forewords follows no established pattern.

Table of contents and list of illustrations

If a report is long enough for a guide to its contents to be helpful, it should have a table of contents (see Appendix D–1). This table is the report outline in its finished form (as discussed in Chapter 7) with page numbers. If the report has a number of tables, charts, illustrations, and the like, a separate table of contents may be set up for them. The mechanics for construction of both of these contents units are fully described in Chapter 12.

Synopsis

The synopsis (also called summary, abstract, epitome, and précis) is the report in miniature. It concisely summarizes all the essential ingredients of the report. It includes all the major facts, as well as major analyses and conclusions derived from these facts. Primarily it is designed for the busy executive who may not have time to read the whole report, but it may also serve as a preview or review for those who very carefully read the report text.

In constructing the synopsis, report writers simply reduce the parts of the report in order and proportion. As their objective is to cut the report to a fraction of its length (usually less than one eighth), much of the writers' success is determined by their skill in directness and word economy. With space at a premium, loose writing is costly. But in their efforts to achieve conciseness, writers are likely to find their writing style dull. Thus, they must work hard to give this concise bit of writing a touch of color and style interest to reflect the tone of the main report.

Although most synopses simply present the report in normal order (normally from introduction to conclusion), there is now some usage of a more direct opening (see Figure 8–2). Such a plan shifts the major findings, conclusions, or recommendations (as the case may be) to the major position of emphasis at the beginning. From this direct beginning, the summary moves to the introductory parts and thence through the report in normal order.

FIGURE 8–2.   Diagram of the synopsis in normal order and in direct order

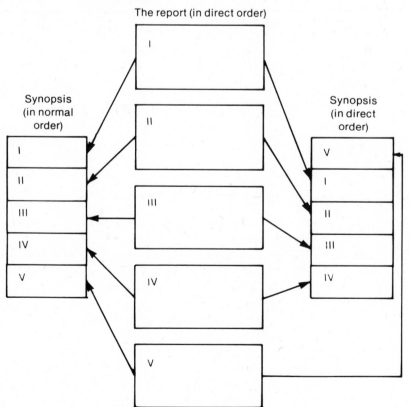

CONTENT OF THE REPORT PROPER

Presentation of the report contents may follow any of a number of arrangements. Some companies prefer to prescribe a definite arrangement for all reports, particularly for the technical ones. As may be expected, these arrangements vary with the needs and whims of the companies involved. Descriptions of two such reports, the technical memorandum report and the staff study, appear in Appendix D–6 and Chapter 9, respectively.

Other companies prefer to follow the traditional, time-honored arrangements. The best known of these is the *indirect* (also called logical and inductive) arrangement. This order of presenting the report material begins with whatever introductory comments are needed to prepare the reader for the information that follows (see the long, formal report in Appendix D–1). Next comes the information gathered. Here the information collected is applied to the problem. It is analyzed and interpreted. The final section of a report written in logical order achieves the report objective. Depending on the objective, this section may summarize, conclude, and/or recommend.

The *direct* arrangement is a second conventional pattern of report structure. It differs from the indirect (also called psychological and deductive) arrangement mainly by its beginning. Instead of introducing the problem, the direct order of report leads off with the major message of the report. That is, the report may begin with a recommendation, conclusion, or summary of findings, whichever the objective of the report happens to involve.

All these variations in the form of the report body are largely rearrangements of the contents of the conventional logical pattern. Thus, the following review of the makeup of the logical report arrangement should equip the student to adapt to the other patterns.

Introduction

The purpose of the introduction of the report is to orient the reader to the problem at hand. In this undertaking, it may include scores of possible topics, for anything may logically be included to help the reader to understand and appreciate the problem. Although the possible contents are varied, report writers should consider the following general topics.

Origin of the report. In many reports, the first part of the introduction presents a review of the facts of authorization. In this section are such facts as when, how, and by whom the report was authorized; who wrote the report; and when the report was submitted. This section is particularly useful in reports that have no letter of transmittal, but some writers prefer its inclusion in all report introductions, even though duplication of information is the result.

Purpose. The first section of many report introductions is a description of the purpose of the investigation. Called by other names (objective, problem, object, aim, goal, mission, assignment, proposal, project, and the like), the purpose of the report is the value to be attained by solving the problem. That value may be a long- or short-term value or a combination of both.

One may state the purpose of a report in various ways. For example, one may state it in an infinitive phrase (To propose standards of corporate annual reports), or in the form of a well-phrased question (What retail advertising practices do Centerville consumers disapprove of?) Usually this major purpose requires no more than a single sentence.

The writers also may cover collateral, or secondary, purposes in this section. If the report solves a major problem, it may at the same time achieve collateral values. By stating these values, the writers help to convince the reader of the worthwhileness of the report. In other words, the writers use a positive approach by telling all that the solved-problem can do for the reader.

Scope.   If the scope of the problem is not clearly covered in any of the other introductory sections, the writers may devote a separate section to it. By *scope* is meant the boundaries of the problem. In good, clear language, the writers describe the problem in regard to its exact coverage. Thus, the reader is told exactly what is and what is not a part of the problem.

Sources and methods of collecting data.   It is usually advisable to tell the reader how the report information was collected, whether through bibliographical research, through interviewing, and such. If bibliographical research was used, for example, the report writers could note the library sources consulted. If the publications list is long, however, a bibliography appended to the report may be a better means of listing. Or, another example, if interviewing was used, the description would cover such areas of the survey as sample determination, construction of the questionnaire, procedures followed in interviewing, facilities for checking returns, and so on. Whatever the technique used, it should be in sufficient detail to allow the reader to evaluate the quality of the work done.

Limitations.   With some problems, there are limitations of sufficient importance to warrant their presentation as a separate section of the introduction. By *limitations* is meant anything that in some way has worked to impede the investigation or in some way has a deterring effect on the report. An illustrative list of limitations to a report investigation problem may include an inadequate supply of money for conducting the investigation, insufficient time for doing the work, unavoidable conditions that hampered objective investigating, or limitations within the problem.

Historical background.   Sometimes a knowledge of the history of the problem is essential to a thorough understanding of the problem. Thus, a section on the problem's history frequently is a part of the report introduction. The general aim of this part is to acquaint the reader with some of the issues involved, some of the principles raised, and some of the values that may be received from the research. Also, this section orients the reader and helps give a better understanding of the problem. A better understanding should help the reader and the writers to solve similar problems that may arise in the future.

Definitions.   If a report is to use words likely to be unfamiliar to the reader, the report should define these words. One practice is to define each such word at the time of its first use in the text. Another practice is to set aside in the introduction a special section for definitions.

Report preview.   In many reports, the final part of the introductory section presents a preview of the report presentation. In this section, the writers tell the reader how the report will be told—what topics will be taken up first, second, third, and so on. And of even greater importance the writers explain the reasons for this plan. Thus, the reader receives a clear picture of the road ahead so that one may logically relate the topics of the report as they come up.

As previously noted, the sections discussed are only suggestions for introduction content. In few reports will one need all of the topics mentioned. And in some instances, one may need to combine some of the topics; in other instances, one may need to split them further into additional sections. In summary, report writers should tailor each introduction to fit the needs of the one situation.

The report body

The part of the report that presents the information collected and relates it to the problem is the report body. Normally it comprises the bulk of the content of a report. In fact, in a sense, this part is the report.

Specifically the report body consists of the presentation of findings of the research. It includes the analysis of these findings and application of them to the problem. It is all that appears in the logical order report between the introduction and conclusion sections, including the supporting tables and charts that relate to this part. Truly it is the heart of the report. Because it is so very important, it is the subject of many of the remaining chapters of this textbook.

The ending of the report

The ending of a report usually consists of a summary, conclusions, recommendations, or a combination of the three.

Summary. For some reports, particularly those that do little more than present fact, the end may consist of a summary of the major findings. Frequently these reports follow the practice of having minor summaries at the ends of major divisions. When this practice is followed, the final summary simply recaps these summaries. But one should not confuse this form of summary with the synopsis. Like the summary, the synopsis presents a summary of major findings; but unlike the summary it contains a gist of the major supporting facts.

Conclusions. The report writers draw conclusions by inference (induction or deduction) from the facts and discussion in the body. Conclusions follow facts, even though in some reports they appear at the beginning (the psychological arrangement).

Some writers prefer to tabulate the conclusions—that is, they make the conclusions stand out by listing them or in some other way distinguishing them from the remainder of the report. But the order of listing them in such an arrangement is open to question. Sometimes it is appropriate to place the most important ones first; sometimes it is better to list them according to the arrangement discussed in the findings. There also may be justification for combining them with the recommendations. In some cases, when the conclusion is obvious, it is wise to omit it and to present only a recommendation.

Recommendations.   The recommendations are the writers' section. Here they state their opinions based on the conclusions. Of course, writers may not state recommendations if they are not asked; but if they are asked, they state them completely, including who should do what, when, where, why, and sometimes how.

Alternative courses of action may be included. Since they are familiar with the findings, the writers should not leave their reader on the horns of dilemma. They should state their desired action and then leave the reader to choose a course of action. Since writers are usually in staff positions, they should give their advice for a line person to accept.

APPENDED PARTS

Sometimes it is desirable that special sections be appended to the report. The presence of these parts is normally determined by the specific needs of the problem concerned.

Appendix

The appendix, as its name implies, is a section tacked on. It is used for supplementary information that supports the body of the report but has no logical place within the body of the report. Possible contents include questionnaires, working papers, summary tables, additional references, other reports, and so on.

As a rule, the charts, graphs, sketches, and tables that directly support the report should not be in the appendix. Instead they should be in the body of the report where they support the findings. Reports are best designed for the convenience of the reader. Obviously it is not convenient for the reader to thumb through many pages in order to find an appendix illustration to the facts presented in the report body.

Bibliography

Investigations that make heavy use of bibliographical research normally require a bibliography (an identifying list of the publications consulted). The construction of this formal list appears in detail in Chapter 13.

Index

An index is an alphabetical guide to the subject matter of a manuscript. It is used primarily with long manuscripts in which it would be difficult to find a specific topic were a subject guide not available. But few reports are long enough to justify use of the index.

SUMMARY REVIEW OF REPORT CONSTRUCTION

In summary, it is with these ingredients that report writers build the report described at the top step in the diagram (Figure 8–1). By systematically dropping and changing some of them, report writers can adapt their reports to meet the formality needs of each situation. The description, of course, is oversimplified. Many companies prescribe differing report arrangements. Some, for example, may remove acknowledgements from the letter of transmittal or preface and place them in a separate section. They may break up the synopsis and present conclusions, recommendations, and findings in separate prefatory sections. And some may include special prefatory sheets for intercompany routing purposes. Nevertheless, the progression described captures the nature of the relationship of all reports. And it should serve as a good general guide in planning them.

QUESTIONS

1. Discuss the model used in the chapter to show progression of report change. Trace the steps in it and explain each.
2. Select three of the report problems at the end of the text (preferably the long ones) and write a report title for each. Use the title checklist to explain and defend your title.
3. It has been said that the shorter a report is, the longer its title needs to be. Do you agree? Defend your decision.
4. Discuss the content of the title page. Why is this page the last of the prefatory parts to leave the report?
5. Discuss the contents of the letter of transmittal.
6. Explain the differences in letters of transmittal, forewords, and prefaces. Why would you use each?
7. Discuss and justify the differences in writing style in the letter of transmittal and the text of the report.
8. What determines whether a report should have a table of contents?
9. Tell how to construct a synopsis.
10. Discuss the objectives of the introduction to a report.
11. How would the introduction of a report written for only one reader who knows the problem well differ from that written for a dozen readers, some of whom know little about the problem?
12. What effect does the life of a report (the time it is kept on file) have on the introduction content?
13. Discuss each of the introduction topics mentioned in the text, bringing out the considerations that would determine the use of each.
14. Why is it important that the sources of information used and the methods of investigation followed be fully described?
15. What is meant by the "limitations" of a report problem?
16. Explain the content and role of a preview in the introduction of a report.
17. Name and distinguish between the conventional types of report endings. Explain in what types of reports each should be used.
18. What is the role of the appendix in a report?
19. When may a report have a bibliography? When is an index considered appropriate?

Constructing short and special reports

Most reports written in industry are short, informal types. They are quite different from the long, formal type described in detail in Chapter 8. To be sure, long, formal reports are written—often. But they simply do not compare in number with the less imposing types. Thus, because of their importance this chapter is devoted to a review of these less formal reports. And because certain special report types also are likely to be encountered in business, some of these reports also are covered.

To some, the emphasis that has been placed on the long, formal report may appear to be disproportionate. "If the long, formal report is not among the types most frequently used," they may ask, "why is it given such major emphasis? Why is not the major stress placed on the types most common in day-to-day business activity?"

The answers to these questions should be apparent from the approach taken in Chapter 8. As the diagram in Figure 8–1 shows, the long, formal report is related to other types. The relationship of its form to that of the other report types is clear. The techniques of organizing it are much the same as those for the lesser types. The writing that goes into it likewise is similar. In fact, all that goes into the long, formal report has some application in constructing the lesser forms. Thus, by learning to write and to construct this the most complex of all reports, one is prepared to work on the lesser types. The process may be likened to the work of a carpenter. Having built a mansion, the carpenter finds it easy to build a bungalow, a barn, or a lean-to.

MAJOR DIFFERENCES IN SHORT AND LONG REPORTS

Even though much of what has been learned concerning the long, formal report applies equally well to the other forms, certain differences do exist. By concen-

109

trating on these differences, one can quickly adapt one's knowledge of report writing to the wide variety of short, informal reports. Four areas of such differences stand out as most significant: (1) less need for introductory material, (2) predominance of direct (psychological and deductive) order, (3) more personal writing style, and (4) less need for coherence aids.

Less need for introductory material

One major content difference in the shorter report forms is their minor need for introductory material. Most reports at this level concern day-to-day problems. Thus, these reports have a short life. They are not likely to be kept on file for posterity to read. They are intended for only a few readers, and these few know the problem and its background. The reader's interests are in the findings of the report and any action they will lead to.

This is not to say that all shorter forms have no need for introductory material. In fact, some have very specific needs. In general, however, the introductory need in the shorter and more informal reports is less than that for the more formal and longer types. But no rule applies across the board. Each case should be analyzed individually. In each case, writers must cover whatever introductory material is needed to prepare the reader to receive the report. In some shorter reports, an incidental reference to the problem, authorization of the investigation, or such will do the job. In some extreme cases, a detailed introduction comparable to that of the more formal report may be needed. There are reports, also, that need no introduction whatever. In such cases, the nature of the report serves as sufficient introductory information. A personnel action, for example, by its very nature explains its purpose. So do weekly sales reports, inventory reports, and some progress reports.

Predominance of direct order

Because usually they are more goal-oriented, the shorter more informal reports are likely to use the direct order of presentation. That is, typically the goals of such a report are to handle a problem—to make a specific conclusion or recommendation of action. This conclusion or recommendation is of such relative significance that it by far overshadows the analysis and information that support it. Thus, it deserves a leadoff position.

As noted earlier, the longer forms of reports may also use a direct order. In fact, many of them do. The point is, however, that most do not. Most follow the traditional logical (introduction, body, conclusion) order. As one moves down the structural ladder toward the more informal and shorter reports, however, the need for direct order increases. At the bottom of the ladder, direct order is more the rule than the exception.

The decision of whether or not to use the direct order is best based on a consideration of the readers' likely use of the report. If the readers need the report conclusion or recommendation as a basis for action they must take, directness will speed these efforts. Direct presentations will permit them to receive quickly the most important information. If they have confidence in the work of the writers, they may not choose to read beyond this point, and they can quickly take the action the report supports. Should they desire to question any part of the report, however, it is there for their inspection. The obvious result would be to save the valuable time of busy executives.

On the other hand, if there is reason to believe that the readers will want to arrive at the conclusion or recommendation only after a logical review of the analysis, the writers should organize the report in the indirect (logical) order. Especially would this arrangement be preferred when the readers do not have reason to place full confidence in the writers' work. A novice working in a new assignment, for example, would be wise to lead the readers to the recommendation or conclusion by using the logical order.

More personal writing style

Although the writing that goes into all reports has much in common, that in the shorter reports tends to be more personal. That is, the shorter reports are likely to use the personal pronouns *I, we, you,* and such rather than a strict third-person approach.

The explanation of this tendency toward personal writing in short reports should be obvious. In the first place, the situation that gives rise to a short report usually involves more personal relationships. Such reports tend to be from and to people who know each other—people who normally address each other informally when they meet and talk. In addition, the shorter reports by their nature are apt to involve a personal investigation. The finished work represents the personal observations, evaluations, and analyses of the writers. The writers are expected to report their work as their own. A third explanation is that the shorter problems tend to be the day-to-day routine ones. They are by their very nature informal. It is logical to report them informally, and personal writing tends to produce an informal effect.

As is explained in Chapter 11, report writers should decide on the question of whether to write in personal or impersonal style on the basis of the circumstances of the situation. They should consider the expectations of those who will receive the report. If the recipients expect formality, the writers should write impersonally. If the recipients expect informality, the writers should write personally. Second, when report writers do not know reader preferences, they should consider the formality of the situation. Convention favors impersonal writing for the most formal situations.

From this analysis, it should be apparent that either style can be appropriate for reports ranging from the shortest to the longest type. The point is, however, that short report situations are more likely to justify personal writing.

Less need for coherence aids

As is pointed out in Chapter 11, the longer forms of reports need some type of coherence plan to make the parts stick together. That is, because of the complexities brought about by length, report writers must make efforts to relate the parts. Otherwise, each paper would read like a series of disjointed minor reports. What report writers should do is to use special coherence aids such as summaries and introductory forward-looking sentences and paragraphs at key places. Thus, the readers are able to see how each part of the report fits into the whole scheme of things.

The shorter the report becomes, the less is its need for coherence aids. This is not to say that coherence is not vital in short reports. Coherence is vital to all reports. But in the shorter reports it is not necessary to use the special coherence aids (introductory sentences and paragraphs, summaries, and the like) to achieve it. In fact, in the extremely short forms (such as memorandum and letter reports), little in the way of wording is needed to relate the parts. In such cases, the information is so brief and simple that a logical and orderly presentation clearly shows the plan of presentation.

Although coherence plans are less frequently used in the short forms of reports, the question of whether to include them should not be arbitrarily determined by length alone. Instead, the matter of need should guide writers in making a choice. Whenever the presentation contains organization complexities that can be made clear by summaries, introductions, and relating parts, these coherence elements should be included. Thus, need rather than length is the major determinant. But it is clearly evident that need for coherence aids decreases as the report length decreases.

SHORT FORMS OF REPORTS

Of the conventional short forms of reports, three in particular deserve special attention. They are the three at the bottom of the illustration stairway of report progression (Figure 8–1): the short report, the letter report, and the memorandum report. Varying widely in form and arrangement, they make up the bulk of the reports written in industry.

The short report

One of the more popular of the less imposing reports is the conventional short report (see illustration, Appendix D–2). Representing the fifth step in the diagram of report progression, this report consists of only a title page and the report text. Its popularity may be explained by the middle-ground impression of formality it gives. Inclusion of the one most essential of the prefatory parts gives the report at least a minimum appearance of formality. And it does this without the tedious work of preparing the other prefatory pages. It is ideally suited for the short but somewhat formal problem.

Like most of the less imposing forms of reports, the short report may be organized in either the direct or indirect order, although direct order is by far the most common plan. As illustrated by the report in Appendix D–2, this most common plan begins with a quick summary of the report, including and emphasizing conclusions and recommendations. Such a beginning serves much the same function as the synopsis of a long, formal report.

Following the summary are whatever introductory remarks are needed. As noted previously, sometimes this part is not needed at all. Usually, however, there follows a single paragraph covering the facts of authorization and a brief statement of the problem and its scope. After the introductory words come the findings of the investigation. Just as in the longer report forms, the findings are presented, analyzed, and applied to the problem. From all this comes a final conclusion and, if needed, a recommendation. These last two elements—conclusions and recommendations—may be presented at the end, even though they are also presented in the beginning summary. Sometimes not to do so would end the report abruptly. It would stop the flow of reasoning before reaching the report's logical goal.

The mechanics of constructing the short report are about the same as those for the more formal, longer types. As illustrated in Appendix D–2, this report uses the same form of title page and the same layout requirement. Like the longer reports, it uses captions. But because of the report's brevity, the captions rarely go beyond the two-division level. In fact, one level of division is most common. Like any other report, its use of graphic aids, appendix parts, and bibliography depends on its need for them.

Letter reports

As the wording implies, a letter report is a report written in letter form (see illustration, Appendix D–4). Primarily it is used to present information to someone outside the company, especially when the report information is to be sent by mail. For example, a company's written evaluation of one of its credit customers may well be presented in letter form and mailed to the one who requests it. An outside consultant may write his or her analysis and recommendations in letter form. Or an organization officer may elect to report certain information to the membership in letter form.

Normally letter reports are used to present the shorter problems—typically those that require three or four pages or less. But no hard and fast rule exists on this point. Long letter reports (ten pages and more) have often been used successfully.

As a general rule, letter reports use the personal style (*I, you, we* references). Exceptions exist, of course, as when one is preparing such a report for an august group, such as a committee of the U.S. Senate or a company's board of directors. Other than this point, the writing style recommended for letter reports is much the same as that for any other report. Certainly clear and meaningful expression is a requirement for all reports.

Letter reports may be arranged either in the direct or indirect order. If the report is to be mailed, there is some justification for using an indirect approach. As such reports arrive unannounced, an initial reminder of what they are, how they originated, and such is in order. A letter report written to the membership of an organization, for example, may appropriately begin with these words.

As authorized by your Board of Directors last January 6, the following review of member company expenditures for direct mail selling is presented.

If one elects to begin a letter report in the direct order, one would be wise to use a subject line. The subject line consists of some identifying words, which appear at the top of the letter, usually immediately after or before the salutation. Although they are formed in many ways, one acceptable version begins with the word "Subject" and follows it with descriptive words that identify the problem. As the following example illustrates, this identifying device helps to overcome any effect of confusion or bewilderment the direct beginning may otherwise have on the reader.

Subject: Report of direct mail expenditures of
           association members, authorized by Board of
           Directors January 1981
Association members are spending 8 percent more on direct mail advertising this year than they did the year before. Current plans call for a 10 percent increase for next year.

Another possibility is to work the introductory identifying information into the direct opening material.

Regardless of which beginning is used, the organization plan for letter reports corresponds to those of the longer, more formal types. Thus, the indirect order letter report follows its introductory buildup with a logical presentation and analysis of the information gathered. From this presentation, it works logically to a conclusion and/or recommendation in the end. The direct order letter report follows the initial summary-conclusion-recommendation section with whatever introductory words are appropriate. For example, the direct beginning illustrated above could be followed with these introductory words.

These are the primary findings of a study authorized by your Board of Directors last January. As they concern information vital to all of us in the association, they are presented here for your confidential use.

Following such an introductory comment, the report would present the supporting facts and their analyses. The writer would systematically build up the case that supported the opening comment. With either order, when the report is sent as a letter, it may close with whatever friendly goodwill comment is appropriate for the one occasion.

Memorandum reports

Memorandum reports are merely informal letter reports. They are used primarily for routine reporting within an organization, although some organizations use them for external communicating. Because they are internal communications, often they are informally written. In fact, they frequently are hurried, handwritten messages from one department or worker to another department or worker. The more formal memorandum reports, however, are well-written and carefully typed compositions (see Appendix D–3) that rival some more imposing types in appearance.

As far as the writing of the memorandum is concerned, all the instructions for writing letter reports apply. But memorandum reports tend to be more informal. And because they usually concern day-to-day problems, they have very little need for introductory information. In fact, they frequently begin reporting without any introductory comment.

The memorandum report is presented on somewhat standardized interoffice memorandum stationery. The words *From, To,* and *Subject* appear at the page top (Appendix D–3), usually following the company identification. Sometimes, the word *Date* also is a part of the heading. Like letters, the memorandum may carry a signature. In many offices, however, no typed signature is included, and the writer merely initials the heading.

SPECIAL REPORT FORMS

As noted previously, this review describes only generally the forms of the reports used in business. Countless variations exist. Of these variations, a few deserve special emphasis.

The staff report

One of the most widely used reports in business is the staff report. Patterned after a form traditional to the technical fields, the staff report is well adapted to business problem solving. Its arrangement follows the logical thought processes used in solving the conventional business problems. Although the makeup of this report varies by company, the following arrangement recommended by a major metals manufacturer is typical.

Identifying information: As the company's staff reports are written on inter-company communication stationery, the conventional identification information (To, From, Subject, Date) appears at the beginning.

Summary: For busy executives who want their facts fast, a summary begins the report. Some executives will read no further. Others will want to trace the report content in detail.

The problem (or objective) : As in all good problem-solving procedures, the report text logically begins with a clear description of the problem—what it is, what it is not, what are its limitations, and such.

Facts: Next comes the information gathered in the attempt to solve the problem.

Discussion: Analyses of the facts and applications of the facts and analyses to the problem follow. (Frequently the statement of facts and the discussion of them can be combined.)

Conclusions: From the preceding discussion of facts comes the final meanings as they apply to the problem.

Recommendation: If the objective of the problem allows for it, a course of action may be recommended on the basis of the conclusions.

Perhaps the major users of staff reports are the branches of the armed forces. In all branches, this report is standardized. As shown in Figure 9–1, the military version differs somewhat from the business arrangement just described.

FIGURE 9–1.   Military form of staff study report

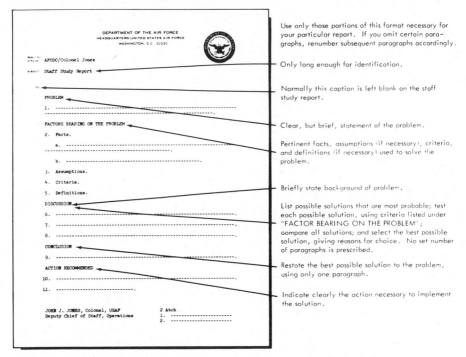

Source: *Air Force Pamphlet* 10–1, Department of the Air Force, Washington, D.C., July 1969, p. 192.

The corporate annual report

Although they are not likely to participate in writing them, business students should know the general forms and contents of corporate annual reports. These reports, which are prepared for most of the nation's leading corporations, tell the operations stories for the companies concerned. The reports are designed to help the investor, the employees, and the public to understand and appreciate the business enterprise. And as all business students will some day fall into one or more of these categories, each would do well to be able to understand these reports.

Originally designed to present only the financial operating facts of the firm, annual reports now cover all areas of a company's operations. Most companies prepare these reports by choice, for although annual reports are required by regulations of the Securities and Exchange Commission and by listings agreements with stock exchanges, these companies want to keep the public closely informed of their activities. They see in the annual report both a public service and a public relations tool.

The audit report

The short-form and long-form audit reports are well known to accountants. The short-form report is perhaps the most standardized of all reports—if, indeed, it can be classified as a report. Actually it is a stereotyped statement verifying an accountant's inspection of a firm's financial records. The wording of the short-form audit report can be seen in the financial section of most corporate annual reports.

Composition of the long-form audit report is as varied as the short form is rigid. In fact, a national accounting association, after studying practices, concluded that no typical form exists. Although it covers a somewhat simple and limited audit, the audit report illustrated in Appendix D–5 shows one acceptable form.

The technical report

Although often treated as a highly specialized form of report, the technical report differs from other reports primarily in its subject matter. Its form variations correspond to most of those discussed in this and the preceding chapter (see Appendix D–6). Even so, a somewhat conventional arrangement of the more formal research report has emerged.

This conventional arrangement begins much like the traditional formal report described in Chapter 8. First come the title pages, although frequently a routing or distribution form for intercompany use may be worked into them or perhaps added to them. A letter of transmittal is likely to come next, followed by a table of contents and illustrations. From this point on, however, the technical report is likely to differ from the traditional one. These differences are mainly in the treatment of information usually presented in the synopsis and in the organizations plan of the report text.

Instead of the conventional synopsis, the technical report often presents the summary information in various parts. There may be, for example, a separate prefatory section covering findings, conclusions, and recommendations. Also, parts of the conventional introduction may appear as prefatory sections—especially objectives and acknowledgements.

Organization of the text of the technical report typically follows a standard order. Although no one order is universal, the most common one is the following:

Introduction.

Methodology (or methods and materials).

Facts.

Discussion.

Conclusion.

Recommendations.

QUESTIONS

1. What are the major differences in the construction of the short and long reports?
2. Why do the shorter forms of reports usually require less introductory material than do the longer reports?

3. Defend the use of direct order in the shorter forms of reports.

4. What should determine whether one should use the direct order in a report?

5. Explain the logic of using personal style in some reports.

6. What should determine whether one should use personal style in a report?

7. What should determine whether one should use a coherence plan in a report?

8. Describe the structure of a typical short report.

9. Distinguish between letter and memorandum reports.

10. Discuss and illustrate (with examples other than those in the text) two contrasting types of beginnings for the letter report.

11. Describe the makeup of the traditional staff report. Can you think of any advantages of this plan?

12. Discuss the purposes of the typical corporate annual report.

13. How do technical reports differ from other business reports? How are they similar?

10
Techniques of readable writing

After the researchers have organized their findings, they know what the facts of the problem are, what the facts mean, and how they will apply them to the problem. Thus, the story the report will tell is clear in their minds. Now their task is to communicate the story to those who should receive it.

Of all the tasks researchers must perform, this is the one they are most likely to perform poorly. Yet, regardless of how well they have worked to this point, unless they communicate the results of their work, they will fail in their objective. But communicating is not easy.

THE FUNDAMENTAL NEED FOR ADAPTATION

The difficulty of communicating was stressed in our introductory review of the communication process (Chapter 2). From this review it is clear that communication is not a precise activity—that some degree of miscommunication is the rule rather than the exception. It is clear also that communication involves fitting the message to the reader's mind—that is, using words and concepts which the reader knows and understands. This approach to communication is called adaptation. It is a fundamental concept that should govern one's use of all the writing suggestions made in following pages.

In order to adapt their writing, skilled report writers begin by visualizing their readers. Thus, they determine such things as who their readers are, how much they know about the subject, what are their educational levels, and how they think. Then, keeping these images of their readers in mind, they tailor their writing to fit these people.

The writers' task is relatively simple when they write to a single reader or homogeneous group of readers. But what if they write to a group with varying characteristics? What if, say, the audience comprises people ranging from college

119

graduates to grade school graduates? The answer should be obvious. In such cases, writers have no choice but to aim at the lowest level of the group. To aim higher would be to exclude the lower levels from the message.

When report writers are better educated or better informed on the subject area than the readers, adaptation means simplification. A company executive writing to the rank-and-file employee, for example, must write in the simple words the reader understands. Likewise, a technician writing to a nontechnical reader must simplify the writing. But when technicians write to fellow technicians, they do well to use the technical vernacular easily understood and expected by such people. As the following examples show, few technical writers were better aware of this fundamental rule than the late Dr. Albert Einstein. In writing on a tecnical subject to a nontechnical audience, he skillfully wrote down to their level.

What takes place can be illustrated with the help of our rich man. The atom M is a rich miser who, during his life, gives away no money (energy). But in his will he bequeaths his fortune to his sons M' and M", on condition that they give to the community a small amount, less than one thousandth of the whole estate (energy or mass). The sons together have somewhat less than the father had (the mass sum M' and M" is somewhat smaller than the mass M of the radioactive atom). But the part given to the community, though relatively small, is still so enormously large (considered as kinetic energy) that it brings with it a great threat of evil. Averting that threat has become the most urgent problem of our time.[1]

But when writing to fellow scientists, he wrote in words they understood and expected.

The general theory of relativity owes its existence in the first place to the empirical fact of the numerical equality of the inertial and gravitational mass of bodies, for which fundamental fact classical mechanics provided no interpretation. Such an interpretation is arrived at by an extension of the principle of relativity to co-ordinate systems accelerated relatively to one another. The introduction of co-ordinate systems accelerated relatively to inertial systems involves the appearance of gravitational fields relative to the latter. As a result of this, the general theory of relativity, which is based on the equality of inertia and weight, provides a theory of the gravitational field.[2]

SUPPORT OF THE READABILITY STUDIES

As we also noted in Chapter 2, the readability studies conducted over past years strongly support the need for adaptation. They show conclusively that writing that communicates is writing that fits the readability of the reader. More precisely, these studies show that readability of writing is determined mainly by two major factors. One is word choice. The other is sentence length. These two factors

---

[1] Albert Einstein, *Out of My Later Years,* Philosophical Library, Inc., New York, 1950, p. 53.

[2] Albert Einstein, *Essays in Science,* Philosophical Library, Inc., New York, 1934, p. 50.

form the basis for the following review of readability techniques. A third factor, paragraphing, also is covered. Although not so directly supported by the readability studies, paragraphing also affects readability.

Before taking up these specific techniques, however, one qualifying point should be stressed. One should not apply these techniques mechanically. Instead one must temper them with reason. Writing is not routine work to be done by the numbers, by rules, or by formulas. Rather it is to some extent an art. As in all forms of art, mastery of techniques is a prerequisite to good performance. In writing, perhaps more than in any other art, one must apply the techniques with good judgment.

WORD SELECTION

In general, the writer's task is to produce in the reader's mind the meanings formulated in the writer's mind. To do this, the writer uses written symbols of meaning (words). Thus, the writer's task is largely one of selecting words that exactly relate the intended meanings.

The very nature of words, however, makes this task difficult. A glance at the size of an unabridged dictionary dramatically explains this difficulty. In addition to the great number of words in the language, the writer's difficulty is intensified by the complexity of the word meaning. As pointed out in Chapter 2, words are at best inexact symbols of meanings. A single word may have a dozen dictionary definitions. In fact, it is said that the 500 most commonly used English words have a total of 14,000 dictionary definitions—an average of 28 meanings per word. No doubt, individual minds add to this number with countless shades of difference in meaning. Contributing further to this difficulty is the inexactness with which most people use words.

This complex nature of words makes the writer's task more difficult. Perhaps this difficulty is too much involved for even the best writers to overcome completely. But certainly writers can improve their communication ability by understanding these limitations and by making deliberate effort to overcome them.

Select words the reader understands

A major requirement of writing that communicates is that the words used mean the same to both writer and reader. In many instances in business, this requirement means simplifying the writing. Certainly simplification is justifiable in writing for those on a lower intellectual level. Even in writing to intellectual equals, there may be some need for simplification.

This suggestion of simplifying writing, however, should in no way be interpreted as an unqualified endorsement of primer writing. In writing for technical or other learned people on subjects about which they are well informed, one should write in words they expect and understand. But even in such cases, some degree of simplification is the key to quick and correct communication. As noted in Chapter 2, the readability studies support simplified writing. They show conclusively that writing communicates best when it is slightly below the comprehension level of the reader. Specifically they show that simplification is achieved through a general preference for the familiar over the unfamiliar, for the short over the long, and for the nontechnical over the technical word. Although these distinctions between words overlap considerably, they are discussed separately for reasons of emphasis.

Use strong, vigorous words. Like people, words have personality. Some words are strong and vigorous; some are dull and weak; and others fall in between these extremes. Skilled writers are constantly aware of these differences. They become students of words, and they select their words to produce just the right effect. They recognize, for example, that "tycoon" is stronger than "eminently successful business executive," that "bear market" is stronger than "generally declining market," and that a "boom" is stronger than a "period of business prosperity." The skilled writers make the strong words predominate.

Of all the forms of speech, the verb is the strongest, and it is closely followed by the noun. The verb is the action word, and action by its very nature commands interest. Nouns, of course, are the doers of action—the characters in the story, so to speak. As doers of action, they attract the reader's attention.

Contrary to what many novice writers think, adjectives and adverbs should be used sparingly. These words add length to the sentence, thereby distracting the reader's attention from the key nouns and verbs. As Voltaire phrased it, "The adjective is the enemy of the noun." In addition, adjectives and adverbs both involve subjective evaluations, and, as previously noted, the objective approach should be evident throughout the report.

Prefer the familiar to the unfamiliar word. As a general rule, the familiar everyday words are the best for report writers to use. Of course, the definition of familiar words varies by persons. What is everyday usage to some people is likely to appear to be high-level talk to others. Thus, the suggestion to use familiar language is in a sense a specific suggestion to apply the principle of adapting the writing to the reader.

Unfortunately many business writers do not use enough everyday language. Instead they tend to change character when they begin to put their thoughts on paper. Rather than writing naturally, they become stiff and stilted in their expression. For example, instead of using an everyday word like "try," they use the more unfamiliar word like "endeavor." They do not "find out"; they "ascertain." They "terminate" rather than "end," and they "utilize" instead of "use."

Now there is really nothing wrong with the hard words—if they are used intelligently. They are intelligently used when they are clearly understood by the reader, when they are best in conveying the meaning intended, and when they are used with wise moderation. Perhaps the best suggestion in this regard is that report writers use words they would use in face-to-face communication with the reader. Another good suggestion is that writers use the simplest words that carry the thought without offending the reader's intelligence.

The communication advantages of familiar words over the formal complex ones is obvious from the following contrasting examples.

Formal and complex	Familiar words
The conclusion ascertained from a perusal of the pertinent data is that a lucrative market exists for the product.	The data studied show that the product is in good demand.
The antiquated mechanisms were utilized for the experimentation.	The old machines were used for the test.
Company operations for the preceding accounting period terminated with a substantial deficit.	The company lost much money last year.

Prefer the short to the long word.   Short words tend to communicate better than long words. Certainly there are exceptions. Some long words like *hypnotize, hippopotamus,* and *automobile* generally are well known; some short words like *verd, vie, id,* and *gybe* are understood only by a few. On the whole, however, word length and word difficulty clearly are correlated. Also, the heavier the proportion of long words to short words, the harder the writing is to understand. This is true even when the reader understands the long words. As the readability studies clearly show, a heavy proportion of long words tends to slow up the reading and makes understanding difficult. Thus, wise report writers will use long words with caution. They will make certain that the long words they use are well known to their readers. And especially will they work to avoid using a heavy proportion of long words, even when these words are understood.

The following contrasting sentences clearly show the effect of long words on writing clarity. Educated readers are likely to understand long words, but the heavy proportion of long words makes heavy reading and slow communication. Without question, the simple versions communicate better.

Heavy or long words	Short and simple words
A decision was predicated on the assumption that an *abundance* of *monetary funds was forthcoming.*	The decision was *based* on the *belief* that there would *be more money.*
They *acceded* to *the proposition to terminate* business.	They *agreed* to *quit* business.
During the preceding year the company *operated at a financial deficit.*	*Last year* the company *lost money.*
Prior to accelerating productive operation, the foreman inspected the machinery.	*Before speeding up production,* the foreman inspected the machinery.
Definitive action was *affected subsequent to* reporting date.	*Final* action was *made after* the reporting date.

Use technical words with caution.   Every field has its own jargon. To those in the field, much of the jargon is a part of the everyday working vocabulary. Certainly it is logical to use this jargon in writing to members of the field. Even so, an overuse of specialized words can make reading hard for the technician. Frequently technical jargon is made up of long and high-sounding words. When used heavily, such words tend to dull the writing and to make the message hard to understand. This difficulty seems to increase as the proportion of technical words increases. The following sentence written by a physician illustrates this point.

> It is a methodology error to attempt to interpret psychologically an organic symptom which is the end-result of an intermediary change of organic processes instead of trying to understand these vegetative nervous impulses in their relation to psychological factors which introduce a change of organic events resulting in an organic disturbance.

No doubt the length of this sentence contributes to its difficulty, but the heavy proportion of technical terms also makes understanding difficult. The conclusion that may be drawn here is obvious. Technical writers may use technical terms in writing to fellow technicians, but they should use such words in moderation.

In writing to those outside of the field, technical writers must write in the language of the layman. Physicians might well refer to a "cerebral vascular accident" in writing to fellow physicians, but they would do well to use "stroke" in writing to laymen. Accountants who write to nonaccountants may also need to avoid the jargon of the profession. Even though terms like "accounts receivable," "liabilities," and "surplus" are elementary to accountants they may be meaningless to some people. So, in writing to such people, accountants would be wise to use nontechnical descriptions, such as "how much is owed the company," "how much the company owes," and "how much was left over." Similar examples can be drawn from any specialized field.

Bring the writing to life with words

Writing must hold the undivided interest for the best possible communication result. Certainly subject matter is a major determinant of the interest of writing. But even lively topics can be presented in writing so dull that interested readers cannot keep their minds on the subject.

To bring the writing to life and make it interesting is no simple undertaking. In fact, it involves techniques that practically defy description—techniques that even the most accomplished writers never completely master. In spite of the difficulty of this undertaking, however, three simple but important suggestions for bringing writing to life can be given. In preliminary summary form, they are the preference of the concrete to the abstract, the use of action words, and the avoidance of camouflaged verbs.

Use the concrete word.   Interesting report writing is marked by specific words —words that form sharp and clear meaning in the reader's brain. Such words are concrete. Concrete words are the opposite of abstract words, which are words of fuzzy and vague meanings. In general, concrete words stand for things readers perceive—things they can see, feel, hear, taste, or smell. Concrete words hold interest, for they move directly into the readers' experiences. Because concrete words are best for holding interest, report writers should prefer them to abstract words wherever possible.

To a large exent, concrete words are the short, familiar words previously discussed. In addition to being more meaningful to readers, such words generally have more precise meaning than the other words. For example, this sentence is filled with long, unfamiliar words: "The magnitude of the increment of profits was the predominant motivating factor in the decision." Written in shorter and more familiar words, the idea becomes more concrete: "The size of the profit gained was the chief reason for the decision."

But concreteness involves more than simplicity, for many of the wellknown words are abstract. Perhaps a clear distinction between concrete and abstract wording can be made by illustration. In the writeup of the results of an experiment, a chemist may refer to the bad smell of a certain mixture as a "nauseous odor." But these words do little to communicate a clear mental picture in the reader's mind, for "nauseous" is a word with many different meanings. Were the chemist to say it smelled like "decaying fish" these words would be likely to communicate a clear meaning in the reader's mind. One of the best-known examples of concreteness is in the advertising claim that Ivory soap is "99.44 percent pure." Had the company used abstract words such as "Ivory is very pure," few would have been impressed. But they used specific words, and millions took notice. Similar differences in abstract and concrete expressions are apparent in the following.

Abstract	*Concrete*
A sizable profit	A 22 percent profit
Good accuracy	Pinpoint accuracy
The leading student	Top student in a class of 90
The majority	53 percent
In the near future	By Thursday noon
A worksaving machine	Does the work of seven men
Easy to steer	Quick steering
Light in weight	Featherlight

Prefer active to passive verbs. Of all the parts of speech, verbs are the strongest, and verbs are at their strongest when they are in the active voice. Thus, the best in vigorous, lively writing makes good use of active-voice verbs.

Active-voice verbs show their subject doing the action. They contrast with the dull passive forms that act on their subjects. The following contrasting sentences illustrate the distinction.

Active: The auditor inspected the books.
Passive: The books were inspected by the auditor.

The first example clearly is the stronger. In this sentence, the doer of the action acts, and the verb is short and clear. In the second example, the helping word "were" dulls the verb, and the doer of the action is relegated to a role in a prepositional phrase. The following sentences give additional proof of the superiority of active over passive voice.

Passive	Active
The new process is believed to be superior by the investigators.	Investigators believe that the new process is superior.
The policy was enforced by the committee.	The committee enforced the policy.
The office will be inspected by Mr. Hall.	Mr. Hall will inspect the office.
A gain of 30.1 percent was recorded for soft lines sales.	Soft lines sales gained 30.1 percent.
It is desired by this office that this problem be brought before the board.	This office desires that the secretary bring this problem before the board.
A complete reorganization of the administration was effected by the president.	The president completely reorganized the administration.

In no way should one interpret this emphasis of active voice to mean that passive voice should be eliminated or that it is incorrect. It has its place (as illustrated in the preceding sentence); and it most certainly is correct. The point is that report writers tend to overwork passive voice—that they could have livelier, more interesting writing if they would use more active voice.

Neither should one interpret the foregoing discussion to mean that there are not situations in which passive voice is preferable. There are. For example, when the identification of the performer is unimportant to the message, passive voice gives the parts of the message their proper emphasis:

Advertising often is criticized for its effect on prices.
Petroleum is refined in Texas.

Passive voice also may be preferable when the performer is unknown, as in these examples:

During the past year, the equipment has been sabotaged seven times.
Anonymous complaints have been received.

Yet another situation in which passive voice may be preferred is one in which the writer prefers not to name the performer:

The interviews were conducted on weekdays between noon and 6 P.M.
Specimens of performance were collected for each equipment type.

And there are other instances in which for reasons of style passive voice is preferable.

Avoid overuse of camouflaged verbs.   Closely related to the problem of overusing abstract words and passive voice is the problem of camouflaged verbs. A verb is camouflaged when it appears in the sentence as an abstract noun rather than in verb form. For example, in the sentence "Elimination of the excess material was effected by the crew," the noun "elimination" is made out of the verb "eliminate." Although there is nothing wrong with nouns made from verbs, in this case the noun form carries the strongest action idea of the sentence. A more vigorous phrasing uses the pure verb form: "The crew eliminated the excess material." Likewise, it is stronger to "cancel" than to "effect a cancellation"; it is stronger to "consider" than to "give consideration to"; and it is stronger to "appraise" than to "make an appraisal." These sentences further illustrate the point.

Camouflaged verbs	Clear verb form
Amortization of the account was effected by the staff.	The staff amortized the account.
Control of the water was not possible.	They could not control the water.
The new policy involved the standardization of the procedures.	The new policy involved standardizing the procedures.
Application of the mixture was accomplished.	They applied the mixture.

From these illustrations and those of the preceding discussion of passive voice, one gleans two helpful writing rules. The first is to make the subjects of most sentences either persons or things. For example, rather than to write "consideration was given to . . . ," one should write "we consider. . . ." The second rule is to write most sentences in normal (subject, verb, object) order and with the real doer of action as the subject. It is when writers attempt other orders that involved, strained, passive structures are most likely to result.

Select words for precise communication

Obviously clear writing requires some mastery of language—enough at least to enable the writer to convey meaning precisely. Unfortunately too many writers take their knowledge of language for granted. They select words as a matter of mechanical routine. All too often, they use words without really thinking of the meanings communicated. Sometimes they use words they really do not understand. Certainly the resulting writing must be as fuzzy as their knowledge of language.

Thus, good writers must become students of words. They must learn the precise meanings of words. Especially must they learn the shades of differences in the meanings of similar words and the different meanings that various arrangements of words can bring about. For example, they must learn that "fewer" pertains to smaller numbers of units or individuals, and that "less" relates to value, degree, or quantity. They must know of the differences in connotation of similar words such as *secondhand, used,* and *antique; slender, thin,* and *skinny; suggest, tell,* and *inform; tramp, hobo,* and *vagabond.*

SENTENCE CONSTRUCTION

Arranging words into sentences that communicate clearly and easily is a goal of report writers. The task is largely a mental one, for the sentence is the form human beings devised to express their thought units. Since sentences are verbalized thought units, they reflect the thinking they express. Clear and orderly sentences are the product of clear and orderly thinking; vague and disorderly sentences represent vague and disorderly thinking.

The techniques of good thinking do not reduce to routine steps, procedures, formulas, or the like, for the process is too little understood. But the sentences that are the product of good thinking do have clearly discernible characteristics. These characteristics suggest the general guidelines for good sentence construction that appear in the following paragraphs.

Keep the sentences short

More than any other characteristic of a sentence, length is most clearly related to sentence difficulty. The longer a sentence is, the harder it is to understand. The explanation of this relationship is simple. The human mind is capable of holding at one time only a limited amount of subject matter. When an excess of information or excessive relationships are presented in a single package, the mind cannot grasp it all. At least, the mind cannot grasp it all on a single reading. Thus, like food, written material is best consumed in bite sizes.

Just what is bite size for the mind, however, depends on the mental capacity of the reader. Most current authorities agree that sentences aimed at the middle level of adult American readers should average about 16 to 18 words in length. For more advanced readers, the average can be higher. And it must be lower for those of lower reading abilities. Of course, these length figures do not mean that short sentences of six or so words are taboo, nor do they mean that one should avoid long sentences of 30 or more words. Occasionally short sentences may be effective to emphasize an important fact. And long sentences may be skillfully constructed to subordinate some less important information. It is the average that should be in keeping with the readability level of the reader.

Differences brought about by sentence length are emphatically illustrated by the following contrasting sentences. Notice how much better the shorter versions communicate.

Long and hard to understand	*Short and clear*
This memorandum is being distributed with the first-semester class cards, which are to serve as a final check on the correctness of the registration of students and are to be used later as the midsemester grade cards, which are to be submitted prior to November 16.	The accompanying cards will serve now as a final check on student registration. Later you will use them for midsemester grades which are due before November 16.
Some authorities in personnel administration object to expanding normal salary ranges to include a *trainee* rate' because they fear that probationers may be kept at the minimum rate longer than is warranted through oversight or prejudice and because they fear that it would encourage the spread from the minimum to maximum rate range.	Some authorities in personnel administration object to expanding the normal salary range to include a trainee rate for two reasons. First, they fear that probationers may be kept at the minimum rate longer than is warranted through oversight or prejudice. Second, they fear that it would in effect increase the spread from the minimum to the maximum rate range.

Regardless of their seniority or union affiliation, all employees who hope to be promoted are expected to continue their education either by enrolling in special courses to be offered by the company, which are scheduled to be given after working hours beginning next Wednesday, or by taking approved correspondence courses selected from a list, which may be seen in the training office.

Regardless of their seniority or union affiliation, all employees who hope to be promoted should continue their education in either of two ways. (1) They should enroll in special courses to be given by the company. (2) They should take approved correspondence courses selected from the list which may be seen in the training office.

Use words economically

Of the many ways in which every thought may be expressed, the shorter ways are usually the best. In general, the shorter wordings save the reader time, they are clearer, and they make more vigorous and interesting reading. Thus, good report writers strive for economy in the use of words.

Learning to use words economically is a matter of continuing effort. Good writers are constantly aware of the need for word economy. They carefully explore and appraise the many ways of expressing each thought. And although they know that the possibility of word economy depends on the subject matter in each case, they know that certain ways of expression simply are not economical. These they avoid. The more common of these ways of expression are discussed in the following paragraphs.

Cluttering phrases.   Our language is cluttered with numerous phrases that are best replaced by shorter expressions. Although the shorter forms may save only a word or two here and there, the little savings over a long piece of writing can be significant. As the following sentences illustrate, the shorter substitutes are better:

The long way	*Short and improved*
In the event that payment is not made by January, operations will cease.	*If* payment is not made by January, operations will cease.
In spite of the fact that they received help, they failed to exceed the quota.	*Even though* they received help, they failed to exceed the quota.
The invoice was *in the amount of* $50,000.	The invoice was *for* $50,000.

Here are other contrasting pairs of expressions:

Long	*Short*
Along the lines of	Like
For the purpose of	For
For the reason that	Because, since
In the near future	Soon
In accordance with	By
In very few cases	Seldom
In view of the fact that	Since, because
On the occasion of	On
With regard to, with reference to	About

Surplus words. Words that add nothing to the sentence meaning should be eliminated. In some instances, however, eliminating the words requires recasting the sentence, as some of the following examples illustrate.

Contains surplus words	*Surplus words eliminated*
It will be noted that the records for the past years show a steady increase in special appropriations.	The records for past years show a steady increase in special appropriations.
There are four rules *which* should be observed.	Four rules should be observed.
In addition to these defects, numerous other defects mar the operating procedure.	Numerous other defects mar the operating procedure.
His performance was good enough *to enable him* to qualify for the promotion.	His performance was good enough to qualify him for promotion.
The machines *which were* damaged by the fire were repaired.	The machines damaged by the fires were repaired.
By *the* keeping *of* production records, they found the error.	By keeping production records, they found the error.

Roundabout construction. Of the many ways of saying anything, some are direct and to the point; others cover the same ground in a roundabout way. Without question, the direct ways are usually better and should be used. Although there are many ways of making roundabout expressions (some overlap the preceding causes of excess wording), the following illustrations clearly show the general nature of this violation.

Roundabout	*Direct and to the point*
The departmental budget *can be observed to be decreasing* each new year.	The departmental budget *decreases* each year.
The union is *involved in the task of reviewing* the seniority provision of the contract.	The union is *reviewing* the seniority provision of the contract.
The president is *of the opinion that* the tax was paid.	The president *believes* that the tax was paid.
It is essential that the income be used to retire the debt.	The income *must* be used to retire the debt.
The supervisors should *take appropriate action to determine* whether the time cards are being inspected.	The supervisor *should determine* whether the time cards are being inspected.
The price increase will *afford the* company *an opportunity* to retire the debt.	A price increase will *enable* the company to retire the debt.
During the time she was employed by this company, Miss Carr was absent once.	*While* employed by this company, Miss Carr was absent once.
He criticized everyone he *came in contact with.*	He criticized everyone he met.

Unnecessary repetition.   Repetition of words or thoughts is best avoided. Exceptions to this rule, however, are justified when writers repeat for special effect or for emphasis.

Needless repetition	*Repetition eliminated*
The provision of section five *provides* for a union shop.	Section five provides for a union shop.
The assignment of training the ineffective worker is *an assignment* he must carry out.	Training the ineffective worker is an assignment he must carry out.
Modern, up-to-date equipment will be used.	Modern equipment will be used.
In the office they found supplies *there* which had never been issued.	In the office they found supplies which had never been issued.
He reported for work Friday *morning* at 8 A.M.	He reported for work Friday at 8 A.M.
In my opinion I think the plan is sound.	I think the plan is sound.
One must not neglect the *important essentials.*	One must not neglect the essentials.

Give the facts proper emphasis

The numerous facts, assumptions, analyses, conclusions, and such that go into a report vary in their importance to the report's's objective. Some, such as conclusions, play major roles. Other areas supply supporting details. Still others are only incidental. The writers' task is to determine the importance of each bit of information in the report and then to communicate this emphasis in the writing. Giving the facts proper emphasis is largely a matter of sentence design.

The short, simple sentences carry more emphasis than longer, more involved sentences. Shorter sentences stand out and call attention to their contents. They are especially strong when placed in positions of emphasis—that is, at beginnings or ends of paragraphs.

A single sentence that covers two or more items gives less emphasis to each item than separate sentences for each item. Within these sentences, varying emphasis may be given each item. Those items placed in independent clauses get major emphasis. Those placed in subordinate structures (dependent clauses, parenthetic structures, modifiers, and the like) are relegated to less important roles. Thus, by skillful design, or by a lack of it, the same facts may be presented in distinctly different ways, as shown by the following illustrations.

In the first illustration, separate sentences present each item of information. Each item gets special emphasis by this treatment, but, because all are treated the same, none stands out. Also, the items obviously are not equally important and should not receive equal emphasis. In addition, the writing is elementary to the point of being ridiculous.

The Mann building was inspected on October 1. Mr. George Wills inspected the building. Mr. Wills is a vice president of the company. He found that the building has 6,500 square feet of floor space. He also found that it has 2,400 feet of storage space. The new store must have a minimum of 6,000 square feet of floor space. It must have 2,000 square feet of storage space. Thus, the Mann building exceeds the space requirement for the new store. Therefore, Mr. Wills concluded that the Mann building is adequate for the company's need.

In the next illustration, some of the information is subordinated, but not logically. The facts of real importance do not receive the emphasis they deserve. Logically the points that should be emphasized are (1) the conclusion that the building is large enough and (2) the supporting evidence, showing that floor and storage space exceed the minimum requirements.

Mr. George Wills, who inspected the Mann building on October 1, is a vice president of the company. His inspection, which supports the conclusion that the building is large enough for the proposed store, uncovered these facts. The store has 6,500 square feet of floor space and 2,400 square feet of storage space, which is more than the minimum requirements of 6,000 and 2,000 respectively, for floor and storage space.

The next illustration gives good emphasis to the pertinent points. The short, simple sentences placed for emphasis at the beginning present the conclusion. The supporting facts that the new building exceeds the minimum floor and storage space requirements receive main-clause emphasis. Incidentals such as the identifying remarks about Mr. Wills are relegated to subordinate roles.

The Mann building is large enough for the new store. This conclusion, made by Vice President George Wills, following his October 1st inspection of the building, is based on these facts. The building's 6,500 square feet of floor space is 500 more than the 6,000 set as a minimum. The 2,400 square feet of storage space is 400 more than the 2,000 minimum requirement.

The following sentences illustrate more specific violations of logical emphasis. The first shows how placing an important idea in an appositional construction weakens the idea. Notice the increased emphasis given the idea (by position and by construction) in the second sentence.

Weak emphasis: Hamilton's typewriter, a machine which has been used daily for over 40 years, is in good condition.

Strong emphasis: Although Hamilton's typewriter has been used daily for 40 years, it is in good condition.

The next sentence shows how placement in a participial construction subordinates an idea. The idea receives more emphasis as a dependent clause in the second sentence.

Weak emphasis: Having paid the highest dividends in its history, the company anticipates a rise in the value of its stock.

Stronger emphasis: Because it paid the highest dividends in its history, the company anticipates a rise in the value of its stock.

Arrange the words correctly for clarity

Short and clear sentences generally conform to the conventional rules of the grammar of a language. Contrary to what many novice writers think, the rules of grammar are not merely arbitrary requirements set by detail-minded scholars. Rather, the rules are statements of logical relationships between words. Dangling participles, for example, confuse meaning by modifying the wrong word. Unparallel constructions leave erroneous impressions of the relationships of the parts. Pronouns without clear antecedents have no definite meaning. The evidence is quite clear: business writers must know and follow the conventional standards of their language.

Unfortunately too many business writers know very little about the conventional rules of English grammar. Why so many have avoided this subject through years of drill at all levels of education is a mystery to educators. Obviously the area is too broad for complete coverage in this book. Some of the points with which most writers have trouble, however, are presented for quick review in Chapter 16. Their importance should not be ignored.

Place related words close together

One requisite for unmistakable clarity in writing is to keep related words as close together as practical. Of course, all related words cannot be placed exactly together, for frequently two or more words or groups of words are related to the same words. In deciding what to do in such cases, writers must follow their good logic. They must appraise the possible meanings conveyed by the arrangement possibilities, and they must select the one arrangement that carries the one meaning intended. That placement of words makes a real difference in meaning is illustrated by the following series of sentences. In this series, the words are the same but the orders change. The order changes thoroughly alter the sentence meanings.

If at the end of this quarter the workers vote to strike, the plant will close.

As the sentence stands, the phrase "at the end of this quarter" logically relates to the verb "vote." In the following sentence, the shift of the phrase to a position between "workers" and "vote" produces confusion. Here the phrase could modify either word.

If the workers at the end of this quarter vote to strike, the plant will close.

Similar confusion is evident when the phrase comes between "vote" and "to strike." It could be construed to modify either the preceding or the following word.

If the workers vote at the end of this quarter to strike, the plant will close.

By moving the phrase further down the sentence, yet another form of confusion is made. Here the phrase could modify "strike" alone or it could modify the whole group "vote to strike."

If the workers vote to strike at the end of this quarter, the plant will close.

Still another meaning is formed by moving the phrase to the end of the sentence. Here it modifies "close."

If the workers vote to strike, the plant will close at the end of this quarter.

It is quite clear, then, that the positions of words in the sentence can make a significant difference in the thoughts communicated. Good writers carefully keep related words close together so there is no possible confusion of meaning.

CARE IN PARAGRAPH DESIGN

Clear sentences do not alone assure clear writing, for the sentences must be built logically into clear paragraphs. The techniques of building paragraphs are not easily put into words. Whether many of these techniques can be reduced to meaningful rules and instructions is questionable, for much of paragraph writing depends on the writers' mental ability to organize logically and relate facts. Nevertheless, the following concrete suggestions can be given.

Give the paragraph unity

Unity is the primary requirement of the paragraph. Unity, of course, means oneness. When applied to paragraph construction, it means that the paragraph should build around a single topic or idea. Thus, a paragraph should include only this major topic or idea plus the supporting details that help to develop it. Exceptions to the rule of unity are the transitional paragraphs whose objectives are to relate foregoing and succeeding topics.

Just what constitutes unity is not always easy to determine. All of a report, for example, may deal with a single topic and therefore have unity. The same could be said for each major division of the report as well as for the lesser subdivisions. Paragraph unity, however, concerns smaller units than these—usually the lowest level of a detailed outline. That is, in reports written with detailed outlines, each paragraph may well cover one of the lowest outline captions. In any event, one good test of a paragraph is to reduce its content to a single topic statement. If this statement does not cover the paragraph content, unity is not likely to be there.

Keep the paragraphs short

Short paragraphs are best for most business writing. They help the readers to follow the organizational plan of the paper. Specifically they help readers to see the beginnings and ends of the items covered, and they give added emphasis to the facts covered. In addition, short paragraphs are more inviting to the eye. People simply prefer to read material that gives them frequent breaks. This is true so long as the breaks are not too frequent. A series of very short paragraphs would leave an equally offensive choppy effect.

FIGURE 10–1.   Contrasting pages, showing psychological effects of long and short paragraphs

 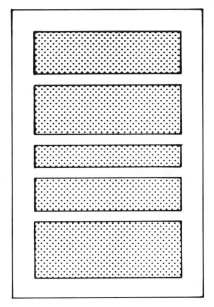

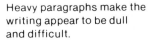

Heavy paragraphs make the writing appear to be dull and difficult.

Short paragraphs give well-organized effect–invite the reader to read.

A glance at Figure 10–1 quickly shows the psychological effect of paragraph length. The full page of solid type appears to be more difficult and generally less inviting than the one marked by short paragraphs. Even if both contained exactly the same words, the difference would be present. Perhaps this difference is largely psychological. Psychological or not, the difference is real.

Just how long a paragraph should be is, of course, dependent on the topic. Some topics are short, others are long. Even so, this general guide can be given on paragraph length: Most well-organized and well-paragraphed reports have paragraphs that average about eight to ten lines. Some good paragraphs may be quite short—even a single line. And some may be well above the eight to ten average.

One good rule of thumb is to question the unity of all long paragraphs—say, those exceeding 12 lines. If inspection shows that only one topic is present, no change should be made. But if inspection shows that the paragraph covers more than one topic, additional paragraphing is in order.

Put topic sentences to good use

One prominent sentence, the topic sentence, expresses the main idea of most well-written paragraphs. Around this topic sentence, the details that support or elaborate the main idea build in some logical way. Exactly how a given paragraph should build from the topic sentence largely depends on the information to be covered and on the writers' plan in covering it. Obviously much of paragraph design must come from the mental effort of the writers. They would profit, however, by being generally acquainted with the paragraph plans most commonly used.

Topic sentence first.   The most widely used paragraph plan begins with the topic sentence. The supporting material then follows in some logical order. As this arrangement gives good emphasis to the major point, it is the most useful to report writers. In fact, some company writing manuals suggest the use of this arrangement almost altogether. As the following paragraph illustrates, this arrangement has merit.

> *A majority of the economists consulted think business activity will drop during the first quarter of next year.* Of the 185 economists interviewed, 13 percent look for continued increases in business activities; and 28 percent anticipate little or no change from the present high level. The remaining 59 percent look for a recession. Of this group, nearly all (87 percent) believe the downcurve will occur during the first quarter of the year.

Topic sentence at end.   Another logical paragraph arrangement places the topic sentence at the end, usually as a conclusion. The supporting details come first and in logical order build toward the topic sentence. Frequently such paragraphs use a beginning sentence to set up or introduce the subject, as in the following illustration. Such a sentence serves as a form of topic sentence, but the real meat of the paragraph comes in the final sentence.

> The significant role of inventories in the economic picture should not be overlooked. At present, inventories represent 3.8 months supply. Their dollar value is the highest in history. If considered in relation to increased sales, however, they are not excessive. In fact, they are well within the range generally believed to be safe. *Thus, inventories are not likely to have a downward drag on the economy.*

Topic sentence within the paragraph.   Some paragraphs are logically arranged with the topic sentence somewhere within. These paragraphs are not often used and usually for good reason. In general they fail to give proper emphasis to the key point in the paragraph. Even so, they sometimes produce good effect, as in this example.

> Numerous materials have been used in manufacturing this part. And many have shown quite satisfactory results. *Material 329, however, is superior to them all.* Built with material 329, the part is almost twice as strong as when built with the next best material. Also, it is 3 ounces lighter. And most important, it is cheaper than any of the other products.

Make the paragraph move forward

Forward movement is an essential quality of good report writing. Good report writing makes the readers feel that they are moving systematically through the subject matter—that each new idea or fact moves them progressively toward the objective. Thus, good report writers know how to put good movement into their writing.

Good movement is the result of good paragraph design. Individual sentences have little movement, for they cover only single thoughts. An orderly succession of single thoughts, however, produce movement. In addition, good movement is helped by skillful use of transition, by smoothness in writing style, and by a general proficiency in word choice and sentence design.

Perhaps the quality of movement is easier to see than to describe. In general, it is present when the readers are made to feel at the paragraph end·that they have made one sure step toward the objective. Although many arrangements can illustrate good paragraph movement, the following illustration does the job quite well.

> Three major factors form the basis for the decision to relocate. First, the supply of building rock in the Crowton area is questionable. The failure of recent geological explorations in the area appears to confirm suspicions that the Crowton deposits are nearly exhausted. Second, distances from Crowton to major consumption areas make transportation costs unusually high. Obviously any savings in transportation cost will add to company profits. Third, obsolescence of much of the equipment at the Crowton plant makes this an ideal time for relocation. New equipment could be moved directly to the new site, and obsolete equipment could be scrapped in the Crowton area.

QUESTIONS

Instructions for questions 1 through 45: Revise the following sentences to make them conform with the principles discussed in the text. They are grouped by the principles they illustrate.

Using understandable words

(Assume that these sentences are written for high school level readers.)

1. Recent stock acquisitions have accentuated the company's current financial crisis.
2. Mr. Coward will serve as intermediary in the pending labor-management parley.
3. Miss Smith's idiosyncracies supply adequate justification for terminating her employment.
4. Requisites for employment by this company have been enhanced.
5. The unanimity of current forecasts is not incontrovertible evidence of an impending business acceleration.
6. Man's propensity to consume is insatiable.
7. The company must desist its deficit financing immediately.
8. This antiquated merchandising strategy is ineffectual in contemporary business operations.
9. Percent return on common stockholders equity averaged 23.1 for the year.
10. The company's retained earnings last year exceeded $2,500,000.

Selecting concrete words

11. Some years ago he made good money.
12. His grade on the aptitude test was not high.
13. Here is a product with very little markup.
14. Damage from the fire was significant.
15. We will need the new equipment soon.

Limiting use of passive voice

16. It is believed by the writer that this company policy is wrong.
17. The union was represented by Cecil Chambers.
18. These reports are prepared by the salespeople every Friday.
19. Success of this project is the responsibility of the research department.
20. Our decision is based on the belief that the national economy will be improved.

Avoiding camouflaged verbs

21. Implementation of the plan was effected by the crew.
22. Acceptance of all orders must be made by the chief.
23. A committee performs the function of determining the award.
24. Adaptation to the new conditions was performed easily by all new personnel.
25. Verification of the amount is made daily by the auditor.
26. The president tried to effect a reconciliation of the two groups.

Keeping sentences short

27. The upswing in business activity that began in 1980 is expected to continue and possibly accelerate in 1981, and gross national products should rise by $65 billion, representing an 8 percent increase over 1980, which is significantly higher than the modest 5½ percent increase of 1979.
28. As you will not get this part of medicare automatically, even if you are covered by social security, you must sign up for it and pay $3 per month, which the government will match, if you want your physician's bills to be covered.
29. Students with approved excused absences from any of the hour examinations have the option of taking a special makeup examination to be given during dead week or of using their average grade on their examinations in the course as their grade for the work missed.
30. Although we have not definitely determined the causes for the decline in sales volume for the month, we know that during this period construction on the street adjacent to the store severely limited traffic flow and that because of resignations in the advertising department promotion efforts dropped well below normal.

Using words economically

31. In spite of the fact that the bill remains unpaid, they placed another order.
32. We expect to deliver the goods in the event that we receive the money.

33. In accordance with their plans, company officials sold the machinery.
34. This policy exists for the purpose of preventing dishonesty.
35. The salespeople who were most successful received the best rewards.
36. The reader will note that this area ranks in the top 5 percent in per capita income.
37. Our new coats are made of a fabric which is of the water repellent variety.
38. Our office is charged with the task of counting supplies not used in production.
39. Their salespeople are of the conviction that service is obsolete.
40. Losses caused by the strike exceeded the amount of $14,000.
41. This condition can be assumed to be critical.
42. Our goal is to effect a change concerning the overtime pay rate.
43. Mr. Wilson replaced the old, antiquated machinery with new machinery.
44. We must keep this information from transpiring to others.
45. The consensus of opinion of this group is that Wellington was wrong.

Discussion and performance questions

46. Select a paragraph of at least three sentences. Alter its sentence structures in two ways to show varying emphasis in its content.
47. Write a sentence that will change in meaning when the order of its words is altered.
48. What is meant by paragraph unity?
49. Summarize the case for the short paragraph.
50. Select a paper you have written of at least eight paragraphs. Underscore the topic sentences. Criticize your paragraph designs.

Qualities of effective report writing

In addition to writing readably, report writers can do other things to improve communication effectiveness. That is, they can give their writing certain qualities which aid in communicating. More specifically, they can write objectively. They can place all the facts of the report logically and consistently in time. They can structure and relate the facts so that they tell a coherent story. And they can write in a way that holds reader interest. These four topics are reviewed in detail in the following pages.

THE ESSENTIAL QUALITY OF OBJECTIVITY

A basic quality of good report writing, objectivity concerns both the attitude of the writers and writing style. Writers maintain an objective attitude by divorcing their prejudices and emotions from their work and by fairly reviewing and interpreting the information they have uncovered. Thus, they approach the problem with an open mind and look at all sides of each question. Their role is much like that of a judge presiding over a court of law. They are not moved by personal feelings. They seek truth, and they leave no stone unturned in quest of it. They make their decisions only after carefully weighing all of the evidence uncovered.

Objectivity as a basis for believability

A report built on the quality of objectivity has another ingredient essential to good report writing. That ingredient is believability. Perhaps biased writing can be in language that is artfully deceptive and may at first glance be believable. But such writing is risky. If at any spot in the report the readers detect bias, they will be suspicious of the whole work. Painstaking objectivity, therefore, is the only sure way to believable report writing.

Objectivity and the question of impersonal versus personal writing

Recognizing the need for objectivity, the early report writers worked to develop a writing style that would convey this attitude. They reasoned that the source of the subjective quality in a report is the human being. And they reasoned that objectivity is best attained by emphasizing the factual material of a report rather than the personalities involved. So they worked to remove the human being from their writing. Impersonal writing style was the result. By impersonal writing is meant writing in the third person—without I's, we's, or you's.

Perhaps the distinction between impersonal and personal writing is best made by illustration.

Personal	*Impersonal*
Having studied the various advantages and disadvantages of using trading stamps, I conclude that your company should not adopt this practice. If you use the stamps, you would have to pay out money for them. Also you would have to hire additional employees to take care of the increase in sales volume.	A study of the advantages and disadvantages of using trading stamps supports the conclusion that the Mills Company should not adopt this practice. The stamps themselves would cost extra money. Also, use of stamps would require additional personnel to take care of the increase in sales volume.

In recent years, some writing authorities have strenuously questioned impersonal writing. These writers point out that personal writing is more forceful and direct than is impersonal writing. They contend that writing that brings both reader and writer into the picture is more like conversation and therefore more interesting. And in regard to objectivity they answer that objectivity is an attitude of mind and not a matter of person. A report, they say, can be just as objective when written in personal style as when written in impersonal style. Frequently they counter with the argument that impersonal writing leads to an overuse of passive voice and a generally dull writing style. This last argument, however, lacks substance. Impersonal writing can and should be interesting. Any dullness it may have is wholly the fault of the writer. As proof one has only to look at the lively styles used by the writers for newspapers, news magazines, and journals. Most of this writing is impersonal—and usually it is not dull.

As in most cases of controversy, there is some merit to the arguments on both sides. There are situations in which personal writing is better. There are situations in which impersonal writing is better. And there are situations in which either style is appropriate. Report writers must decide at the outset which style is right for each situation.

The report writers' decisions should be based on the circumstances of each report situation. First, they should consider the expectations or desires of those for whom they are preparing the report. More than likely they will find a preference for the impersonal style, for, like most human beings, business people have been slow to break tradition. Next, the writers should consider the formality of each report situation. If the situation is informal, as when the report is really a personal communication of information between business associates, personal writing is appropriate. But if the situation is formal, as is so with most major reports, the conventional impersonal style is better.

Avoiding dullness and awkwardness in impersonal writing

Even though impersonal style often is desirable, one must use it with care. As noted previously, it can and should be interesting. But all too often it is not. All too often it is dull and awkward.

Writing interestingly when using the impersonal style generally involves emphasizing active voice (recall the active-passive voice discussion in Chapter 10). As these two contrasting paragraphs illustrate, the difference in effect can be significant:

Impersonal writing, heavy passive voice	*Impersonal writing, emphasis on active voice*
Sales in all outlets in the Southwest Region were observed to be 10 to 30 percent higher than last month. Outlets in the Dallas-Fort Worth district were found to have the lowest increase, averaging 13.7 percent. This lower increase is believed to have been due in part to the fact that all construction in the area decreased significantly. The highest increase was determined to be in the Houston district, which averaged 25.3 percent. This high average was concluded to be a result of this area's sharp upswing in home construction.	Sales of all Southwest Region outlets increased from 10 to 30 percent. Outlets in the Dallas-Fort Worth district increased least, averaging 13.7 percent. This low increase resulted from a general decline in construction in the area. Leading all districts, the Houston district averaged a 25.3 percent increase. A boom in home construction explains the increase.

An awkward effect often results when writers refer to themselves in impersonal writing. Rarely are such references necessary. In fact, usually they can be omitted without any loss of message. These contrasting sentences illustrate the point:

Awkward references	*References omitted*
In the opinion of the writer this conclusion supports the need for additional research funding.	This conclusion supports the need for additional research funding.
Because of the inconclusiveness of these findings, the author suggests additional research.	The inconclusiveness of these findings calls for additional research.
It is believed by the author that in view of the evidence sales will increase.	The evidence indicates that sales will increase.

These and the preceding illustrations and comments on the question of personal-impersonal writing and active-passive voice support a concluding comment. No right or wrong exists on these matters. Both impersonal and personal styles are correct and appropriate. And both active and passive voice have their place in good communication. Report writers need to understand each of them. And they should exercise care in using them for the best possible communication effect.

LOGICAL CONSISTENCY IN TIME VIEWPOINT

Choosing the proper time viewpoint for presenting the information in a report is a problem for even seasoned writers. For example, should one report survey findings as past or present? Should one write "Twenty-one percent of Matson's women employees are (present) college graduates"? Or should one write ". . . were (past) college graduates"? One could argue logically that the research has been completed—that the findings were current only at the time of the investigation. But one could also argue logically that in all likelihood the information is true at the time of writing and can be reported as current.

What we have seen illustrated is the matter of time viewpoint. By time viewpoint is meant the place in time from which all the information in a report is viewed. This position may be either past or present. Authorities do not agree on which one is the better.

In the past time viewpoint, one treats the research, findings, and writing as past. Thus one would write results from a recently completed survey in this way: "Seven percent of the workers favored a change." And one would refer to another part of a report in words such as these: "In Chapter 3 this conclusion was reached." Other like information also would be viewed as being in the past, with two exceptions. One is universal truths. By universal truths we mean prevailing concepts or proven conclusions. For example, one could write "Sales of ski equipment decline in the summer months." And one could write "Relative humidity exceeding 90 percent increases the toxic effect of the fumes." The other exception is the case of references to future happenings. These, of course, are logically worded in future tense: "At this rate, the water supply will be exhausted by 1994," and "If the next ten years are like the past ten years, we will not be able to penetrate the market."

In present time viewpoint, one places all information presented in its logical position in time at the moment of writing. Information that is current at the time of writing is written in present tense. Thus, if one can assume that survey results remain true, these words could report a finding: "Seven percent of the workers favor a change." And a reference to another part of the report might be worded "In Chapter 2 this conclusion is reached." Information clearly in the past or in the future would be in a past or future tense. For example, survey findings likely to be obsolete at the time of writing may be worded thus: "In 1939, 44.2 percent of the managers *favored* this plan." Or a predicted figure for the future may be reported in these words: "According to this projection, the value of these assets will exceed $32 million by 1986." A present time viewpoint should in no way be interpreted to mean that every verb must be in the present tense. Nor should it ever result in placing a single event awkwardly in time. Adherence to this viewpoint simply involves placing all facts in their logical place in time at the time of writing.

Which time viewpoint to use is a matter of preference. Authorities do not agree on the matter, although writers in the sciences appear to prefer past time viewpoint. The important thing is consistency. Shifting from one to the other is illogical as well as confusing. One should select one viewpoint—and stay with it throughout the report.

STRUCTURAL AIDS TO REPORT COHERENCE

Smoothness in the flow of information presented is an essential characteristic of good report writing. In the well-written report, each fact is in its logical place, and the relationship of each fact to other facts and to the plan of the report is clear to the reader. Thus, the parts of the report fit together, and the report reads as a unified composition. The writing quality that gives the report this smoothness of connection is commonly called coherence.

Perhaps the one best contributor to coherence is good organization—a topic discussed in detail in an earlier chapter. By relating facts in a logical, natural sequence, some degree of coherence is given to the writing. But logical arrangement of facts alone is not always enough. Particularly is this true in the long and involved report when the relationships of the parts are complex and are not so easily grasped by the reader. In such reports, writers need to make special effort to structure the report so that the relationships are clear. Specifically, they can structure the report story by using concluding and summary paragraphs to mark the report's progress. They can use introductory and preview paragraphs to show major relationships. And they can use transitional sentences and words to show relationships between the lesser parts.

The use of introductory, concluding, and summarizing sections

The extent of use of introductory, concluding, and summarizing sections depends on the report. Perhaps the best rule for report writers to follow is to use them whenever they are needed to relate the parts of the report or to move the report message along. In general, these sections are more likely to be needed in the longer and more involved reports. In such reports, report writers are likely to follow a traditional plan of connecting structure.

This plan, as described in Figure 11–1, uses these special sections to tie together all the parts of the report. Because it serves to keep readers aware of where they have been, where they are, and where they are going, the plan helps the readers to find their way through complex problems. Also, placement of forward-looking and backward-glancing sections permits casual readers to dip into the report at any place and quickly get their bearing.

As noted in the diagram, three types of sections (usually a paragraph or more) may be used to structure the report. One is the introductory preview. Another is the section introduction. And still another is the conclusion or summary sections, either for the major report parts or for the whole report.

For the longer reports a section of the report introduction may be used (see

FIGURE 11–1.   Diagram of the structural coherence plan of a long, formal report

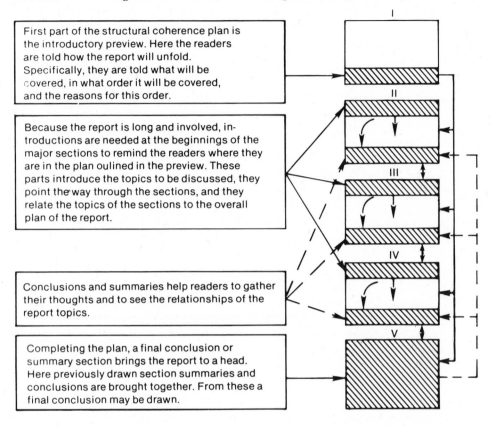

First part of the structural coherence plan is the introductory preview. Here the readers are told how the report will unfold. Specifically, they are told what will be covered, in what order it will be covered, and the reasons for this order.

Because the report is long and involved, introductions are needed at the beginnings of the major sections to remind the readers where they are in the plan oulined in the preview. These parts introduce the topics to be discussed, they point the way through the sections, and they relate the topics of the sections to the overall plan of the report.

Conclusions and summaries help readers to gather their thoughts and to see the relationships of the report topics.

Completing the plan, a final conclusion or summary section brings the report to a head. Here previously drawn section summaries and conclusions are brought together. From these a final conclusion may be drawn.

Chapter 8) to tell the readers of the report's plan of organization. Generally this preview covers three things: topics to be discussed, their order of presentation, and the logic for this order. Having been informed of the basic plan, the readers are then able to understand quickly how each new subject they encounter in the following pages fits into the whole. Thus, a connection between the major report parts is made. The following paragraphs do a good job of previewing a report comparing four brands of automobiles for use by a sales organization.

A comparison of data on cost, safety, and dependability serves as the bases for the decision as to which light car Allied should buy. The following analysis breaks down each of these factors into component parts and applies each part to the three brands considered.

Because it is the most tangible factor, cost appears first. This section compares initial and trade-in values. Then it takes up the matter of operating costs as determined by gasoline mileage, oil usage, and repair expense. In a second major section, similar comparisons determine car safety. Here driver visibility, special safety features, brakes, steering quality, acceleration rate, and traction serve as major considerations. A third section measures car dependability on the basis of repair records and salespeople's time lost because of automobile failure. A final section reaches the decision as to the best brand to buy through a procedure of assigning weights to the foregoing comparisons.

In addition to the introductory preview, relationships between the major report captions may be helped by introductory and summary sections placed at convenient spots throughout the report. These sections may be used occasionally to remind the readers of where they are in the progress of the report. Also, these sections may elaborate on the relationships between the report parts and, in general, give detailed connecting and introductory information. The following paragraph, for example, serves as an introduction to the final section of a report of an industrial survey. Note how the paragraph ties in with the preceding section, which covered industrial activity in three major geographic areas, and justifies covering secondary areas.

> Although the great bulk of industry is concentrated in three areas (Grand City, Milltown, and Port Starr), a thorough industrial survey needs to consider the secondary, but nevertheless important, areas of the state. In the rank of their current industrial potential, these areas are the Southeast, with Hartsburg as its center; the Central West, dominated by Parrington; and the North Central, where Pineview is the center of activities.

The following summary-conclusion paragraph gives an appropriate ending to a major section. The paragraph brings to a head the findings presented in the section and points the way to the subject of the next section.

> These findings and those pointed out in preceding paragraphs all point to one obvious conclusion. Small business executives are concerned primarily with subject matter which will aid them directly in their work. That is, they favor a curriculum slanted toward the practical subjects. They do, however, insist on some coverage of the liberal areas. Also, they are convinced of the value of studying business administration. On all of these points they are clearly out of tune with the bulk of big business leaders who voiced their positions in this matter. Even the most dedicated business administration professors would find it difficult to support such an extremely practical concept. Nevertheless, these are the small business executives' opinions on the subject, and as they are the consumers of the business education product, their opinions should at least be considered. Likewise, their specific recommendations on courses (subject of the following chapter) deserve careful review.

Proper use of paragraphs such as these forms a network of connection throughout the work. The longer the report, the more effective they are likely to be.

Communication value of transition

Transition, which literally means a bridging across, may be formed in many ways. In general, transitions are made by words, or sentences, placed in the writing to show the relationships of the information presented. They may appear at the beginning of discussion on a new topic and may relate this topic to what has been discussed. They may appear at the end as a forward look. Or they may appear internally as words or phrases that in various ways tend to facilitate the flow of subject matter.

Whether a transition word or sentence should be used depends on the need for relating the parts concerned. Because the relationship of its parts may be seen merely from a logical sequence of presentation, a short report may require only a few transitional parts here and there. A long and involved report, on the other hand, may require much more transitional help.

A word of caution.   Before more specific comment on transition is given, one fundamental point must be made clear. Transitions should in no way be made mechanically. They should be used only when there is a need for them or when leaving them out would produce abruptness in the flow of report findings. Transitions should not appear to be stuck in; instead, they should blend in naturally with surrounding writing. For example, transitional forms of this mechanical type should be avoided: "The last section has discussed topic X. In the next section topic Y will be analyzed."

Transitional sentences.   Throughout the report, writers can improve the connecting network by the judicious use of sentences. Sentence transitions are especially useful in forming the connecting link between secondary sections of the report, as illustrated in the following example of transition between Section B and C of a report. The first few lines of this illustration draw a conclusion for Section B. Then, with smooth tie-in, the next words introduce Section C and relate this topic to the report plan.

[*Section B, concluded*]
. . . Thus the data-show only negligible difference in the cost for oil consumption [*subject of Section B*] for the three brands of cars.
[*Section C*]
Even though costs of gasoline [*subject of Section A*] and oil [*subject of Section B*] are the more consistent factors of operation expense, the picture is not complete until the cost of repairs and maintenance [*subject of Section C*] are considered.

Additional examples of sentences designed to connect succeeding parts are the following. By making a forward-looking reference, these sentences set up the following subject matter. Thus, the resulting shifts of subject matter are both smooth and logical.

These data show clearly that Edmond's machines are the most economical. Unquestionably their operation by low-cost gas and their record for low-cost maintenance give them a decided edge over competing brands. *Before a definite conclusion as to their merit is reached, however, one more vital comparison should be made.*

(The final sentence clearly sets up the discussion of an additional comparison.)

. . . *At first glance the data appear to be convincing, but a closer observation reveals a number of discrepancies.*

(Discussion of the discrepancies is logically set up by this final sentence.)

Placement of topic sentences at key points of emphasis is still another way of using a sentence to improve the connecting network of the report. Usually the topic sentence is most effective at the paragraph beginning, where the subject matter can very quickly be related to its spot in the organization plan described in the introductory preview or the introduction to the section. Note in the following example how the topic sentences emphasize the key information. Note also how the topic sentences tie the paragraphs with the preview (not illustrated), which no doubt related this organization plan.

Brand C accelerates faster than the other two brands, both on level road and on a 9 percent grade. According to a test conducted by Consumption Research, Brand C attains a speed of 60 miles per hour in 13.2 seconds. To reach this same speed, Brand A requires 13.6 seconds and Brand B requires 14.4 seconds. On a 9 percent grade, Brand C reaches the 60-miles-per-hour speed in 29.4 seconds and Brand A in 43.3 seconds. Brand B is unable to reach this speed.

Because it carries more weight on its rear wheels than the others, Brand C has the best traction of the three. Traction, which means a minimum of sliding on wet or icy roads, is most important to safe driving, particularly during the cold, wet winter months. As traction is directly related to the weight carried by the rear wheels, a comparison of these weights should give some measure of the safety of the three cars. According to data released by the Automobile Bureau of Standards, Brand C carries 47 percent of its weight on its rear wheels. Brands B and A carry 44 percent and 42 percent, respectively.

Transitional words. Although the major transition problems concern connection between sections of the report, there is need also for transition between lesser parts. If the writing is to flow smoothly, there is frequent need for relating clause to clause and sentence to sentence and paragraph to paragraph. Transitional words and phrases generally serve to make these connections.

The transitional words that report writers may use are too numerous to relate, but the following review gives a clear picture of what these words are and how they can be used. With a little imagination to supply the context, one can easily see how such words relate succeeding ideas. For better understanding, the words are grouped by the relationships they show between subjects previously discussed and those to be discussed.

Relationship	*Word examples*
Listing or enumeration of subjects	In addition
	First, second, etc.
	Besides
	Moreover
Contrast	On the contrary
	In spite of
	On the other hand
	In contrast
	However
Likeness	In a like manner
	Likewise
	Similarly

Cause-result	Thus
	Because of
	Therefore
	Consequently
	For this reason
Explanation or elaboration	For example
	To illustrate
	For instance
	Also
	Too

THE ROLE OF INTEREST IN REPORT COMMUNICATION

Like all forms of good writing, report writing should be interesting. Actually the quality of interest is as important as the facts of the report, for without interest, communication is not likely to occur. If interest is not held—if the mind is allowed to stray—readers cannot avoid missing parts of the message. And it does not matter how much the readers want to read the report message; nor is their interest in the subject enough to assure communication. The writing must maintain their interest. The truth of this reasoning is evident to students who have tried to read dull writing in studying for an examination. How desperately they wanted to learn the subject, but how often the mind strayed away!

Perhaps writing interestingly is an art. But if it is, it is an art in which report writers can gain some proficiency if they work at it. If they are to develop proficiency, they need to work watchfully to make their words build concrete pictures, and they need to avoid the rubber-stamped jargon or technical talk so often used in business. They need to cultivate a feeling for the rhythmic flow of words and sentences. They need to remember that back of every fact and figure there is some form of life—people doing things, machines operating, a commodity being marketed. The secret to interesting writing is to bring the real life to the surface by concrete diction and vigorous active-voice verbs insofar as it is possible. But at the same time writers should work to achieve interest without using more words than are necessary.

Here a word of caution may be injected. Attempts to make writing style interesting can be overdone. Such is the case whenever the reader's attention focuses on how something is said rather than on what is said. To be effective, good style simply presents information in a clear, concise, and interesting manner. Possibly the purpose and definition of style can best be summarized by this objective of the report writer: Writing style is at its best when the readers are prompted to say, "Here are some interesting facts," rather than "Here is some beautiful writing." Specific suggestions for writing interestingly appear in Chapter 10.

QUESTIONS

1. Discuss the need for objectivity in report writing.
2. Summarize the arguments on the question of using personal or impersonal writing

in reports. What should determine the writer's decision to use personal or impersonal writing?

3. Explain how the question of impersonal versus personal writing involves the use of active and passive voice.

4. Explain and illustrate present and past time viewpoints.

5. What advice would you give a report writer on the matter of time viewpoint.

6. Using as a guide the diagram (Figure 11–1), summarize the coherence plan of the report.

7. Discuss how words, sentences, and paragraphs may be used to form transitions in reports.

8. Show your knowledge of transition by constructing three pairs of connecting sentences—one sentence in each pair ending a paragraph and one sentence beginning the following paragraph.

12

Physical presentation of a report

As far as physical appearance is concerned, the report is very much like a public speaker. When a speaker appears before a group, even before a word is uttered, the audience forms an initial impression. Such an impression is the result of what the audience sees—things such as dress, bearing, and facial characteristics. These impressions may be favorable if what is seen is pleasing, or they may be unfavorable if what is seen is not pleasing. The impressions created here set the stage for the success of the speech that follows.

Once the words begin to flow, there is, of course, the chance that the initial impressions may be altered. But even so, the chances of change coming about are related to the strength of the initial impressions. And to make it even harder for change to occur, the eyes of the listeners remain fixed on the source of the first impressions throughout the presentation.

The same story may be told of a report. A report, too, first impresses its readers with its appearance. Likewise, these first impressions are lasting ones. They, too, are made more difficult to overcome because the readers are constantly looking at what formed the first impression.

Undeniably true as this observation is, the value of an attractive report is not universally accepted by those who engage in report writing. There are writers of reports who believe the message is all that counts and that "trivial" things such as form, neatness, and general attractiveness are immaterial. But possibly because this attitude is typical of their overall thinking and ability, these people are usually found well down the organization ladder. On the other hand, top executives who do not appreciate the importance of good physical appearance are likely to be misfits in their positions. Since it is the top executives who must be satisfied in most instances, report writers should be thoroughly acquainted with all those mechanical considerations that go into a report's physical appearance. A general review of these considerations appears in the following pages.

GENERAL INFORMATION ON PHYSICAL PRESENTATION

Because most business reports are typed, a general knowledge of the mechanics involved in typing manuscripts is essential to report writers. Even if they do not have to type their own reports, writers should know enough about report makeup to be certain that justice is done to their work. Certainly they cannot be assured that their reports meet high standards unless they are familiar with such standards.

Choice of cover

The first part of any report seen by the reader is the cover. Thus, if the first impression made by the report is to be favorable, care in the selection of a cover must be exercised. Numerous types of covers are available commercially, and most of these are adequate.

In selecting a cover for use, one should consider three basic qualities: the type of fastening used, the protection offered, and the physical appearance. The fastening device used must be of the type that will hold the report pages firmly in place. As a rule, fasteners that hold through perforations in the pages do this job better than clamp-type devices. Most types of covers available furnish adequate protection for most reports, but occasionally a report may need an especially tough cover to protect it from unusual handling. For these, extra durable covers made of plastic or cloth are available. Selection of the right cover from the standpoint of physical appearance is an easy task, for nearly all the covers available are adequate for most occasions. But there may be times when a special color or type may be best suited for a particular project.

Care in paper selection

Paper is not just paper, as many people are likely to believe. Differences in grades, sizes, weights, and such are so numerous that they defy adequate coverage here. But a few general hints should suffice to guide the report writers in their selections of paper.

Typing paper comes in two conventional sizes—8½ by 11 inches and 8½ by 13 inches. The first size is by far the more popular of the two and is used in most typed reports. The long (8½ by 13 inch) size is used principally for reports that require long tabular displays or illustrations.

There are many good grades and varieties of paper; so report writers are best guided by their own inspection. Almost any good-quality typing paper is acceptable. A good-quality watermarked, rag content bond is preferable to coated varieties. As a rule, a 20- or 16-pound weight is best, although quality paper of a lighter weight may be acceptable in certain circumstances. The added expense of good paper may be justified by the appearance advantage it gives the finished work. Good paper makes typing stand out sharply, and it makes erasures easy and unnoticeable.

With little exception, white paper is used in business communications. In some companies, however, colored paper is used to identify work from certain departments or for special types of reports.

Unlike printed matter, manuscript is usually typed on one side of the page. Only if opaque paper is used could typing on both sides be justified for only then would the type impressions not be visible through the sheet.

Conventional page layout

For the typical text page in the report, a conventional layout is one that appears to fit the page as a picture in a frame (see Figure 12–1). This eye-pleasing layout fits the page space not covered by the binding of the report. Thus, the typist must allow an extra ⅔ inch or so on the left margins of the pages of a left-bound report and at the top of the pages of a top-bound report.

As a general rule, top, left, and right margins should be equal and uniform. For double-spaced manuscripts, about an inch is recommended. From 1¼ to 1½ inches is ideal for single-spaced work (see Figure 12–2). Bottom margins customarily are larger than those at the top—about a half again as much. The left margin, of course, is easily marked by the characters that begin the line. The right margin is formed by the average lengths of the full lines. As near as is possible, the right margin should be straight—that is, without dips or bulges.

Typists may find it advisable to mark off in black ink a rectangle the size of the layout. Then they may place the rectangle beneath each page as it is typed so that they can see the dimensions they are using and can end the typed lines appropriately.

Special page layouts

Certain pages in the text may have individual layouts. Pages that display major titles (first pages of chapters, tables of contents, synopses, and such) conventionally have an extra half inch or so of space at the top (see Figure 12–3). This technique has long been followed by publishers and is illustrated in almost all published books.

Letters of transmittal and authorization also may have individual layouts. They are typed in any conventional letter form. In more formal reports they may be carefully arranged to have the same general outline or shape as the space on which they appear (see Figure 12–7).

Choice of typing form

It is conventional to double-space typed reports. This procedure stems from the old practice of double spacing to make typed manuscripts more easily read by the proofreader and printer. The practice has been carried over into typed work that is not to be reproduced further. Advocates of double spacing claim that it is easy to read because the readers are not likely to lose their line place.

154

FIGURE 12–1.   Recommended layout for normal double-spaced page

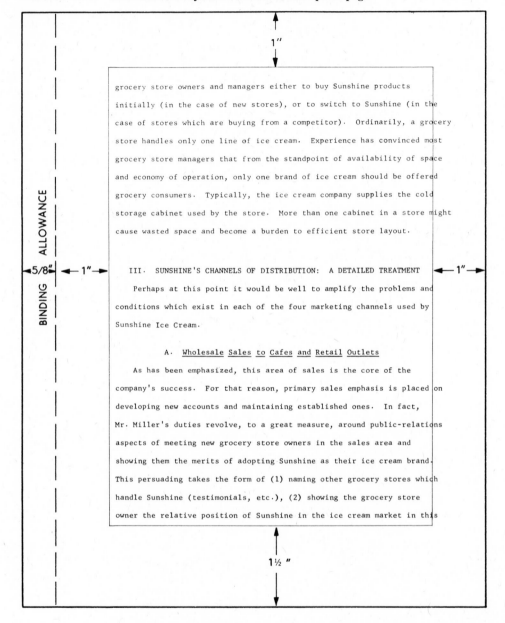

grocery store owners and managers either to buy Sunshine products initially (in the case of new stores), or to switch to Sunshine (in the case of stores which are buying from a competitor). Ordinarily, a grocery store handles only one line of ice cream. Experience has convinced most grocery store managers that from the standpoint of availability of space and economy of operation, only one brand of ice cream should be offered grocery consumers. Typically, the ice cream company supplies the cold storage cabinet used by the store. More than one cabinet in a store might cause wasted space and become a burden to efficient store layout.

III. SUNSHINE'S CHANNELS OF DISTRIBUTION: A DETAILED TREATMENT

Perhaps at this point it would be well to amplify the problems and conditions which exist in each of the four marketing channels used by Sunshine Ice Cream.

A. <u>Wholesale</u> <u>Sales</u> <u>to</u> <u>Cafes</u> <u>and</u> <u>Retail</u> <u>Outlets</u>

As has been emphasized, this area of sales is the core of the company's success. For that reason, primary sales emphasis is placed on developing new accounts and maintaining established ones. In fact, Mr. Miller's duties revolve, to a great measure, around public-relations aspects of meeting new grocery store owners in the sales area and showing them the merits of adopting Sunshine as their ice cream brand. This persuading takes the form of (1) naming other grocery stores which handle Sunshine (testimonials, etc.), (2) showing the grocery store owner the relative position of Sunshine in the ice cream market in this

FIGURE 12-2.   Recommended layout for a normal single-spaced page

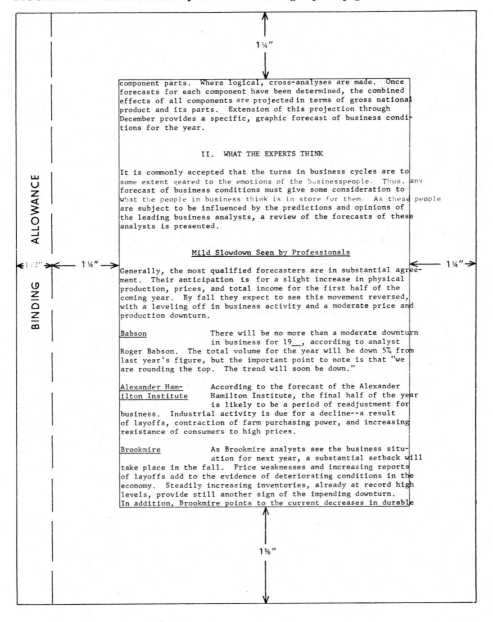

156

FIGURE 12-3.   Recommended layout for a double-spaced page with title displayed

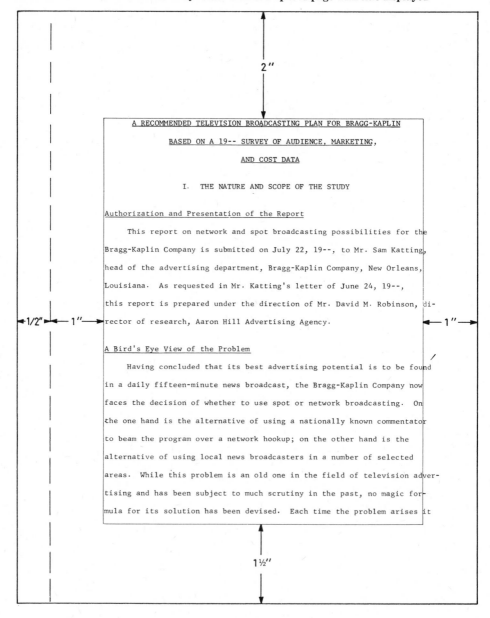

In recent years, the use of single spacing has gained in popularity. The general practice is to single-space the paragraphs, double-space between paragraphs, and triple-space above all centered heads. Supporters of single spacing contend that it saves space and facilitates fast reading, since it approximates the printing most people are accustomed to reading.

Patterns of indentation

Double-spaced typing should be indented to show the paragraph beginnings. On the other hand, because its paragraphs are clearly marked by extra line spacing, single-spaced typing usually is blocked.

There is no generally accepted pattern of indentation. Some sources advocate a distance of four spaces; some prefer five; some like eight; others like ten and more. Any decision on the best distance is purely arbitrary and left up to the writers, although a writer would do well to follow the practice established in the office, group, or school for which one writes the report. Whatever the selection, the important rule to follow is that of consistency.

Possibilities in type selection

When report writers have a choice of typewriters, they may profit from knowing some general information about type and typewriting. Not all typewriters present the same form of finished copy, for type forms and sizes differ. The most widely used types are pica, which has 10 characters to the inch, and elite, which has 12 characters to the inch. Both types take up six lines to the inch; thus, the difference between the two is wholly in the width of the characters.

In addition to these two major types, numerous special size and styles of type exist. There are some very small types, such as Micro Elite, Miniature Gothic, and Bank type. These types are especially useful in typing tables, forms, and such, which would crowd a full page of larger sized type. Then there are some very dark types (Boldface or Book) and some very large types (Magnatype, Bulletin, Amplitype, and Great Primer). Typewriters may even be equipped with Old English or other unusual and distinctive types. Although most of these type sizes and styles are not used for typing the text of the business report, they may serve some special need in unusual instances.

Neatness in typed work

Even with the best typewriter available, the finished work is no better than the efforts of the typist. But this statement does not imply that only the most skilled typists can turn out good work. Even inexperienced typists can produce neat manuscripts simply by exercising care.

Typists should take care in correcting their mistakes, for obvious corrections (strikeovers, erasure holes in the page, and such) stand out in the manuscript like sore thumbs. With a bit of care, this operation can be done so well that casual readers do not detect the errors.

Possibly nothing detracts more from a report than type that the eye must strain to see. So typists should take care to see that their typewriters are equipped with good, black ribbons—ribbons that will make legible letters. A medium-inked ribbon is best for most typing work. Because the ink is likely to smear a bit on the first few pages typed with a new ribbon, it may be wise to type really important work only after a ribbon has had the excess ink worn off. Because of the sharp contrast in type it would cause, typists should avoid changing ribbons in the midst of a manuscript.

For neat and clearly legible typing, typists should regularly clean the type faces. Ink from the ribbon tends to collect and dry in the type faces. If allowed to remain, it will fill the enclosed portions of the type characters. Smudged or fuzzy typing is the result. Any small brush may be used for this purpose.

Numbering of pages

Two systems of numbers are used in numbering the pages of the written report. Arabic numbers are conventional for the text portion, normally beginning with the first page of the introduction nad continuing through the appendix. Small roman numerals are used for the pages that precede the text. Although all these prefatory pages are counted in the numbering sequence, the numbers generally are not placed on the pages preceding the table of contents. It is optional to place them on the table of contents pages.

Placement of numbers on the page varies with the binding used for the report. In reports bound at the top of the page, all page numbers usually are centered at the bottom of the page, a double or triple space below the text layout.

For the more widely used left-side binding, page numbers appear in the upper right corner of the page, a double space above the top line of the layout and in line with the right margin. Exception to this placement is customarily made for special layout pages that have major titles and an additional amount of space displayed at the top. Included in this group may be the first page of the report text; the synopsis; the table of contents; and, in very long and formal works, the first page of each major division or chapter. Numbers for such pages as these are centered a double or triple space below the imaginary line marking the bottom of the layout.

Display of captions

Captions, or headings as they are sometimes called, are titles to the various divisions of the report. They represent the organization steps worked out previously and are designed to help readers find their way through this organization plan. Thus, it is important that the captions show the readers at a glance the importance of their part in the report.

This importance of captions is emphasized in two ways—by type and position. Any logical combination of type and position will show differences in the importance of captions. In actual practice, however, a few standard orders of captions have become widely used.

There are four major positions of captions, as shown in Figure 12–4. Highest of these four in order of rank is the centered caption. This caption is on a line by itself and is centered between left and right margins. Next in order is the marginal caption. Beginning on the left margin, this caption is also on a line by itself. The box caption is third in this ranking, but it normally is used only in single-spaced copy. It begins on the left margin and is surrounded by a box of space formed by indenting the first few lines of the text. The box indentations are kept of equal width throughout the report, although the heights of the boxes will vary with the number of words in the captions enclosed. Fourth in importance is the run-in caption. This caption simply runs into the first line of the text it covers and is distinguished from the text only by underscoring.

Were the report to be printed, there would be a wide variety of type faces and

FIGURE 12–4.   Caption positions in order of importance

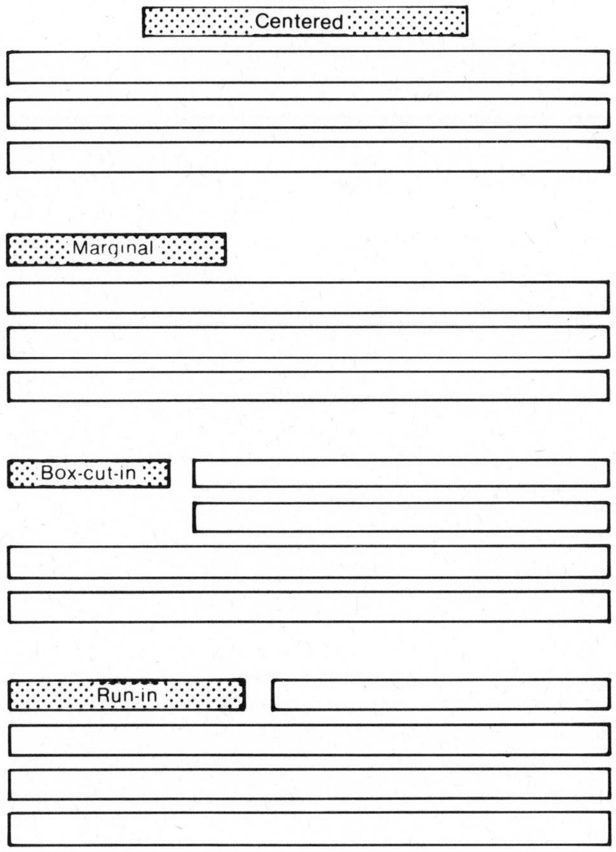

sizes that one could use to show different degrees of importance in the captions. But most reports are typed and thereby limited by what type variations can be made with an ordinary typewriter. Except when unusual type faces are available, typists can show type distinctions primarily in two ways—by the use of capitals and by the underscore. Spacing between letters is sometimes used, although the space requirements of this technique normally eliminate it from consideration. But even though typists are limited to two means of showing importance by type selection, they are able to construct these four distinct ranks of type.

SOLID CAPITALS UNDERSCORED

SOLID CAPITALS

Capitals and Lowercase Underscored

Capitals and Lowercase

In theory, any combination of type and position that shows the relative importance of the caption at a glance is acceptable. The one governing rule to follow in considering types and positions of captions is that no caption may have a higher ranking type or position than any of the captions of a higher level. It is permissible, however, that two successive steps of captions appear in the same type if their difference is shown by position, or in the same position if their difference is shown by type selection. Also, there is no objection to skipping over any of the steps in the progression of type or position.

Although the possibilities of variation are great, some practices have become almost conventional, possibly because they excel in showing each caption's importance at a glance. Also, these practices no doubt are widely accepted because of their simplicity of construction. One such scheme of captioning is the following, which is appropriate for use in reports with three orders of division.

The first order of captions in this scheme is on a separate line, centered, and typed in solid capital letters. Although solid capitals underscored would be all right, this high type normally is reserved for the report title, which is the highest caption in the report. Second-order captions are also on separate lines, beginning with the left margin and typed with capitals and lowercase underscored. Third-degree captions are run into the paragraphs they cover. To distinguish the line from the text, underscoring is used. The caption ends with a strong mark of punctuation, usually the period.

Other acceptable schemes include the following.

1. Centered, solid capitals.
2. Centered, capitals and lowercase underscored.
3. Marginal, capitals and lowercase underscored.
4. Run-in, capitals and lowercase underscored.

1. Centered, solid capitals.
2. Marginal, capitals and lowercase underscored.
3. Box cut-in, capitals and lowercase underscored.
4. Run-in, capitals and lowercase underscored.

1. Centered, solid capitals.
2. Centered, capitals and lowercase underscored.
3. Box cut-in, capitals and lowercase.
1. Centered, solid capitals.
2. Marginal, capitals and lowercase underscored.
3. Box cut-in, capitals and lowercase underscored.

MECHANICS AND FORMAT OF THE REPORT PARTS

The foregoing notes on physical appearance apply generally to all parts of the report. But for individual construction of specific report pages, additional special notes are needed. So that the student may be able to understand these special notes, there follows a part-by-part review of the physical construction of the formal report. Much of this presentation is left to illustration, for volumes could be written about the minute details of construction. Major points, however, are indicated.

Title fly

Primarily used in the most formal reports, the title fly contains only the report title. The title appears slightly above the vertical center of the page in an eye-pleasing arrangement, and all its lines are centered with regard to left and right margins. It is typed in the highest ranking type used in the report (usually solid capitals underscored) and is double spaced if more than one line is required.

Title page

The title page normally contains three main areas of identification (Figure 12–5), although some forms present the same information in four or five spots on the page (Figure 12–6). In the typical three-spot title page, the first item covered is the report title. It is best typed in the highest ranking type used in the report, usually solid capitals underscored. The title is centered. If the title requires more than one line, the lines are broken between thought units and both lines are centered. The lines are appropriately double spaced.

The second area of identification names the individual or group for whom the report is prepared. It is preceded by an identifying phrase such as "Prepared for" or "Submitted to"—words that indicate the individual's role in the report. In addition to the name, identification by title or role, company, and address may be included, particularly if the writer and recipient are from different companies. If the information below the identifying phrase requires three or more lines of type, single spacing is recommended; fewer than three lines may be double spaced. But regardless of how this information is spaced, the identifying phrase appears best set off from the facts below it by a double space.

The third area of information identifies the report writer. It, too, is preceded by an identifying phrase. "Prepared by," "Written by," or any such wording may

FIGURE 12–5. **Good layout for the three-spot title page**

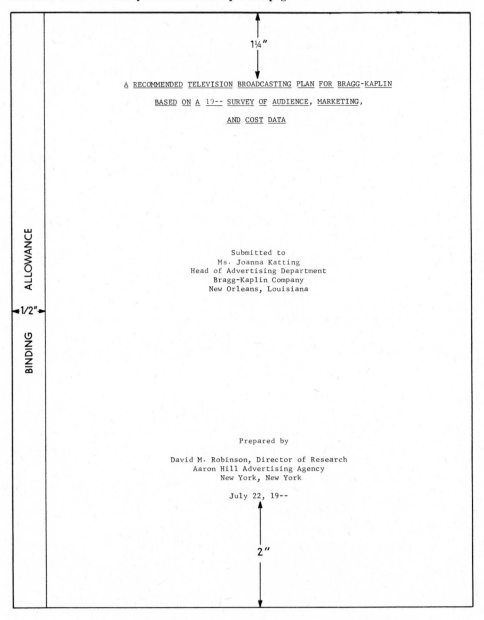

FIGURE 12-6.   Good layout for the four-spot title page

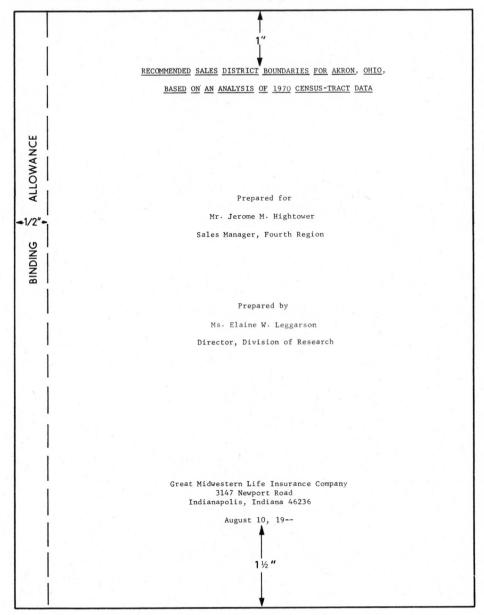

be used to describe this person's role in the report. The writer's title or role, company, and address may also appear here. Finally, in this group of information, the date of publication usually is included. This identification information also is single spaced if four lines are required and double spaced if it involves three lines or less. Likewise, its identification phrase is set off with a double space. The date-line is preferably double spaced from the information preceding it, regardless of previous spacing. Placement of the three spots of information on the page should conform to an eye-pleasing arrangement.

One such arrangement begins the title about 1¼ inches from the top of the page. The final spot of information ends about 2 inches from the page bottom. The center spot of information splits the space between the top and bottom units with a two-to-three ratio, the bottom space being the larger. Line lengths of the information units, of course, are largely governed by the information contained; yet, the writer will have some opportunity to combine or split units. Preferably the lines will have sufficient length to keep the units from having an overall skinny appearance.

Letters of transmittal and authorization

As their names imply, the letters of transmittal and authorization are actual letters. Therefore, they should appear as letters. They may be typed in any acceptable letter form—pure block, modified block, or indented. A layout plan recommended for at least the more formal reports is one that fits the letter into a rectangle of the same shape as the space on which it is typed (see Figure 12–7). This rectangle is marked by the dateline at the top, the initial characters of type at the left, the average of the line lengths at the right, and the last line in the signature at the bottom. For the best optical effect, the rectangle should ride a little high on the page, with a ratio of top margin to bottom of about two to three.

Acknowledgments

When writers are indebted to the assistance of others, it is fitting that they acknowledge the indebtedness somewhere in the report. If the number of individuals involved is small, they may be acknowledged in the introduction of the report or in the letter of transmittal. In the rare event that a writer may need to make a number of acknowledgments, a special section may be constructed for this purpose. Such a section is headed with the single capital-letter title "Acknowledgments" and may be typed with the same layout as any other text page that has a title displayed.

Table of contents

The table of contents is the report outline in its polished, finished form. It lists the major report captions with the page numbers on which these captions appear.

FIGURE 12-7.   Letter of transmittal fitted to the shape of the space in which typed

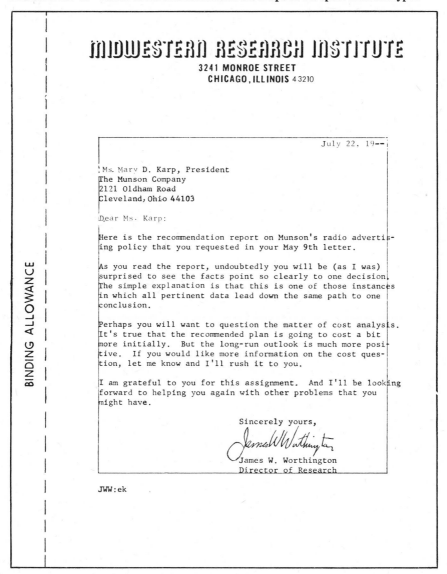

BINDING ALLOWANCE

MIDWESTERN RESEARCH INSTITUTE
3241 MONROE STREET
CHICAGO, ILLINOIS 4 3210

July 22, 19--

Ms. Mary D. Karp, President
The Munson Company
2121 Oldham Road
Cleveland, Ohio 44103

Dear Ms. Karp:

Here is the recommendation report on Munson's radio advertising policy that you requested in your May 9th letter.

As you read the report, undoubtedly you will be (as I was) surprised to see the facts point so clearly to one decision. The simple explanation is that this is one of those instances in which all pertinent data lead down the same path to one conclusion.

Perhaps you will want to question the matter of cost analysis. It's true that the recommended plan is going to cost a bit more initially. But the long-run outlook is much more positive. If you would like more information on the cost question, let me know and I'll rush it to you.

I am grateful to you for this assignment. And I'll be looking forward to helping you again with other problems that you might have.

Sincerely yours,

James W. Worthington

James W. Worthington
Director of Research

JWW:ek

Although not all reports require a table of contents, one should be a part of any report long enough for a guide to be helpful to the readers.

The page is appropriately headed by the capital-letter caption "Contents" or "Table of Contents," as shown in Figure 12–8. The page layout is that used for any report page with a title displayed. Below the title are two columns. One contains the captions, generally beginning with the first report part following the table of contents. The captions may or may not include the outline letters and numbers. If numbers are used, the entries are arranged so that the last digits of compound

FIGURE 12–8.   Good layout and mechanics in the first page of the table of contents

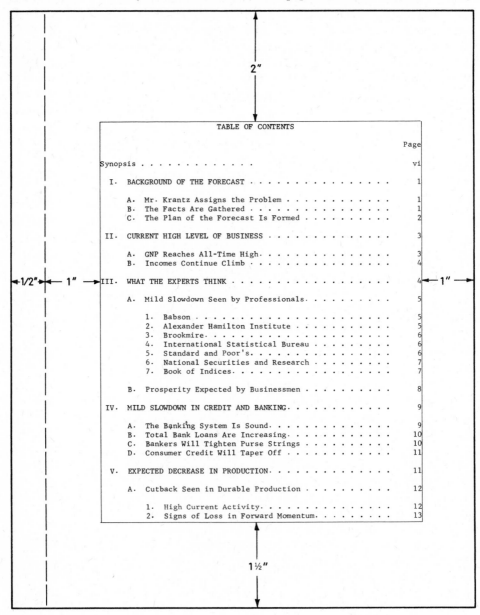

2"

1/2"   1"

1"

1½"

numbers are aligned. The other column, which is brought over to the right margin and headed by the caption "Page," contains the page numbers on which the captions appear. These numbers are aligned on their right digits. The two columns connect by leader lines of periods, preferably with spaces intervening.

As a rule, all captions of the highest level of division have line spaces above and below. Captions below this level are uniformly single spaced or double spaced, depending on the overall lengths of the captions. If the captions are long, covering most of the line or extending to a second line, uniform double spacing between captions is recommended. Short captions may be typed in a consistent single-spaced form. Some authorities, however, prefer to double space all the contents entries when double spacing is used in the text.

In the table of contents, as in the body of the report, variations in the type used to distinguish different levels of captions are permissible. But the type variations used in the contents need not be the same as those in the text typing. Usually the highest level of captions is distinguished from the other levels, and sometimes second-degree captions are distinguished from lower captions by type differences. It is not at all wrong to show no distinction by using plain capitals and lowercase throughout.

Table of illustrations

The table of illustrations is constructed either as a continuation of the table of contents or as a separate table. This table, as shown in Figure 12–9, lists the graphic aids presented in the report in much the same way as the report parts are listed in the table of contents.

The table is headed with an appropriately descriptive capital-letter title such as "Table of Charts and Illustrations," or "List of Tables and Charts," or "Table of Figures." If the table is on a separate page, the page layout is the same as that for any text page with title displayed. And if it is a continued part of the table of contents, the table of illustrations begins after spacing four or more lines from the last contents entry.

The table consists of two columns—one for the graphic-aid title and the second for the page on which the aid appears. Heading the second column is the caption "Page." The two columns are also connected by leader lines of spaced periods. Line spacing in the table is optional, again depending on the line lengths of the entries. Preceding each entry title is that entry's number; and should these numbers, roman or otherwise, require more than one digit, the digits are appropriately aligned on their right member. In reports which use two or more illustration types (tables, charts, maps, and such), if each type has its own numbering sequence, the entries may be listed successively by types.

VARIATIONS IN FORMS OF REPORTS

Much of the discussion to this point has been about the long, formal report form—the form that contains numerous prefatory and appended parts in addition

168

FIGURE 12–9. Good layout and mechanics in the last page of the table of contents, showing the table of illustrations attached

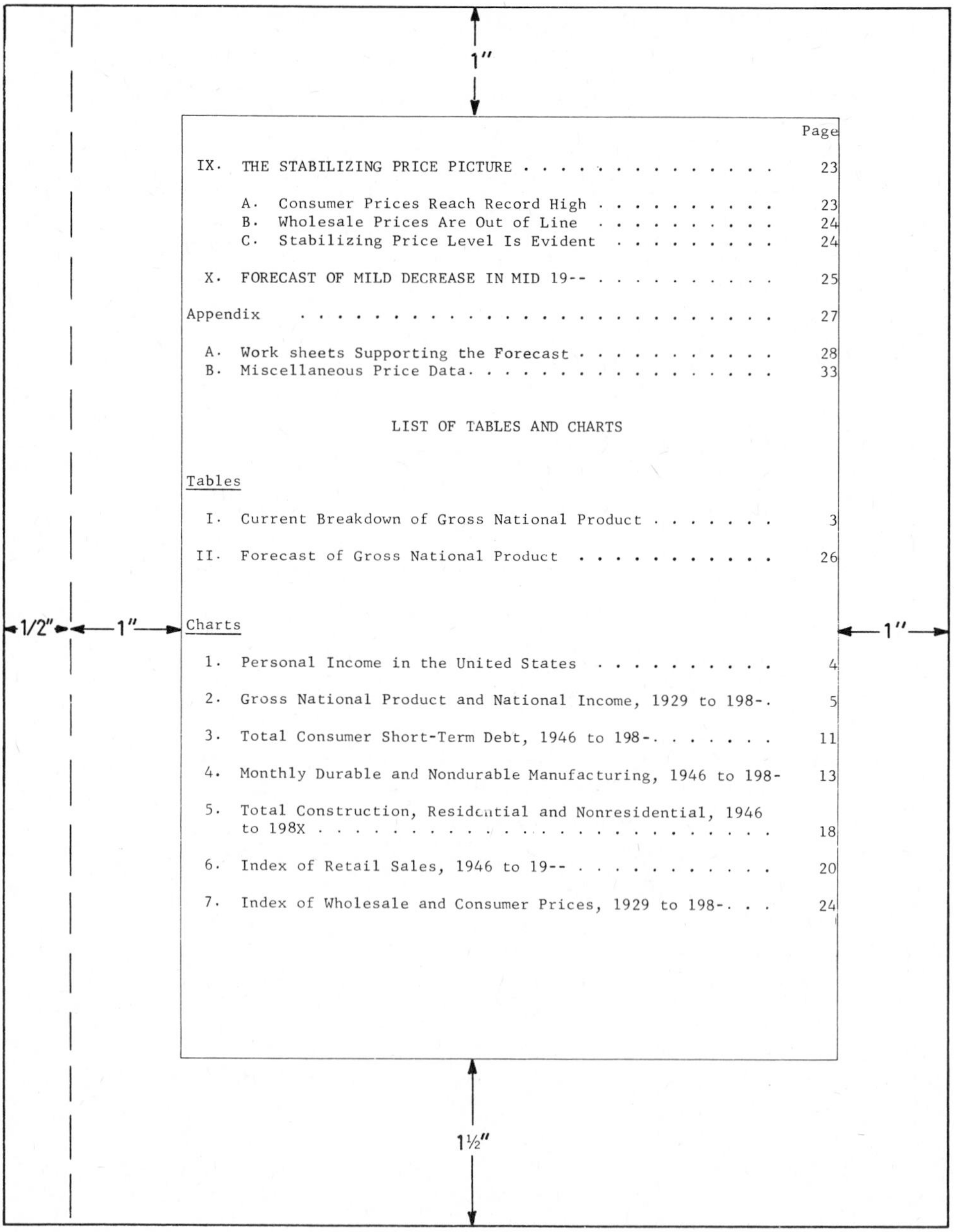

1"

1/2"   1"   1"

1½"

FIGURE 12–10.   Good form for a memorandum report

Campus Correspondence

LOUISIANA STATE UNIVERSITY

FROM: Committee on Courses and Curricula
           J. William Hughes, Chairperson

TO: Faculty, College of   DATE: December 15, 19--
           Business Administration

SUBJECT: Report of progress and plans on the study of the business
           administration curricula

Progress for the Period October 1 to December 15

On October 10 the Committee mailed questionnaires (copy attached) to the
deans of 24 selected colleges of business administration. To date, 21 of
the deans have returned questionnaires.

Professors Byrd, Calhoun, and Creznik have tabulated the replies received
and are now analyzing the findings.

Future Plans

Professors Byrd, Calhoun, and Creznik will present their analyses to the
Committee at its February 4th meeting. At this time, the Committee expects
to study these analyses and to make final recommendations.

Professor Byrd will record the Committee's recommendations in a written
report. The Committee will distribute copies of this report to all voting
members of the faculty at least one week before the faculty meeting scheduled
for May 9.

to a complete text. As was noted in Chapter 9, however, most of the reports written are not of this type. Most of them are shorter and more informal. Even so, they use much the same form requirements for the parts they have in common. The two major exceptions are the memorandum and letter reports. The physical layout requirements of the letter report are the same as those for any other letter (see Appendix D–4). Any conventional letter form is appropriate, and, as was explained in the discussion of layout of the transmittal and authorization letters, the letter report may well approximate the shape of the space in which it is typed.

Memorandum reports, although they are a type of informal letter, do not necessarily follow conventional letter format. The most popular form (see Figure 12–10) uses the military arrangement of introductory information: From, To, Subject. Generally this information is followed by informal presentation of facts in organized fashion. Other forms of the memorandum vary widely. Some resemble questionnaires in that they are comprised of lists of topics or questions, with spaces provided for the written answers. Others are simply handwritten notes on standard interoffice communication forms.

QUESTIONS

1. "Business readers want facts. They could care less about the form in which the facts are presented." Comment on the logic of this evaluation.
2. Describe the layout of an ideal conventional page in a report. How does this differ from the layout of a special page?
3. Summarize the arguments on the question of whether to single or double space the report.
4. Describe the page numbering procedure of a formal report, beginning with the title fly and ending with the last page of the appended parts.
5. Discuss the two basic ways of giving emphasis to the captions in a report.
6. Work up two schemes of caption emphasis that are different from those illustrated in the text. Evaluate them critically.
7. Discuss the content and layout considerations of a title page.
8. Describe the form of the letter of transmittal.
9. In what ways may acknowledgments be handled?
10. Summarize the layout and mechanics of the table of contents.
11. Describe the structure of a letter report. Do the same for a memo report.

Mechanics of documentation and bibliography construction

In most forms of scholarly research (excluding certain areas of the pure sciences), facts, opinions, and ideas gathered from outside sources comprise much of the information presented. All report writers should know the conventional techniques of handling this information.

PLACEMENT OF QUOTED AND PARAPHRASED INFORMATION

Report writers use information from secondary sources in two ways. They may paraphrase it (cast in the words of the report writer); or they may use it verbatim (exactly as the original author worded it). Paraphrasing is most often used, for usually the exact words of the reference source do not say exactly what the writer wants to say. But quoting sometimes is desirable, especially in two types of situation. One is when the exact words of the source are precisely what the writer wants to use. The other is when the quoted words will add credibility to the information presented (for example, when the source quoted is authoritative).

Paraphrased material need not be distinguished from the remainder of the report text, although its source frequently must be given. Materials used verbatim, however, must be clearly distinguished from the surrounding text. The conventional rule for making this difference is simple. Quoted passages of four lines or less in length are typed with the report text and are distinguished from the normal text by quotation marks. Longer quotations (five lines and more) are set in from both left and right margins (about five spaces) but without quotation marks. If the text is double spaced, the quoted passage is further distinguished from the report writer's work by single spacing, as illustrated in Figure 13–1.

Frequently report writers find it best to break or use only fragments of the quoted work. Because omissions may distort the meaning of a passage, report

FIGURE 13–1. Segment of a report showing mechanics of typing a quoted message

```
of those opposing the issue, Logan Wilson makes this penetrating ob-

servation:

          It is a curious paradox that academicians display a
          scientific attitude toward every universe of inquiry
          except that which comprises their own profession. . . .
          Lacking precise qualitative criteria, administrators
          are prone to fall back upon rather crude quantitative
          measures as a partial substitute.⁵

     These logical, straightforward, and simple arguments of the pro-

ponents of teacher evaluation appear to be irrefutable.
```

writers must clearly show such omissions. They make these omissions clear by use of the ellipsis (a series of periods, usually three, sometimes typed with intervening spaces) at the points of omission. A passage with numerous such omissions is the following.

... many companies have undertaken to centralize in the hands of specially trained correspondents the handling of the outgoing mail. Usually centralization has been accomplished by the firm's employment of a correspondence supervisor. . . . The supervisor may guide the work of correspondents . . . or the company may employ a second technique. . . .

In long quotations, it is conventional to show omissions of a paragraph or more in either of two ways. One way is to show the omission by a full line of periods. The other is to end the paragraph preceding the omission with four ellipsis points.

CONSTRUCTION OF SOURCE FOOTNOTES

As great importance is placed on the honesty of the report and the validity of the information used in it, it is customary to inform the reader of the source of paraphrased and quoted material. This may be done in either of two ways—by explanation in the text or by a source footnote. Explanation within the text is normally used only for general reference to a source or authority and not for reference to a specific passage or page in published material. For the more specific source references, the footnote is extensively used.

When to footnote

Report writers determine whether to use source footnotes mainly on the basis of giving credit where credit is due. If the words and context are solely theirs, report writers need not recognize sources. But if the information presented originates from an outside source, they should give credit to that source.

Following this reasoning of giving credit where credit is due, it is apparent that all material quoted should be footnoted. Such words are obviously the contribution of another and not of the author who repeats them. Failure to conform to this practice is to commit plagiarism—the highest of academic crimes.

Paraphrased material, too, is usually footnoted. Exceptions to this practice, however, are made when the material used is general knowledge in the field and is not the contribution of one particular source. For example, it is general knowledge in the field of advertising that one advantage in using sales letters is that advertisers may pick their audience in advance. If this information were presented in written form, even though the writer had read it in the work of another writer, no footnote would be needed so long as the information were paraphrased. The writer might elect to footnote here, however, if one felt it desirable to show authority for such a statement. If the same information were quoted, recognition of the source would be imperative.

Mechanics of the footnote

The most favored placement for the footnote is at the page bottom, separated from the text by a 1½- or 2-inch line which begins at the left margin. Obviously footnotes on the page of reference are easily used by the reader, for one can read them with a minimum of effort. One does not have to turn pages, as some other placements require; thus, one is not likely to break the continuity of one's reading or to lose one's place. Because bottom-of-page placement requires that the typist stop typing high enough on the page to allow the footnote to fit inside the page layout, typists frequently do not like this arrangement.

A second placement of the footnote is within the text and as near as possible to the spot of citation. One such form sets off the note from the text by top and bottom lines which extend the full width of the page. These techniques are convenient to the reader; and obviously they please typists.

Also gaining in popularity is a third practice—that of placing all footnotes at the end of the manuscript (or at the end of chapters in longer works). This form clearly benefits the typist, for it simplifies the typing work. For the readers, however, it is most inconvenient. It requires that they turn pages each time they choose to read a footnote. Although the form is gaining in popularity, it is hard to justify it for business use. In business reporting, one major objective of the writer is to save the valuable time of the reader. This practice simply does not do that.

A fourth practice inserts the note in parentheses immediately following the text reference. Because it is both useful to the reader and easy for the typist, this placement is most commendable and is likely to gain in use in the years ahead. Even so, because it remains the most popular, bottom-of-page placement is emphasized in this book.

When bottom-of-page placement is used, the footnote appears below the separating line. Always it is single spaced, even though the text may be double spaced. When two or more entries appear together, a double space separates them. If the text is in block form (as it may be if single spacing is used), the footnotes also are blocked. And if indented form is used (this is the rule with conventional double spacing), the footnote also is indented.

The footnotes are keyed with their text references by means of superscripts, which are arabic numerals a half line above the normal line. These numbers are first placed in the text directly after the last typed character or punctuation mark in the word or words cited. The numbering of superscripts may be consecutive throughout the paper; or it may begin anew with each chapter or with each page.

Variation in footnote makeup

Unfortunately there is no one generally accepted order for footnote form. Variations occur from school to school, from department to department, and from authority to authority. Thus, the procedures outlined below cannot conform with all of these groups. They may be looked on, however, as possibly the simplest of the generally accepted arrangements. These simplified footnote arrangements have two forms—one to be used when there is a bibliography appended to the paper and the other to be used when no bibliography is present.

Footnote form with bibliography

When a bibliography is included in the paper, the footnote references need contain only these parts: (1) author's surname; (2) title of the article, bulletin, book; and (3) page number.

[3] Wilson, *The Report Writer's Guide,* p. 44. (Book reference.)
[4] Allison, "Making Routine Reports Talk," p. 71. (Periodical reference.)

Should the reader want to know more about the source cited, he or she may turn to the bibliography. It is the writer's option, however, to use the complete footnote entry, regardless of the presence of a bibliography.

Form of the footnote without bibliography

A complete footnote is necessary for all first references to a source in a paper without a bibliography. But, as is pointed out on a following page, repeated references to the same source may be shortened. Because complete references to books, periodicals, articles, and such differ on certain points of their content, footnote instructions on each of these types are presented separately. All the items that could possibly be placed in each type of entry are listed in the order of arrangement. But not all these items are always available or essential to a footnote. Thus, there should be no alarm concerning items that are not present or are not essential to specific identification. One should simply pass over these. In other words, the following lists are intended to give the maximum contents and the order or arrangement of the footnote entries. In the simplified procedure recommended here, only the comma is used to separate the entries, and a period ends the list. Abbreviations are appropriate if consistently followed.

Book entry.
1. Superscript. (Arabic numeral keyed with the text reference and placed before the first part of the entry without spacing.)
2. Name of the author, in normal order. (If two or more authors are involved, all may be presented. If the number of authors is too great to list, the first author followed by the Latin *et al.* or its English equivalent "and others" may be used.)
3. Capacity of the author. (Needed only when contribution to the publication is not truly that of the author, such as *editor, translator,* or *compiler.*)
4. Chapter name. (Necessary only in rare instances when the chapter name helps the reader to find the source, such as in references to encyclopedias.)
5. Book name. (Book names are placed in italics. In typewritten work, italics are indicated by underscoring or by solid caps.)
6. Edition. (Only if other than a first edition.)
7. Publishing company.
8. Location of publisher. (If more than one office, one nearest the writer should be included. Cities in the United States alone are sufficient if population execeds 500,000; city and state are best given for smaller places.)
9. Date. (Year of publication. If revised, year of latest revision.)
10. Page or pages. (Specific page or inclusive pages on which the cited material is found.)

Examples:

(A typical book)

[1] Raymond V. Lesikar, *Report Writing for Business,* 6th ed., Richard D. Irwin, Inc., Homewood, Ill., 1981, pp. 13–15.

(A book written by a staff of writers under the direction of an editor. Chapter title is considered helpful.)

[2] W. C. Butte and Amos Buchannan, editors, "Direct Mail Advertising," *An Encyclopedia of Advertising,* Binton Publishing Company, New York, 1981, p. 99.

(Book written by a number of coauthors)

[3] E. Butler Cannais and others, *Anthology of Public Relations,* Warner-Bragg, Inc., New York, 1980, p. 137.

Periodical entry.
1. Superscript.
2. Author's name. (Frequently no author is given. In such cases, the entry may be skipped, or if it is definitely known to be anonymous, the word "anonymous" may be placed in the entry.)
3. Article name. (Typed in quotation marks.)
4. Periodical name. (Placed in italics, which are made by underscoring typed work.)
5. Publication identification. (Volume number in consistent arabic or roman numbers, followed by specific date of publication in parentheses.)
6. Page or pages.

Examples:
[1] James C. Kinnig, "A New Look at Retirement," *Modern Business,* vol. 37 (July 31, 1979), pp. 31–32.

[2] William O. Schultz, "How One Company Improved Morale," *The Business Leader,* vol. 17 (Aug. 31, 1981), p. 17.

[3] Don Mitchell, "Report Writing Aids," *ABCA Bulletin,* October 1980, p. 13.

Newspaper article.
1. Superscript.
2. Source description. (If article is signed, give author's name. Otherwise give description of article, such as "United Press Dispatch" or "editorial.")
3. Main head of article. (Subheads not needed.)
4. Newspaper name. (City and state names inserted in brackets if place names do not appear in newspaper title. State names not needed in case of very large cities, such as New York, Chicago, and Los Angeles.)
5. Date of publication.
6. Page. (May even include column number.)

Examples:
[1] United Press Dispatch, "Rival Unions Sign Pact," *The* [Baton Rouge, Louisiana] *Morning Advocate,* September 3, 1980, p. 1–A.

[2] Editorial, "The North Moves South," *The Austin* [Texas] *American,* October 3, 1980, p. 2–A.

Letters or documents.
1. Nature of communication.
2. Name of writer.   ⎫ With identification by title and
3. Name of recipient. ⎭ organization where helpful.
4. Date of writing.
5. Where filed.

Example:
[1] Letter from J. W. Wells, President, Wells Equipment Co., to James Mattoch, Secretary-Treasurer, Southern Industrialists, Inc., June 10, 1981, filed among Mr. Mattoch's personal records.

The types of entries discussed in the preceding paragraphs are those most likely to be used; yet, many unusual types are likely to be found in any extensive research project. Government publications, bulletins, special publications of learned societies, essays, and the like may afford countless special problems. Although writers may find help for such special cases in the various books available on style, usually they can work the problem logically. They can do this by keeping in mind that their objective in constructing the footnote is to make it possible for readers to find the cited source should they choose to do so. As a rule, writers will profit by classifying each problem as either a book or a periodical, depending on which it appears to approximate. Then they should attempt to construct the appropriate entry, leaving out the parts they feel do not help to identify the source and inserting any additional information they feel should be included for completeness. Example:

A writer wants to make reference to a paper read at the 1981 Computer Science Conference held at Louisiana State University, Baton Rouge, Louisiana, and published in the proceedings of that organization. The paper was by John S.

White, Chief Accountant, Exxon Company, and reference is to page 24 of the proceedings. As the published proceedings are written in what appears to approach periodical form (it contains a number of articles and is published annually), the following entry may be made.

[1] John S. White, "Organizing and Planning for Electronic Data Processing Systems," *Proceedings of the Computer Science Conference, 1981,* held and sponsored by Louisiana State University, Baton Rouge, Louisiana, p. 24.

Double sources

Sometimes one wants to cite a passage written by someone other than the author whose name appears on the work consulted. The passage may be a quotation that the author of the consulted work may have borrowed from another author. Or it may be that the source is a collection of papers written by various people and only edited by the one whose name appears on the publication (such as a book of readings). In such cases, the usual procedure is to make what amounts to a double reference. First is the true author's name and the identification of his or her work (as much as is available). Next are some appropriate relating words, such as "quoted in" or "cited in." Finally there is the description of the reference in which the passage was found. Such a reference may look like this.

[3] John W. Benning, "How Green Were the Years," presidential address, 13th annual meeting, Academy of Social Sciences, Boulder, Colorado, 1980, as cited in Henry A. Tucker, *New Concepts in the Social Sciences,* Walthrup Press, Inc., New York, 1981, p. 314.

Standard reference forms

If it becomes necessary to cite a source more than once in a manuscript, as it frequently does, repetition may be kept to a minimum by the use of standard reference abbreviations. Although these abbreviations serve a very worthwhile purpose in their attempt to simplify the footnote construction, it is unfortunate that they are of Latin origin and, therefore, understood only in scholarly circles. Because these forms are so little known, many writers prefer not to use them, even at the expense of repeating whole footnote entries. Possibly in time some simplified English substitutes will become generally accepted. But until that time, those who write research papers should understand at least the more common of those entries.

Ibid. (ibidem). Literally *ibid.* means "in the same place." It is used to refer the reader to the preceding footnote. The entry consists of the superscript, *ibid.,* and the page number.

Op. cit. (opere citato). Meaning "in the work cited," this form is used to refer to a previously cited footnote, but not the one directly preceding. That is, the two similar citations are separated by at least one intervening footnote to another source. The entry consists of the superscript, last name of the author, *op. cit.,* and page number.

Loc. cit. (loco citato). This form means "in the place cited" and its use follows its literal meaning. The form refers to a preceding entry, either the one directly preceding or one farther back in the footnote series. It is used only when the page numbers of the two references to the same source are the same. If the entry refers to the footnote directly preceding, *loc. cit.* alone is used. If the form is used to refer to an entry farther back in the series, the author's last name plus *loc. cit.* make up the entry.

The following series of entries illustrates these possibilities.

[1] James Smith, *How to Write the Annual Report,* Small-Boch, Inc., Chicago, p. 173.

[2] *Ibid.,* p. 143. (Refers to Smith's book but to different page.)

[3] William Curtis, "An Experiment with Records," *Business Leader,* vol. XIX (Dec. 5, 1980), p. 28.

[4] Smith, *op. cit.,* p. 103. (Refers to Smith's book but to different page than in footnote 2.)

[5] Curtis, *loc. cit.* (Refers to Curtis's article and to same page as in footnote 3.)

[6] *Loc. cit.* (Refers to Curtis's article and to same page as in footnotes 3 and 5.)

Other abbreviation forms are frequently used in footnote entries. Some of these are particularly useful in making reference to text passages or to other footnotes. Such references are generally made in discussion footnotes, which are quite different from the source footnotes discussed in the preceding pages. The most widely used of these abbreviations are as follows.

Cf.—compare (directs reader's attention to another passage).
Cf. ante—compare above.
Cf. post—compare below.
ed.—edition.
e.g.—for example.
et al.—and others.
et passim—and at intervals throughout the work.
et seq.—and the following.
i.e.—that is.
idem—the same.
infra—below.
l., ll.—line, lines.
Ms., Mss.—manuscript, manuscripts.
n.d.—no date.
n.n.—no name.
n.p.—no place.
p., pp.—page, pages.
f., ff.—following page, pages.
supra—above.
vol., vols.—volume, volumes.

DISCUSSION FOOTNOTES

In sharp contrast with source footnotes are the discussion footnotes. Through the use of discussion footnotes, writers strive to explain a part of the text, to amplify discussion on a phase of the presentation, to make cross references to other parts of the paper, and the like. This material is not placed in the text principally because to place it there would tend to slow down or complicate the presentation. But one should take care that not too much of the writing is relegated to a role in a footnote. Material presented in footnote form obviously does not receive the emphasis that material presented in text form receives. Thus, unless writers use discretion in selecting the points for footnote presentation, the major story of the paper will suffer.

No standard form could possibly be devised for presentation of the discussion footnote. Of course, the note should be as concise and clear as it possibly can be. But general instructions can go no further than these points, for each footnote differs because of contents. These examples illustrate some possibilities of this footnote type.

(Cross reference)	[1] See the principle of focal points on page 72.
(Amplification of discussion and cross reference)	[2] Lyman Bryson says the same: "Every communication is different for every receiver even in the same context. No one can estimate the variation of understanding that there may be among receivers of the same message conveyed in the same vehicle when the receivers are separated in either space or time." See *Communication of Ideas,* p. 5.
(Comparison)	[3] Compare with the principle of the objective: Before starting any activity, one should make a clear, complete statement of the objective in view.

THE BIBLIOGRAPHY

A bibliography is an orderly list of published material on a particular subject. In a formal paper, the list covers writings on the subject of the paper. The entries in this list very closely resemble source footnotes, but one should not confuse the two.

The bibliography normally appears as an appended part of a formal paper and follows the appendix. Usually a fly page containing the one word "Bibliography" in capital letters precedes it. The page that begins the list is headed by the main caption "Bibliography," usually typed in solid capital letters. Below this title, the publications are presented by broad groups and in alphabetical order within the groups. Usually such groupings as books, periodicals, and bulletins may be used. But the determination of groups should be based solely on the types of publications collected in each bibliography. If, for example, a bibliography includes a large number of periodicals and government publications plus a wide assortment of diverse publication types, the bibliography could be divided into three parts: periodicals, government publications, and miscellaneous publications.

As with footnotes, variations in bibliography form are numerous. A simplified form recommended for business use follows the same procedure as that described above for source footnotes, with four major exceptions.

1. The author's name is in reverse order, surname first, for the purpose of alphabetizing. If coauthors are involved, however, only the first name is reversed.

2. The entry is generally typed in hanging indention form. That is, the second and all following lines of an entry begin some uniform distance (usually about five spaces) to the right of the beginning point of the first line. The purpose of this indented pattern is to make the alphabetized first line stand out.

3. The bibliography entry gives the inclusive pages of the article, book, bulletin, or such and does not refer to any one page or passage.

4. A uniform line indicates second and subsequent references to publications of the same author (see bibliography illustration). In typed manuscripts, this line may be formed by the underscore struck ten consecutive times. But this line is appropriate only if the entire authorship is the same in the consecutive publications. For example, the line could not be used when consecutive entries have one common author but different coauthors.

An illustration of a bibliography is as follows.

BIBLIOGRAPHY

BOOKS

Burton, Hal, *The City Fights Back,* The Citadel Press, New York, 1980, 318 pp.
Converse, Paul D., Harvey W. Huegy, and Robert V. Mitchell, *The Elements of Marketing,* 5th ed., Prentice-Hall, Inc., New York, 1952, 968 pp.
Kiernan, Gladys M., *Retailers Manual of Taxes and Regulation,* 13th ed., Institute of Distribution, Inc., New York, 1981, 345 pp.
Koontz, Harold D., *Government Control of Business,* Houghton Mifflin Company, New York, 1976, 937 pp.
Surrey, N. M. M., *The Commerce of Louisiana during the French Regime, 1699–1763,* Columbia University Press, New York, 1916, 476 pp.

GOVERNMENT PUBLICATIONS

U.S. Bureau of the Census, "Characteristics of the Population," *Eighteenth Census of the United States: Census of Population,* Vol. II, Part 18, U.S. Government Printing Office, Washington, D.C., 1971, 248 pp.
———, *Statistical Abstract of the United States,* U.S. Government Printing Office, Washington, D.C., 1978, 1057 pp.
United States Department of Commerce, *Business Statistics: 1971,* U.S. Government Printing Office, Washington, D.C., 1971, 309 pp.
———, *Survey of Current Business: 1977 Supplement,* U.S. Government Printing Office, Washington, D.C., 1977, 287 pp.

PERIODICALS

Montgomery, Donald E., "Consumer Standards and Marketing," *The Annals of the American Academy of Political and Social Science,* vol. 7 (May 1980), pp. 141–49.
Phillips, Charles F., "Major Areas of Marketing Research," *The Journal of Marketing,* vol. 44 (July 1980), pp. 21–26.

————, "Some Studies Needed in Marketing," *The Journal of Marketing,* vol. 5 (July 1940), pp. 16–25.

MISCELLANEOUS PUBLICATIONS

Bradford, Ernest S., *Survey and Directory, Marketing Research Agencies in the United States,* Bureau of Business Research, College of the City of New York, 1972, 137 pp.

Reference Sources on Chain Stores, Institute of Distribution, Inc., New York, 1980, 116 pp.

Smith, T. Lynn, *Farm Trade Centers in Louisiana,* 1901 to 1975, Louisiana Bulletin No. 234, Louisiana State University, Baton Rouge, 1972, 56 pp.

THE ANNOTATED BIBLIOGRAPHY

Frequently in scholarly writing, a brief comment on the value and content of the entry follows each bibliography entry. That is, the bibliography is annotated. No definite rules may be given for the composition of the annotation. The comments should, in as brief a fashion as is practical, point out the content and value of each entry. Short descriptive phrases are generally used rather than complete sentences, although sentences are acceptable. The annotation, like the bibliography entry, is single spaced, but it is separated from the entry by a double space. It, also, is indented from the initial line of the entry, as illustrated below.

Donald, W. T., editor, *Handbook of Business Administration,* McGraw-Hill Book Co., New York, 1976, 731 pp.

Contains a summary of the activities in each major area of business. Written by foremost authorities in each field. Particularly useful to the business specialist who wants a quick review of the whole of business.

Brown, Stanley M., and Lillian Doris, editors, *Business Executive's Handbook,* Hamm Publishing Company, New York, 4th ed., 1980, 651 pp.

Provides answers to most routine executive problems in explicit manner and with good examples. Contains good material on correspondence and sales letters.

QUESTIONS

1. In what two ways may quoted material be placed within the text of a report?
2. Distinguish between paraphrased and verbatim use of secondary information.
3. Explain the use of the ellipsis. Illustrate its use at the beginning of a passage, at the end of a passage, and within a passage.
4. How are omissions of a paragraph or more conventionally indicated?
5. What is the major determinant of when a source footnote is needed?
6. Distinguish between the need for footnotes for paraphrased material and for quoted material.
7. Describe the mechanical arrangement of the footnote on the page.
8. What is the superscript? Describe its role in the footnote.

9. From the garbled information presented below, construct (*a*) a series of footnote entries for material with a bibliography and (*b*) a series of entries for a paper without a bibliography. The entries are all within the space of three consecutive pages.

> First entry: reference to page 132 of a book written by Lloyd Peabody, James Melton, and William Byrd; published by Jones Publishing Company, Atlanta, Georgia; entitled *Advanced Personnel Management;* 4th edition; published 1981.

> Second entry: reference to page 71; a magazine article appearing in *Management News;* October 7, 1980, "An Experiment with Incentive Plans"; written by Kirk Tobin; Volume 71.

> Third entry: second reference to Peabody's book, this time to page 33.

> Fourth entry: another reference to page 33 of Peabody's book.

> Fifth entry: a second reference to page 71 of Tobin's article.

10. Construct bibliography entries for the text books you are using.

11. Construct bibliography entries for five magazine articles in your major field of study.

12. Find and construct the bibliography entries for five sources which you believe involve unusual problems in footnoting. (Publications other than books or periodicals are most likely to meet this requirement.)

13. Distinguish between the discussion footnote and the source footnote.

14. Using hypothetical information, construct discussion footnotes used (*a*) to make a cross reference, (*b*) to amplify discussion, and (*c*) to make a comparison.

15. Define the annotated bibliography. What is its purpose?

16. From the information below, make the entry as it would appear
    a. In a bibliography.
    b. As a footnote (No. 2) referring to page 374 (no bibliography).
    c. As a footnote that is No. 4 in a series in which No. 2 referred to the same book and the same page.
    d. As a footnote that is No. 5 in the same series, but reference is to another page page (p. 411).
    > Book title—*A History of Modern Business.*
    > Author—James W. Gordon.
    > Date of publication—1981.
    > Edition—1st.
    > Total pages—567.
    > Publisher—Maybery Publishing Company, Boston.

14

Graphic aids for reports

G raphic aids[1] are an essential part of most reports. Even though it is generally true that the report story is best told in words, words alone usually are not adequate. In such instances, report writers may use some form of graphic aid to help put over the meanings of the words. Thus, the primary function of graphic aids in the report is that of assisting the words to communicate the report contents.

In addition to their vital role in communication, graphic aids also serve to cover minor supporting detail not considered in the text words. Or they may serve to give special emphasis to certain points of coverage. Even though they should not be included for this reason alone, they serve to improve the physical appearance of the report, thereby making the report more inviting and readable.

FORESIGHT IN PLANNING THE ILLUSTRATIONS

If graphic aids are to be effective, report writers must plan them with foresight and care. Such planning is part of the task of organizing the report, and report writers do it at the time they organize the report.

The task of planning the graphic presentation should never be allowed to become arbitrary or routine. Never should writers arbitrarily select some random number of illustrations to include. Nor should the completeness of graphic presentation be judged solely on the number of illustrations used. Instead, each graphic device planned for presentation in the report should have a definite reason for being. And this reason for being should be judged by one, and only one, criterion; that criterion is need. Only if the graphic aid is needed—that is, if it helps to communicate the report story—should one include it.

---

[1] The term *graphic aids* is used here in its broadest meaning and includes all forms of illustration designed to supplement the text. By this definition, tables (which are not truly graphic) are included as graphic aids.

A major part of planning the graphic aids is determining the type of illustration to use. As will become clear in the pages ahead, all types are not equally good for a given case. Some are clearly superior in some instances and clearly inferior in others. Thus, it is the report writer's task to review the possibilities available in each case and to select the one form of graphic aid that does the very best job of communicating the information.

RELATIONSHIP OF NEED TO THE PLAN

Just what graphic aids are needed to communicate a report story, however, is not easy to determine. Much depends on the overall plan of the writers. If the writers plan to cover the subject in detail, the role of the graphic aids is to emphasize and to supplement. Specifically the graphic aids point up the major facts discussed and present the detailed data not covered in the writing. On the other hand, if the writers plan to present the facts in summary form, they may use the graphic aids to work more closely with the text.

The first of these arrangements (complete text supplemented by graphic aids) is conventional and is best for all studies when completeness is a main requirement. The second plan (summary text closely helped by graphic aids) is gaining in importance. It is especially used in popular types of reports, such as those addressed to the general public. As illustrated in Figure 14–1, this plan produces fast-moving, light reading—the kind the public likes. In addition to the public, many top executives prefer this plan. With the increasing demands on their time, these executives prefer that the reports they read give them the facts quickly and easily. Short summary reports, helped by an abundance of clear graphic aids, do this job best. Frequently, because of the need for a complete report for future reference and the need for presenting summary information to top executives, both kinds of reports are written for the same problem.

PREFERRED PLACEMENT WITHIN THE REPORT

The graphic aids designed primarily to help the report story should appear within the report text and near the text they illustrate. If the illustration is small, taking up only a portion of the page, it should be surrounded by the writing that covers it. And if the illustration requires a full page, it should come immediately following the page on which it is discussed. When the discussion covers several pages, however, the full-page illustration ought to be on the page following the first reference to its content.

Another acceptable placement of a full-page illustration is on the obverse side of a page and facing the text it supports. When this placement is used, either of two page arrangements is acceptable. The illustration page may be affixed to the preceding page so that it turns with that page and appears as its reverse side. Or the reverse side of the illustration page may be left blank. These arrangements cause some problem in numbering the pages, however. In the first arrangement,

FIGURE 14–1. Page from a popular report illustrating use of a summary text closely helped by graphic aids

Long Industry Lead Times

In considering measures to ease the energy supply situation (section VI), the importance of long lead times cannot be overemphasized. In some activities a sufficient concentration of brains and money can solve problems through "crash" action. In the oil industry, however, as the diagram below shows, planners must think in terms of several years, not months. An understanding of the time factor in oil operations is fundamental.

CHART 15

Lead Times in Oil Industry Developments.

Geophysical work to find commercial field 1-3 years	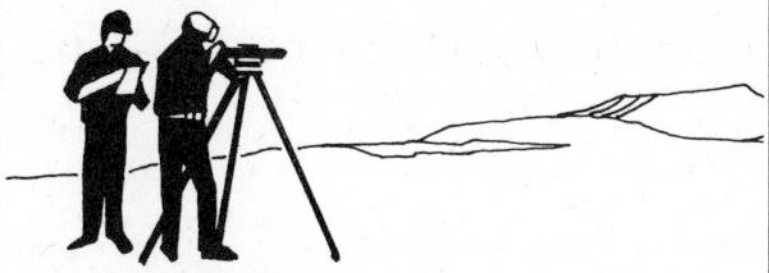
Offshore drilling 1-2 years to drill wells 6-18 months to set platforms 2-3 years in development	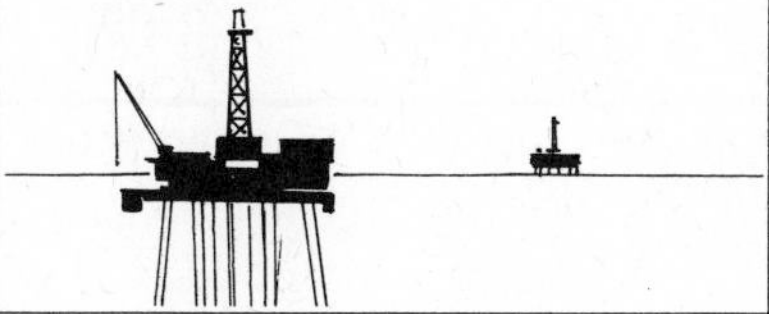
Refinery Construction 3 years to obtain site, to design, and to get permits 2-4 years for construction	
Marine Terminals 3 years upwards	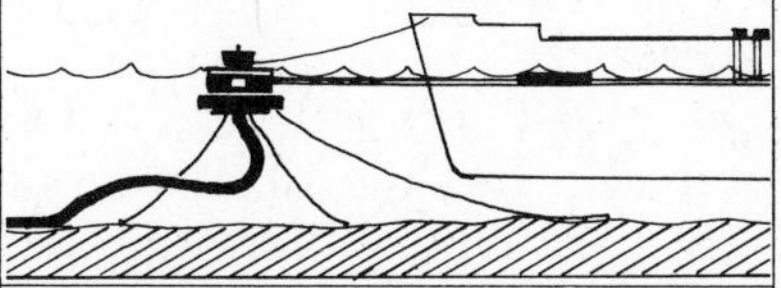
Tanker construction 2-3 years	

the page may be given the next number in sequence. In the second arrangement, the word *obverse* and the page number may appear on the blank side of the page in the spot where the number normally would go.

There is some acceptance of the report arrangement in which all the illustrations are in the appendix. Aside from the time saved by the typist, little can be said for this practice. Certainly it does not work for the convenience of the readers, who must flip through pages each time they want to see the graphic presentation of a part of the text.

Graphic aids that are not designed specifically to help tell a part of the report story should be in the appendix. Included in this group are all graphic aids that belong within the report for completeness, yet have no specific spot of coverage within the study. As a rule, this group largely comprises long and complex tables that may cover large areas of information. These tables may even cover the data displayed in a number of charts and other more graphic devices generally constructed to illustrate very specific spots within the report.

COORDINATION OF THE PICTURES AND THE WORDS

As noted earlier, the role graphic aids play in communicating report information can be major. But just how much of the report message should they tell? How much should the written words tell? Report writers must answer these key questions as they construct the report.

In answering these questions, a good two-part working rule to consider is the following: (1) Tell the complete report story (all that is really significant) in words, (2) use illustrations to supplement the high points as well as to cover the incidental details that would merely clutter the text if they were made a part of the report story. Obviously, applying these rules is a somewhat subjective matter and must be governed by the logic of the writers.

Because the written and visual parts of the report work together as a team in communicating, they should be coordinated in the report plan. A part of coordinating involves considerations of strategy and placement previously discussed. It also involves keying the words with the illustrations. Keying words with illustrations means that the writers should call the reader's attention to each illustration at the ideal place in the report. More specifically, the writers should invite the reader to look at the illustrations when the illustrations will make their best communication effect. One makes such references best as incidental remarks in sentences that state significant comments about the data shown in the illustration. Although numerous incidental wordings may be used, the following word groups are acceptable.

    . . . , as shown in Chart 4, . . .
    . . . , indicated in Chart 4, . . .
    . . . , as a glance at Chart 4 reveals, . . .
    . . . (see Chart 4).

GENERAL MECHANICS OF CONSTRUCTION

In planning the illustrations, and later in the actual work of constructing them, report writers must face numerous questions of mechanics. Many of these questions they must solve through intelligent appraisal of the conditions concerned in each instance. But the mechanics fall into general groups, the most conventional of which are summarized in the following paragraphs.

Size determination

One of the first decisions involved in constructing a graphic aid is that of determining how large the illustration should be. The answer to this question should not be arbitrary, nor should it be based solely on the convenience of the writers. Instead the writers should seek to give the illustration the size that its contents justify. If, for example, an illustration is relatively simple, comprising only two or three quantities, a quarter page might be adequate. Certainly a full page would not be needed to illustrate the data. But if the illustration displays a dozen or so quantities, a larger illustration would be justified—possibly even a full page.

With extremely complex and involved data, it may be necessary to make the graphic aid larger than the report page. Such long presentations must be carefully inserted and folded within the report so that they open easily. The fold selected will, of course, vary with the size of the page. There is no one best fold. The writers will do well to survey whatever possibilities are available to them.

Layout arrangement

The layout of any graphic aid is influenced by how much information is to be illustrated. But whenever practical, it is best to keep the layout of the illustration within the normal page layout.

Rules and borders

Proper placement of rules and borders can help display and make clear the data in most illustrations. But there are no hard-and-fast rules on how to place them. As a general practice, however, graphic aids of less than a page are set off from the text by a line border, which completely encloses the illustration and its captions. This practice is useful for full-page illustrations as well, although with such pages the border does not serve so practical a purpose. As previoulsy noted in the discussion of layout, the borders should not extend beyond the normal page margins. Ah exception to this rule is, of course, the unusual instances in which the volume of data to be illustrated simply will not fit into an area less than the normal page layout.

Color and cross-hatching

Appropriate use of color or cross-hatching helps the reader to see the comparisons and distinctions. In addition, they give the report a boost in physical attractiveness. Color is especially valuable for this purpose and should be used whenever practical.

One easy way of applying color or cross-hatching to graphic aids is by using any of a variety of adhesive materials on the market. Available in a wide assortment of colors and cross-hatch patterns, these adhesives are easily cut into bar, pie, or other shapes and stuck to the areas of the graphic aids where color or design is needed. Also available are a variety of adhesive letters, numerals, border designs, and such. When properly used, these adhesives produce a truly professional appearing graphic aid.

Numbering

Except for minor tabular displays that are actually a part of the text, all illustrations in the report are numbered. Numerous schemes of numbering are appropriate, depending on the makeup of the graphic aids.

If sufficient numbers of two or more graphic aid types are used in a report, each type may be numbered consecutively. For example, if a report is illustrated by six tables, five charts, and six maps, these graphic aids might be numbered Table I, Table II, . . . Table VI; Chart 1, Chart 2, . . . Chart 5; and Map 1, Map 2, ... Map 6.

But if the illustrations used are a wide mixture of types, they may be numbered in two groups—tables and figures. To illustrate, consider a report that contains three tables, two maps, three charts, one diagram, and one photograph. One could group and number these graphic aids as Table I, Table II, and Table III, and Figure 1, Figure 2, . . . Figure 7. By convention, tables are never grouped with other forms of presentation. *Figures* represent a sort of miscellaneous grouping which may include all illustration types other than tables. It would not be wrong to group and number as figures all graphic aids other than tables, even if the group contains sufficient subgroups (chart, maps, and such) to warrant separate numbering of each of these subgroups.

As the preceding examples illustrate, tables are conventionally numbered with capital roman numerals (I, II, III, and so on). All other forms of illustration use the arabic numerals (1, 2, 3, and so on). There is some tendency now, however, to use arabic numerals for all forms. Obviously the most important rule to follow in regard to numbering is that of consistency.

Construction of title captions

Every graphic aid should have a title caption that adequately describes the contents. Like the captions used in other parts of the report, the title to the graphic aid has the objective of concisely covering the illustration contents. As a check of content coverage, report writers may well use the journalist's five Ws—*who, what, where, when, why.* Sometimes they may include *how* (the classification principle). But as conciseness of expression is also desired, it is not always necessary to include all the Ws in the caption. A title of a chart comparing annual sales volume of Texas and Louisiana stores of the Brill Company for the 1979–1981 period may be constructed as follows.

Who—Brill Company.
What—annual sales.
Where—Texas and Louisiana.
When—1979–1981.
Why—for comparison.

The caption may read, "Comparative Annual Sales of Texas and Louisiana Branches of the Brill Company, 1979–1981."

Placement of titles

Titles of tables are conventionally placed above the tabular display. Titles to all other graphic presentations usually are placed below the illustration. There is convention, too, for placing table titles in a higher type (usually solid capitals without the underscore in typewritten reports) than titles of all other illustrations. But now these conventional forms are not universally followed. There is a growing tendency to use lowercase type for all illustration titles, and to place titles of both tables and charts at the top. These more recent practices are simple and logical; yet, for formal reports the conventional way is recommended.

Footnotes and source acknowledgments

Occasionally parts of a graphic aid require special explanation or elaboration. When these conditions come up, just as when similar explanations are made within the text of the report, a footnote is used. Such footnotes are nothing more than concise explanations placed below the illustration and keyed to the part explained by means of a superscript (raised number) or asterisk (as shown in Figure 13–1). Footnotes for tables are best placed immediately below the graphic presentation. Footnotes for other graphic forms follow the illustration when the title is placed at the top of the page, and they follow the title when the title is placed at the bottom of the page.

When the source of the information in the graphic aid deserves acknowledgment, a source note appears as the bottom entry below the graphic aid. The entry consists simply of the word *Source,* followed by a colon and the source name. A source note for data based on information from the U.S. Department of Agriculture might read like this: Source: U.S. Department of Agriculture. If the data were collected by the writers or their staff, either of two procedures is appropriate. The writers may identify the source as primary, using this source note: Source: Primary. Or the writers simply may omit the source note.

CONSTRUCTION OF TABLES

A table is any systematic arrangement of quantitative information in rows and columns. Although tables are not truly graphic in the literal meaning of the word, they are instrumental in communicating information. Therefore, they are appropriately considered a part of the graphic aids planning of a report. The purpose of a table is to present a broad area of information in convenient and orderly fashion. Such an arrangement simplifies the information and makes the comparisons easier to see.

Two basic types of tables are available to report writers—the general-purpose table and the special-purpose table. General-purpose tables are arrangements of a broad area of data collected. They are repositories of detailed statistical data and have no special analytical purpose. As a rule, general-purpose tables appear in the report appendix.

Special-purpose tables, as their name implies, are prepared for a special purpose —to help illustrate a particular part of the text. Usually they consist of data carefully drawn from the general-purpose tables. Typically they include only those data pertinent to the writers' analysis, and they arrange or regroup these data to illustrate their special purpose. Such tables usually appear within the text near the writing they illustrate.

Aside from the title, footnotes, and source designation previously discussed, the table consists of stubs, captions, and columns and rows of data, as shown in Figure 14–2. Stubs are the titles to the rows of data, and captions are the titles to the columns. The captions, however, may be divided into subcaptions, or column heads, as they are sometimes called.

As the text tables should be specially planned, their construction is largely influenced by their illustration purpose. Nevertheless, a few general construction rules may be listed.

1. If rows tend to be long, the stubs may be repeated at the right.

2. The dash (—) or the abbreviation "n.a.," but not the zero, is used to indicate data not available.

3. Footnote references to numbers in the table should be keyed with asterisks, daggers, double daggers, and such. Numbers followed by footnote reference numbers may cause confusion.

4. Totals and subtotals should appear whenever they help the purpose of the table. The totals may be for each column and sometimes for each row. Usually row totals are made at the right, but, when the totals need emphasis, they may be placed at the left. Likewise, column totals generally appear at the bottom, but they may appear at the top of the column when writers want to emphasize them. A ruled line (usually a double one) separates the totals from their data.

5. Units in which the data are recorded must be clear. Unit descriptions (bushels, acres, pounds, and such) appropriately appear above the columns, as part of the captions or subcaptions. If the data are in dollars, however, the dollar mark ($) placed before the first entry in each column is sufficient.

Tabulated information need not always be presented in formal tables. In fact,

FIGURE 14–2.   Good arrangement of the parts of a
typical table

TABLE NO. TITLE OF TABLE				
Stub head	SPANNER HEAD			
	Column head	Column head	Column head	Column head
Stub	X X X	X X X	X X X	X X X
Stub	X X X	X X X	X X X	X X X
Stub	X X X	X X X	X X X	X X X
Stub	X X X	X X X	X X X	X X X
"	"	"	"	"
"	"	"	"	"
"	"	"	"	"
"	"	"	"	"
"	"	"	"	"
"	"	"	"	"
TOTAL	X X X	X X X	X X X	X X X
Footnotes				
Source note:				

short arrangements of data may be presented more effectively as parts of the text. Such arrangements generally are made in either of two ways: as leaderwork or as text tabulations.

Leaderwork is the presentation of tabular material in the text without titles or rules. Typically a colon precedes the tabulation, as in this illustration:

August sales for representatives of the Western Region were as follows:

Charles B. Brown	$13,517
Thomas Capp	19,703
Bill E. Knauth	18,198

Text tabulations are simple tables, usually with headings and some rules. But they are not numbered, and they have no titles. They are made to read with the text, as in this example:

August sales for the representatives in the Western Region increased sharply from the preceding month, as these figures show:

Representative	July sales	August sales	Increase
Charles B. Brown	$12,819	$13,517	$ 698
Thomas Capp	17,225	19,703	2,478
Bill E. Knauth	16,838	18,198	1,360

THE SIMPLE BAR CHART

Simple bar charts are graphic means of comparing simple magnitudes by the lengths of equal-width bars. Such charts are used to show quantity changes over time, quantity changes over geographic distance, or quantitative distances.

The principal parts of the bar chart are the bars and the grid. The bars may be arranged horizontally or perpendicularly, and each has in its beginning a title to identify the quantity being illustrated. The grid on which the bars are placed is simply a field carefully ruled by line marks arithmetically scaled to the magnitude illustrated. Usually construction of a finely marked grid is a preliminary step in making a bar chart. Then the bars are placed on the grid. But for best visual effect the final drawing of the chart should show only sufficient grid lines to help the reader's eye measure the magnitudes of the bar. These scale grid lines are carefully labeled with numerals. A scale caption appearing below the values in a vertical bar chart and above the values in a horizontal bar arrangement indicates the unit in which the values are measured.

Although there are numerous acceptable variations in bar chart construction, a basic pattern should serve as a helpful guide to novice writers (see Figure 14–3).

FIGURE 14–3.   Illustration of good arrangement of the parts of a simple bar chart

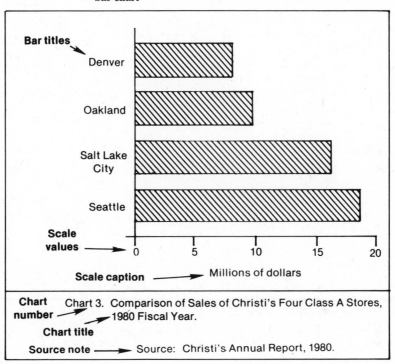

VARIATIONS OF THE BAR CHART

In addition to the simple bar chart just described, a number of other types of bar charts are useful in presenting a report. The more commonly used of these variants are the multiple bar chart, the bilateral bar chart, and the subdivided or component-part bar chart.

Multiple bar charts

Comparisons of two or three variables within a single bar chart are possible through the use of multiple bars distinguished by cross-hatching, shading, or color. That is, the bars that represent each of the variables being compared are distinguished by these mechanical means, as illustrated in Figure 14–4. The key to the variables is given in a legend, which normally appears within the illustration or below it, depending on where space is available. Generally it is confusing and therefore inadvisable to make multiple comparisons of this type when more than three variables are involved.

FIGURE 14–4. Multiple bar chart

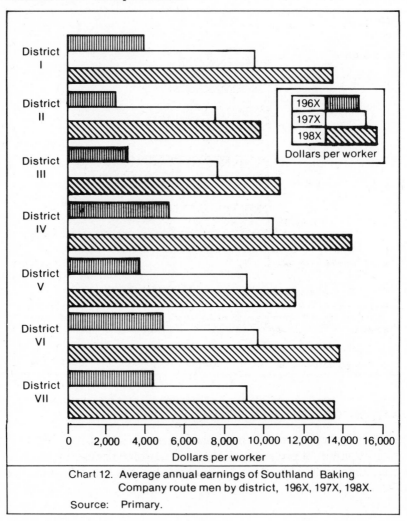

Chart 12. Average annual earnings of Southland Baking
Company route men by district, 196X, 197X, 198X.

Source: Primary.

Bilateral bar charts

When it is necessary to show plus or minus deviations, bilateral bar charts may be used. In these charts, the bars begin at a central point of reference and may go either up or down from it, as illustrated in Figure 14–5. Bar titles may be written within, above, or below the bars, depending on which placement best fits the illustration. Bilateral bar charts are especially good for showing percentage change, but they are useful for any series in which minus quantities are present.

FIGURE 14–5.   Bilateral bar chart

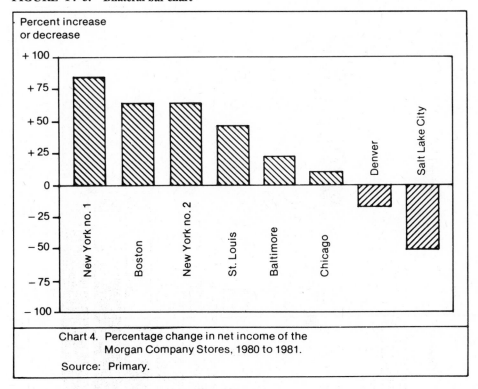

Chart 4. Percentage change in net income of the
          Morgan Company Stores, 1980 to 1981.

Source: Primary.

Subdivided bar charts

If it is desirable to show the composition of magnitudes being compared, sub-divided bar charts are effective. Cross-hatchings, shadings, or colors are first assigned to each of the parts to be shown; then, the bars are marked off into their component parts, as Figure 14–6 illustrates. As always when cross-hatching or color is used, a legend is employed to guide the reader.

One form of the subdivided bar chart frequently compares the composition of variables by percentages. This chart differs from the typical bar chart principally in that the bar lengths are meaningless in the comparisons. All the bars are of equal lengths, and only the component parts of the bars vary. As depicted in Figure 14–7, the component parts may be labeled. But they may also be explained in a legend.

FIGURE 14–6.   Illustration of a subdivided bar chart

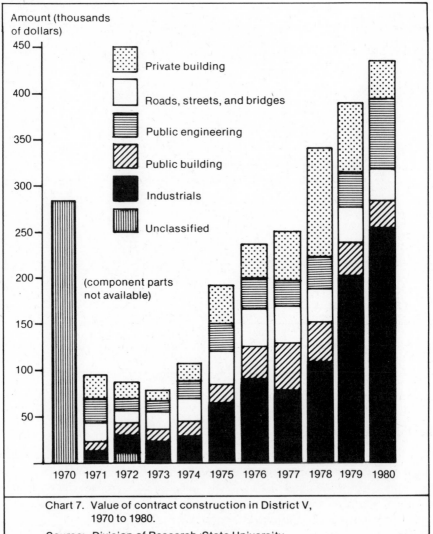

Chart 7. Value of contract construction in District V,
1970 to 1980.

Source: Division of Research, State University.

FIGURE 14–7.   Illustration of a subdivided bar chart

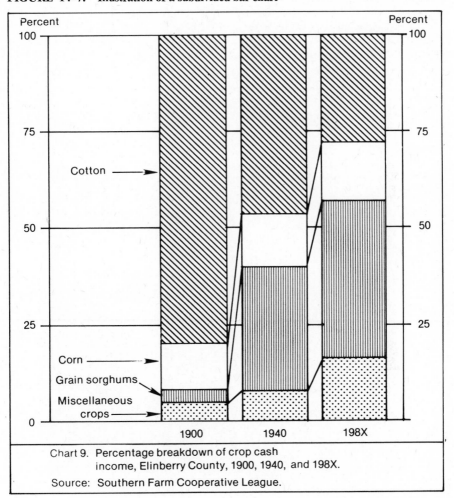

Chart 9. Percentage breakdown of crop cash
income, Elinberry County, 1900, 1940, and 198X.

Source: Southern Farm Cooperative League.

PIE CHART CONSTRUCTION

Also of primary importance in comparing the percentage composition of variables is the pie chart (Figure 14–8). As the name implies, the pie chart illustrates the magnitude as a pie, and it shows the component parts of this whole as slices of the pie. The slices may be individually labeled, or cross-hatching or coloring with an explanatory legend may be used. As it is difficult to judge the value of each slice with the naked eye, it is advisable to include the units of value within each slice. A good rule is to begin slicing the pie at the 12 o'clock position and to move around clockwise. It is usually best to show the slices in descending order of magnitude.

FIGURE 14–8.   Illustration of a pie chart

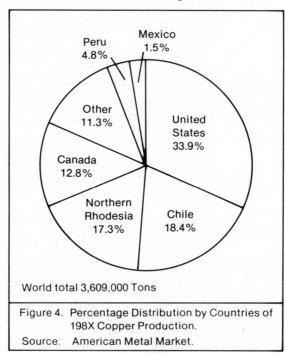

World total 3,609,000 Tons

Figure 4.   Percentage Distribution by Countries of
198X Copper Production.

Source: American Metal Market.

Pie diagrams never should show comparisons of two or more wholes by means of varying the areas of wholes. Such comparisons are almost meaningless. The human eye is totally inadequate in judging the relative areas of most geometric shapes.

ARRANGEMENT OF THE LINE CHART

Line charts are best used to show the movements or changes of a continuous series of data over time, such as changes in prices, weekly sales totals, and periodic employment data. They may be plotted on an arithmetic, semilogarithmic, or logarithmic grid; but since the arithmetic plot is most common to business reports, it is described here.

In a line chart, the item to be illustrated is plotted as a continuous line on a grid. On the grid, time is plotted on the horizontal *(X)* axis; the values of the series are plotted on the vertical *(Y)* axis. The scale values and time periods appear on the axis lines, as shown in Figure 14–9.

FIGURE 14–9.   A line chart with one series

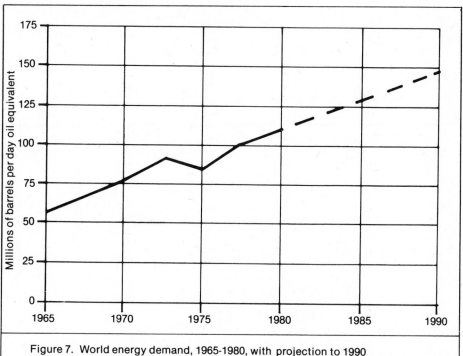

Figure 7. World energy demand, 1965-1980, with projection to 1990

Source: Public Affairs Department, Exxon Corporation.

Line charts also can show comparisons of two or more series (Figure 14–10) on the same grid. In such a comparison, the lines should be clearly distinguished by color or form (dots, dashes, dots and dashes, and the like) and should be clearly labeled or explained by a legend somewhere in the chart. But there is a limit on the number of series that may be compared on a single grid. As a practical rule, four or five series on a single grid should be a maximum.

FIGURE 14–10. Line chart comparing more than one series

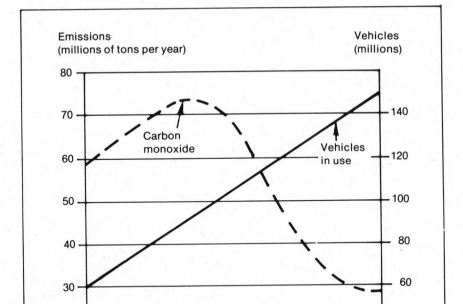

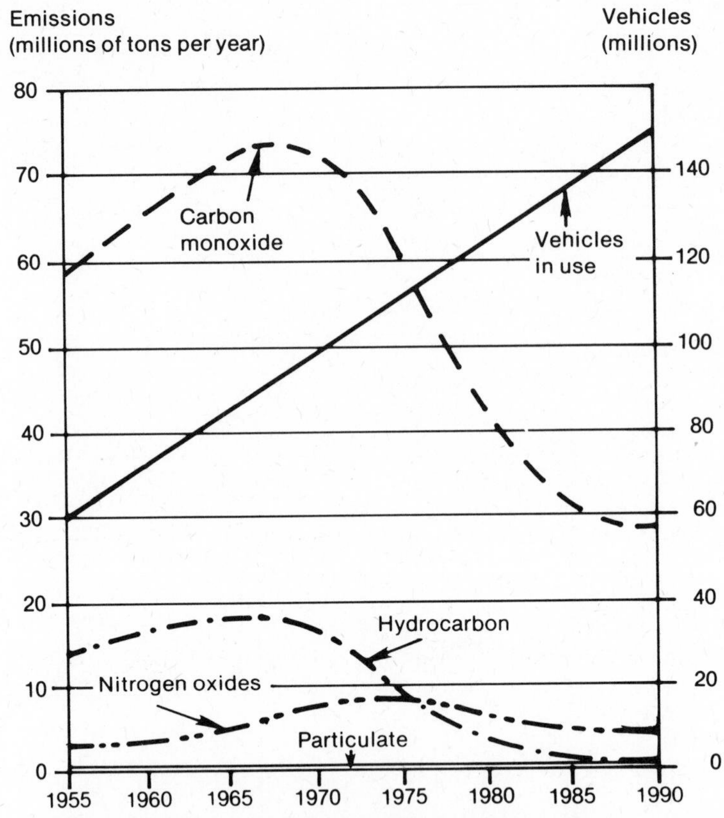

Chart 7. Vehicles and vehicle emissions in the United
States, actual and projected, 1955-1990.
Source: National Petroleum Council.

It is possible, also, to show component parts of a series by use of a line chart, sometimes called a belt chart. Such an illustration, however, is limited to showing the components of one series. This type of chart, as shown in Figure 14–11, has a top line representing the total of the series; then, starting from the base, it cumulates the component parts, beginning with the largest and ending with the smallest. Typically it uses cross-hatching or coloring to distinguish the parts. The differences between the cumulative totals show the values of the last component part brought into the cumulation.

Even though the line graph is one of the simplest charts to construct, three common pitfalls should be warned against. First of these is the common violation of the rule of zero origin. The *Y* scale (vertical axis) must begin at zero, even though the points to be plotted are relatively high in value. If most of the points to

FIGURE 14–11.   Illustration of a component-part line chart

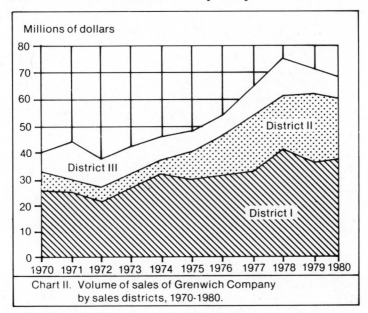

FIGURE 14–12.   Two methods of showing scale breaks

be plotted are relatively high in value, the comparison may be made by breaking the scale somewhere between zero and the level of the lowest plotted value. Of the numerous means of illustrating scale breaks, the two techniques shown in Figure 14–12 are recommended.

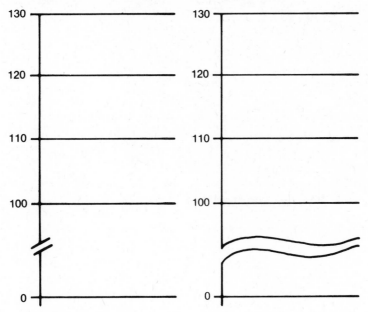

FIGURE 14–13. Illustration of a statistical map showing quantitative differences of areas by cross-hatching

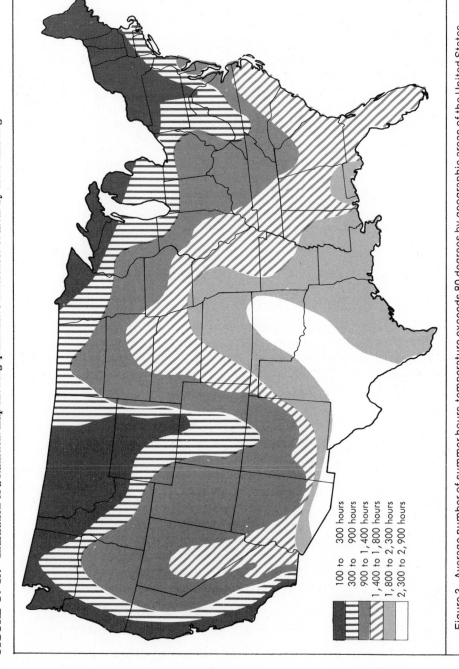

100 to   300 hours
300 to   900 hours
900 to 1,400 hours
1,400 to 1,800 hours
1,800 to 2,300 hours
2,300 to 2,900 hours

Figure 3. Average number of summer hours temperature exceeds 80 degrees by geographic areas of the United States.

Source: Bureau of Business Research, the University of Texas.

Second, equal magnitudes on both X and Y scales should be represented on the grid by equal distances. Any deviation from this rule would distort the illustration, thereby deceiving the reader.

A third common violation of good line chart construction concerns the determination of proportions on the grid. It is easy to see that by expanding one scale and by contracting the other, impressions of extreme deviation can be made. For example, data plotted on a line chart with time intervals $\frac{1}{16}$ inch apart certainly appear to show more violent fluctuations than the same data plotted on a chart with time intervals $\frac{1}{2}$ inch apart. Only the application of common sense can prevent this violation. The grid distances selected simply must be such as will tend to make presentation of the data realistic.

DESIGN OF THE STATISTICAL MAP

Maps may also serve to communicate quantitative information. Primarily they are useful for comparing quantitative information by geographic areas. On such maps, the geographic areas are clearly outlined, and the differences between areas are shown by some graphic technique. Of the numerous techniques used, four are most common.

1.   Possibly the most popular technique is that of showing quantitative differences of areas by color, shading, or cross-hatching (Figure 14–13). Such maps, of course, must have a legend to explain the quantitative meanings of the various colors, cross-hatchings, and so on.

2.   Some form of chart may be placed within each geographic area to depict the quantities representative of that area, as illustrated in Figure 14–14. Bar charts and pie charts are commonly used in such illustrations.

FIGURE 14–14.   Statistical map, showing comparisons by charts within geographic areas

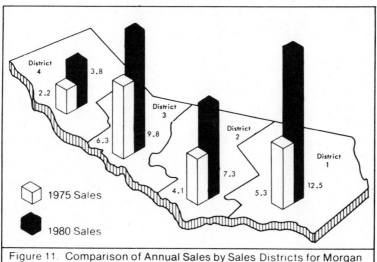

Figure 11. Comparison of Annual Sales by Sales Districts for Morgan Distributors, Inc. 1975 and 1980, in Millions of Dollars.

FIGURE 14–15. Statistical map, showing quantitative differences using numbers placed within geographic areas

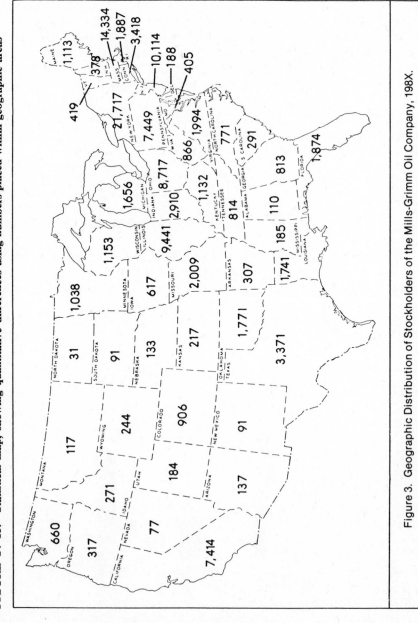

Figure 3. Geographic Distribution of Stockholders of the Mills-Grimm Oil Company, 198X.

3.   Placing the quantities in numerical form within each geographic area, as shown in Figure 14–15, is another widely used technique.

4.   Dots, each representing a definite quantity (Figure 14–16), may be placed within the geographic areas in proportion to the quantities to be illustrated for each area.

FIGURE 14–16.   Illustration of a statistical map, using dots to show quantitative differences by geographic areas

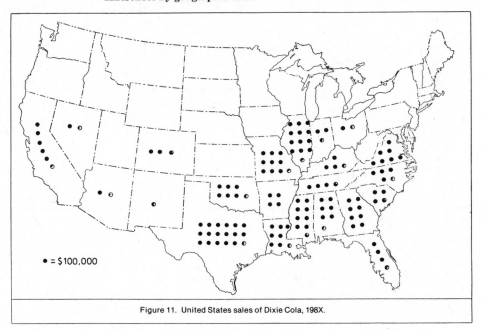

Figure 11. United States sales of Dixie Cola, 198X.

CONSTRUCTION OF THE PICTOGRAM

A pictogram is a bar chart that uses pertinent pictures rather than bars to put over the information. For example, a company that seeks to show graphically its profits on the sales dollar could use a simple bar chart for the purpose. Or instead of bars they could use a line of coins equal in length to the bars. Coins would be appropriate because they depict the information to be illustrated. This resulting graphic form, as illustrated in Figure 14–17, is the pictogram.

Normally construction of pictograms follows the general procedure used in constructing bar charts. But two special rules should be followed. First, all of the picture units used must be of equal size. The comparisons must be made wholly on the basis of the number of illustrations used and never by varying the areas of the individual pictures used. The reason for this rule is obvious. The human eye is

FIGURE 14–17. Illustration of the pictogram

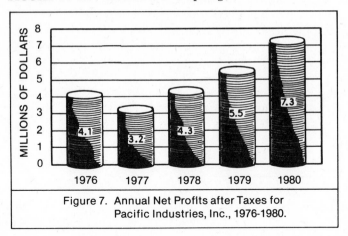

Figure 7. Annual Net Profits after Taxes for
Pacific Industries, Inc., 1976-1980.

grossly inadequate in comparing areas of geometric designs. Second, the pictures or symbols used must appropriately depict the quantity to be illustrated. A comparison of the navies of the world, for example, may use miniature ship drawings. Cotton production may be shown by bales of cotton. Obviously the drawings used must be immediately interpreted by the reader.

MISCELLANEOUS GRAPHIC AIDS

The graphic aids discussed thus far are those most commonly used. Others sometimes help to communicate the report information. Photographs and drawings (see Figure 14–18) may sometimes serve a useful communication purpose. Diagrams, also (see Figure 14–19), may help to make simple a complicated explanation or description, particularly when technological procedures are being communicated. Then there are many almost nameless types of graphic presentation, most of which are combinations of two or more of the commoner techniques. Since anything in the way of graphic design is acceptable as long as it helps to communicate the true story, the possibilities of graphic aid design are almost unlimited.

QUESTIONS

1. Discuss the bases for determining what graphic aids should be used in a report.
2. A report writer placed all graphic aids in the appendix. Discuss the merits and demerits of this placement.
3. Discuss what a report writer should do to direct the reader's attention to the graphic aids. Illustrate the techniques.
4. What criterion should govern the size of a graphic aid. Justify this guideline.
5. How would you number the graphic aids in a report that has three maps, two diagrams, two charts, and five tables.

FIGURE 14–18.   Illustration of a drawing

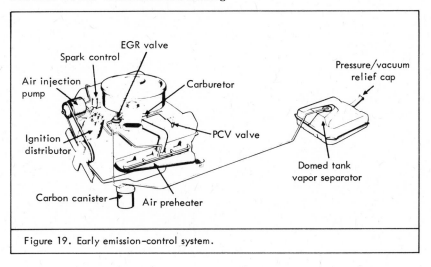

Figure 19. Early emission-control system.

FIGURE 14–19.   Example of the use of a diagram

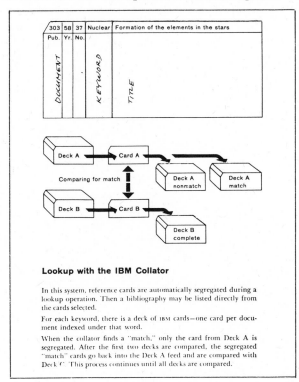

Lookup with the IBM Collator

In this system, reference cards are automatically segregated during a lookup operation. Then a bibliography may be listed directly from the cards selected.

For each keyword, there is a deck of IBM cards—one card per document indexed under that word.

When the collator finds a "match," only the card from Deck A is segregated. After the first two decks are compared, the segregated "match" cards go back into the Deck A feed and are compared with Deck C. This process continues until all decks are compared.

6. How would you number the graphic aids in a report that has seven charts and six tables.

7. Construct a title for a table that shows graduates of your college by major field for the past ten years.

8. Assume that in the table prepared for Question 7 you decide to use a footnote to explain that two curricula were combined in the early years covered by the report. Construct such a footnote and discuss its placement in the table.

9. Where should the titles of graphic aids be placed?

10. Distinguish between the two basic types of tables. Discuss the use of each.

11. For each of the types of graphic aids listed below, (a) describe its construction, (b) comment on what kind of information it shows best, and (c) give an example of some data it could present effectively.
    (1) Simple bar chart.
    (2) Multiple bar chart.
    (3) Bilateral bar chart.
    (4) Subdivided bar chart.
    (5) Pie chart.
    (6) Line chart.
    (7) Component-part line chart.
    (8) Statistical map.
    (9) Pictogram.

12. A report writer wants to present a graphic aid that shows company sales by districts and by product for the past year. (a) What graphic aids might be used? (b) Which ones should be ruled out? (c) What is your recommendation and why?

13. What graphic aid types would be most useful in showing total company sales, including sales by product, over a ten-year period.

14. Which of the graphic aid types would you use to show changes over a three-year period in the percentages of consumer expenditures for clothing, food, recreation, transportation, housing, and miscellaneous expenses?

15. The writer of an annual report for a major corporation wants to use a chart to show how the company's income dollar was spent. What graphic aid form should be used?

16. What techniques may be used to show scale breaks? Why should they be used?

17. Discuss the need to take care in determining proportions on a grid.

18. What techniques may be used to show quantitative differences by area on a statistical map?

19. Discuss the strong and weak points of a pictogram.

20. For each of the following sets of facts (a) determine the graphic aid (or aids) that would be best, (b) defend your choice, and (c) construct the graphic aid.
    (1) Average (mean) amount of life insurance owned by Fidelity Life Insurance Company policyholders. Classification is by annual income.

Income	Average life insurance
Under $5,000	$ 5,245
$ 5,000– 9,999	14,460
10,000–14,999	26,680
15,000–19,999	39,875
20,000–24,999	51,440
25,000 and over	76,390

(2)   Profits and losses for D and H Food Stores, by store, 1976–1980, in dollars.

| | Store | | |
Year	Able City	Baker	Charleston	Total
1976	13,421	3,241	9,766	26,428
1977	12,911	−1,173	11,847	23,585
1978	13,843	−2,241	11,606	23,208
1979	12,673	2,865	13,551	29,089
1980	13,008	7,145	15,482	35,635

(3)   Share of real estate tax payments by ward for Bigg City, 1975 and 1981, in thousands of dollars.

	1975	1981
Ward 1	17.1	21.3
Ward 2	10.2	31.8
Ward 3	19.5	21.1
Ward 4	7.8	18.2
City total	54.6	92.4

(4)   Percentage change in sales by salesperson, 1979–1981, District IV, Abbott, Inc.

Salesperson	Percentage change	Salesperson	Percentage change
Joan Abraham	+ 7.3	Wilson Platt	+ 7.4
Wilson Calmes	+ 2.1	Carry Ruiz	+11.5
Todd Musso	− 7.5	David Schlimmer	− 4.8
Mary Nevers	+41.6	Helen Dirks	− 3.6

(5)   Net income from operations of seven largest U.S. banks, with percentage of profit derived from foreign operations, 1979–1981.

Bank	1979 Operations net (millions)	Foreign (percent)	1981 Operations net (millions)	Foreign (percent)
Bank America	$178.4	25%	$166.5	20%
1st Nat'l City	168.2	42	145.1	38
Chase Manhattan	147.7	20	139.3	15
J. P. Morgan	109.1	30	102.0	25
Mfgrs. Hanover	77.9	28	85.2	24
Chemical	72.5	15	77.4	10

15
Oral reports

Not all business reports are of the written types described in the preceding chapters. Many are oral. In fact, if the more informal presentations of information are viewed as reports, most are oral. However one views them, oral reports are a most important part of an organization's communications. And, because they are so important, a knowledge of how best to present them is obviously vital to the business student.

THE NATURE OF ORAL REPORTS

A logical first step in the study of oral reporting is to define the term. Certainly it makes sense to understand clearly just what is being studied. And because the preceding chapters have covered written reports extensively, a logical second step is to distinguish between written and oral reports. Thus, in following paragraphs these two topics serve as a logical introduction to this review of oral reporting.

A definition of oral reports

In its broadest sense, an oral report is any presentation of factual information using the spoken word. A business oral report logically would limit coverage to "factual business information." By this definition, an oral business report covers much of the information exchanged daily in the conduct of business. It varies widely in degree of formality involved. At one extreme it covers the most routine and informal reporting situations. At the other, it includes the highly formal and proper presentations that take place in business. As the more informal exchanges are little more than routine conversations, the emphasis in the following pages is on the more formal ones. Clearly these are the reports which require the most care and skill in preparation and presentation. They are the ones most deserving of formal study.

Differences between oral and written reports

As written reports have been covered thoroughly in preceding chapters, a logical next step in studying oral reports is to note differences between written and oral reports. Differences do exist; and they are significant. Three in particular stand out.

Visual advantages of the written word.   The first major difference between oral and written reports concerns the differences between the written and spoken word. It is that the written word permits greater use of visual aids to communication than do spoken words. With the written word, reporters use paragraphing to show the reader the structure of the message and to make the thought units stand out. In addition, by writing the message, reporters can use punctuation to show relationships, subordination, and qualification of the information. The result of these techniques is to improve the communication effect of the entire message.

On the other hand, when reporters make oral presentations, they use none of these techniques. Of course, they can use others—techniques peculiar to oral communication. For example, they can use inflection, pauses, volume emphasis, and changes in rate of delivery. Depending on the situation, both oral and written techniques are effective in aiding communication. But the point is, they are different.

Reader control of written presentation.   A second difference in oral and written reporting is that in a written report the readers control the pace of the communication. They can pause, reread, change their rate of reading, or stop as they choose. Since readers set their pace, writers can develop their communications stylistically and with some complexity and still communicate. When receiving oral reports, people cannot control the pace of the presentation. They must grasp the meaning intended as the speakers choose to present the words. Because of this limiting factor, good oral reporting must be relatively simple and gauged for quick, easy understanding.

Emphasis on correctness in writing.   A third difference in oral and written reporting is in the degree of correctness permitted in each. Because their work is likely to receive considerable scrutiny and study, report writers are likely to work for a high degree of correctness. That is, they are apt to follow carefully the recognized rules of grammar, punctuation, sentence structure, and so on. Oral reporters, on the other hand, are permitted to be much more lax in following these recognized rules. For one reason, their work is not recorded for others to scrutinize at their leisure. For another, established oral communication standards permit a less rigid application of established rules.

Other differences exist, of course, but these are the ones which are most significant. Hopefully they serve as foundation from which to explain the techniques of oral reporting. At least, they give some basic understanding of the relative nature of these two forms of reporting. In addition, they point to some of the topics of concern in studying oral reporting. As will become obvious in the pages ahead, much of the coverage of the subject deals with these basic differences.

GENERAL ASPECTS OF ORAL REPORTING

In beginning to work on an oral report, wise reporters carefully consider all the factors which combine to determine the effectiveness with which they perform their tasks. Such factors are many; they are complex; and they may be considered in many different arrangements. The arrangement selected for this review begins with the logical first step in all endeavor—the planning of the effort. Next, it takes up the personal aspects which bear upon the effectiveness of the oral presentation. Then it reviews the aspects of audience analysis which can influence the report.

Planning the oral report

As in written reports, planning is a logical first step in the work on an oral report. For the short, informal report, of course, planning may be minimal. But for the more formal presentations, particularly those involving audiences of more than one, proper planning is likely to be as involved as that for a comparable written report.

Determination of report objective.   Logically the report writers' first step in planning an oral report is to determine their objective. Just as was described for the written report in Chapter 3, in this step the reporters clearly state the report goal in clear, concise language. And then they clearly state the factors involved in achieving this goal. These steps give them a clear guide to the information they must gather and to the framework around which they will build their presentation.

In the process of determining specific goals, the oral reporters must be aware of their general objective. That is, they must decide on the general purpose in making the presentation. Is it to persuade? To inform? To recommend? Their conclusion here will have a major influence on the development of the material for presentation and perhaps even on the presentation itself.

An example used in Chapter 3 ("Bases of Comparison" section) well illustrates this procedure. It is the problem of comparing three cities to determine which is best for locating a new plant. For this specific purpose the reporters might come up with statement and factors like those given in the section in Chapter 3 just cited. In determining their general purpose, they would review the authorization facts of the case. If the executives authorizing the investigation asked for a decision, the reporters' general goal would be to convince their listeners of the logic of their decision. As a second possibility, if they were authorized only to gather information on the problem, the reporters would have the general purpose of informing and, in the process, of assisting others to make the decision. They would resist the temptation to do anything beyond merely informing. For a third possibility, if the authorizing executives asked the reporters only to gather information on the problem, the reporters would have presenting the information as their general purpose. They would purposely stay clear of any effort which might be interpreted as persuasion.

Gathering the report information.   With the report purpose clearly in mind, the reporters next turn to the task of gathering the information they need to achieve this purpose. The task may involve any of the formal research methods. As these methods were described in some detail in Chapters 4 and 5, they need no further comment here. The researchers' task also may involve informal research—that is, personal inspection and study of a problem; perhaps with suggested solutions. Production engineers, for example, might carefully study a certain production problem applying their specialized knowledge. They would work out a proposed solution. Then they would try to explain and justify.

Organizing the content.   After the reporters have all the information they need for the report, their next step is to give it order. Again, the procedure is quite the same as that used in written reports. They may follow either of the organization plans used in written reports (direct, indirect), but the organization requirements for the same report information presented both orally and in writing are not necessarily the same. Time pressure, for example, may justify direct presentation for an oral report. The same report problem presented in writing might be best arranged in indirect order. Obviously a reader can always skip to the conclusion or ending of a report. The listener does not have this choice.

Although oral reports may use either direct or indirect order, the indirect is by far the most widely used order as well as the most logical. Because the audience typically is not likely to be acquainted intimately with the problem, some introductory comments are needed to prepare the audience to receive the message. In addition, the oral reporters may need introductory words to arouse interest, stimulate curiosity, or to impress the audience with the importance of the subject. The main purpose of the introductory remarks, of course, is to state the purpose, define unfamiliar terms, explain limitations, describe scope, and generally cover all of the necessary introductory subjects (see discussion of introduction, Chapter 8).

In the body of the oral report, the reporters develop the goals they have set. Here, also, there is much similarity with the written report. Division of subject matter into comparable parts, logical order, introductory paragraph, concluding paragraph, and such are equally important to both forms.

The major difference in organization of the oral and written report is in the ending. Both forms may end with a conclusion, a recommendation, a summary, or a combination of the three. But the oral report is likely to have a final summary tacked on regardless of whether it has a conclusion or a recommendation. In a sense, this final summary serves the purpose of a synopsis by bringing together all the really important information, analyses, conclusions, and recommendations in the report. It serves also to assist the memory by placing added emphasis on the points that should stand out.

Consideration of personal aspects

After the oral reporters organize the content of the report, they may next turn to the matter of how best to present the information. And in this process one would do well to consider oneself as a speaker. In a well-written report, the reporter is behind the scenes. But in an oral report, the speaker is in a very real sense a part of the message. The audience takes in not only the words communicated but also what they see in the speaker. And what they see in the speaker can have a most significant effect on the meaning that develops in their minds. Thus, wise oral reporters carefully evaluate their personal effect on the message they present, and they do whatever they can to detect and overcome shortcomings and to sharpen any strengths they might have.

In attempting to improve personal effectiveness in communicating, reporters would be wise to compare themselves objectively with what they know to be effective speaker characteristics. Although the following summary of such characteristics may prove to be useful, most reporters know these characteristics from experience. They easily recognize the good qualities and the bad. The problem is to some extent recognizing these characteristics, or the lack of them, in themselves. To a greater extent, it is doing something about improving one's bad characteristics when they are recognized. Hopefully the following review will help to pinpoint these problem areas and will give some practical suggestions of how to overcome them.

Confidence.   A primary characteristic of effective oral reporting is confidence. Included are the speaker's self-confidence as well as confidence of the audience in the speaker. Actually the two are complementary, for a speaker's self-confidence tends to produce an image that gives the audience confidence in the speaker. Similarly an audience's confidence in a speaker can give the speaker a sense of security, thereby making him or her more confident.

Confidence of an audience in a speaker typically is earned over periods of association. But there are things reporters can do to project an image which invites confidence. For example, they can prepare the presentation diligently, and they can practice it thoroughly. Such careful preliminary work produces confidence. Having confidence leads to more effective communication, which in turn builds confidence in the listener's mind. Another thing speakers can do to gain confidence is to check carefully their physical appearance. Unfair and illogical as it may be, certain manners of dress and certain hair styles create strong images in people's minds ranging from one extreme to the other. Reporters who want to communicate effectively analyze the audience they seek to reach; and they work to develop the physical appearance which projects an image in which the audience can have confidence. Yet another suggestion for being confident is simply to talk in strong, clear tones. Such tones do much to project an image of confidence, and, although most people can do little to change their natural voices, they can try to add sufficient volume.

Sincerity.   Listeners are quick to detect insincerity in a speaker. And when they detect it, they are likely to give little credence to what is said to them. On the other hand, sincerity is a valuable aid to conviction, especially if the audience has confidence in the speaker's ability. As to what one can do to project an image of sincerity, the answer is clear and simple. One must *be* sincere. Rarely is pretense of sincerity successful.

Thoroughness.   A speaker who is thorough in her presentation generally is better received than one known for scant or hurried coverage. Thorough coverage gives the impression that time and care have been taken, and such an impression tends to make the message believable. But thoroughness can be overdone. If the information is presented in too much detail, the listener may become lost in a sea of information. The secret is to select the significant information and to leave out the cluttering trivia. To do this, of course, requires that reporters exercise good judgement. They must place themselves in the listeners' shoes and ask themselves just what do the listeners need to know and what do they not need to know.

Friendliness.   A speaker who projects an image of friendliness has a significant advantage in communicating. People simply like people who are friendly, and they are more receptive to what friendly people say. Like sincerity, friendliness is difficult to feign. It must be honest if it is to be effective. But with most people, friendliness is honest, for most people want to be friendly. Some just are not able to project the friendly image they would like to project. With a little self-analysis, a little mirror watching as one speaks, most people can find ways of improving the friendliness of their image.

These are but some of the characteristics that aid the oral reporter. There are others such as interest, enthusiasm, originality, and flexibility. But the ones mentioned are the most significant and the ones most speakers need to work on. Through self-analysis and dedicated effort to improve the personal aspects of oral reporting, speakers can make marked improvement in their communication ability.

Audience analysis

Equally as important as considering one's own communication characteristics is the oral reporters' need to be alert to the unique aspects of the audience. The end goal of the report, of course, is a specific audience response. Thus, what goes on inside the listener as the communication takes place is a key part of oral reporting. Unfortunately all too often reporters are so preoccupied with their problem (their nervousness, importance of their task, selection of graphic aids, and such) that they give little thought to the uniqueness of the audience.

Preliminary audience analysis.   For best communication results, oral reporters should learn the pertinent characteristics of their audience in advance. What is pertinent will vary by situation. It is the speakers' task to learn the pertinent characteristics in each case and to adapt the presentation to them.

Determining the pertinent characteristics is a thought problem requiring the use of good logic. Speakers merely analyze the audience, searching for any characteristics which would have any effect on the best manner of presenting the report. For example, size of the audience may be a significant characteristic, for the manner of presentation, use of graphic aids, detail of explanation, and formality of the communication are influenced by the number of listeners involved. Similarly the personal characteristics of the audience can be vital to communication effectiveness—characteristics such as age, experience, extent of knowledge, and interest. With such information in mind, reporters can aim their words for the one audience. The importance to speakers of being informed about their listeners has been stressed for centuries. It was Aristotle, in fact, who advised speakers to consider carefully the characteristics of men in youth, in the prime of life, and in old age. And he admonished speakers to remember the differences in interest and experience in planning their messages.[1] His advice remains good.

Audience analysis during presentation.   The reporters can benefit further by continuing audience analysis into the presentation. Called feedback, this phase of audience analysis gives the reporters information which allows them to adjust the report as they present it to the audience.

The reporters' eyes and ears will give feedback information as the reporters talk to their audience. They can gain from facial expressions some indication of how the listeners receive the information. They can detect from sounds coming from the audience whether the speakers have their attention, whether the audience understands, whether the audience is listening, and the like. If questions are in order, they can learn directly how their message is received and how they must alter it. In general, by being intensely alert to the audience as they communicate with them, oral reporters can make adjustments in their presentation to improve the communication of their message.

PRESENTATION OF THE ORAL REPORT

Report planning and consideration of personal and audience aspects give oral reporters some general guides to the presentation of their message. But the most significant part of the oral reporting procedure is the presentation itself. It is, so to speak, the final product—the end result of all the work that preceded it. Good technique in this effort is vital to success.

What is good technique generally is known by most intelligent people. Most can recognize good speaking when they hear it. And most heads will nod in agreement when they hear the following techniques of good oral presentation reviewed. Even so, most people do not follow these techniques as well as they could. Thus, it is worthwhile for speakers to put them in mind any time they face an audience.

There are many such techniques, and they may be classified in various ways. In the following review of them, they are arranged in four groups: (1) use of language, style, and conversational mode; (2) bodily action; (3) voice quality; and (4) characteristics of good and bad delivery.

Language style and the conversational mode

It is an elementary point to note that language is the principal medium used in oral communication. And whether a report is confused or clear, weak or forceful depends heavily on the words selected and on their arrangement. Without question, the language used in oral reporting is most vital to the success of the communication. It deserves most careful consideration.

---

[1] Lane Cooper, *The Rhetoric of Aristotle,* Appleton-Century Crofts Co., New York, 1932, pp. xx–xxi.

Just as in written communication, oral report language should be adapted to the audience. That is, it should be in words that are easily understood by the listeners—preferably words that are in their speaking vocabularies. And these words should be arranged clearly in sentences no more involved than the readers' ability to comprehend. In fact, these techniques of adaptation apply even more to oral reporting, for the spoken message cannot be reviewed as can a written message. Communication must occur as the words are spoken or it does not occur.

In addition to selecting words and structures readers easily comprehend, speakers should also work for a variety in sentence forms. Variety adds interest to the presentation; and interest is an aid to communication. In acquiring variety, speakers should develop an interesting mixture of sentence types. Or, more specifically, they will develop an interesting rhythm of alternating loose and periodic sentences. What is an interesting pattern is difficult to describe. It is a matter of what is pleasing to the mind and to the ear. Good speakers and good writers recognize it. They have a feel for it. But they are not able to explain precisely what it is. Novice writers or speakers have no choice but to try to acquire an understanding of it.

In giving the spoken sentence the variety that produces interest, reporters should mix the two basic forms of sentence—the *loose* and the *periodic*. The periodic sentence is one in which meaning is not clear until the very end. In contrast, the loose sentence gives the essentials at the beginning and has the supporting and modifying parts at the end. Illustrating these two forms are these two sentences:

Periodic	*Loose*
During the business convention, right in the middle of Robert's presentation about the new advertising proposal, Harry fainted.	Harry fainted during the business conference, right in the middle of Robert's presentation about the new advertising proposal.
In a case like this, without giving further consideration, our company should sue.	Our company should sue, in a case like this, without giving further consideration.

Each of these forms of sentence arrangement has advantages. The periodic sentence structure is best for holding attention, for marshaling thought, and for giving added emphasis. The loose arrangement is best for bringing out essential ideas sooner. But it is not a question of using one arrangement or the other. The well-presented oral report will have a pleasing mixture of both, as well as of other contrasting techniques. More specifically, it will have loose sentences mixed with periodic sentences, comparisons mixed with contrasts, negations mixed with positives, and simple thoughts interspersed with complex ideas.

In selecting the proper words and arrangements to communicate the message, reporters should use a technique previously discussed—feedback. As they deliver their message, they should continuously be alert to any sign of miscommunication that comes from the audience. When they detect signs of misunderstanding, they must adjust to it on the spot. Perhaps they will need to repeat a point;

218

they may say it in a different way; they may illustrate by example; or they may need to elaborate. Whatever they sense that must be done, they do.

Because oral reporting is similar to conversation, usually it is best done in a conversational manner. The ways of conversation are familiar to all people, and they communicate best. But this is not to say that informality is always desired. In conversation, informality is not always the rule. Some conversation is highly formal. And so it is with oral reporting. Reporters should follow the degree of formality appropriate for the situation. It would be inappropriate to be too formal; and it would be inappropriate to be too informal. Thus, they should work to develop a conversational style appropriate for each situation.

Bodily actions

In face-to-face oral communication some degree of visual communication takes place. In everyday conversation, bodily actions are a significant part of the communication. So significant are they, in fact, that some people would be sorely limited if the use of their hands, shoulders, facial muscles, and so on, were denied them. As oral reporting is a form of face-to-face oral communication, bodily actions are an important communication technique. Reporters should know them. They should be aware of how to use them; and they should use them to the best advantage.

General impressions. In reviewing bodily actions, the general impression one makes while speaking deserves mention. Although not bodily action in a literal sense, the general impression speakers make on a listener has much the same communication effect. Clearly, it is a part of the visual message the listener receives. The general impression created by oral reporters is a synthesis of all the elements that are communicated to the audience. Included are momentary things over which speakers have no control, such as the lighting, the stage fixtures, the sound equipment, and so on. But there are some relatively simple things over which speakers have some control and which may contribute importantly to the general impression created. One of these is the problem of dress. The watchword here is "appropriate." Certainly speakers should not appear conspicuous, and they should live up to the standards of dress the audience expects of them.

Another contributor to the general impression speakers form is the speaking position they take. They have two choices: They may sit, or they may stand. Small, informal audiences may prefer that reporters sit while speaking; in fact, speakers might feel awkward standing on a platform with only a few people in the audience. On the other hand, some small groups may be affronted if the speakers sit. Such a group may get the general impression that the speakers think that the listeners are not important enough for a stand-up presentation. Generally there is less risk in standing, even before a small group.[2] The speakers have no choice but

---

[2] Raymond S. Ross, *Speech Communications: Fundamentals and Practice,* 3 ed. Prentice-Hall, Inc., Englewood Cliffs, N.J., 1974, p. 120.

to appraise the situation carefully and to take the position that appears to be most appropriate.

Posture.   Posture is another part of the image speakers communicate to their audience. Not only does it influence meaning in the listeners' minds but also it has an effect on the speakers' reactions to themselves as they speak, and such reactions can have a negative effect on communication effectiveness. Most people recognize good posture. But all too many do not recognize bad posture in themselves. Self-analysis is the answer along with a conscious effort to improve.

In an effort to improve their posture, speakers should keep in mind what must go on within their body to form a good posture. Their body weight must be distributed in a comfortable and poised way consistent with the impression they want to make. They should keep their body erect without appearing stiff, and comfortable without appearing limp. Their bearing should be self-poised, alert, and communicative. And they should do all this naturally. The great danger with posture, as with all studied bodily action, is that of appearing artificial, conspicuous, or out of place.

Walking.   The way one walks before an audience can create meanings in the listeners' minds both before and during the presentation. A strong, sure walk to the speaker's stand can project an image of confidence; hesitant, awkward steps can convey the opposite impression. During the presentation, speakers may employ walking as a form of physical punctuation. They may reinforce transitions and pauses with a few steps to the side, and they may emphasize a point with a step forward. Additionally walking has emphatic qualities for the audience, as the movement may break the monotony of the presentation. Too much walking, however, calls attention to the walking and detracts from the message. In determining the amount and kind of walking desired, a good rule to follow is this: the more formal the situation, the less pronounced the walking should be; the larger the audience, the more definite the steps may be.[3]

Facial expression.   Probably the most apparent and communicative bodily movements are facial expressions. The problem is, however, that speakers may unconsciously use facial expressions which convey meanings not intended. For example, frightened speakers may tighten their jaws unconsciously and begin to grin. The effect may be an out-of-taste image that detracts from the entire communication effort. A smile, a grimace, a puzzled frown all convey clear messages. Without question, they are effective communication devices and should be used.

Equally important in considering facial expressions is the matter of eye contact. The eyes have long been considered "mirrors of the soul" and provide most observers with information about the speaker's sincerity, goodwill, and flexibility. Some listeners tend to shun speakers who refuse to look at them, perhaps in the belief that the communicators should not be trusted or that they do not really care for the listeners. On the other hand, discriminate eye contact tends to show that speakers have a genuine interest in their audience.

---

[3] Ibid., p. 121.

Gestures.   As does posture, gestures add to the message communicated. Just what they add, however, is hard to say, for they have no definite or clear-cut meanings. A clinched fist, for example, clearly adds emphasis to a strong point. But it also can be used dramatically to convey defiance, to make a threat, or to signify respect for a cause. And so it is with other gestures. They register vague meanings.

Even though the meanings of gestures are vague, they are strong and they appear to be natural adjuncts to communication. It appears quite natural, for example, for speakers to emphasize a plea by gesturing with palms up. And it is equally natural to support verbal rejection or disagreement with a palms-down movement. Speakers may reinforce a division of points by using first one hand and then the other. Or they may use only one hand and with vertical palm suggest several divisions as they slice the air, moving one hand on a level plane from left to right. The general stereotype in using such gestures usually is recognizable, although no two people will use all gestures exactly alike.

In summary, it should be clear that body movements can be used effectively to aid in communicating. Just which movements one should use in a given situation, however, is difficult to say, for they are clearly related to personality, physical makeup, and to the size and nature of the audience. A very formal speaker appearing before a formal group would wisely use poised but relatively restricted bodily action. Grandiose movements, grand sweeps of the arms, and such would be inappropriate. An informal speaker appearing before an informal audience could use effectively a much wider range of action. In general, the larger the audience, the more gross and unrestricted the bodily action may become. Just what individual speakers should do on a given occasion is a matter for them to work out through their own logical interpretation of the situation.

Use of voice

Good vocal quality is an obvious requirement of good oral reporting. Like bodily movements, the voice should not hinder the listener's concentration on the message presented. More specifically, it should not call attention away from the message to itself. Voices that cause such difficulties fall generally into four areas of fault: (1) lack of pitch, (2) lack of variety in speaking speed, (3) lack of emphasis by variation in volume, and (4) unpleasantness in voice quality.

Lack of pitch variation.   Speakers who talk in a monotone are not likely to hold the interest of their listeners for long. Most voices are capable of wide variations in pitch; so the problem rarely is a physiological one. Most often it is primarily a matter of habit—of voice patterns developed over long years of talking without being aware of effect.

Lack of variation in speaking speed.   Determining how fast to talk is a major problem in oral reporting. As a general rule, that part of the message that can be understood easily is presented at a fairly rapid rate. If such information is presented at a deliberately slow pace, the effect is likely to be irritating and distracting. Some information, however, by its very nature is complex and requires a slower pace. Thus, the speaker would do well to vary the pace with the difficulty of the material.

A common problem related to the pace of speaking is the incorrect use of pauses. Of course, pauses used at the appropriate time and place are effective. When properly used, they add emphasis to the upcoming subject matter, and they are an effective means of gaining attention. But frequent pauses at points where they add little or nothing to the presentation are irritating, and they break the listener's flow of comprehension. The error compounds when the speaker fills in the pauses with "uh's" or other meaningless sounds.

Lack of vocal emphasis. A secret of good oral reporting is to give the words the emphasis due them by variations in the manner of speaking. Speakers achieve this desired effect by employing three techniques: (1) varying the pitch of the voice, (2) varying the pace of the presentation, and (3) varying the volume of the voice. As the first two have been discussed, only the use of voice volume requires comment.

Obviously speakers must talk loudly enough for all in the audience to hear. Thus, the loudness (voice force) for a large group is different from that used for a small group. Regardless of group size, however, variety in force is essential for interest and emphasis. It produces contrast, which is one means of giving emphasis to the subject matter. Some reporters incorrectly believe that the only way to gain emphasis is to get louder and louder. But just as much emphasis may be had by going from loud to soft. It is the contrast with what has gone on before that provides the emphasis. Again, variety is the watchword in making the voice more effective.

Unpleasant voice quality. It is a hard fact of communication that some voices are more pleasing than others. Fortunately most voices are reasonably pleasant. But there are some that are raspy, nasal, or in some other way unpleasant. Although therapy often is effective in improving such voices, some speakers are destined to live with what they have. Even so, most people do not do as well as they can with what they have. By concentrating on variations in pitch, speed of delivery, and volume, even the most unpleasant voices can be effective.

Improvement through self-analysis. All of the foregoing voice problems can be overcome through hard work and concentration. The technique is through simple self-analysis. In this day of tape recorders, it is easy to hear oneself talk. And since most people know good speaking when they hear it, it should be easy for one to improve one's presentation. Certainly some people have vocal limitations; but few speakers learn to do the best that is possible with the abilities they have.

USE OF VISUAL AIDS

As was noted earlier, the spoken word is severely limited in communication effectiveness. Sound is here a brief moment and it is gone. If the message is missed, there may be no chance to hear it again. Because of this severe limitation, oral reporting often needs strong visual support—charts, tables, blackboards, film, and so on. Using them may be as vital to success of the presentation as the words themselves.

Proper use of design

Effective visual aids are those drawn from the message. They fit the one report and the one audience. To be shunned are any picked up from similar reports. Rarely do they fit.

In selecting visual aids, oral reporters should follow generally the procedure report writers should follow. That is, they should search through their presentation for topics that appear vague or confusing. Whenever a picture or other form of visual aid will help to clear up this vagueness, reporters should use one. Visual aids are truly a part of the reporters' message, and they should be looked upon as such.

After they have decided that a topic deserves visual support, reporters determine the form the support should take. That is, should it be a chart, a slide, a picture, or what? They should base their decision primarily on the question of which form best communicates the message. As simple and obvious as this point may appear, all too often reporters violate it. All too often they select visual aids more for their appearance and dramatic effect than for their communication effect.

Forms of visual aids to consider

Because no one form of visual aid is best for all occasions, reporters should have a flexible attitude toward these aids. They should know the good and bad qualities of each; and they should know how each may be used most effectively.

In considering selection of a visual aid, one should keep in mind the types available. First, there are the various forms of photographed or drawn illustrations—charts, graphs, tables, diagrams, pictures, and so on. Each of these forms has its own special strengths and weaknesses, as was described in Chapter 14. Each may be displayed in various ways—by slide, overhead, or opaque projector; by flip chart; by easel display; on a blackboard; on a felt board; or in other ways. And each of these display forms has its own strengths and weaknesses. In addition, visual aids may take the form of motion pictures, models, samples, demonstrations, and the like. There is no shortage of possibilities.

Because so many forms of visuals and means of displaying them exist, a review of the subject would be somewhat voluminous and perhaps trivial. It is more logical to suggest that reporters plan their visual displays by first determining the possibilities available to them. In doing so, they would need to take into account factors of time, cost, availability, practicality, and such. Then they should consider the strengths and weaknesses of each possibility available to them. Especially should they consider the strengths and weaknesses relative to their own unique abilities to use the techniques. Such a logical thought process should lead them to select the most appropriate visuals for the one case.

Techniques in using visuals

As properly designed visuals carry key parts of the report message, they are properly points of emphasis in the reporters' oral presentation. Reporters use them to illustrate key points. Reporters point out key parts of them. Generally oral reporters blend them in with their words to communicate their findings. How they do all of this is to some extent an individual matter, for techniques vary. They vary so much, in fact, that it would be illogical to study the techniques used. It is more practical to review some general procedures—some do's and don't's—which can be applied to most individual techniques. Such a list is the following:

1. Make certain the visual aids are clearly visible to all in the audience. Too many or too light lines on a chart, for example, can be difficult to comprehend. Too small an illustration can be meaningless to people far from the speaker.
2. Explain the visual if there is any likelihood of misunderstanding it.
3. Organize the visuals as a part of the presentation. Fit them into the plan of the presentation.
4. Emphasize the visual aids. Point to them with bodily action and with words.
5. Talk to the audience—not to the visual aids. Look at the visuals only when the audience should look at them.
6. Avoid blocking the listener's view of the visual aids. Make certain that lecterns, pillars, chairs, and such do not block anyone's view. And take care not to stand in anyone's line of vision.

A SUMMARY CHECKLIST

The foregoing review of oral reporting is scant at best. The subject is a broad one. In fact, entire books are devoted to it. But hopefully this review has covered the high points—especially those that are easily transferred into practice. Certainly more concise and perhaps even more practical is a summary checklist of good and bad reporting practices. Such a checklist is the following:

1. Organize the report so that it leads the hearer's thoughts logically to the conclusion.
2. Move surely and quickly to the conclusion. Do not leave a conclusion dangling, repeat unnecessarily, or appear unable to close.
3. Use language specifically adapted to the audience.
4. Articulate clearly, pleasantly, and with proper emphasis. Avoid mumbling and the overuse of "ah," "er," "uh," and so on.
5. Speak correctly, using accepted grammar and pronunciation.
6. Maintain an attitude of alertness, displaying appropriate enthusiasm and confidence.
7. Employ bodily action to best advantage. Use it to emphasize points and to assist in communicating concepts and ideas.

8. Avoid stiffness or rigidity of bodily action.
9. Look the audience in the eye and talk directly to them.
10. Avoid excessive movements, fidgeting, and signs of nervousness.
11. Punctuate the presentation with reference to visual aids. Make them a part of the report story.
12. Keep the temper even, even when faced with unfair opposition. To lose your temper is to lose control of the presentation.

QUESTIONS

1. Explain the principal differences between written and oral reports.
2. Compare the typical organization plans of oral and written reports. Note the major difference between the two plans.
3. Explain how one's personal aspects influence the meanings of one's spoken words.
4. A reporter presented an oral report to an audience of 27 middle and upper level administrators. Then he presented the same information to an audience consisting of the three top executives in the company. Note some of the differences that probably took place in these two presentations.
5. What is meant by the language style of an oral report? What advice would you give to one trying to achieve good style?
6. Explain the role of feedback in oral reporting.
7. Discuss how the general impression one receives of a reporter has an effect on the message received.
8. By description (or perhaps by example) identify good and bad postures and walking practices for speaking.
9. Explain how facial expressions can miscommunicate.
10. Give some illustrations of gestures that can be used for multiple meanings. Demonstrate them.
11. "We are born with voices—some good, some bad, and some in between. We have no choice but to accept what we have been given." Comment.
12. What should be the determining factor in the use of a visual aid?
13. Discuss (or demonstrate) some good and bad techniques of using visual aids.
14. In presenting an oral report to a group made up of her peers as well as a few of her superiors, a speaker is harassed by the questions of one of her peers. Apparently this person is just trying to embarrass the reporter. What advice would you give this reporter? Would your advice be different if the critic were one of her superiors? What if it were one under her in position?

See end of Appendix C for oral report problems.

16

Correctness of punctuation and grammar in reporting

Experienced report writers see correctness in grammar and punctuation as standards that when followed will help to communicate their messages. They realize that these so-called rules of grammar and punctuation are generally accepted by learned people. More than likely, the readers of their reports will be literate people. If such people are to accept a report as coming from a well-informed source, the writing must conform to their standards. Thus, it stands to reason that readers of reports are apt to judge the overall standards of writers and their work by the standards of the writers' writings.

THE NEED FOR CORRECTNESS

Experienced writers know, also, that their standards of writing are for the most part logical. All the conventional writing rules, they know, serve to guard against misunderstanding and aid in presenting facts clearly and quickly. They know that these standards have a very practical place in their work.

The practical importance of writing standards is dramatically illustrated by any one of the numerous court cases that have centered around the changed meaning of contract words brought about by grammar or punctuation error. Possibly an even better illustration is the classic example of two sentences of directly opposing meanings. The words in the sentences are the same; only the punctuation differs. But what a difference the punctuation makes!

"The teacher," said the student, "is stupid."
The teacher said, "The student is stupid."

So that one can get a measure of one's need for improving writing correctness, a brief diagnostic test appears at the end of this chapter. Its goal is to point out which of the more significant standards one knows and does not know. Then by selectively studying the standards violated, one can save study time. But because the test covers only the more frequently used standards, one would be wise to scan all of the standards in this chapter.

STANDARDS FOR CLARITY THROUGH PUNCTUATION

The pages that follow present a review of the punctuation standards most likely to be useful to report writers. No attempt is made to include all possible points; so this presentation should in no way be considered a complete English handbook. For the finer points not included here (and every report writer at some time will run into writing situations that require such information), report writers should consult any of a number of current handbooks. The standards that follow are coded with letters and numbers that are useful as grading marks to explain the errors when they are made.

Apos (Apostrophe)

Apos 1   Use the apostrophe to show the possessive case of nouns and indefinite pronouns. If the word does not end in *s,* add an apostrophe and an *s.* If the word ends in *s,* add only an apostrophe.

Nominative form	*Possessive form*
company	company's
employee	employee's
companies	companies'
employees	employees'

Apos 2   Proper names and singular nouns which end in *s* sounds are exceptions. To such words, you may either add the apostrophe and the *s* or just the apostrophe. To the nominative plural, add only an *s.*

Nominative form	Possessive form
Texas (singular)	*Texas', Texas's*
Jones (singular)	*Jones', Jones's*
Joneses (plural)	*Joneses'*
countess (singular)	*countess', countess's*

Use an apostrophe to mark the place in a contraction where letters are omitted.

$$\text{has not} = \text{hasn't}$$
$$\text{cannot} = \text{can't}$$
$$\text{it is} = \text{it's}$$

Bkts (Brackets)

Set off in brackets words which the author wishes to insert in a quotation.

"Possibly the use of this type of supervisor [the trained correspondence expert] is still on the increase."

"At least direct supervision has gained in importance in the past decade [the report was written in 1970], during which time 43 percent of the reporting business firms that started programs have used this technique."

Cln (Colon)

Cln 1   Use the colon to introduce a statement of explanation, an enumeration, or a formal quotation.

> *Statement of explanation:*   At this time the company was pioneering a new marketing idea: it was attempting to sell its products direct to consumers by means of vending machines.
>
> *Enumeration:*   There are four classes of machinists working in this department: apprentice machinist, journeyman machinist, machinist, and first-class machinist.
>
> *Formal quotation:*   President Hartung had this to say about the proposal: "Any such movement which fails to have the support of the rank-and-file worker in this plant fails to get my support."

Cln 2   Do not use the colon when the thought of the sentence should continue without interruption. If it is a list that is being introduced by a colon, the list should be in apposition to a preceding word.

> *Below standard:*   Cities in which new sales offices are in operation are: Fort Smith, Texarkana, Lake Charles, Jackson, and Biloxi.
>
> *Acceptable:*   Cities in which new sales offices are in operation are Fort Smith, Texarkana, Lake Charles, Jackson, and Biloxi.
>
> *Acceptable:*   Cities in which new sales offices are in operation are as follows: Fort Smith, Texarkana, Lake Charles, Jackson, and Biloxi.

Cma (Comma)

Cma 1   Use a comma to separate principal clauses connected by a coordinating conjunction. The coordinating conjunctions are *and, but, or, nor,* and *for.* (A principal clause has subject and verb, and it stands by itself.)

> Only two of the components of the index declined, and these two account for only 12 percent of the total weight of the index.
>
> New automobiles are moving at record volumes, but used car sales are lagging well behind the record pace set two years ago.

Exceptions may be made to this rule, however, in the case of compound sentences consisting of short and closely connected clauses.

> We sold and the price dropped.
> Sometimes we profit and sometimes we lose.

Cma 2.1   Separate the elements listed in series by commas. In order to avoid misinterpretation in rare instances when some of the elements listed have compound constructions, it is best to place the comma between the last two items (before the final conjunction).

Good copy must cover facts with accuracy, sincerity, honesty, and conviction.

Direct advertising can be used to introduce salespeople, fill in between salespeople's calls, cover territory where salespeople cannot be maintained, and keep pertinent reference material in the hands of prospects.

A survey conducted at the 1980 automobile show indicated that black and cream, blue and gray, dark maroon, and black cars were favored by the public. (Note how this example illustrates the need for a comma before the final conjunction.)

Cma 2.2   Separate coordinate adjectives in series by commas when they modify the same noun and if there is no *and* connecting them. A good test to determine whether adjectives are coordinate is to insert an *and* between the words. If the *and* does not change the meaning of the expression, the words are coordinate.

Miss Pratt has been a reliable, faithful, efficient employee for 20 years.

We guarantee that this is a good, clean car.

Light green office furniture is Mr. Orr's recommendation for the stenographic pool. [If *and* were placed between *light* and *green,* the word meaning would be changed.]

A big Dawson wrench proved to be best for the task. [The *and* won't fit between *big* and *Dawson.*]

Cma 3   Set off nonrestrictive modifiers from the sentence by commas. By a nonrestrictive modifier is meant a modifier which could be omitted from the sentence without changing the meaning of the sentence. Restrictive modifiers (those which restrict the words they modify to one particular object) are not set off by commas. A restrictive modifier cannot be left out of the sentence without changing the sentence meaning.

Restrictive: The salesperson who sells the most will get a bonus. [*Who sells the most* restricts the meaning to one particular salesperson.]

Nonrestrictive: James Smithers, who was the company's top salesperson for the year, was awarded a bonus. [If the clause *who was the company's top salesperson for the year* is omitted, the statement is not changed.]

Restrictive: J. Ward & Company is the firm which employs most of the physically handicapped in this area.

Nonrestrictive: J. Ward & Company, the firm which employs most of the physically handicapped in this area, has gained the admiration of the community.

Notice how some modifiers could be either restrictive or nonrestrictive, depending on the meaning intended by the writer.

Restrictive: All of the suits which were damaged in the fire were sold at a discount. [Implies that a part of the stock was not damaged.]

Nonrestrictive: All of the suits, which were damaged by the fire, were sold at a discount. [Implies that all the stock was damaged.]

Cma 4.1   Use commas to set off parenthetic expressions. A parenthetic expression consists of words which interrupt the normal flow of the sentence. In a sense, they appear to be "stuck in." In many instances they are simply words out of normal order. For example, the sentence "A full-page, black-and-white advertisement was run in the *Daily Bulletin*" contains a parenthetic expression when the word order is altered: "An advertisement, full-page and in black and white, was run in the *Daily Bulletin*."

> This practice, it is believed, will lead to ruin.
> The Johnston Oil Company, so the rumor goes, has cut back sharply its exploration activity.

Although you may use the dash and the parentheses for similar reasons, the three marks differ as to the degree to which they separate the enclosed words from the rest of the sentence. The comma is the weakest of the three, and it is best used when the material set off is closely related to the surrounding words. Dashes are stronger marks than commas and are used when the words set off tend to be long or contain internal punctuation marks. Parentheses, the strongest of the three, are primarily used to enclose material which helps to explain or supplement the main words of the sentence.

Cma 4.2   Use commas to set off an appositive (a noun or a noun and its modifiers inserted to explain another noun) from the rest of the sentence. In a sense, appositives are forms of parenthetic expressions, for they interrupt the normal flow of the sentence.

> The Baron Corporation, our machine parts supplier, is negotiating a new contract.
> St. Louis, home office of our Midwest district, will be the permanent site of our annual sales meeting.
> President Carthwright, a self-educated woman, is the leading advocate of our night school for employees.

But appositives which identify very closely are not set off by commas.

> The word *liabilities* is not understood by most laboring people.
> Our next shipment will come on the steamship *Alberta*.

Cma 4.3   Set off parenthetic words such as *therefore, however, in fact, of course, for example,* and *consequently* with commas.

> It is apparent, therefore, that the buyers' resistance has been brought about by an overvigorous sales campaign.
> After the first experiment, for example, the traffic flow increased 10 percent.
> The company will, however, be forced to abandon the old pricing system.

Included in this group of introductory words may be interjections (*oh, alas*) and the responsive expressions (*yes, no, surely, indeed, well,* etc.). But if the words are strongly exclamatory or are not closely connected with the rest of the sentence, they may be punctuated as a sentence. (*No. Yes. Indeed.*)

> Yes, the decision to increase production has been made.
>
> Oh, contribute whatever you think is adequate.

Cma 4.4   When more than one unit appears in a date or an address, set off the units by commas.

> *One unit:*   December 30 is the date of our annual inventory.
>
> *One unit:*   The company has one outlet in Ohio.
>
> *More than one unit:*   December 30, 1906, is the date the Johnston Company first opened its doors.
>
> *More than one unit:*   Richmond, Virginia, is the headquarters of the new sales district.

Cma 5.1   Use commas to separate subordinate clauses preceding main clauses.

> Although it is durable, this package does not have eye appeal.
>
> Since there was little store traffic on Aisle 13, the area was converted into office space.

Cma 5.2   Place commas after introductory verbal phrases. A verbal phrase is one which contains some verb derivative, a gerund, a participle, or an infinitive.

> *Participle phrase:*   Realizing his mistake, the supervisor instructed the workers to keep a record of all salvaged equipment.
>
> *Gerund phrase:*   After gaining the advantage, we failed to press on to victory.
>
> *Infinitive phrase:*   To increase our turnover of automobile accessories, we must first improve our display area.

Cma 6.1   Use the comma only for good reason. It is not a mark to be inserted indiscriminately at the whims of the writer. As a rule, use of commas should always be justified by one of the standard practices previously noted.

Cma 6.1.1   Do not be tripped into putting a comma between subject and verb.

> The thought that he could not afford to fail spurred him on. [No comma after *fail*.]

Cma 6.2   Take exception to the preceding standards whenever insertion of a comma will help clarity of expression.

> *Not clear:*   From the beginning inventory methods of Hill Company have been haphazard.
>
> *Clear:*   From the beginning, inventory methods of Hill Company have been haphazard.
>
> *Not clear:*   When eating your hands should be clean.
>
> *Clear:*   When eating, your hands should be clean.

Dsh (Dash)

Use the dash to set off an element for emphasis or to show interrupted thought. Particularly use it with long parenthetic expressions or those containing internal punctuation. With the typewriter, make the dash by striking the hyphen twice, without spacing before or after.

Budgets for some past years—1974, for example—were prepared without consulting the department heads.

The test proved that the new process is simple, effective, accurate—and more expensive.

Only one person—the supervisor in charge—has authority to issue such an order.

If you want a voice in the government—vote.

Ex (Exclamation mark)

Use the exclamation point at the end of a sentence or an exclamatory fragment to show strong emotion. But use this mark sparingly; never use it with trivial ideas.

We've done it again!

No! It can't be!

Hpn (Hyphen)

Hpn 1   Indicate division of a word at the end of a line by the hyphen. You must divide between syllables. It is generally impractical to leave a one-letter syllable at the end of a line (*a-bove*) or to carry over a two-letter syllable to the next line (*expens-es*).

Hpn 2   Place hyphens between the parts of some compound words. Generally, the hyphen is used whenever its absence would confuse the meaning of the words.

Compound nouns: *brother-in-law, cure-all, city-state*

Compound numbers under 100 and above 20: *thirty-one, fifty-five, seventy-seven*

Compound adjectives (two or more words used before a noun as a single adjective): *long-term* contract, *50-gallon* drum, *door-to-door* selling, *end-of-month* clearance.

Prefixes (most have been absorbed into the word): *de-emphasize, exchairman, viceroy, antilabor*

Hpn 2.1   A proper name used as a compound adjective needs no hyphen or hyphens to hold it together as a visual unit for the reader: The capitals perform that function.

Correct: A Lamar High School student

Correct: A United Airlines pilot

Hpn 2.2 Two or more modifiers in normal grammatical form and order need no hyphens. Particularly, a phrase consisting of an unmistakable adverb (one ending in *ly*) modifying an adjective or participle which in turn modifies a noun shows normal grammatical order and is readily grasped by the reader without the aid of the hyphen. But an adverb not ending in *ly* had better be joined to its adjectives or participle by the hyphen.

> *No hyphen needed:*   A poorly drawn chart
> *Use the hyphen:*   A well-prepared chart

Ital (Italic)

Ital 1   For the use of italics for book titles, see QM 4. Note that italics are also used for names of periodicals, of works of art or music, and of naval vessels and aircraft.

Ital 2   Italicize foreign words and abbreviations thereof—if you must use them. Italicize standard foreign (usually Latin) words and abbreviations used in footnotes and book references. This list includes, *circa, c.* ("about"); *et al.* ("and others"); *ibidem, ibid.* ("in the same place"); *idem* ("the same"); *infra* ("below"); *supra* ("above"); *loco citato, loc. cit.* ("in the place cited"); *opere citato, op. cit.* ("in the work cited"); *passim* ("here and there"); *sic* ("so," "thus"); *quod vide, q.v.* ("which see"). But the commonly used "versus," or "vs.," "v." does not require italics.

Ital 3   Italicize a word, letter, or figure used as its own name. Without this device, we could not write this set of rules. Note the use of italics all through to label name words.

> The little word *sell* is still in the dictionary.
> The pronoun *which* should always have a noun as a clear antecedent. [Try reading that one without the italics: it becomes a fragment ending in mid air!]

Paren (Parenthesis)

Use the parentheses to set off words which are parenthetic or which are inserted to explain or to supplement the principal message (see Cma 4.1).

> Dr. Samuel Goppard's phenomenal prediction (*Business Week,* June 20, 1980) has made some business forecasters revise their techniques.
> Smith was elected chairman (the vote was almost 2 to 1), and immediately he introduced his plan for reorganization.

Pd (Period)

Pd 1   Use the period to indicate the end of a declarative sentence.
Pd 2   Use periods after abbreviations or initials.

> Ph.D., Co., Inc., A.M., A.D., etc.

Pd 3   Use the ellipsis (a series of periods) to indicate the omission of words from a quoted passage. If the omitted part consists of something less than a paragraph, three periods are customarily placed at the point of omission (a fourth period is added if the omission comes at the sentence end). If the omitted part is a paragraph or more, however, a full line of periods is used. In either case the periods preferably are typed with intervening spaces.

> Logical explanations, however, have been given by authorities in the field. Some attribute the decline . . . to the changing economy in the state during recent years. . . .
>
> . . . .
>
> Added to the labor factor is the high cost of raw material, which has tended to eliminate many marginal producers. Also, the rising cost of electric power in recent years may have shifted many of the industry leaders' attention to other forms of production.

Q (Question mark)

Q 1   Place a question mark at the end of sentences which are direct questions.

> What are the latest quotations on Ewing-Bell common stock?
> Will this campaign help to sell Dunnco products?

But do not use the question mark with indirect questions.

> The president was asked whether this campaign will help to sell Dunnco products.
> He asked me what the latest quotations on Ewing-Bell common stock were.

QM (Quotation mark)

QM 1   Use quotation marks to enclose the exact words of a speaker or, if the quotation is short, the exact words of a writer.
    By short written quotations is meant something four lines or less. Longer quoted passages are best displayed without quotation marks and with additional right and left margins (see Chapter 13).

> *Short written passage:*   H. G. McVoy sums up his presentation with this statement: "All signs indicate that automation will be evolutionary, not revolutionary."
> *Verbal quotation:*   "This really should bring on a production slowdown," said Ms. Kuntz.

If the quoted words are broken by explanation or reference words, each quoted part is enclosed in question marks.

> "Will you be specific," he asked, "in recommending a course of action?"

QM 2   Enclose a quotation within a quotation with single quotation marks.

> President Carver said, "It has been a long time since I have heard an employee say, 'Boss, I'm going to beat my quota today.' "

QM 3 Always place periods and commas inside quotation marks. Place semi-colons and colons outside the marks. Place question marks and exclamation points inside if they apply to the quoted passage and outside if they appy to the whole sentence.

"If we are patient," he said, "prosperity will some day arrive." [The comma is within the quotes; the period is also within the quotes.]

"Is there a quorum?" he asked. [The question mark belongs to the quoted passage.]

Which of you said, "I know where the error lies"? [The question mark applies to the entire sentence.]

I conclude only this from the union's promise to "force the hand of man-agement": Violence will be their trump card. [Here the colon is not a part of the quotation.]

QM 4 Enclose in quotation marks the titles of the parts of a publication (articles in a magazine, chapters in a book). Place titles of a whole publication, how-ever, in italics. Use underscoring to show italics in typewritten material.

The third chapter of the book *Elementary Statistical Procedure* is entitled "Concepts of Sampling."

Joan Glasgow's most recent article, "A Union Boss Views Automation," appears in the current issue of *Fortune*.

SC (Semicolon)

SC 1 Separate by a semicolon independent clauses that are not connected by a conjunction.

Cork or asbestos sheeting must be hand cut; polyurethane may be poured into a mold.

The new contract provides substantial wage increases; the original con-tract emphasized shorter hours.

Covered by this standard are clauses connected by *however, nevertheless, therefore, then, moreover, besides* (conjunctive adverbs, not conjunctions).

The survey findings indicated a need to revise the policy; nevertheless the president vetoed the amendment.

Small-town buyers favor the old models; therefore the board concluded that both models should be manufactured.

SC 2 You may separate by a semicolon independent clauses joined by *and, but, or, for, nor* (coordinating conjunctions) if the clauses are long or if they have other punctuation in them. You also may use the semicolon in this situation for special emphasis.

The FTU and the IFL, rivals from the beginning of the new industry, have shared almost equally in the growth of membership; but the FTU predom-inates among workers in the petroleum-products crafts, including pipeline construction and operation, and the IFL leads in memberships of chemical workers.

The market price was $4; but we paid $7.

SC 3 Separate by semicolons the parts in a list when the parts have commas in them.

> The following gains were made in the February year-to-year comparison: Fort Worth, 7,300; Dallas, 4,705; Lubbock, 2,610; San Antonio, 2,350; Waco, 2,240; Port Arthur, 2,170; and Corpus Christi, 1,420.
>
> Elected for the new term were Anna T. Zelnak, attorney from Cincinnati; Wilbur T. Hoffmeister, stockbroker and president of Hoffmeister Associates of Baltimore; and William P. Peabody, a member of the faculty of the University of Georgia.

SC 4 Use the semicolon between equal (coordinate) units only. Do not use it to attach a dependent clause or phrase to an independent clause.

STANDARDS FOR CORRECTNESS IN GRAMMAR

Maintaining high standards of grammar is vital to the business writer who desires to excel at her or his work. Although it is not always necessary that high standards of grammar be followed in order to communicate, little can be said in favor of abandoning these standards. To illustrate, the statement "He ain't never done nothing to nobody" has little chance of not communicating its message. But doesn't it communicate more than the message intended? Doesn't it also communicate some idea as to the intellectual level of the writer? Certainly, such impressions would not help the communication of a typical report or letter.

As with the review of punctuation standards, the following summary of grammar standards is not intended to be a complete handbook on the subject. Rather, it is a summary of the major trouble spots encountered by most business writers. Mastery of these grammar principles would almost assure the business writer of achieving the high standards which are vital to the communication of reports and letters.

AA (Adjective-adverb confusion)

Do not use adjectives for adverbs, nor adverbs for adjectives. Adjectives modify only nouns and pronouns; and adverbs modify verbs, adjectives, or other adverbs.

Possibly the chief source of this confusion is in statements where the modifier follows the verb. If the modifier refers to the subject, an adjective should be used. If it limits the verb, an adverb is needed.

> *Below standard:*   She filed the records *quick.*
> *Acceptable:*   She filed the records *quickly.* [Refers to the verb.]
> *Below standard:*   John doesn't feel *badly.*
> *Acceptable:*   John doesn't feel *bad.* [Refers to the noun.]
> *Below standard:*   The new cars look *beautifully.*
> *Acceptable:*   The new cars look *beautiful.* [Refers to the noun.]

It should be noted that many words are both adjective and adverb (*little, well, fast, much*). And some adverbs have two forms: One form is the same as the adjective, and the other adds the *ly* (*slow* and *slowly, cheap* and *cheaply, quick* and *quickly*).

> *Acceptable:*   All of our drivers are instructed to drive *slow*.
> *Acceptable:*   All of our drivers are instructed to drive *slowly*.

Agmt SV (Agreement of subject and verb)

Nouns and their verbs must agree in number. A plural noun must have a plural verb form; a singular noun must have a singular verb.

> *Below standard:*   *Expenditures* for miscellaneous equipment *was* expected to decline. [*Expenditures* is plural, so its verb must be plural.]
>
> *Acceptable:*   *Expenditures* for miscellaneous equipment *were* expected to decline.
>
> *Below standard:*   The *president,* as well as his staff, *were* not able to attend. [*President* is the subject, and the number is not changed by the modifying phrase.]
>
> *Acceptable:*   The *president,* as well as his staff, *was* not able to attend.

Compound subjects (two or more nouns joined by *and*) require plural verbs.

> *Below standard:*   The *welders* and their *foreman* is in favor of the proposal. [*Welders* and *foreman* are compound subjects of the verb, but *is* is singular.]
>
> *Acceptable:*   The *welders* and their *foreman are* in favor of the proposal.
>
> *Below standard:*   *Received* in the morning delivery *was a typewriter and* two *reams* of letterhead paper. [*Reams* and *typewriter* are the subjects; the verb must be plural.]
>
> *Acceptable:*   *Received* in the morning delivery *were a typewriter and* two *reams* of letterhead paper.

Collective nouns may be either singular or plural, depending on the meaning intended.

> *Acceptable:*   The *committee have* carefully *studied* the proposal. [*Committee* is thought of as separate individuals.]
>
> *Acceptable:*   The *committee has* carefully *studied* the proposal. [The *committee* is considered as a unit.]

As a rule, the pronouns *anybody, anyone, each, either, everyone, everybody, neither, nobody, somebody,* and *someone* take a singular verb. The word *none* may be either singular or plural, depending on whether it is used to refer to a unit or to more than a unit.

> *Acceptable:*   *Either* of the advertising campaigns *is* costly.
> *Acceptable:*   *Nobody* who watches the clock *is successful.*

AN (Adverbial noun clause)

Do not use an adverbial clause as a noun clause. Clauses beginning with *because, when, where, if,* and similar adverbial connectives are not properly used as subjects, objects, or complements of verbs.

> *Not this:* He did not know *if* he could go or not.
> *But this:* He did not know *whether* he could go or not.
> *Not this:* The reason was *because* he did not submit a report.
> *But this:* The reason was *that* he did not submit a report.
> *Not this:* A time-series graph is *where* [or *when*] changes in an index such as wholesale prices are indicated.
> *But this:* A time-series graph is the picturing of. . . .

Awk (Awkward)

Avoid awkward writing. Writing is awkward when its word arrangement is unconventional or uneconomical, or simply not the best for quick understanding.

Dng (Dangling modifiers)

Avoid the use of modifiers which do not logically modify a word in the sentence. Such modifiers are said to dangle. They are both illogical and confusing. Usually, you can correct sentences containing dangling constructions in either of two ways: You can insert the noun or pronoun which the modifier describes, or you can change the dangling part to a complete clause.

> *Below standard:* Believing that credit customers should have advance notice of the sale, special letters were mailed to them.
> *Acceptable:* Believing that credit customers should have advance notice of the sale, we mailed special letters to them. [Improvement is made by inserting the noun modified.]
> *Acceptable:* Because we believed that credit customers should have advance notice of the sale, we mailed special letters to them. [Improvement is made by changing the dangling element to a complete clause.]

Dangling modifiers are of four principal types: participial phrases, elliptical clauses, gerund phrases, and infinitive phrases.

> *Below standard:* Believing that District 7 was not being thoroughly covered, an additional salesperson was assigned to the area. [Dangling participial phrase.]
> *Acceptable:* Believing that District 7 was not being thoroughly covered, the sales manager assigned an additional salesperson to the area.
> *Below standard:* By working hard, your goal can be reached. [Dangling gerund phrase.]
> *Acceptable:* By working hard, you can reach your goal.

> *Below standard:* To succeed at this job, long hours and hard work must not be shunned. [Dangling infinitive phrase.]
> *Acceptable:* To succeed at this job, one must not shun long hours and hard work.
> *Below standard:* While waiting on a customer, the radio was stolen. [Dangling elliptical clause—a clause without noun or verb.]
> *Acceptable:* While the salesperson was waiting on a customer, the radio was stolen.

There are, however, a few generally accepted introductory phrases which are permitted to dangle. Included in this group are *generally speaking, confidentially speaking, taking all things into consideration,* and such expressions as *in boxing, in welding,* and *in farming.*

> *Acceptable:* Generally speaking, business activity is at an all-time high.
> *Acceptable:* In farming, the land must be prepared long before planting time.
> *Acceptable:* Taking all things into consideration, this applicant is the best for the job.

Frag (Sentence fragment)

Avoid the sentence fragment. Although the sentence fragment may sometimes be used for effect, as in sales writing, it is best omitted by all but the most skilled writers. The sentence fragment consists of any group of words which cannot stand up alone as a complete and independent statement. Probably the most frequent violation of this rule results from the use of a subordinate clause as a sentence.

> *Below standard:* Believing that you will want an analysis of sales for November. We have sent you the figures.
> *Acceptable:* Believing that you will want an analysis of sales for November, we have sent you the figures.
> *Below standard:* He declared that such a procedure would not be practical. And that it would be too expensive in the long run.
> *Acceptable:* He declared that such a procedure would not be practical and that it would be too expensive in the long run.

Pn (Pronouns)

Pn 1 Make certain that the word each pronoun refers to (its antecedent) is clear. Failure to conform to this standard causes confusion, particularly in sentences where two or more nouns are possible antecedents or where the antecedent is far away from the pronoun.

> *Below standard:* When the president objected to Mr. Carter, he told him to mind his own business. [Who told whom?]
> *Acceptable:* When the president objected to Mr. Carter, Mr. Carter told him to mind his own business.

Below standard: The mixture should not be allowed to boil; so when you do it, watch the temperature gauge. [*It* doesn't have an antecedent.]

Acceptable: The mixture should not be allowed to boil; so when conducting the experiment, watch the temperature gauge.

Below standard: The model V is being introduced this year. Ads in *Time, The Saturday Evening Post,* and big-city newspapers over the country are designed to get sales off to a good start. It is especially designed for the novice boatman who is not willing to pay a big price.

Acceptable: The model V is being introduced this year. Ads in *Time, The Saturday Evening Post,* and big-city newspapers over the country are designed to get sales off to a good start. The new model is especially designed for the novice boatman who is not willing to pay a big price.

Confusion may sometimes result from using a pronoun with an implied antecedent.

Below standard: Because of the disastrous freeze in the citrus belt, it is necessary that most of them be replanted.

Acceptable: Because of the disastrous freeze in the citrus belt, it is necessary that most of the citrus orchards be replanted.

Except when their reference is perfectly clear, it is best to avoid using the pronouns *which, that,* and *this* to refer to a whole idea of a preceding clause. Many times you can make the sentence clear by using a clarifying noun following the pronoun.

Below standard (following a detailed presentation of the writer's suggestion for improving the company suggestion box plan): This should be put into effect without delay.

Acceptable: This suggestion box plan should be put into effect right away.

Pn 2   The number of the pronoun should agree with the number of its antecedent. If the antecedent is singular, its pronoun must be singular. If the antecedent is plural, its pronoun must be plural.

Below standard: Taxes and insurance are necessary evils in any business, and it must be considered carefully in anticipating profits.

Acceptable: Taxes and insurance are necessary evils in any business, and they must be considered carefully in anticipating profits.

Below standard: Everybody should make plans for their retirement. [Words like *everyone, everybody, anybody* are singular.]

Acceptable: Everybody should make plans for his or her retirement.

Pn 3   Take care to use the correct case of the pronoun. If the pronoun serves as the subject of the verb, or if it follows a form of the infinitive *to be,* use a nominative case pronoun. (Nominative case of the personal pronouns is *I, you, he, she, it, we, they.*)

Acceptable: He will record the minutes of the meeting.

Acceptable: I think it will be he.

If the pronoun is the object of a preposition or a verb, or if it is the subject of an infinitive, use the objective case. (Objective case for the personal pronouns is *me, you, him, her, us, them*.)

Below standard: This transaction is between you and *he*. [*He* is nominative and cannot be the object of the preposition *between*.]
Acceptable: This transaction is between you and *him*.

Below standard: Because the investigator praised Ms. Smith and *I*, we were promoted.
Acceptable: Because the investigator praised Ms. Smith and *me*, we were promoted.

The case of relative pronouns (*who, whom*) is determined by the pronoun's use in the clause it introduces. One good way of determining which case to use is to substitute the personal pronoun for the relative pronoun. If the case of the personal pronoun which fits is nominative, use *who*. If it is objective, use *whom*.

Acceptable: George Cutler is the salesperson who won the award. [*He* (nominative) should be substituted for the relative pronoun; therefore, nominative *who* should be used.]
Acceptable: George Cutler is the salesperson *whom* you recommended. [Objective case *him* would substitute. Thus, objective case *whom* is used.]

Usually the possessive case is used with substantives which immediately precede a gerund (verbal noun ending in *ing*).

Acceptable: Our selling of the stock frightened some of the conservative members of the board.
Acceptable: Her accepting the money ended her legal claim to the property.

Prl (Parallelism)

Parts of a sentence that express equal thoughts should be parallel (the same) in grammatical form. Parallel constructions are logically connected by the coordinating conjunctions *and, but,* and *or*. Care should be taken to see that the sentence elements connected by these conjunctions are of the same grammatical type. That is, if one of the parts is a noun, so should the other parts be nouns. If one of the parts is an infinitive phrase, so should the other parts be infinitive phrases.

Below standard: The company objectives for the coming year are to match last year's production, higher sales, and improving customer relations.
Acceptable: The company objecitves for the coming year are to match last year's production, to increase sales, and to improve customer relations.

Below standard: Writing copy may be more valuable experience than to make layouts.
Acceptable: Writing copy may be more valuable experience than making layouts.

Below standard: The questionnaire asks for this information: number of employees, what is our union status, and how much do we pay.

Acceptable: The questionnaire asks for this information: number of employees, union affiliation, and pay scale.

Tns (Tense)

Tns   The tense of each verb, infinitive, and participle used should reflect the logical time of happening of the statement: Every statement has its place in time. If this place in time is to be exactly communicated, you must be careful of your selection of tense.

Tns 1   Use present tense for statements of fact that are true at the time of writing.

Below standard: Boston was not selected as a site for the aircraft plant because it *was* too near the coast. [Boston still is near the coast, isn't it?]

Acceptable: Boston was not selected as a site for the aircraft plant because it *is* too near the coast.

Tns 2   Use past tense in statements covering a definite past event or action.

Below standard: Mr. Burns *says* to me, "Bill, you'll never make an auditor."

Acceptable: Mr. Burns *said* to me, "Bill, you'll never make an auditor."

Tns 3   The time period reflected by the past participle (*having been . . .*) is earlier than that of its governing verb. For the present participle (*being . . .*), the time period reflected is the same as that of the governing verb.

Below standard: These debentures are among the oldest on record, *being* issued in early 1937.

Acceptable: These debentures are among the oldest on record, *having been* issued in early 1937.

Below standard: Ms. Sloan, *having been* the top salesperson on the force, was made sales manager. [Possible but illogical.]

Acceptable: Ms. Sloan, *being* the top salesperson on the force, was made sales manager.

Verbs in subordinate clauses are governed by the verb in the principal clause. When the main verb is in the past tense, usually you should place the subordinate verb also in a past tense (past, present perfect, or past perfect). Thus, if the time of the subordinate clause is the same as that of the main verb, use past tense.

Acceptable: I *noticed* [past tense] the discrepancy, and then I *remembered* [same time as main verb] the incidents which caused it.

If the time of the subordinate clause is previous to that of the main verb in past tense, use past perfect tense for the subordinate verb.

Below standard: In early July we *noticed* [past] that he *exceeded* [logically should be previous to main verb] his quota three times.

Acceptable: In early July we *noticed* that he *had exceeded* his quota three times.

The present perfect tense is used for the subordinate clause when the time of this clause is subsequent to the time of the main verb.

Below standard: Before the war we *contributed* [past] generously, but lately we *forget* [should be time subsequent to the time of main verb] our duties.

Acceptable: Before the war we *contributed* generously, but lately we *have forgotten* our duties.

The present perfect tense does not logically refer to a definite time in the past. Instead, it indicates time somewhere in the indefinite past.

Below standard: We *have audited* your records on July 31 of 19___ and 19___.

Acceptable: We *audited* your records on July 31 of 19___ and 19___.

Acceptable: We *have audited* your records twice in the past.

WU (Word use)

Misused words call attention to themselves and detract from the writing. Although the possibilities of error in word use are infinite, the following list contains a few of the most common ones.

Don't use	*Use*
a long ways	a long way
and etc.	etc.
anywheres	anywhere
different than	different from
have got to	must
in back of	behind
in hopes of	in hope of
in regards to	in regard to
inside of	within
kind of satisfied	somewhat satisfied
nowhere near	not nearly
nowheres	nowhere
off of	off
over with	over
seldom ever	seldom
try and come	try to come

STANDARDS FOR THE USE OF NUMBERS

Quantities may be spelled out or they may be expressed in numeral form. Whether to use one form or the other is often a perplexing question. Especially is it perplexing to the business writers, for much of their work is with quantitative subjects. Because the means of expressing quantities is so vital to business writers, the following notes on the use of numbers are presented.

No (Numbers)

No 1   Although authorities do not agree on number usage, business writers would do well to follow the rule of ten. By this rule, you spell out numbers ten and below. You use figures for numbers above ten.

> *Correct:*   The auditor found 13 discrepancies in the stock records.
> *Correct:*   The auditor found nine discrepancies in the stock records.

No 2   Make an exception to the rule of ten when a number begins a sentence. Spell out all numbers in this position.

> *Correct:*   Seventy-three bonds were destroyed.
> *Correct:*   Eighty-nine men picketed the north entrance.

No 3   In comparisons keep all numbers in the same form. The form should be the one that according to the rule of ten occurs most often in the series.

> *Correct:*   We managed to salvage three lathes, one drill, and thirteen welding machines.
> *Correct:*   Sales increases over last year were 9 percent on automotive parts, 14 percent on hardware, and 23 percent on appliances.

No 4   When two series of numbers appear in one sentence, spell out one (preferably the smaller) and present the other in numeral form.

> *Correct:*   Three salespersons exceeded $1,500, fourteen exceeded $1,000, and thirty-one exceeded $500.

No 5   Present days of the month in figure form when the month precedes the day.

> *Correct:*   July 3, 19___

When they appear alone, or when they precede the month, the days of the month may be either spelled out or in numeral form according to the rule of ten.

> *Correct:*   I shall be there on the 13th.
> *Correct:*   The union scheduled the strike vote for the eighth.
> *Correct:*   Ms. Millican signed the contract on the seventh of July.
> *Correct:*   Sales have declined since the 14th of August.

OTHER COMMON ERRORS

Sp (Spelling)

Spell words correctly. Consult your dictionary whenever you are in doubt.

Cap (Capitalization)

Capitalize all proper names and the beginning words of a sentence.

244

QUESTIONS

Correct any punctuation or grammar errors you can find in the following sentences. Explain your corrections.

1. Charles E. Baskin the new member of the advisory committee has been an employee for seven years.

2. The auditor asked us, "If all members of the work group had access to the petty cash fund?"

3. Our January order consisted of the following items; two dozen Norwood desk calendars, note size, one dozen desk blotters, 20 by 32 inches, and one dozen bottles of ink, permanent black.

4. The truth of the matter is, that the union representative had not informed the workers of the decision.

5. Sales for the first quarter were the highest in history, profits declined for the period.

6. We suggest that you use a mild soap for best results but detergents will not harm the product.

7. Employment for October totaled 12,714 an increase of 3.1 percent over September.

8. It would not be fair however to consider only this point.

9. It is the only water-repellant snag-proof and inexpensive material available.

10. Henry Thatcher a supervisor in our company is accused of the crime.

11. Mr. Goodman made this statement, "Contrary to our expectations, Smith and Company will lose money this year."

12. I bought and he sold.

13. Soon we saw George Sweeny who is the auditor for the company.

14. Manufactured in light medium and heavy weights this razor has been widely accepted.

15. Because of a common belief that profits are too high we will have to cut our prices on most items.

16. Such has been the growth of the cities most prestigious firm, H. E. Klauss and Company.

17. In 1968 we were advised in fact we were instructed to accept this five year contract.

18. Henrys playing around has got him into trouble.

19. Cyrus B. Henshaw who was our leading salesperson last month is the leading candidate for the position.

20. The worker who completes the most units will receive a bonus.

21. The word 'phone which is short for telephone should be avoided in formal writing.

22. In last months issue of Modern Business appeared Johnson's latest article What Systems Theory Means to You.

23. Yes he replied this is exactly what we mean.

24. Why did he say John it's too late?

25. Place your order today, it is not too late.

26. We make our plans on a day to day basis.

27. There is little accuracy in the 60 day forecast.
28. The pre Christmas sale will extend over twenty six days.
29. We cannot tolerate any worker's failure to do their duty.
30. An assortment of guns, bombs, burglar tools, and ammunition were found in the cellar.
31. If we can be certain that we have the facts we can make our decision soon.
32. This one is easy to make. If one reads the instructions carefully.
33. This is the gift he received from you and I.
34. A collection of short articles on the subject were printed.
35. If we can detect only a tenth of the errors it will make us realize the truth.
36. She takes shorthand good.
37. There was plenty of surprises at the meeting.
38. It don't appear that we have made much progress.
39. The surface of these products are smooth.
40. Everybody is expected to do their best.
41. The brochures were delivered to John and I early Sunday morning.
42. Who did he recommend for the job.
43. We were given considerable money for the study.
44. He seen what could happen when administration breaks down.
45. One of his conclusions is that the climate of the region was not desirable for our purposes.
46. Smith and Rogers plans to buy the Bridgeport plant.
47. The committee feels that no action should be taken.
48. Neither of the workers found their money.
49. While observing the workers, the assembly line was operating at peak perfection.
50. The new building is three stories high, fifteen years old, solid brick construction and occupies a corner lot.
51. They had promised to have completed the job by noon.
52. Jones had been employed by the Sampson Company for twenty years.
53. Wilson and myself will handle the job.
54. Each man and woman are expected to abide by this rule.
55. The boiler has been inspected on April 1 and May 3.
56. To find problems and correcting them takes up most of my work time.
57. The carton of canned goods were distributed to the workers.
58. The motor ran uneven.
59. All are expected except John and she.
60. Everyone here has more ability than him.

A DIAGNOSTIC TEST

The following test is designed to give you a quick measure of your ability to handle some of the most troublesome punctuation and grammar situations. First, correct all errors in each sentence. Then turn to Appendix E for the recommended corrections and the symbols to the punctuation and grammar standards involved. Next, you should study the standards that you violate.

1. An important fact about this typewriter is, that it has the patented "feather touch".
2. Goods received on Invoice 2741 are as follows; three dozen white shirts, size 15–33, four mens felt hats, brown, size 7; and five dozen assorted ties.
3. James Silver president of the new union started the campaign for the retirement fund.
4. We do not expect to act on this matter however until we hear from you.
5. Shipments through September 20, 1976 totaled 69,485 pounds an increase of 17 percent over the year ago total.
6. Brick is recommended as the building material but the board is giving serious consideration to a substitute.
7. Markdowns for the sale total $34,000, never before has the company done anything like this.
8. After long experimentation a wear resistant run proof and beautiful stocking has been perfected.
9. Available in white green and blue this paint is sold by dealers all over the country.
10. George Steele who won the trip is our most energetic salesperson.
11. Good he replied, sales are sure to increase.
12. Hogan's article Retirement? Never!, printed in the current issue of Management Review, is really a part of his book A Report on Worker Security.
13. Formal announcement of our pre Easter sale will be made in thirty two days.
14. Each day we encounter new problems. Although they are solved easily.
15. A list of models, sizes, and prices of both competing lines are being sent you.
16. The manager could not tolerate any employee's failing to do their best.
17. A series of tests were completed only yesterday.
18. There should be no misunderstanding between you and I.
19. He run the accounting department for five years.
20. This report is considerable long.
21. Who did you interview for the position?
22. The report concluded that the natural resources of the Southwest was ideal for the chemical industry.
23. This applicant is six feet in height, twenty-eight years old, weighs 165 pounds, and has had eight years' experience.
24. While reading the report, a gust of wind came through the window blowing papers all over the room.
25. The sprinkler system has been checked on July 1 and September 3.

A grading checklist for reports

The following checklist should serve two purposes. First, it should serve as a guide to preparing reports. Second, it should serve as an aid to grading reports. (Your instructor can use the symbols to mark errors.) The checklist covers all types of reports—from the simple memorandums to the long, analytical reports. For each report type, you need only to use the items that apply.

TITLE (T)

T 1 Complete? The title should tell what one may expect to find in the report. Use the five Ws as a check for completeness (*who, what, where, when, why*—sometimes *how*).

T 2 Too long. This title is longer than it needs to be. Check it for uneconomical wording or unnecessary information.

LETTER OF TRANSMITTAL (LT)

LT 1 More directness needed in the opening. The letter should present the report right away.

LT 2 Content of the letter needs improvement. Comments which help the reader to understand or appreciate the report are appropriate.

LT 3 Do not include findings unless the report has no synopsis.

LT 4 A warm statement of your attitude toward the assignment is appropriate —often expected. You either do not make one, or the one you make is weak.

LT 5 A friendlier, more conversational style would improve the letter.

SYNOPSIS (S)

S 1 (If direct order assigned) Begin directly—with a statement of finding, conclusion, or recommendation.

S 2 (If indirect order assigned) Begin with a brief review of introductory information.

S 3 The summary of highlights should be in proportion and should include major findings, analyses, and conclusions. Your coverage here is (*a*) scant or (*b*) too detailed.

S 4 Work for a more interesting and concise summary.

ORGANIZATION—OUTLINE (O)

O 1 This organization plan is not the best for this problem. The main sections should form a logical solution of the problem.

O 2 The order of the parts of this outline is not logical. The parts should form a step-by-step route to the goal.

O 3 These parts overlap. Each part should be independent of other parts. Although some repetition and relating of parts may be desirable, outright overlap is a sign of bad organization.

O 4 More subparts are needed here. The subparts should cover all the information covered by the major part.

O 5 This subpart does not fit logically under this major part.

O 6 These parts are not equal in importance. Do not give them equal status in the outline.

O 7 (If talking captions assigned) These captions do not talk well.

O 8 Coordinate captions should be parallel in grammatical structure.

O 9 This (these) caption (s) is (are) too long.

O 10 Varying the wording of the captions to avoid monotonous repetition.

INTRODUCTION (I)

I 1 This introduction does not cover exactly what the reader needs to know. Although the needs vary by problem, these topics usually are important: (*a*) origin of the problem, (*b*) statement of the problem, (*c*) methods used in researching the problem, and (*d*) preview of the presentation.

I 2 Coverage of this part is (*a*) scant or (*b*) too detailed.

I 3 Important information has been left out.

I 4   Findings, conclusions, and other items of information are not a part of the introduction.

COVERAGE (C)

C 1   The coverage here is (*a*) scant or (*b*) too detailed.

C 2   More analysis is needed here.

C 3   Here you rely too heavily on a graphic aid. The text should cover the important information.

C 4   Do not lose sight of the goal of the report. Relate the information to the problem.

C 5   Clearly distinguish between fact and opinion. Label opinion as opinion.

C 6   Your analyses and conclusions need the support of more fact and authoritative opinion.

WRITING (W)

W 1   This writing should be better adapted to your readers. It appears to be (*a*) too heavy or (*b*) too light for your readers.

W 2   Avoid the overuse of passive voice.

W 3   Work for more conciseness. Try to cut down on words without sacrificing meaning.

W 4   For this report more formal writing is appropriate. You should write consistently in impersonal (third person) style.

W 5   A more personal style is appropriate for this report. That is, you should use more personal pronouns (I's, we's, you's).

W 6   The change in thought is abrupt here.
   a.   Between major parts, use introductions, summaries, and conclusions to guide the reader's thinking.
   b.   Use transitional words, phrases, or sentences to relate minor parts.

W 7   Your paragraphing is questionable. Check the paragraphs for unity. Look for topic sentences.

GRAPHIC AIDS (GA)

GA 1   You have (*a*) not used enough graphic aids, or (*b*) used too many graphic aids.

GA 2   For the information presented this graphic aid is (*a*) too large or (*b*) too small.

GA 3   This type of graphic aid is not the best for presenting the information.

GA 4   Place the graphic aid as near as practical to the place where its contents are discussed.

GA 5   The appearance of this graphic aid needs improvement. Possibly this is your best work, but it does not make a good impression on the reader.

GA 6   Refer the readers to the graphic aids at the times they should look at them.

GA 7   Preferably make the reference to the graphic aids incidental, as subordinate parts of sentences which comment on the content of the graphic aids (for example ". . . , as shown in Chart 5," or (see Chart 5).

LAYOUT AND MECHANICS (LM)

LM 1   The layout of this page is (*a*) too fat, (*b*) too skinny, or (*c*) too low, high, or off center (as marked).

LM 2   Neat typing? Strikeover, smudges, and erasures detract from the message.

LM 3   Make the margins straighter. The roughness here offends the eye.

LM 4   The spacing here needs improvement. (*a*) Too much space here. (*b*) Not enough space here.

LM 5   Your page numbering is not the best. See the text for specific instructions.

LM 6   This page appears (*a*) choppy, or (*b*) heavy.

LM 7   Your selection of type and position for the captions is not the best.

LM 8   This item of form is not generally acceptable.

Appendix B

Statistical techniques for determining sample size and reliability

The reliability of sample results as well as the adequacy of sample size may be measured by statistical and some less technical techniques (as described in Chapter 5). Although a thorough review of sampling statistics would require more space than is available in this summary, two of the basic measures are described in the following paragraphs. Both are special adaptations of the standard deviation, which is a measure of the spread of the normal distribution.

Each of these two basic formulas contains a symbol for the numbers in the sample and a measure of error. Thus, the formulas may be worked for either of these values when the value is unknown. Also, each application of the formulas tests only one characteristic of the study at a time. Thus, in determining the desired size of a sample many applications may need to be made. In a study involving a questionnaire of ten questions, for example, ten separate applications could be made—one for each question. Although it is seldom necessary to test every question in the study, enough should be tested to assure a reasonable degree of reliability for the whole.

The first of these formulas is the standard error of the percentage. As its name implies, it is a measure used when the findings are recorded in percentage form. It is expressed in the following formula:

$$\sigma_p = \sqrt{\frac{pq}{N}}.$$

Explanation of the symbols is as follows.

σ_p is the standard error of the percentage (the maximum allowable error either way in percentage points).

p is the frequency of occurrence of the phenomenon measured expressed as a percentage of the whole.

q is $1 - p$.

N is the number of cases in the sample.

When used to obtain the number required for a given allowable error rather than the standard error, the formula becomes:

$$N = \frac{pq}{\sigma_p^2}.$$

The sample size computed by this formula gives results within the limits of error specified about 68 out of 100 times. For greater accuracy, the investigators could work the formula for two standard errors, which ensures that the answer has a 95 out of 100 chance of being within the error allowed. The formula then becomes:

$$N = \frac{pq}{\left(\dfrac{\sigma_p}{2}\right)^2}.$$

As an illustration of its practical application, a consumer preference study of a new soap may be used. Any of the question in this study could be tested individually; and one such question might be "Do you like the odor of ——— soap? The investigators, possibly observing the first returns as they come in, estimate the probable ratio of answers. Possibly for the question on soap odor preferences, such an estimate could be 60 percent yes and 40 percent no or don't know. Thus, p expressed in decimal form would be 0.60, and q $(1 - p)$ would be 0.40. The investigators would then have to decide the percentage of error that they would tolerate. In this instance, a 5 percent (.05 in decimal form) error (σ_p) might be selected. If the investigators want to be about 95 percent confident that their results will be within the error they will tolerate, the problem becomes:

$$N = \frac{0.60 \times 0.40}{\left(\dfrac{0.05}{2}\right)^2} = \frac{0.24}{0.000625} = 384.$$

The second formula used is the standard error of the mean. It is used to determine error of findings expressed as means as well as the sample size needed in obtaining such findings. It is expressed in this formula:

$$\sigma_{\bar{x}} = \frac{\sigma}{\sqrt{N}}.$$

N is the size of the sample.
σ is the standard deviation of the items in the sample.
$\sigma_{\bar{x}}$ is the standard error of the mean.

In working the formula, the investigators must first find values for the two unknowns, the standard deviation (σ) and the standard error of the mean (σ_x). If they are statistically inclined, they can compute this value by using the conventional statistical formula.[1] But if they do not know statistics, they can make a rough but usually satisfactory approximation of the standard deviation. They can esti-

---

[1] The formula for the standard deviation is

$$\sigma = \sqrt{\frac{\Sigma x^2}{N}}.$$

Σx^2 is the summation of the deviations from the mean squared. N is the number of units.

mate the standard deviation to be one sixth of the range (R) of the values—that is, one sixth of the difference between the largest and smallest items in the sample. Thus, their formula becomes:

$$\sqrt{N} = \frac{\dfrac{R}{6}}{\sigma_{\bar{x}}}.$$

For the standard error of the mean $\sigma_{\bar{x}}$, they simply decide how much error (in units in which the data are given) they can permit and still have satisfactory results.

A study of average weekly incomes of factory workers illustrates this technique. In a preliminary survey, the investigators find incomes ranging from $60 to $150. Although this information is scant, it gives the investigators something to work with. So they assume a range of $90 ($150 less $60). Next, the investigators decide that they want the mean value of the sample to be no more than $1 away from the true mean value. With these quantities determined, they then apply them to the formula:

$$\sqrt{N} = \frac{\dfrac{R}{6}}{\sigma_{\bar{x}}} = \frac{\dfrac{90}{6}}{1} = \frac{15}{1}.$$
$$N = 15^2 = 225$$

Thus, the investigators need a sample of 225 to get the accuracy they want. This size of sample will produce the accuracy desired in about 68 cases out of 100. If the investigators want to be more than 68 percent certain, they can work the formula for an N with 95 percent certainty. This they may do by dividing the standard error by 2—in this case, 1 divided by 2, or 0.5. The computation with this new value produces an N of 900.

From the illustrations used for the two measures, two general observations may be made. First, in both cases the estimates of sample size were based on scant preliminary information. The investigators would do well to apply the formula again after more of the survey information has been collected. Second, to cut in half the range of error in a sample, one must quadruple the size of the sample. That is, if the range of error of a sample is to be improved from 4 percent to 2 percent, the sample must be increased 4 times.

Table for determining sample size* (sample size necessary to ensure, with 95 percent certainty, that the survey proportions are within a given number of percentage points of the true value)

Maximum percentage error either way	*Frequency with which phenomenon occurs*					
	5 or 95 percent	*10 or 90 percent*	*20 or 80 percent*	*30 or 70 percent*	*40 or 60 percent*	*50 percent*
0.5	7,600	14,400	25,600	33,600	38,400	40,000
1.0	1,900	3,600	6,400	8,400	9,600	10,000
2.0	475	900	1,600	2,100	2,400	2,500
3.0	211	400	711	933	1,067	1,111
4.0	119	225	400	525	600	625
5.0	76	144	256	336	384	400
10.0	19	36	64	84	96	100

* When findings are expressed in percentage form.

Appendix C

Report problems

SHORT PROBLEMS

1. Advising on whether to buy new or used automobiles. Since taking over as sales manager for Hamm Distributors, Inc., Loomis H. Hogan has introduced a number of revolutionary ideas for helping this regional sales organization get out of financial difficulties. The current idea is to buy used automobiles for its sales representatives rather than new ones. Hogan argues that the salespeople have small territories and average only 10,000 miles per year. He acknowledges that the old ones are likely to be less dependable and less prestigious. But he feels that the main problem now is one of finances and that the used automobiles would save money.

Because he seeks support for his ideas, Mr. Hogan turned to you, a research associate with Morrison Research, Inc. Thus it is your task to gather information on the subject and to submit the information to your client along with your analyses and recommendation.

Gathering the information was easy, for you had only to find the file copy of research your office did for Econo-Kar Auto Rental, Inc. (The Econo Kar people have authorized you to use these data.) As summarized in table 1, these data show clearly the costs of automobiles and their operation. The information is not so current as you'd like. But you feel the conclusions they support are valid. In addition to these data, you will include in your analysis the other considerations involved in the problem—dependability of old automobiles, prestige, image, and such.

Your task now is to present your information with appropriate analyses, conclusions, and recommendations. Of course, you will present the information in appropriate report form—probably as a conventional short report (title page plus text).

TABLE 1.   Per-mile ownership and operating costs

Age of automobile at purchase	Purchase price	Car kept 3 years	Percent saving	Car kept until junked	Percent saving
New	$7,296	42.1	—	26.8	—
1 year	5,968	37.9	10%	26.0	6%
2 years	3,881	29.5	30	22.5	21
3 years	2,061	21.9	48	20.4	32
4 years	1,547	20.9	51	20.1	37
5 years	1,250	20.3	52	19.8	43
6 years	923	19.8	53	19.8	49
7 years	693	19.7	53	—	53

Note: All figures are based on prices and costs of an intermediate-sized car driven 10,000 miles a year. The percentage saved until junked at ten years reflects driving the used car the same number of years as the new car is driven; that is, the saving for a year-old car driven nine years and then junked is the saving over the cost of driving a new car for nine years.

2.   Reporting on energy conservation to the board of regents.   Five years ago the board of regents of State University authorized the Office of Physical Plant to begin a massive energy-saving program. Physical Plant responded by taking a number of energy-saving actions. It raised thermostats in summer months and lowered them in winter. It installed a computer-controlled power management system. It conducted extensive energy conservation campaigns. And it did other things. All available information indicates the efforts were reasonably successful.

Now the board of regents wants a report on these energy-saving efforts. And as chief engineer, Office of the Physical Plant, you have the job of doing the reporting.

You begin by collecting the data for energy consumption over the five-year period. Since the university has added some buildings during the period, you are careful to distinguish between energy used for the buildings existing five years ago and for buildings added since. You will report on costs also; but here you will be careful not to confuse. Energy costs have almost tripled over the five-year period. Your data are summarized in Table 2.

TABLE 2.   State University energy consumption for past seven years

	Therms* of energy consumption		Energy costs ($000,000)
	Old buildings	New buildings	
Last year	9.1	2.5	$5.8
2 years ago	8.8	2.1	4.2
3 years ago	8.7	2.2	3.3
4 years ago	9.6	0.3	2.3
5 years ago	9.5	0.2	2.0
6 years ago	9.7	—	1.8
7 years ago	11.2	—	1.6

* Therm = 100,000 Btu's.

Make your report to the board and point out what has happened. Probably the board also will want some words on the future. Here you cannot be optimistic. State Utility Company projects costs to increase to $0.09 per kwh. (today's cost is

$0.03). Although you and your office have done most of the easy things to conserve, you could do some of the more difficult. You will gladly report on these suggestions to the board—if they want such a report.

Now you are ready to begin writing the report. You will present consumption data so that it forms a picture of the success of the conservation plan. And you will report cost data, taking care to emphasize the effects of price changes over the years. Present your information in the form of a short report (title page plus text). Probably you will use some graphic aids to emphasize the data. Address the report to the Board of Regents, Wilma L. Sullivan, Chairperson.

3. Presenting and analyzing differences in grades of dorm and nondorm students. As director, Office of Campus Housing, State University, your current task is to report on grade point averages of dorm and nondorm students. You have the data neatly assembled (Table 3). Now you must organize it for analysis and presentation in a report to Dr. Theodore Hobbs, dean for Academic Affairs.

TABLE 3. Grade point averages (4.0 basis)

	Freshmen	*Sophomores*	*Juniors*	*Seniors*
Men				
Dormitory	2.15	2.40	2.51	2.78
Nondormitory	1.90	2.14	2.39	2.66
Women				
Dormitory	2.34	2.54	2.68	3.06
Nondormitory	2.17	2.36	2.60	2.91

As you review the data, you quickly see that dorm students perform better than nondorm students. You will present this information fully, of course; and you will also explain why. Here you will move into the area of subjective interpretation. That is, you will use your best judgment to explain the grade differences. You will take care to label your judgments for what they are.

Write the report on State University's memorandum stationery.

4. Recommending a scholarship recipient. Assume the role of executive secretary, the DeLong Foundation. It is your job to recommend to the Foundation's board of directors a recipient for the DeLong Scholarship at your school. This scholarship is one of the better ones. It pays well, and it covers the remaining years of the recipient's undergraduate education.

Following the initial announcement of the scholarship award four weeks ago, 31 applications came in. You carefully evaluated all of them, and you interviewed the top 11. Now you have narrowed the selection to two people: Hazel McNutt and Mark Klammer. You will present these two students to the board, along with a comparative review of their background facts and your recommendation. In summary form, the facts you have assembled on your note pad are as follows:

Hazel McNutt. Age 19. Second semester sophomore. Grade point average, 3.6. Memberships: University Methodist Church (president Wesley Foundation Association), Young Republicans (secretary-treasurer), Marketing Club (membership chairperson). Dean's List all semesters. Major in Marketing. Father deceased and mother works as secretary. Two younger sisters at home. Mother unable to help with finances. Hazel works 20 hours a week busing tables at local cafeteria. An attractive woman—an extrovert. Very pleasing personality. Friendly smile. Polite. Respectful. Check of professors reveals only favorable comments—good student, hard worker. Character references all report favorably—a young woman of good character and high morals.

Mark Klammer.   First semester junior. Grade point average, 3.8. Memberships: Accounting Club, University Choral Club, Southside Baptist Church. Major in Accounting. Age 20. Works 30 hours per week as night clerk in downtown hotel. From large family (five younger brothers and sisters). Father employed as mechanic; mother works as salesclerk in department store. Parents able to give only limited financial help (20 percent). A small, slightly built young man. Friendly but somewhat reserved. Appears to be timid. Evaluations of professors are exceptionally high—a diligent, intelligent, outstanding scholar. Character references attest to his high morals and ideals—a truly fine young man.

Using your very best objectivity, now you will evaluate the two people. You will present your evaluations in an objective memorandum report addressed to Kenneth Kendall, chairperson of the board.

5.   Justifying the purchase of a typewriter with magic correcting tape.   You are the manager of the executive typing pool at Cherokee Manufacturing Company. Under your supervision are 15 typists who handle the typewriting needs of all except the company's highest executives. (These have their own secretaries.) Mainly your employees type letters, memoranda, and reports.

At the moment it is time to order five new typewriters (you replace the machines routinely at three-year intervals). You have decided to purchase Continental Business Machines' new Standard III model with magic correcting tape feature. The company has used the Continental Standard III for years, but not with the correcting tape feature. In fact, the company's purchasing agent has negative opinions on such "expensive frills" (his words).

It is true, the correcting tape adds $92 to the basic cost of $680 (plus tax) for the Standard III. You think the extra feature is worth the difference by enabling the typist to make corrections without erasing (merely by setting the machine in a split second and typing over the error). And the corrections cannot be detected with the naked eye.

Knowing that you will have to sell Mr. Cecil W. Tweedy (the purchasing agent) on the idea, you will write him a report justifying the purchase and, of course, seeking his approval.

In order to build a convincing case, you conducted a brief observation study of your typists at work. After a total of three hours of uninterrupted watching, you found that the average typist makes about nine errors per hour. Total lost time for erasures and retyping is about three minutes per hour (20 seconds per error). The magic correcting tape would make each correction easily in five seconds. You believe the time saved will soon pay for the added cost, considering the fact that the typists now average $5.20 per hour in salary.

So your task now is to look over the facts you have assembled, organize them logically, and present them in a report which will convince Mr. Tweedy that this purchase is justified.

6.   Recommending dress and grooming regulations.   Move into the role of director of employee relations for City National Bank and write a memorandum on dress and grooming regulations for all employees (male and/or female, as your instructor directs). At last week's executive committee meeting the discussion centered on the inappropriate attire and grooming of too many of the employees. The general feeling was that the bank's image is suffering.

The meeting concluded with President Lorraine Wukash directing you to prepare appropriate dress and grooming regulations. "Be careful not to make us appear to be prudes," she warned you. "But give us something that will protect the image of City Bank. Send your recommendations to me first. I'll send them to the employees under my signature."

Now you must use your best judgment in preparing these regulations. Be careful to cover all important matters. And make the regulations so clear that all will understand. Write them in a memorandum report addressed to President Wukash.

7.   Writing the results of an evaluation study of a department head.   You are personnel director of Conway Industries, Inc., and your office has just completed a performance evaluation of all department heads. These evaluations were made using a nine-statement questionnaire, which was distributed to all subordinates of each department head. The subordinates were instructed to mark on a scale of 0–100 the position his or her department head would place relative to the statement.

Now you have tabulated all the data and have the results for each department head. For purposes of comparison, you also have the averages of all department heads at Conway. Your next step is to present this information to each department head, pointing out his or her strengths and weaknesses. You will present this review in a memorandum report. The first department head to be reported is Eilene Abernathy. (Table 4.)

8.   Selecting the best outlet for Cerdan's Cravats.   Assume the role of special assistant to Mr. Julian P. Pitts, sales manager for Cerdan's Cravats, Inc. Your present assignment is to investigate two retail outlets in Metroville and to recommend to Mr. Pitts the one you think should be awarded the Cerdan dealership for the city. Each of the two stores has indicated an interest in handling Cerdan's quality products, but the Cerdan dealership policy forbids more than one outlet in a city the size of Metroville (60,000 population).

For the past two days you have been in Metroville where you very carefully inspected the two stores involved. As you conducted your investigation, you kept foremost in mind that Cerdan's enviable sales record and its reputation as a tie for style-conscious men are attributed to careful selection of outlets. Cerdan's customers are men of some means, usually coming from the upper middle- and high-income groups. So, traditionally, Cerdan has selected outlets catering to these groups.

TABLE 4. Subordinates' evaluations of Eilene Abernathy

Statement	Rating for Eilene Abernathy*	Average ratings for all department heads*
1. The quality of human relationships, such as being fair, objective, honest	59	71
2. Quality of leadership	52	54
3. Quality of communication in both oral and written forms and the willingness to be communicative	55	58
4. Quality of support of employee development	66	71
5. The way in which the budget is planned and administered in regard to both equity and efficiency	41	55
6. The way in which the administrative unit is represented to higher administration	92	87
7. The efficiency of operation of the administrative offices	67	80
8. The extent to which this administrator keeps abreast of matters within the department	58	78
9. Your personal estimate of the confidence which your colleagues have in this administrator	56	54

* Scale of 0 to 100.

Exclusiveness of customers, however, is not your only consideration. Certainly, you are seeking an outlet that can move Cerdan's Cravats in volume, and you want an outlet that gives the kind of service for which Cerdan dealers are noted. You will also want to consider a number of other factors—things like store location, growth potential, and physical plant. Now you are ready to begin your analysis of the facts. The facts, in the garbled form in which you noted them, look like this:

Metroville Man's Shop

A small, exclusive shop. Sells only quality lines of men's and boy's clothing. Stocks two other brands of ties—Pennington (middle to high quality), and the popular High Fashion (middle quality). Is willing to drop the Pennington brand if given Cerdan dealership. Store is owned by its founder, Cornelius W. Hodge, who appears to be in mid-60s. Mr. Hodge is very personable and gregarious—likes to wait on customers personally. Stresses service and quality. Two other salespeople, both in their 20s. Selling atmosphere is leisurely—no pressure. Customers appear to be mostly mature, conservative, and successful business executives and professionals. Only high-quality merchandise sold. Annual sales approximately $550,000. Advertises weekly (usually in Sunday edition of local daily)—average a quarter page per week. No TV or radio. Ads are dignified and stress quality and style. Sales floor is small (40 x 75 feet) and old, but clean and well-maintained. Store located at heart of downtown. Downtown merchants have suffered from development of suburban shopping centers, but this store has prospered, probably because of presence of business executives and professionals in area. Store opened 37 years ago. Building has attractive, modern front. The fixtures are old but well kept. Mahogany-paneled walls give dignified but dreary appearance. Stock is neatly arranged, but store has crowded appearance.

Clifton's Haberdashery

A new men's store located in the West End Shopping Center, the new shopping mall. Floor space about 45 x 130 feet. Modern design—bright and attractive interior. Neat arrangement of merchandise. Spacious. Store owned by Hansel Sylvester—young (mid-30s) and aggressive. Sales force consists of three full-time and one part-time salespeople. Sales tactics involve some pressure, but service also stressed. Merchandise ranges from top quality to low-middle. Four brands of ties now carried; Dapper Dan (low-middle), Paree (middle), King's Crown (middle), and Bayman (middle-high). Not willing to drop any of these brands if Cerdan dealership awarded. Store sales about $1 million annually. It caters heavily to young business executives and college students. Emphasizes young (mod) styles, but also carries some conservative clothing. Advertises heavily —total of 1¼ pages per week—usually ¼ page on Thursdays and full page on Sundays. Some radio spot ads. Ads are smart, smooth, appealing. Stress style and price.

You will write up the analysis and your recommendation in the company memorandum form Mr. Pitts will expect. Because Pitts is a man who likes his answers fast, you plan to present your recommendation right off. And because he is the thorough man that he is, you plan to follow your recommendation with a logical analysis of the facts which will support your decision.

9. Justifying the purchase of a riding mower. As manager of the operation and maintenance department at the Macon Tire & Rubber Company, you recently purchased a riding lawn mower for the department. As company policy requires that all expenditures over $250 be justified in writing, you must write a justification report to Mr. Benjamin Cox, director of purchasing. Mr. Cox will then keep the report on file for the auditors or for whomever else may wish to see it.

Here are the facts around which you will build your case. Previously you had been using two self-propelled, walking-type mowers, 24-inch cut. They cost $345 new, have a three-year life and a trade-in value of $50. The mowers were used about 120 hours each year. The two operators received $4.10 per hour for this work. Average annual repair cost for each mower is $68.

The riding mower, which has a life of about six years, was purchased for $1,140. As it has a 60-inch cut, it can more than do the work of the two other mowers. With it, one operator can take care of all the company's lawn in about 100 hours each year. But one of the smaller mowers will be kept for close work. With such limited use, this one old mower should last another three years. Upkeep costs for this mower are apt to be $120 per year. The difference in operating costs between the mowers is negligible. Write up the report in Macom's standard memorandum form.

10. Recommending a sales manager for Mason-Platt Pharmaceuticals, Inc. As sales manager for the Western region of Mason-Platt Pharmaceuticals, Inc., you must recommend one of your better salespeople for the vacant position of district manager for the Valley City area. After carefully screening the records of your seven eligibles, you determine the top three. Now you have to evaluate them, rank them for the job, and pass on your recommendation to Naomi Guerra, the marketing vice president for Mason-Platt. You know the three top candidates fairly well. All three are personable, ambitious people. Judging from impressions you have of them, there is not much to choose between them. So you will make your recommendation on the basis of the factual information you have assembled from their personal records (see summary below). You will write up your analysis and recommendations in the standard memorandum form used for all Mason-Platt intercompany reports. And you will use the conclusion-first approach which you know Ms. Guerra prefers.

	George MacFarren	Mary Toops	Joe W. Rush
Age	33	28	35
Sales experience	3½ years, Glad Publishing Co.; 4 years, Mason-Platt	6 years, Mason-Platt	4 years, Central Insurance; 5 years, Lund Pharmaceutical; 4 years, Mason-Platt
Education	High school diploma; City Community College, Associate of Arts in general business	B.B.A. degree, Northern State University, major in marketing	B.S. degree, Steward University, major in psychology
Record with Mason-Platt (percent of sales quota)	1st yr., no quota 2d yr., 117 3d yr., 106 4th yr., 121	1st yr., no quota 2d yr., 105 3d yr., 98 4th yr., 121 5th yr., 107 6th yr., 137	1st yr., no quota 2d yr., 137 3d yr., 141 4th yr., 140
Score on Management Potential Test (60 = passing, 70 = above average, 80+ = outstanding)	81	88	77

11.   Writing a personnel action report on an erring subordinate.   You don't like to do such things, but you must report one of your subordinates for general inefficiency and neglect of duty. In fact, you conclude that you must recommend discharge of the fellow.

As supervisor of Department 7 (the office supply department of the Boulder Insurance Company), you have been putting up with the antics of Wingate P. Throckmorton III for nearly all of the seven months he has been with your company. The two quarterly evaluation reports on Throckmorton showed that his work was below standard from the start. He received "inferior" ratings both times. These were not your judgments, but those of Throckmorton's immediate superior, Martha Kay Bennett. Perhaps Throckmorton has the ability (he made a fair score on the company's aptitude test), but he just has not produced. He has made numerous costly errors in his assignment of writing purchase orders (you may use your imagination to bring in these details); and he resents, to the point of belligerence, any criticism of his errors.

During the past three months he has been absent from work 13 days. Only one of these absences was excusable. Twice he reported to work intoxicated and had to be sent home. On one of these occasions (it happened just yesterday) he had to be forcibly ejected. This last act was the final straw. Although he reported to work today all apologetic and promising to do better, you have no more hope for him. He made similar promises the last time you had him in your office for frank discussions of his problems.

Now you will write a personnel action report recommending that Throckmorton be discharged. You will use the company's memorandum form and will address your report to Eleanor A. Gandy, director of personnel. Standard practice in the company is to write such reports with the conclusion first and then to justify the conclusion with facts and analyses.

12. Investigating a personnel problem in Department 77. Today's assignment in your role as special assistant to Mildred Kammer, director of employment relations, Southwestern Aircraft, Inc., takes you to Department 77. Your objective is to investigate charges brought to you by Tim Cory, the union steward representing the workers of this department. According to Cory, union members in Department 77 have been discriminated against in the awarding of overtime work. Nonunion workers have been getting the lion's share of overtime.

Upon arriving at the department, you discuss the matter with Stanley Krause. Krause's version of the story goes like this. Of the eight workers in the department, five are members of the union and three are not. The three nonunion workers have had more overtime than the others; but they deserve it. Krause claims that he gave overtime on the basis of seniority and productivity—nothing else. This policy, he points out, is permitted in the contract with the union. If the nonunion employees got more of the overtime, it is because they have seniority and are better workers.

After talking to Krause you go to the files containing the department's records. Here you find data that should prove or disprove Krause's claim, and in fact, should point to the solution to the whole problem. After an hour or more of pouring over these records covering the past six months, your summary notes look like this:

Employee and union status*	Hours of overtime work	Years employed	Productivity (average daily units performed)	Percent rejection (not meeting inspection)
George Graves (U)	0	14	30	0.08
W. Wilson Davis (U)	0	1	21	0.09
Kermit Crowley (U)	10	3	32	0.07
Walter H. Quals (U)	60	8	26	0.01
Hugo Detresanti (U)	60	7	30	0.03
Ralph A. Andrews (NU)	40	35	26	0.02
Will O. Rundell (NU)	70	17	35	0.03
Thomas A. Baines (NU)	90	12	43	0.03

* U—union, NU—nonunion.

Now your task is to analyze these data and to present your findings to Ms. Kammer in the form of the standard memorandum report used by the company.

In addition to analyzing the data, you will recommend a course of action on the problem.

13. Which commercial is better for EZ-Clean? The research department of the Alman-Beaty Advertising Agency has completed an experiment with two 60-second TV commercials for EZ-Clean, a liquid window cleaner. Not being able to decide between two approaches for promoting the product, the agency decided to try out each commercial in a different test city. Petroville and River City were selected for the test. After the commercials were run, a representative sample of viewers was interviewed by telephone in an attempt to determine the effectiveness of the advertisements.

One of the commercials (Commercial A) is a humorous cartoon strip depicting the use of the product by popular comic-strip charatcers. It depicts one character, an animated mouse, gleefully cleaning a large plate of glass with an "old-fashioned" glass cleaner. Then the mouse runs into the next room, gets the attention of his perpetual adversary, a cat, and gets the cat to chase him. His plan to get the cat to run into the glass plate fails when the cat sees dirt on the glass. The cat then lectures to the mouse on the virtues of EZ-Clean and then walks away. While walking out of the room, however, the cat runs into a glass door, knocking himself out. The commercial ends with the mouse standing by the door, holding a can of EZ-Clean, and winking at the TV viewers.

The second commercial (Commercial B) is a conventional family scene. It shows a husband and wife sitting in their parlor and looking out of the "largest picture window in town." Their view is limited, however, for the window is dirty. They try everything—ammonia, water, other products; but nothing does the job until they try EZ-Clean. The final scene shows the couple watching a parade as it passes by their clean window.

The results of the test are now in (see Tables 5 and 6) and it is your job to study

TABLE 5. **Commercial A, recall of viewers 24 hours later, test sample of 1,000 female viewers, Columbus, Ohio**

	Percent
Remembered commercial 24 hours after viewing	88.3
Product story recall	72.3
Video (recall of specific incidents)	
Mouse cleaning window with "old-fashioned" cleaner	68.5
Cat detecting glass	70.0
Cat lecturing to mouse about EZ-Clean	64.3
Mouse gleefully viewing scene	60.2
Cat running into glass door	71.3
Mouse holding can of EZ-Clean	36.4
Audio (recall of specific appeals)	
Simple/easy to use	8.3
Not messy	2.3
Gets glass clean, cleaner	11.7
Cleans well/best cleaner	3.2
Glass stays clean, clear longer	6.3
Leaves no film/leaves glass clean, clear	16.1
Glass seems to disappear	2.3

TABLE 6.   Commercial B, recall of viewers 24 hours later, test sample of 1,000 female viewers, Indianapolis, Indiana

	Percent
Remembered commercial 24 hours after viewing	68.4
Product story recall	56.4
Video (recall of specific incidents)	
Demonstration: Saw window being cleaned/couple man and woman clean window	45.1
Window cleaned with EZ-Clean	21.1
Window cleaned with old-fashioned cleaners, ammonia, soap and water, vinegar	18.8
Saw couple in living room/couldn't see out of dirty windows	21.8
Saw outdoor scene, parade passing by after cleaning window	12.0
Different sizes of EZ-Clean	5.3
Spray can	3.8
Audio (recall of specific appeals)	
Simple/easy to use	36.8
Not messy	7.5
Gets glass clean, cleaner	28.6
Cleans well/best cleaner	11.3
Glass stays clean, clear longer	10.5
Leaves no film/leaves glass clean, clear	9.8
Glass seems to disappear	5.3

them and to report on your analyses and conclusions to the agency. Your conclusions will be based on which ad will be likely to sell more EZ-Clean. And, of course, you will present your work in good report form.

14.   Determining the Advertising Effectiveness of a Cooking School.   Until recently the manufacturers of Mrs. Walker's Shortening have depended almost totally on newspaper and magazine advertising to sell their product. Six months ago, however, the company's management decided to try a new form of advertising —a televised cooking school.

Before going into this form of advertising on a big scale, the company management decided to experiment with the plan. Thus, they designed a before-after with control group experiment, using Millville (65,000 population) as the test city and Harrisburg (61,000 population) as the control city. In each city they selected 20 comparable stores for the study.

Sales of Mrs. Walker's Shortening were recorded for all stores for one week. Then the cooking school was conducted over the Millville television station. Directed by a nationally prominent cooking authority, the school was held during a daytime hour that is popular for consumers' viewing. Although the school was primarily educational, Mrs. Walker's Shortening was subtly suggested in the instructions and strongly recommended in the commercials which were included in the 30-minute program. Weekly results of sales were kept for all of the stores in the experiment during and immediately after the program. Then, to determine long-run effects, additional records were collected 12 weeks and 24 weeks later. This information (Table 7) holds the key to the question of whether television cooking schools are effective means of advertising Mrs. Walker's Shortening.

TABLE 7.   **Records of sales for test and control city stores before, during, and after the experiment**

	Pounds sold in test city stores	Pounds sold in control city stores
January 3–9, before school	2,371	2,031
January 10–16, week of school	2,893	2,076
January 17–23, week after school	2,964	2,047
January 24–30, 2d week after school	2,981	2,088
April 4–10, 12th week after school	2,521	2,107
June 27–July 3, 24th week after school	2,503	2,142

As director of research for Mrs. Walker's Products, Inc., you have the task of analyzing the results of the experiment and of reporting your conclusions to management. Write your report in memorandum form, using the company standard memorandum stationery. Address your report to President George E. Walker.

15.   Recommending a secretary to Ms. Sicili.   As an interviewer in the personnel department of the Mashack-Karner Manufacturing Company, write a memorandum report to Ms. Beatrice Sicili, supervisor, production planning department.

Some days ago Ms. Sicili requested that you find her an experienced secretary as a replacement for one who is resigning. Today, after carefully screening through application blanks, test scores, and your own interview notes of the nine applicants for the job, you select what appears to be the top three people. Now, following standard company policy, you must summarize your analysis on a standard memorandum (To, From, Subject form). This report will rank the three people and will concisely evaluate their suitability for the job in question. Ms. Sicili, however, will make the final decision. As is customary in your company, the report will be written in the direct order and in personal style.

The following are the facts which will form the basis of your evaluation. If you think it is necessary, you may supplement this information with reasonable imagination so long as you do not alter the general picture presented.

Mary Beth Jenkins: Age 41; husband disabled; children 16, 11, and 9; five years as secretary with Butler Realty, lost job when company closed business, excellent references from superiors; neat and fairly attractive; high school and business college graduate; test scores: typing—84 words per minute; shorthand speed—121 words per minute; secretarial aptitude—95 (excellent); good health.

Joe W. Whatley: Age 24; single; high school diploma; Associate of Arts degree from community college, secretarial studies; typing speed—71 words per minute; shorthand speed—108 words per minute; secretarial aptitude test—85 (good); three years secretarial experience with Bentley Electric—excellent references. Neat and personable.

Marie Shaver: Age 21; married, no children; high school, three years' college (major in secretarial studies); no working experience; typing speed—94 words per minute; shorthand speed—133 words per minute; secretarial aptitude test—94 (excellent); very attractive and personable.

16. The coffee break problem at Bruin, Inc. As office manager of Bruin, Inc., you are disturbed over the fact that your 85 office workers are taking long rest periods at 10:00 A.M. and 2:30 P.M. You feel that since Bruin is paying its office workers an average of $280 a week, the company is losing money.

A bit of discreet checking revealed to you that 41 of the 50 workers you observed left the office for their rest period. You observed also that these 41 workers average breaks of 27 minutes. Those taking their breaks within the office area all were back within the 15 minutes allotted. The cause of the long breaks is clear to you. Those going outside the office must wait for a very crowded elevator on their way to the downstairs coffee shop.

An office manager friend of yours recently circumvented a similar problem by installing a vending machine in his office. He told you that the machine he installed has the following characteristics:

1. It costs $1,260, installed, and includes a unit for dispensing instant mixes and a unit for dispensing very hot and very cold water. Mixes dispensed include instant coffee (with a packet of sugar and a packet of instant cream), instant cocoa, and instant chicken or beef bouillon.
2. The two-unit arrangement occupies 20 square feet of floor space.
3. The machines support themselves insofar as cost is concerned, and they provide a small profit which can be distributed to such funds as the Employee Annual Picnic Funds.
    The machines are sold by the Bollon Company, which will supply the necessary coffee, cocoa, and bouillon mixes. The Bollon Company will service the machines as necessary.

On the basis of your personal observation and what your friend told you, you are now prepared to write a memorandum report of your findings to the vice president, administration. You want to write your report in good form, and you will want to cover such essentials as estimated money and work-hours saved as possible justification for installing a vending machine.

17. Should Fidelity use a janitorial service? As assistant to the president of Fidelity Insurance Company, you have been asked to look into the possibility of using a janitorial service instead of the two full-time janitors employed by the company. In recent years the firm has had much difficulty keeping janitors. In fact, five people have filled the two $175-a-week positions within the past two years, the longest lasting ten months. The two janitors currently employed have been with the company for only three and five weeks, respectively.

As you gather the facts, you learn that in addition to the two salaries, the company must pay about $27 a week for janitorial supplies. Then, of course, there are the workers' fringe benefits, which amount to an extra 20 percent. And once each year for major housecleaning extra help costing about $1,600 has to be hired. The Perkins Janitorial Service has offered to do all of the company's work for $475 per week. Your job is to analyze all of the facts involved and to arrive at a decision. You will give the cost factors heavy weight, but you must remember that there are other less tangible reasons which should be considered. Write up your analysis and recommendation in a standard memorandum report addressed to President Joseph E. Ward.

18.   Who should be Raeder Manufacturing Company's new office manager?
As director of personnel for the home office of the Raeder Manufacturing Company, you must recommend someone to serve as office manager. Following company procedure you narrow your selection to the three leading contenders. Next you must evaluate them, determine which one should have the job, and submit your decision with your reasons to Mr. Preston P. Puffer, vice-president in charge of administration.

You know the top three candidates very well. They are all section heads, and they are all competent. Thus the decision will be a close one. Because you will want to keep personalities out of your analysis, you will make your recommendations largely on the basis of factual information you have assembled from the personnel records (see summary below). You will write up your analysis and recommendations in the standard memorandum form used for all Raeder intercompany reports, and you will use the conclusion-first approach which you know Mr. Puffer prefers.

Malvina Krenek

Age: 49

Education: high school graduate, one-year business college course (certificate).

Experience: 8 years as bookkeeper with Parr Plumbing Company; 3 years of personnel records work with Kable Manufacturing Company; 20 years with Raeder in various general office assignments, last 7 as head of personnel records section.

Company ratings[1]: satisfactory, seven years; very satisfactory, nine years; excellent, four years.

Comments from rating sheets: a hard worker, loyal, somewhat limited in ability to grasp problems quickly, works well under pressure, overemphasizes details.

Test scores[2]: administrative potential, 70; office procedure, 89.

Stanley Vitek

Age: 30

Education: B.B.A. from State University, major in personnel management, B+ average.

Experience: two years as pilot in U.S. Air Force, two years of general personnel work with McKee Aircraft, Inc.; five years at Raeder in various general office assignments, last two as head of customer correspondence section.

Company ratings[1]: very satisfactory, two years; excellent, three years.

Comments from rating sheets: a very bright young man, aggressive, thorough and tireless in his work, will not be content with mediocre assignment, good leadership qualities.

Test scores[2]: administrative potential, 92; office procedure, 84.

---

[1] Company ratings are made annually on each employee by his or her supervisor. Classifications used are as follows: excellent, very satisfactory, satisfactory, barely satisfactory, unsatisfactory.

[2] Scale for company tests is as follows:

   below 60, below average
   60– 69, average
   70– 79, above average
   80– 89, well above average
   90–100, exceptional

Willaim A. Heine

Age: 39

Education: high school diploma (completed 12 years ago after 3 years of night school);
   has been attending evening college for past 7 years, 42 semester hours passed, C+
   average, major in general business.

Experience: 9 years in U.S. Army as clerk typist and administrative clerk; 12 years
   with Raeder in various general office assignments, last 7 as head of sales records.

Company ratings[1]: very satisfactory, ten years; excellent, two years.

Comments from rating sheets: a very hard worker, a perfectionist, does not delegate
   work as much as he should, ambitious, works his subordinates hard.

Test scores[2]: administrative potential, 77; office procedure, 80.

PROBLEMS OF MEDIUM LENGTH

19.   Recommending on whether to meet on your campus.   As education director, International Future Business Leaders, your current assignment is to investigate the site for next year's meeting. Every summer this association of university business students meets on a college campus. The meetings are held on campuses between semesters. Typically from 80–100 members attend the one-week program. They meet in classroom buildings, union facilities, and such. Usually they stay in vacant dormitories and eat in campus facilities, although sometimes they have used off-campus lodging and eating facilities.

For next year the organization directors are considering meeting on your campus. They have asked you to gather the pertinent facts for them. Of primary importance are such vital matters as the availability and costs of meeting rooms, dormitory rooms, and meals. The group needs one large meeting room (capacity of 100) and four small rooms (25 capacity). Fifty dormitory rooms will be adequate (two to a room). Men and women will be about equally represented. Meals usually are bought individually, but a weekly rate would be considered.

In addition to these basic needs, organization members are interested in information on after-hours activities. Thus you will report on the recreational, sightseeing, and cultural attractions of the area. Of course, you will emphasize the attractions that are likely to interest college people.

After you have gathered the information, you will organize it and present it in appropriate report form. As the directors must make a decision, you will help them by making your recommendation. Try hard to be objective.

20.   Determining consumer attitudes toward fraudulent practices.   As a research specialist in the Public Relations Office of Central Department Stores, your job is to investigate problems which affect this major department store chain's relations with its customers. Your specific problem of the moment is that of fraudulent behavior of customers (shoplifting, altering price tags, returning worn clothing, and such).

Central management is well aware of the fact that some of its customers deal fraudulently with company stores. Ideas of how to deal with this problem have been numerous, but all involve possible negative results. In fact, it could be that some solutions would produce results worse than the fraud. Before Central management takes any action, it feels that it should know more about the attitudes of consumers toward fraud and how it should be combated. So management has asked you to gather and analyze this information.

You begin the task by surveying 200 Central customers (you may fill in the details of your research procedure). To each of the 200 you presented 15 fraud situations. Then you asked the interviewees for their personal viewpoints on each situation. You asked also for an indication of how their friends would react in each situation—a subtle way of learning the recipients' true feeling on a matter involving morality. The information in Tables 8–10 summarize your findings.

TABLE 8.   Personal attitudes of consumers toward fraudulent practices (percent)

	Attitude			
Fraudulent practice	*Very wrong*	*Not serious*	*Under- standable*	*Not wrong*
Shoplifting	97.0	0.3	2.7	0.0
Returning worn clothing	93.7	2.3	3.3	0.7
Changing or switching price tag	96.7	1.3	2.0	0.0
Writing bad checks	82.3	15.3	2.4	0.0
Eating food in store (without paying)	77.7	18.3	4.0	0.0
Ignoring change error at checkout	76.0	16.7	7.3	0.0
Dishonest use of coupons	64.3	27.7	2.7	5.3
Making invalid warranty claim ..	53.0	35.3	10.0	1.7
Ignoring undercharge	49.3	37.7	8.7	4.3
Ignoring billing error	52.3	35.3	8.7	3.7

TABLE 9.   Percent of customers whose friends would engage in fraudulent practices when opportunity occurs

Fraudulent practice	*Most of time*	*Occasionally*	*Rarely*	*Never*
Shoplifting	10.3	2.3	22.0	65.4
Returning worn clothing	21.0	2.0	4.3	72.7
Changing or switching price tag	12.7	3.7	22.3	67.3
Writing bad checks	5.3	12.0	26.7	56.0
Eating food in store (without paying)	25.7	5.0	37.0	32.3
Ignoring change error at checkout	33.0	17.3	30.7	19.0
Dishonest use of coupons	8.0	21.0	35.3	35.7
Making invalid warranty claim ..	24.7	36.3	22.3	16.7
Ignoring undercharge	39.3	37.0	15.7	8.0
Ignoring billing error	21.0	20.7	31.3	27.0

TABLE 10. Customers' viewpoints of appropriate actions for certain fraudulent practices

Fraudulent practice	Do nothing	Take preventive action	Give warning	Take drastic action
		Action considered most appropriate (percent of customers)		
Shoplifting	1.3	.3	58.7	39.7*
Returning worn clothing	3.0	7.7	11.0	78.3†
Changing or switching price tag	.7	3.7	70.3	25.3*
Writing bad checks	1.0	7.3	59.3	32.3*
Eating food in store (without paying)	4.7	32.3	63.7	.3
Ignoring change error at checkout	1.7	37.0	60.3	1.0*
Dishonest use of coupons	2.7‡	7.0	27.0	63.3‡
Making invalid warranty claim	3.0‡	14.3	28.7	54.0*
Ignoring undercharge	5.7	76.3	18.0	.0
Ignoring billing error	5.0	31.3	63.7	.0

* Notify authorities.
† Refuse.
‡ Accept coupon or claim.

Even though the work was extensive, the information obtained was not. You will present your findings in a short report. Address it to Ms. Madelaine Childs, Director of Public Relations. In general, your report will present and interpret the data you collected. Your goal is to guide management in forming policies regarding fraudulent practices.

21. Evaluating effects of coupon deals on dairy products sales. Assume that you are a trainee in the marketing department of Green Valley Dairies, Inc. For years this national dairy operation has used with cooperating grocers a coupon plan to promote its products. Specifically, this plan is to include coupons in newspaper advertisements of cooperating grocers. The coupons entitle purchasers to discounts on nine categories of Green Valley products. Green Valley covers the discount costs so that the grocers do not lose; but it hopes that the campaign will increase sales, thereby overcoming these costs.

Green Valley management feel the plan has been successful, but they have no hard facts. So they ask your department to come up with some. Your boss, Susan Kron, devised the following research plan (you may add details to this general description).

First, a panel of 500 households was selected. Each was requested to keep a diary of dairy product purchases. Dairy records were submitted to Green Valley covering three periods: (1) the two-week period ending one month before the discount period, (2) the two-week period in which the discount was offered, and (3) the two-week period beginning one month after the discount period. This plan, Ms.

Kron reasoned, should give some of the effects of the offer—short run and long run.

Discount offers were made for each of the nine categories of dairy products over a period of two years (one category at a time). You have the results all neatly arrayed in tables (see Tables 11 and 12). Now your task is to interpret these find-

TABLE 11.   Average quantities of dairy products purchased by households for two-week periods before, during, and after coupon promotion

Product group	Before	During	After
Fluid milk (half gallons)	5.9	7.6	5.9
Cottage cheese (pounds)	1.3	3.7	1.7
Yogurt (half pints)	1.7	5.8	2.2
Ice cream (gallons)	.7	1.5	.9
Ice milk (gallons)	.4	1.2	.6
Process cheese (pounds)	.7	2.9	.7
Natural cheese (pounds)	.7	2.7	1.1
Butter (pounds)	1.2	2.8	1.2
Cream products (pints)	1.2	1.9	1.2

TABLE 12.   Total effects of coupon discount promotion on sales of fluid milk, by demographic characteristic (percentage change from before period)

Demographic characteristic	During	After
Education		
Grade school	+58	+27
High school	+28	+8
College	+20	−1
Occupation		
Labor and crafts	+41	+5
Professional and clerical	+14	−7
Farmer	+41	−9
Retired and unemployed	+69	+17
Race		
White	+27	−3
Nonwhite	+68	+14
Employment status		
Wife employed	+54	+7
Wife unemployed	+6	0
City size		
Less than 2,500	+28	−1
2,500–49,999	+26	−2
50,000–499,999	+28	+9
500,000–999,999	+47	+17
1,000,000 and over	+33	+13
Income of household		
$25,000 and over	+43	+4
$15,000–$24,999	+17	+2
$10,000–$14,999	+21	+1
$5,000–$9,999	+8	+3
Under $5,000	+49	0

ings for management. Especially you want to emphasize the long-run effects of the discount coupons by type of dairy product. And if there are any, you'll want to point out any differences in the effects of discount deals on demographic groups.

Of course, you will present your findings, analyses, and conclusions in appropriate report form—one befitting the top executives who will read it.

22. Evaluating a flexible work-hour plan. Six months ago, Hill Manufacturing Company began experimenting with a flexible work-hour plan. Specifically, the company selected 298 workers from a representative cross section of functions and placed them on flexible work schedules. That is, the workers could come and go as they wished. They are required only to work their usual number of hours per week.

The general feeling at Hill is that the plan is working quite well. At least, this is the information that feeds back to management. But management wants some more concrete information on the matter. As one of two management trainees in Hill's employee relations department, you were given a part of the assignment. The other trainee, Marilyn Matson, was given a second part. Marilyn's task is to look at the concrete evidence—at information concerning such items as turnover, productivity, and absenteeism. Your assignment is to look at the attitudinal side—at what the workers think about the plan.

Your first step was to interview each of the 298 workers involved to get their reactions. Then you interviewed 100 managers (all closely involved with the 298 workers) to get their reactions. Of course, you got from each group the information you felt they could give, although there was some duplication. Your findings are summarized in Tables 13 and 14.

Now you are ready to present your findings. You will analyze the data as well as reach a general conclusion concerning the effectiveness of the plan as revealed

TABLE 13.   Employees' viewpoints concerning certain measures of flexible working-hours plan (percent)

Measure	Viewpoints		
	Increased	Unaffected	Decreased
Driving time	17	24	59
Pressures related to getting to work	6	20	74
Needs to leave work before quitting time	5	33	62
Leisure time	66	23	11
Morale	86	8	6
Attitudes toward company	67	24	9
Productivity	67	22	11
Need for supervision	27	27	46
Cooperation and coordination between departments	42	37	21
Cooperation and coordination between shifts	53	39	8
Abuses	37	33	30

TABLE 14. Managers' viewpoints concerning certain measures of flexible working-hours plan (percent)

	Viewpoints		
Measure	Increased	Unaffected	Decreased
Employees' driving time	3	21	76
Sick-leave use	0	54	46
Productivity	45	50	5
Absenteeism	21	72	7
Supervisor-subordinate relations	11	70	19
Employee leisure time	81	18	1
Employee morale	57	40	3

by your findings. Even though the report will be rather short, it will be important to Hill Management. So you will prepare it in short report form (title page plus text). And you will prepare some graphics to emphasize the highlights. Submit the report to Hudson A. Hill, President.

23. Reporting on international franchise operations. In your job as a research associate for Caldwell Research, Inc., you have been assigned the task of getting information for the Continental Franchise Association. Officers of this organization of Canadian and U.S. franchise owners want information on the expansion of association members into foreign markets and the factors and problems involved in such expansion.

You gather the data for this study by sending questionnaires to the 221 member firms. Sixty-three responded (representing 46,280 franchise units).

The questionnaire was designed to get six areas of information. First you sought to classify the firms by type of franchise (automotive, fast-food, soft drink, and such). Second, you asked for information on the firms' expansion plans—that is, how many and what ownership forms of new units do they plan to open in the next three years. Third, you ask for reasons why some of the firms had no plans for international expansion. Fourth, from those firms with expansion plans, you sought to determine why they elected to get into foreign markets. Fifth, you tried to determine the major problems encountered by firms engaged in foreign franchise operations, current and planned. And sixth, you sought to learn where were the foreign franchise operations, current and planned.

The information you have gathered is exhaustive. All of it will go in a long, analytical report, which you will write later. However, because the board wants a preview of findings right away, you will present only the highlights in a summary report. And you will get the report to the board in time for their quarterly meeting next Monday.

For this report you have assembled the key information in Tables 15 through 20. Now you must analyze this information and organize it for presentation. Address the report to the Board of Directors, Wilma Neeley, Chairperson. Give the report the formal preparatory pages its length and formality justify.

TABLE 15. Classification by respondents' firms by type of franchise system

Type of franchise system	Respondents Number	Percent
Automotive services	2	3.2
Business services	8	12.7
Car rentals	1	1.6
Recreation services	3	4.8
Fast foods	22	34.9
Retailing (food)	3	4.8
Hotels/motels	6	9.5
Soft drinks	—	—
Other	18	28.5
Total respondents	63	100.0

TABLE 16. Number of units planned in next three years (by location and ownership form)

Location	Ownership form Franchisee-owned (no.)	Master or area (no.)	Company-owned (no.)	Joint venture franchisee/majority (no.)	Joint venture franchisee/minority (no.)	Total Number	Percent
In United States and Canada . . .	12,576	129	713	24	32	13,474	83.17
In foreign countries	1,932	616	110	24	45	2,727	16.83
Total number . . .	14,508	745	823	48	77	16,201	
Total percent	89.55	4.60	5.08	0.30	0.47		100.0

TABLE 17. Reasons for no franchises at present in foreign countries

	Reason	Respondents Number	Percent
1.	Government or legal restrictions	14	32.6
2.	Insufficient foreign demand for products (good and/or services)	8	18.6
3.	Lack of market information	16	37.2
4.	Trademark and/or copyright obstacles	2	4.7
5.	Products not adapted to foreign consumers	3	7.0
6.	Excessive geographic distance	20	46.5
7.	Other	13	30.2
	Total respondents	43*	—

* Multiple answers given by some.

TABLE 18.   Reasons for involvement in franchise activities in foreign countries

		Respondents	
	Major problem	*Number*	*Percent*
1.	Increase sales and profits	21	77.8
2.	Returns on investment usually greater than that from domestic operations	2	7.4
3.	Saturated U.S. market for firm's products	1	3.7
4.	Market expansion	22	81.5
5.	Acquisition	1	3.7
6.	Desire to be known as an international firm	14	51.9
7.	Other	3	11.1
Total respondents		27*	—

* Multiple answers given by some.

TABLE 19.   Major problems encountered in establishing franchises in foreign countries (for firms currently engaged in foreign franchise activities)

		Respondents	
	Reason	*Number*	*Percent*
1.	Host government regulations	17	68.0
2.	Patent, trademark, and/or copyright protection	7	28.0
3.	Inadequate local financing	4	16.0
4.	Control of franchisees	8	32.0
5.	Recruitment of franchisees	5	20.0
6.	Adaption of products to local markets	2	8.0
7.	Adaption of franchise package to local markets	4	16.0
8.	High import duties and taxes	9	36.0
9.	Location problems	3	12.0
10.	Training of foreign franchisee personnel	6	24.0
11.	Logistics problems	7	28.0
12.	Language and cultural barriers	9	36.0
13.	Monetary uncertainties and royalty retribution to franchisor	11	44.0
14.	Other	3	12.0
Total respondents		25*	—

* Multiple answers given by some.

TABLE 20.   Location of franchise units, current and planned

	Current	*Planned**
United States and Canada	44,894	14,461
England	481	668
Japan	663	578
West Germany	177	141
France	88	57
Italy	39	31
Remainder of continental Europe	61	88
Other	417	177
Total	46,820	16,201

* Next three years.

24.   Reporting on the status of women in Granite's sales force.   Seven years ago the executives of Granite, Inc., a large marketer of industrial goods, decided to bring women into its sales force "as quickly and expeditiously as possible." Now they want a progress report. In general, management wants an overall picture of the status of women in the Granite sales force. More specifically, they want the answers to questions such as how many women have been hired, what are their characteristics, and how successful they have been.

As administrative assistant to Marvin Stutts, vice president of sales, you have been assigned the chore of doing the reporting. You begin by going through personnel records for each of Granite's 13 sales regions. First, you gather comparative information on the number of men and women salespeople now and for the same time seven years ago (Table 21). Then from the same source you get comparative information of absenteeism and turnover (Table 22), sales experience (Table 23), and personal details (Table 24). Next you go to the sales records file for data on sales performance (Table 25).

TABLE 21.   Number of men and women employed in sales, by region, current year, and seven years ago

	Current year		Seven years ago	
Sales region	Men	Women	Men	Women
A	14	3	11	0
B	19	1	16	0
C	77	12	70	2
D	43	5	39	2
E	92	24	87	1
F	37	10	33	2
G	23	3	19	0
H	51	7	48	1
I	28	3	27	0
J	49	6	43	2
K	35	3	33	1
L	59	17	50	1
M	67	5	61	0
Total	594	99	537	12

TABLE 22. . Absenteeism and turnover, by sex (preceding year)

	Men	Women
Absenteeism (days):		
None	27%	14%
1–5	62	48
6–10	6	29
11–15	4	7
16+	1	2
	100%	100%
Turnover:		
Employees	11.5%	5.4%

TABLE 23. Years of industrial sales experience*
(percent of total male and female)

Years of experience	Men	Women
0–5	13	37
6–10	26	26
11–15	24	17
16–20	19	19
21–25	11	1
Over 25	7	0

TABLE 24. Profile of salespeople (percent)

	Men	Women
Age:		
Under 25	11	27
26–35	34	54
36–50	40	19
Over 50	15	0
Marital status:		
Married	81	16
Divorced, widowed, separated	9	25
Single	10	59
Education (year completed, 12 = high school):		
12	8	0
13	13	0
14	19	16
15	12	12
16	48	69
Over 16	0	3

TABLE 25. Sales performance of men and women meeting or exceeding annual quota (percent)

Percent of annual quota met	Men	Women
130 and over	9	2
120–129	7	9
110–119	18	23
100–110	47	51
90–99	9	11
80–89	8	4
70–79	1	0
Under 70	1	0

In your judgment, information on customer impressions also is essential; so you conduct brief telephone interviews with 302 Granite customers. It appears that your findings (Table 26) give a clear measure of customer viewpoints toward women in selling. You conduct similar interviews among company sales executives.

Now, with all this information tabulated neatly before you, you are ready to

278

TABLE 26. Opinions of sales executives* and customers about overall performance of men and women salespeople (percent)

	Sales executives	Customers† served only by men	Customers† served by one or more women‡
Believe men perform better	23	3	9
Little or no difference	74	75	80
Believe women perform better	7	2	11
Believe men employees cause more problems	10		
Little or no difference	68		
Believe women employees cause more problems	22		

* 13 regional managers and 37 district managers, all men, all supervising one or more women.
† 99 percent men.
‡ Not necessarily women salespeople from Granite.

begin work on the report. Because the report will be read by top management, you will give it the appropriate formal trappings (as specified by your instructor). Address it to Mr. Stutts.

25. Determining the meaning given to nonverbal behavior by interview participants. At last year's meeting of the Personnel Offices Association controversy developed over how nonverbal behavior of job applicants should be interpreted. Opinions varied widely on the topic. In fact, the controversy continued on into the meeting of the board of directors, which concluded the conference. Thus it was that the board members voted to provide the necessary funds and authorized you, its executive director, to conduct a study on the subject.

Soon after the meeting you began the work. First, you designed a questionnaire covering ten statements concerning key attitudes toward nonverbal behavior. The design organized answers by degrees of respondent's agreement with the statements. Next, you mailed two copies of the questionnaire to each of 500 members randomly selected from the association's mailing list of personnel officers (not the association's membership roster, although some on the list are members).[1]

Those receiving the questionnaires were instructed to complete and return one of the two copies and to give the other to a person whom they had interviewed and hired recently. This person also was instructed to complete and return the questionnaire. After receiving 400 usable responses (200 from interviewers and 200 from interviewees), you tabulated the findings. Although you are not convinced that it is meaningful, you organized the responses by sex. Finally you arranged your findings in an orderly table (Table 27).

[1] Actually the data are from Jack D. Eure and Joan Baron, "Nonverbal Cues and the Perceptions of Intelligence in the Employment Interview," *Proceedings of the 1980 Southwest American Business Communication Association Meeting,* San Antonio, Texas.

TABLE 27. Attitudes toward nonverbal behavior in the employment interview (percent)

Attitude statement		Strongly disagree E	Strongly disagree S	Disagree E	Disagree S	No Opinion E	No Opinion S	Agree E	Agree S	Strongly agree E	Strongly agree S
1. A good indicator of intelligence is the length of time a person can hold eye contact during interview.	M	29	18	50	48	21	14	0	20	0	0
	F	13	18	55	46	13	9	19	27	0	0
2. Applicants who lean forward during the interview are more assertive.	M	0	4	43	40	21	16	36	38	0	2
	F	0	0	75	14	6	5	19	73	0	9
3. Facial twitches are signs of insecurity	M	7	4	50	30	29	40	14	20	0	6
	F	6	14	62	55	13	18	13	9	6	5
4. Repeated eyebrow movement indicates a short attention span.	M	14	10	58	64	14	14	14	12	0	0
	F	0	14	63	68	31	18	6	0	0	0
5. Frequent hand gestures indicate a high level of energy.	M	7	6	50	28	0	14	43	46	0	6
	F	0	0	38	14	6	14	43	77	13	0
6. Constant fidgeting by the applicant indicates a lack of self-confidence.	M	7	0	21	26	14	4	50	58	7	12
	F	0	0	37	27	6	5	44	55	13	14
7. Interviewees exhibiting fewer eye shifts are more likely to have greater credibility.	M	14	6	29	28	14	18	43	34	0	14
	F	0	9	37	23	13	23	37	46	13	0
8. Frequent smiling during the interview indicates a friendly personality.	M	7	0	22	10	7	14	50	62	14	14
	F	0	0	38	18	0	0	56	50	6	32
9. Applicants who nod their head during the interview are more attentive.	M	7	4	36	34	14	10	36	50	7	2
	F	0	0	31	14	25	18	44	59	0	9
10. A good indicator of character is the applicant's appearance.	M	0	2	28	12	0	6	36	50	36	30
	F	0	0	25	5	0	5	50	55	25	36

Note: M—male; F—female; E—employee; S—student.

Now you are ready to begin the task of analyzing and organizing the findings for presentation in a report. The report will be rather formal; so you will give it appropriate prefatory sections. Probably you will make good use of visual aids, as the information is quantitative. Probably in time the content of the report will be printed in monograph form and distributed to the membership. For the moment, however, you are submitting information to the board. So address the report to the Board of Directors, Ms. Elizabeth Kipper, Chairperson.

26. Interpreting survey results for Giant's advertising department. As assistant to the director, advertising department, Giant Soap and Glycerine, Inc. of Omaha, you are faced with the task of presenting and interpreting some survey statistics. The statistics were given to you by William A. Kennard, director, who had received them from the research department. Kennard's instructions to you were both brief and precise.

"Here are some figures Research handed me," he said. "They're a part of Research's most recent survey—the part they say we should be interested in. Look them over, digest them, and then tell me what they mean to us in advertising. Have it ready for me before our departmental meeting Friday. Better write it up for the record."

The data (Tables 28–31) are quite significant, for they tell what the consumers think of Giant. Giant, of course, is the company's leading product and ranks among the nation's leading detergents. The statistics tell a lot, too, about the image the buyers have of each of Giant's major competitors. It is your job now to present

TABLE 28. Percentages of households using leading brands of detergents, by use (based on national sample of 1,000)

Brand name	For dishes	For fine fabrics	For laundry
White	220	312	92
Snow	131	94	—
Giant	112	56	251
Surf	83	40	73
Eze	76	—	64
Del	51	261	—
Kleen	—	—	132
Sun	—	—	121

TABLE 29. Major reasons given for liking six leading brands for washing dishes (samples of 100 for each brand)

Reason for liking	White	Snow	Giant	Surf	Eze	Del
Amount of suds	16	8	14	9	19	13
Superior cleaning	13	16	11	36	9	19
Mild on hands	21	2	19	9	0	34
Pleasant odor	0	1	15	0	6	0
Economical	3	0	21	0	0	0

TABLE 30.   Major reasons given for liking five leading brands for washing fine fabrics, hand wash (samples of 100 for each brand)

Reason for liking	White	Snow	Giant	Surf	Del
Right amount of suds	14	11	15	10	14
Superior cleaning	13	12	24	41	12
Mild on hands	62	29	19	11	52
Mild on clothes	51	24	23	14	50
Pleasant odor	3	1	15	0	0
Economical	4	0	22	0	0

TABLE 31.   Major reasons given for liking six leading brands for regular laundry, automatic washer (samples of 100 for each brand)

Reason for liking	White	Giant	Surf	Eze	Kleen	Sun
Amount of suds	33	34	32	15	17	44
Superior cleaning	36	38	39	55	61	67
Mild on clothes	55	52	40	7	3	2
Economical	0	37	0	0	19	0

this information to Mr. Kennard in good orderly fashion pointing out those things which are significant from an advertising point of view.

In analyzing the data, you will want to keep in mind the general advertising Giant has had in recent years. For years the company has promoted Giant as a mild yet extremely effective all-around cleaner—good for dishes as well as for fine and regular fabrics. Giant advertising campaigns have stressed two primary appeals. They have stressed the mildness which makes Giant safe for delicate hands and for the most delicate fabrics. And they have stressed Giant's strong cleaning power—strong enough, they say, to make the dirtiest work clothes come clean without scrubbing. Perhaps the data will show the effectiveness of these claims; or maybe they will point out other appeals which have not yet been used. At least the data will show what consumers like in a soap or detergent.

You plan to write the report in your company's short-report form—title page and text proper, with captions. Because Mr. Kennard likes his facts fast, you consider presenting the conclusions first—or perhaps you will have a brief summary at the report's beginning. Because this is a subsidiary report to the main one Research will present on the survey, there is no need for you to present a description of the research methodology used.

27.   Will contest bring profits to Food King?   John H. Gromman, newly appointed advertising and promotion manager for Food King, Inc., has an idea for increasing sales and thereby increasing profits, for the chain of 142 stores. He thinks that contests at each store, with an abundance of prizes, would more than pay off. Such contests, he concludes, have been tried by other stores—and they appeared to work.

Janice Clemmons, however, does not think very much of the plan; and Janice

Clemmons happens to be Food King's president. So to prove or disprove the value of contests, Ms. Clemmons suggests that the company conduct an experiment. You, as director of research, get the assignment.

The first step is to devise a contest for the experiment. With Gromman's assistance, you settle on a contest involving a simple drawing for prizes. With each purchase of $10 or more, the customers receive entry blanks, which they endorse and deposit in a large box. Drawings are made weekly to determine the winners of such prizes as washing machines, radios, electric mixers, and toasters.

For your experiment you select two comparable and homogeneous groups of five stores—one group as the experimental group and the other as a control group. In one group of stores (Group A) contests are held; none are held in the other stores (Group B). After one month of contests, with weekly drawings and prizes galore, the contests are stopped. Because you believe the contests may have some long-run effect on sales, you decide to analyze operations for the following months. You later find three months to be adequate. Now you assemble the data in preparation for your analysis.

Although you considered using a variety of data (traffic flow, size and numbers of purchases; cost of the contests) you conclude that net profits tell the whole story in summary fashion. The profit figures you assembled are in Table 32.

TABLE 32. Net profits ($000)

Store		Month before contests	Month of contests	Month after	Second month after	Third month after
A	1	32	29	39	34	32
	2	31	27	38	33	30
	3	30	27	33	31	31
	4	33	25	37	34	33
	5	30	28	38	31	29
B	6	29	30	31	30	32
	7	30	32	31	30	30
	8	31	31	30	30	32
	9	33	34	33	32	32
	10	30	31	31	30	30

Write up your analysis of these data, and then conclude from your analysis. Write up your work in a form that is appropriate for this situation.

28. What will business be like during the months ahead? As assistant to the president, De Berry Stores, Inc., you have drawn the assignment of writing a consensus forecast to be presented at the meeting of the board next Wednesday. President Nadine De Berry of this chain of 24 major department stores in the East and Midwest gave you the assignment personally. The company does not employ an economist. De Berry does not believe in such "frills." "Why should we pay for them," she says, "when we can get free forecasts of all the top economists merely by reading through current periodicals."

Ms. De Berry's instructions, as usual, were quite vague; so much of what you will do is left to your good judgment. All she said was that she wants you to survey the predictions of the nation's leading economic forecasters for the months ahead and to present your findings in a clear and meaningful report to the board. She wants the forecasts consolidated as much as it is practical—that is, she does not want merely a succession of individual forecasts. Your coverage will, of course, be largely of a general nature, covering all of the country's economy. But you will give special emphasis to whatever information you can find pertaining especially to department stores and to the eastern and midwestern regions.

In good short-report form your report will begin with a title page. Because the board will want the facts quickly, you will include a fast-moving synopsis. Whether you will need additional prefatory parts will depend on how voluminous your presentation turns out to be.

29.   Should Sage change its formula?   Your employer, E. O. Struman, Inc., has for two generations manufactured a leading line of men's toiletries. During the past few years the company has watched its share of the market diminish. Much of the sales loss, Struman management believes, is a result of the company's failure to change formulas of its products. With only minor exception, Struman products today are the same as they were the day they were introduced. And some were introduced over 40 years ago.

About a year ago, following a reorganization of its management, Struman began a program of product improvement. Its laboratories, heretofore concerned with new product development and production testing, began serious efforts to change the existing products. And to test consumer reaction to their developments, they brought in a research analyst. You are that analyst.

Your first assignment in this capacity is to test a change in formula for Sage, the firm's leading cologne for men. The new formula for this product includes a chemical which produces a cooling, tingling sensation to the skin—something the old formula did not have. According to news in the trade, this sensation is well liked and has been responsible for increased sales of some of Struman's competitors. You have no authentic proof of this effect; so you will need to conduct your own research on the subject.

In order to test the new product you designed a primary research project. You constructed a controlled sample of 500 men carefully selected to represent the male users of cologne. You used ages and education as your primary controls. Then your carefully selected and trained investigators approached the men selected; and they determined how each man rated the new product with the old. Each participant was asked to use each product alternately for a two-week period. After this period an interviewer approached each participant and through questioning determined his reactions to the two products.

Now the results are in and are neatly tabulated and arranged in Tables 33–36. It is time to analyze them and to report your findings to the firm's management. Your major problem, of course, is to advise management on the critical question of whether to change to the new formula. But your analysis of the reasons why men like and disike the two products should be helpful in promoting the products;

TABLE 33. Comparison of preferences for new and old formulas for Sage

	Number preferring new Sage	Number preferring old Sage	Number with no preference
Overall preference	273	210	17
Odor preference	168	313	19
Preference for effect on skin	317	166	17

TABLE 34. Answers to question "What, if anything, do you like about each product?"

	New Sage	Old Sage
Odor:		
Mild	34	0
Strong	0	87
Pleasant	109	207
Other comments about odor	23	13
Skin effect, stimulating:		
Invigorating	134	0
Refreshing	83	23
Other	37	3
Skin effect, comforting:		
Soothing effects	7	96
Doesn't burn, mild	0	82
Cooling effect	93	0
Other	17	23

TABLE 35. Answers to question "What, if anything, don't you like about each product?"

	New Sage	Old Sage
Odor:		
Weak	62	3
Strong	17	69
Dislike (in general)	194	48
Other comments about odor	17	23
Harsh effect on skin:		
Stings	66	0
Burns	51	0
Other comments	13	3
Not enough effect on skin:		
Little or no feeling	0	119
Other comments	5	17

Note: As each respondent could give any number of answers (0, 1, 2, 3, etc.), the totals do not equal 500.

so you will want to emphasize these points en route to your conclusion. You will present your report in a form suitable for top management. Because most of the readers will have little interest in the specific details of your methodology, your introduction will contain only a brief description of method. Address the report to Y. A. Ferguson, President.

TABLE 36.   Answers to questions "What brand of cologne are you now using?" and "How do the two colognes you have sampled compare with your present brand?"

Brand	Number using	Comparison of Sage (new) with present brand			Comparison of Sage (old) with present brand		
		Prefer Sage (new)	*Prefer present brand*	*Like about same*	*Prefer Sage (old)*	*Prefer present brand*	*Like about same*
Sage (old)	118	7	86	25	—	—	—
Royal Purple*	104	21	32	51	2	100	2
Gentry*	86	16	24	46	0	83	3
Sir*	51	9	19	23	2	46	3
Mystic Knight	44	3	40	1	7	21	16
Seven Seas	24	2	18	4	3	13	8
Others	43	4	35	4	8	21	14
Others*	30	7	9	14	0	28	2
Total	500	69	263	168	22	312	48

* Contains chemicals which produce skin tingling effects.

30.   Advising the board on the question of using deal campaigns to help sell food products.   At last week's meeting of the board of directors, Warner Foods, Inc., the major topic of concern was Warner's sagging sales of margarine, shortening, and oils. During the past six months the firm's two major competitors made substantial gains at Warner's expense. So far as Warner can determine, the gains were made through aggressive selling and promotion—factors which the Warner's sales staff feels that it can adjust to. But such adjustments take time. What the Warner directors want now is somehing that will pick up the lost ground in a hurry.

One possible approach, as some of the directors view the situation, is to begin a series of deal campaigns with each product. "Deals" are any form of coupon, gift, or gimmick arrangement designed to stimulate sales. For example, coupons giving a discount on the purchase price of a product may be mass mailed to consumers; or gift certificates may be packed within a product's container. The possible variations are many. They all have one thing in common, however. They are costly, frequently to the point of causing temporary losses. They are effective only if they can cultivate repeat customers.

Although Warner has never used deal campaigns, their competitors have used them extensively. And so have many other manufacturers of foods and other household products. Over the years, however, Warner management has viewed deal campaigns with a high degree of skepticism, especially since Warner products are high in quality and price and appeal to the higher income and social groups.

Because the directors are skeptical about deal campaigns, they are reluctant to begin them without knowing more about them. So, in an effort to become better informed, they have called on the research department for help. You, the senior research specialist, have been given the assignment.

As board chairman Peter Darwin explained it to you, your assignment is to gather the best available information on effectiveness of deals. The board will expect your recommendation, too; but you may wish to qualify it since you are not going into the financial aspects of the problem in detail. Also, any consideration of the financial aspects would depend on the nature of the specific campaign selected.

The board meets again in about two weeks; so there isn't time for primary research. Secondary research will have to be used. After a few hours of fruitless work you give up on your company library; but you find exactly what you want at a nearby university library. It is a report conducted just last year by Professor Mary Cook at Midlands University. In her somewhat brief but information packed tables (Tables 37–39) you see the basis of your analysis.

TABLE 37. Margarine, shortening, and oils (Percent of families reporting specified number of deals and percent of total deals accounted for in each category, during July 198X, Saint Louis, Missouri)

Number of deals per family	Margarine		Shortening		Oils	
	Dealing families	Portion of total deals	Dealing families	Portion of total deals	Dealing families	Portion of total deals
1	29.6	6.6	34.5	11.3	60.2	35.7
2	23.5	10.4	19.5	12.8	24.5	29.1
3	10.7	7.1	17.2	17.0	7.7	13.6
4	8.6	7.7	6.9	9.0	3.4	8.0
5	4.5	5.0	6.9	11.3	3.4	10.1
6	4.1	5.5	6.1	12.1	—	—
7	4.1	6.4	1.1	2.6	0.8	3.5
8	1.7	2.9	2.7	7.1	—	—
9	1.7	3.3	2.7	7.9	—	—
10	1.2	2.8	0.4	1.2	—	—
11	0.4	1.0	0.4	1.4	—	—
12 or more	9.9	41.3	1.6	6.3	—	—
Total	100.0	100.0	100.0	100.0	100.0	100.0

TABLE 38. Sales increases attributed to deal campaigns and effect of campaigns on profits (average [mean] of six companies, one campaign each)

	Percent higher than before campaign
Sales during campaigns	16.3
Sales after campaigns (months):	
1	9.1
3	5.9
6	3.6
12	1.8

Note: Net profit before and after campaign, 5.1 percent of gross sales; net profit during campaign, 2.1 percent of gross sales.

TABLE 39. Dealing and nondealing households by characteristics (percent)

Household characteristics	Buying households		Purchases by dealing households		Purchases by all households	
	Dealing households	Nondealing households	Deal (pounds)	Nondeal (pounds)	Deal (pounds)	Nondeal (pounds)
Race and nationality:						
Native white	54	46	10.0	90.0	6.4	93.6
Foreign-born white	51	49	10.1	89.9	6.0	94.0
Nonwhite	22	78	5.7	94.3	1.6	98.4
Income:						
Low (under $12,000)	39	61	10.0	90.0	4.8	95.2
Medium ($12,000–$25,000)	55	45	9.4	90.6	6.0	94.0
High (over $25,000)	53	47	9.9	90.1	6.1	93.9
Size of household:						
Small (1 or 2 persons)	39	61	14.1	85.9	7.0	93.0
Medium (3 or 4 persons)	53	47	8.9	91.1	5.4	94.6
Large (5 or more persons)	55	45	8.5	91.5	5.1	94.9
Education:						
8 years or less	43	57	11.0	89.0	5.3	94.7
9–12 years	47	53	7.9	92.1	4.4	95.6
13 years or more	59	41	11.6	88.4	8.5	91.5
Age of housewife:						
Under 45 years	54	46	9.2	90.8	5.8	94.2
45–64 years	44	56	11.0	89.0	5.9	94.1
65 years or older	38	62	10.8	89.2	4.4	95.6

288

After you have studied the data and made your analysis, prepare the report for the board. Give the report whatever formality the board is likely to expect; and since the information is largely quantitative, you will support your presentation with appropriate graphic aids.

31.   Solving a problem on your campus (Requires additional research.)   On all college campuses some common problems exist. At least, they exist in the minds of many of the faculty, students, and staff. From the list of problem areas which follows, select one which you regard as a problem at your institution.

For the problem that you select, you will first gather all of the significant information which concerns it. When you are thoroughly acquainted with the facts of your problem you will gather whatever authoritative information you can concerning how it might be solved. Perhaps your research will involve looking through bibliographical sources to find out what has been done on other campuses. It may involve getting information or opinions from the various people on campus who are involved in the problem. When you have all this information, you will carefully analyze your problem in the light of all available knowledge. Then you will arrive at a recommended solution.

So that the situation will appear to be realistic you may assume whatever role or position at your college that is appropriate. Present your work in appropriate report form.

Your problem area possibilities are as follows (some are broad and will need to be made specific):

Traffic regulation and control.
Fire prevention.
Safety on campus.
Crime prevention on campus.
Scholastic honesty.
Attendance policies.
Orientation of new students.
Registration procedures.
Student government.
Grades (appeal procedures, grade inflation).
Faculty-student relations.
Dress and grooming.
Library operations.

LONG PROBLEMS

32.   Searching for unique characteristics of retail executives.   Is there commonality in the backgrounds and characteristics of executives in retail and non-retail companies? This is the question you must answer for the National Retail Merchants Association.

As director of research for the association, you have just completed an extensive survey.[1] Your goal was to gather information which will guide the association's members in selecting personnel for future executive assignments. It would be helpful if the members know whether retail executives are special types or much like other executives. Your survey was designed to do just that; and you think you have been successful.

With your findings neatly summarized before you, your next step is to analyze them for their meaning to your problem. Then you will organize your findings and analyses into the pattern that will produce the most logical and efficient presentation. Certainly you will want to do more than just present a long succession of questions and answers (which is the form your findings are in now). Perhaps you can find some means of arranging the survey questions on the basis of broad types of information involved.

Your analyses will produce an answer to the basic question of whether retail executives are unique. And if they are, it will end with a summary of the major differences—information that retailers can use in selecting people for management training.

The finished report will be rather formal, for it will be duplicated in mass and sent to the membership. It will contain the traditional prefatory parts. But rather than a letter of transmittal, it will have a preface.

Following is a summary of the findings:

Q. How many years have you been employed by your current company?

Average	Nonretail	Retail
19	14.5	23

Q. How many different companies have you worked for during your business career?

Number of companies	Nonretail	Retail
1	26%	23%
2	19	15
3	23	24
4	27	30
5 or more	5	8

Q. If you have worked for more than one company, which factors were most influential in your decision to change positions?

	Nonretail	Retail
Better compensation package	32%	42%
More desirable location	7	3
Increased responsibility	44	48
Increased status	6	5
Increased creativity	9	9
Increased challenge	42	48
More rapid advancement	19	17

---

[1] Actually the survey results presented were gathered by Korn-Frey International, and the UCLA Graduate School of Management. The actual survey comprised responses from 1,708 executives from a cross section of American businesses.

Q. In which functional area did you begin your career?

	Nonretail	Retail
Finance/accounting	28%	26%
Marketing/sales	19	35
Personnel	4	4
Professional/technical	31	16
Production/manufacturing	9	8
International	1	0
General management	4	5
No response	4	6

Q. What is your current functional area?

	Nonretail	Retail
Finance/accounting	22%	19%
Marketing/sales	8	10
Personnel	7	10
Professional/technical	12	15
Production/manufacturing	2	0
International	2	2
General management	44	41
No response	3	3

Q. Which functional area do you believe is currently the "fastest route to the top"? Which one will be in ten years?

	Current		Ten years	
	Nonretail	Retail	Nonretail	Retail
Finance/accounting	33%	32%	30%	35%
Marketing/sales	31	47	20	30
Personnel	0	0	1	2
Professional/technical	7	1	10	7
Production/manufacturing	4	0	4	0
International	2	1	4	2
General management	18	18	23	22
No response	5	1	8	2

Q. Has your workweek increased, decreased, or remained the same over the past ten years?

	Nonretail	Retail
Increased	40%	34%
Decreased	15	15
Remained the same	45	52

Q. Has your business travel time increased, decreased, or remained the same over the past ten years?

	Nonretail	Retail
Increased	47%	52%
Decreased	27	25
Remained the same	26	23

Q. Have you ever been transferred overseas during your business career?

	Nonretail	Retail
Yes	11%	5%
No	89	95

Q. Do you consider overseas business experience valuable in terms of professional growth?

	Nonretail	Retail
Yes	64%	45%
No	34	52
No response	2	3

Q. Have you ever taken a leave of absence from the business community in order to participate in nonmilitary government service?

	Nonretail	Retail
Yes	2%	3%
No	97	97
No response	1	0

Q. Do you believe that government service enhances one's chances for corporate success?

	Nonretail	Retail
Yes	24%	20%
No	74	79
No response	2	1

Q. Has your interest in participating in government service increased, decreased, or remained the same over the past ten years?

	Nonretail	Retail
Increased	21%	25%
Decreased	28	23
Remained the same	49	51
No response	2	1

Q. Is your present position the highest to which you aspire?

	Nonretail	Retail
Yes	67%	61%
No	33	39

Q. If you were financially independent, would you continue in your present position?

	Nonretail	Retail
Yes	68%	75%
No	31	23
No response	1	2

Q. When do you wish to retire?

	Nonretail	Retail
Before age 65	48%	49%
At age 65	31	24
At age 70	4	3
Work as long as possible	17	23
No response	0	1

Q. If you were starting over, would you pursue the same career, a similar career, or a different career?

	Nonretail	Retail
Same	60%	60%
Similar	28	28
Different	12	12

Q. In retrospect, was your formal education worthwhile as it applies to your career?

	Nonretail	Retail
Not worthwhile	1%	1%
Somewhat worthwhile	24	29
Very worthwhile	75	70

Q. In general, do you believe the chances for advancement are greater for the executive who remains with one company for his or her entire career?

	Nonretail	Retail
Yes	27%	30%
No	71	68
No response	2	2

Q. In general, do you believe the "it's who you know, not what you know" theory of career advancement is still valid?

	Nonretail	Retail
Yes	16%	18%
No	83	82
No response	1	0

Q. In general, which traits do you believe enhance an executive's chances for success?

	Nonretail	Retail
Creativity	45%	46%
Desire for responsibility	58	56
Concern for people	49	56
Concern for results	74	75
Ambition	38	45
Integrity	66	56
Loyalty	23	28
Aggressiveness	36	39
Appearance	15	18
Social adaptability	16	17
Exceptional intelligence	20	20

Q. Which level of education have you attained?

	Nonretail	Retail
No college degree	8%	13%
College degree	85	81
Graduate degree	43	33

Q. If you have a college degree, is it a B.A. or a B.S.

	Nonretail	Retail
B.A.	66%	74%
B.S.	34	26

Q. From what type of undergraduate institution did you receive your degree?

	Nonretail	Retail
Small private	29%	24%
Large private	24	27
Small public	9	9
Large public	31	40

Q. From what type of graduate institution did you receive your degree?

	Nonretail	Retail
Small private	13%	14%
Large private	52	49
Small public	4	3
Large public	31	35

Q. Were you employed during your undergraduate education?

	Nonretail	Retail
Yes	68%	68%
No	27	23
No response	5	9

Q. In what region did you spend the major portion of your childhood?

	Nonretail	Retail
Northeast	33%	25%
Southeast	9	9
Midwest	38	39
Southwest	7	10
West	9	16
Other	4	3

Q. In what locality did you spend the major portion of your childhood?

	Nonretail	Retail
Urban	42%	39%
Suburban	34	31
Rural	20	25
No response	5	5

Q. Which of your parents did you live with during your childhood?

	Nonretail	Retail
Father only	1%	0%
Mother only	8	10
Both	89	88
Neither	1	2
No response	1	0

Q. How would you classify your parent's occupations during your childhood?

(Father)	Nonretail	Retail
Professional/technical	22%	18%
Managerial	23	25
Clerical	4	3
Sole proprietor	17	13
Blue collar	21	23
Did not work outside home	0	0
Other	7	7
No response	6	11

Q. Were you an only child, first child, middle child, or last child?

	Nonretail	Retail
Only child	14%	11%
First Child	34	37
Middle child	22	18
Last child	29	33
No response	1	1

Q. Was your precollege education primarily public, parochial or other private?

	Nonretail	Retail
Public	79%	82%
Parochial	12	11
Other private	8	7
No response	7	0

Q. Please indicate your age.

	Nonretail	Retail
Over 60	19%	25%
59–50	48	40
49–40	29	28
Below 40	4	6
No response	0	1

Q. Sex

The nonretail is 99 percent male. Retail is 98 percent male.

Q. Marital status

Both the nonretail and the retail groups are 95 percent married.

Q. Number of children

Both the nonretail and the retail groups have an average of three children, but 8 percent of the nonretail group have one or less children, while 17 percent of the retail respondents have one or less children.

Q. Have you been married more than once?

	Nonretail	Retail
Yes	11%	12%
No	89	88

Q. If currently married, is your spouse employed?

	Nonretail	Retail
Full-time	5% .	7%
Part-time	9	16
Not employed	82	73
No response	4	4

Q. Within the past five years, do you find yourself devoting more time to leisure activities?

	Nonretail	Retail
Yes	32%	28%
No	68	72

Q. Do you feel that you are able to spend an adequate amount of time with your family?

	Nonretail	Retail
Yes	67%	66%
No	32	34
No response	1	0

Q. How important is religion in your daily life?

	Nonretail	Retail
No importance	14%	16%
Limited important	28	18
Moderate importance	34	46
Significant importance	24	20

Q. Religion

	Nonretail	Retail
Protestant	68%	70%
Catholic	22	14
Jewish	6	13
Other	3	3
No response	1	0

Q. On social issues, how do you consider yourself politically?

	Nonretail	Retail
Conservative	74%	61%
Moderate	25	39
Liberal	1	0

Q. What is your political affiliation?

	Nonretail	Retail
Democrat	13%	15%
Republican	68	61
Independent	18	24
No response	1	0

Q. Do you vote regularly?

	Nonretail	Retail
Yes	95%	93%
No	4	7
No response	1	0

Q. How often do you drink?

	Nonretail	Retail
Never	5%	3%
Seldom	16	28
Moderately	63	53
Often	15	13
Very often	2	3

Q. How often do you smoke?

	Nonretail	Retail
Never	58%	61%
Seldom	9	10
Moderately	13	8
Often	13	17
Very often	6	4
No response	1	0

Q. How often do you use tranquilizers?

	Nonretail	Retail
Never	87%	85%
Seldom	10	9
Moderately	2	5
Often	0	0
Very often	0	0
No response	1	1

Q. Compensation—base salary plus bonus.

	Nonretail	Retail
Under $100,000	53%	47%
$100,000–150,000	27	27
$150,000–200,000	11	21
$200,000–250,000	7	11
$Over $250,000	5	11

Note: Rounding sometimes produces totals not precisely 100 percent.

33.   Determining preretirement and retirement practices.   Assume the role of research director for the National Association of Administrators. Your current assignment is to conduct a study of preretirement, retirement, and postretirement practices of the nation's organizations. More specifically, your objective is to get answers to questions such as what are organizations doing to prepare employees for retirement, what do they do for employees at retirement, and what relations do they have with retirees after retirement.

The information you gather will go to the membership in a report to the organization's members. Primarily, the report will be informational, but it will contain some analyses; and it will make whatever conclusions the analyses support.

In your search for the information, you conducted a mail survey of 474 organizations representing the association's membership. You received 267 usuable responses, 47 percent being manufacturing, 31 percent being nonmanufacturing, and 22 percent being nonbusiness organizations (hospitals, universities, government agencies, and such). In your attempt to distinguish among organizations by size, you classified employers of 1,000 or more as large and employers of fewer than 1,000 as small. Based on this classification plan, approximately 40 percent of your respondents were large and 60 percent were small.

You have tabulated your results (Tables 40–45)[1] and are ready to construct the report that will present them. As the report will be written for the total membership, you will give it the appropriate formal parts. You will need to decide whether to use a preface rather than a letter of transmittal. Because the information to be presented is quantitative, you will use graphic aids wherever they help to communicate.

34.   Evaluating the performance of a college dean.   Place yourself in the position of assistant dean in the College of Business Administration, Wayward University. Your boss, Dean Alonzo K. Cuevas, is very much concerned with his faculty's perception of his performance. A man who only recently entered the academic field after a highly successful career in business, Dean Cuevas wants badly to know his strengths. He wants even more to know his shortcomings so that he can correct them. So, to get this information, he asks you to conduct a survey of the full-time faculty that will reveal the information he seeks.

After long and diligent effort and much consulting with various experts on the faculty, you produced a survey instrument consisting of 31 statements. The statements covered key areas of performance. Responses to each statement are based on the extent to which the faculty members agree. The questionnaire provides for five levels of agreement.

After two weeks of persuasively requesting the faculty to respond, you were able to obtain 68 usable responses (out of a possible 87). Your next step was to tabulate the answers.

Now that the tabulating is done (see Table 46), you are ready to prepare your findings for final presentation. You want something better than just a long list of

---

[1] These tables are used with permission from the Bureau of National Affairs and come from a survey of American Society for Personnel Administration members.

TABLE 40. Preretirement counseling and education programs

| | Percent of companies | | | | | |
| | By industry | | | By size | | All |
	Manufacturing	Nonmanufacturing	Nonbusiness	Large	Small	companies
Employer has a preretirement counseling program	39	39	25	57	22	36
Employees participate in program:*						
Six months before retirement	6	3	13	5	8	6
One year before retirement	4	13	13	5	14	8
Two years before retirement	0	0	7	0	3	1
Three years before retirement	0	6	7	2	6	3
Four years before retirement	2	0	0	2	0	1
Five years before retirement	8	0	13	3	11	6
At age 55	27	41	40	35	31	33
At age 60	20	22	0	17	19	18
Anytime, at employee's request	33	31	13	25	42	31
Participants include:*						
All employees nearing retirement	82	97	87	85	92	88
Spouse or other family members	62	63	66	72	50	64
Program was developed:*						
Entirely in-house	61	63	67	60	67	63
Using a packaged program	22	25	7	23	17	21
With help of outside consultant	18	9	27	17	17	17
Tuition aid is available for employees near retirement to develop new interests/activities	28	26	20	26	25	25

* Percentages are of companies that have counseling programs. Percentages add to more than 100 because of multiple responses.

TABLE 41. Topics covered in preretirement counseling programs

| | Percent of companies with programs | | | | | |
| | By industry | | | By size | | All companies |
	Manufacturing	Nonmanufacturing	Nonbusiness	Large	Small	
Social Security benefits	90	94	93	92	92	92
Company pension benefits	94	88	93	93	89	92
Other company benefits/services for retirees	84	91	60	83	81	82
Financial planning	61	59	60	62	58	60
Wills and inheritance provisions	51	59	60	65	39	55
Earning money after retirement	53	50	53	55	47	52
Recreation and hobbies	45	63	53	63	33	52
Health problems of older persons	49	63	33	60	36	51
Organizations for retirees	45	53	60	50	50	50
Mental/emotional aspects of retirement	45	53	47	58	31	48
Where to live after retirement	45	47	27	57	19	43
Volunteer activities	35	53	40	50	28	42
Safety precautions for older persons	22	28	20	33	8	24

TABLE 42. Flexible retirement arrangements

| | Percent of companies | | | | | |
| | By industry | | | By size | | All companies |
	Manufacturing	Nonmanufacturing	Nonbusiness	Large	Small	
Employees may "taper off" working hours prior to retirement	10	15	27	14	16	15
All employees eligible	3	5	19	5	9	7
Certain employees eligible	6	10	8	9	7	8
Employees may continue working on consultant basis after retirement	55	52	46	55	50	52
Employees may be recalled for temporary work after retirement	63	56	66	65	60	62

TABLE 43. Company Retirement Ceremonies

	Percent of companies					
	By industry			By size		All companies
	Manufacturing	Nonmanufacturing	Nonbusiness	Large	Small	
Company sponsors retirement ceremonies	75	89	81	82	80	81
Types of ceremonies:*						
Informal office parties	48	47	56	49	50	50
Luncheon	41	37	31	33	40	38
Dinner	36	37	21	28	36	33
Reception	14	22	31	25	17	20
Company gives retirement awards or gifts	54	67	53	54	60	58

* Percentages are of companies that sponsor retirement ceremonies. Percentages add to more than 100 because of multiple responses.

TABLE 44. Relations with retired employees

	Percent of companies					
	By industry			By size		All
	Manufacturing	Nonmanufacturing	Nonbusiness	Large	Small	companies
Services provided to retired employees:						
Invitations to company functions	68	67	46	66	61	63
Regular employee publications mailed to home	59	63	37	73	44	55
Life insurance coverage	59	56	39	67	45	53
Coverage at reduced amount*	84	87	78	80	88	84
Payment of health insurance to supplement						
Medicare	39	43	32	48	32	39
Discounts on company products or services	26	39	12	29	25	27
Payment of optional Medicare	17	16	5	20	11	14
Company pays all*	45	54	33	52	41	47
Company pays part*	36	23	—	14	47	29
Membership in company recreation						
or social club	16	12	5	17	9	12
Special publications for retired persons	10	12	5	14	7	10
Matching gifts to educational institutions	10	2	—	10	2	6
Free use of company medical dept.	4	1	2	4	2	3
Free physical exams	0.7	1	2	2	0.6	1
Other	11	20	5	16	9	12
Company has a retired employees club	14	9	5	20	4	10

* Percent of companies providing benefit.

TABLE 45. Changes in retirement programs

| | Percent of companies | | | | | |
| | By industry | | | By size | | All companies |
	Manufacturing	Nonmanufacturing	Nonbusiness	Large	Small	
Impact of change in the mandatory retirement age:						
None	39	31	34	29	40	35
Very little	50	58	45	57	48	51
Some	8	10	14	9	11	10
Great	0	1	2	2	0	1
Increase in number of employees electing not to retire since age 70 amendment	17	26	22	29	16	21
Changes in programs for preretired and retired employees in past two years	29	29	22	33	24	28
Anticipate making changes in near future	30	35	32	37	29	32

TABLE 46. Number of faculty members rating dean's performance at different levels under each of 32 propositions

	Agree			Disagree		Unable to evaluate
	Com-pletely	Mostly	Partly	Mostly	Com-pletely	

I. Philosophy and knowledge base:

1. Possesses knowledge and skills in general administration needed to head the College of Business Administration .... 19 | 24 | 7 | 5 | 11 | 2

2. Has adequate understanding of each functional field and its potential contributions .... 6 | 16 | 19 | 16 | 12 | 3

3. Has clear sense of purpose for college and conveys this to departments .... 15 | 17 | 17 | 8 | 9 | 2

4. Demonstrates balanced concern for teaching, research, public service, and university service .... 12 | 19 | 10 | 12 | 14 | 1

5. Demonstrates strong concern for faculty needs in order to function effectively and to develop professionally .... 15 | 17 | 8 | 16 | 12 | 0

6. Demonstrates awareness and sensitivity to differences in faculty talents and to areas in which each may best contribute .... 6 | 14 | 16 | 11 | 16 | 5

7. Demonstrates strong concern for student needs .... 7 | 14 | 12 | 7 | 5 | 23

II. Planning:

8. Provides adequate policy statements for collegewide guidance in important decisions that are common to all departments .... 10 | 19 | 16 | 11 | 8 | 5

9. Sees that goals are set, plans are made, and results are evaluated for the college as a whole .... 12 | 17 | 17 | 10 | 7 | 4

10. Sees that goals are set, plans are made, and results are evaluated for each major study area (for programs, curricula, faculty needs, space needs, budgets, etc.) .... 11 | 10 | 20 | 13 | 8 | 6

11. Maintains continuing program for planning improvements and innovations, both long range and short range .... 13 | 17 | 14 | 7 | 5 | 12

12. Involves people effectively in planning, actively soliciting ideas from all faculty members, or from all who may have useful inputs regarding particular issues .... 8 | 14 | 8 | 11 | 23 | 4

III. Organizing work and providing resources:

13. Sees that faculty resources are used effectively, considering different types and levels of instruction, research, and service, and considering strengths and limitations of individual faculty members .... 7 | 13 | 14 | 14 | 14 | 6

14. Provides adequate policy governing control of class size for type of class, multiple section coordination, load adjustment where justified, instructor assistance where justified, and other support where both needed and feasible .... 5 | 11 | 17 | 8 | 12 | 14

304

TABLE 46. *(continued)*

| | | Agree | | | Disagree | | Unable |
	Com-pletely	Mostly	Partly	Mostly	Com-pletely	to evaluate
15. Supports research to extent needed and possible and gives general encouragement to development of individual creative effort	11	16	17	13	9	2
16. Supports a faculty recruiting program that is based upon carefully planned needs and that generates adequate numbers, quality, university representation of applicants, and diversity of background so as to prevent either inbreeding or limited perspective; and that screens and attracts as many as possible of the best qualified from throughout the nation	14	21	7	12	6	7

IV. Leadership, communication, and evaluation:

	Com-pletely	Mostly	Partly	Mostly	Com-pletely	Unable to evaluate
17. Is action-oriented, a real doer, a person who gets things done	24	20	11	4	6	2
18. Delegates effectively to assistant administrators most of the responsibilities for ongoing operations, yet stays in touch and monitors results	16	19	13	5	5	9
19. Encourages (either directly or through chairmen) each faculty member to realize and utilize individual potential—takes personal interest and is easily approachable . . .	10	13	7	16	18	2
20. Administers reward system fairly and objectively and in terms of preannounced standards; encouraging chairmen and others involved to recognize and reward diverse contributions, not allowing own biases to dominate, not playing favorites; also explains his recommendations to chairmen and faculty	9	11	11	11	16	8
21. Keeps faculty members informed on university, college, departmental, and individual developments likely to be of interest and value to them	15	21	14	10	6	1
22. Invites faculty suggestions and other inputs regarding plans, operating problems, and possible improvements, is genuinely receptive, and considers suggestions seriously and objectively	10	12	12	12	19	1
23. Welcomes differences of opinion and deals with these with an open mind	7	13	10	19	15	3
24. Uses democratic procedures wherever possible and appropriate (gets people involved in making decisions that affect them)	7	10	8	18	21	3
25. Holds well-planned meetings for distributing information, holding constructive group discussions of college problems and needs, and reaching group decisions where appropriate	12	16	20	10	7	2

TABLE 46. *(concluded)*

		Agree			Disagree		Unable
		Com-pletely	Mostly	Partly	Mostly	Com-pletely	to evaluate
26.	Is sensitive to *student* needs and suggestions, including feedback regarding current operations and unfilled needs	7	8	10	8	4	31
V.	External representation:						
27.	Represents college effectively at university levels	20	26	3	6	5	8
28.	Represents college effectively in relations with business groups	25	23	4	3	3	9
29.	Represents college effectively in relations with professional groups	18	24	2	6	4	13

		Con-sidered above average	Somewhat above average	Average	Somewhat below average	Con-sidered below average	Unable to evaluate
30.	Compared to other deans in your knowledge and experience, how would you evaluate the overall performance of Dean Cuevas	19	14	8	7	14	2

questions and answers; so you will first arrange the questions by broad areas of similarity. Then you will present the data with meaningful analyses. Remember that the main concern of Dean Cuevas is what he must do to improve his performance. Thus, your report should lead to some specific recommendations.

As you are hopeful that a good job on this report will get you the advancement you seek, you will give it your best effort. You will dress it up with appropriate prefatory parts. And you will use visual aids wherever they help to communicate.

35. Determining what makes a Mufti service center successful. The management of the Mufti Muffler Company wants to know why some of their automotive service centers are doing much better than others. And it is your job to find out.

You, as research supervisor for Dobbs Research Associates, have been working on the problem for the past four weeks. As orally authorized by Mufti's vice president for sales, Rene C. Cullen, you and your crew have visited 200 manager-owned Mufti operations in the 27-state area served by the company. The stations visited were selected by Mufti executives to be about equal insofar as physical facilities and location are concerned. All are predominantly community stations—that is, they are off main highways. All are about equal in traffic flow past the station, and all have nearly equal competitive situations. But they differ in one major respect— sales volume. One half (100) of the stations have had unusually good sales volumes; the other half (100) have had low volumes.

To find the reasons for high or low volumes, you worked out a detailed plan for collecting data. First you had your investigators visit each station posing as customers. They then observed and recorded such things as the attendants' courtesy, services rendered, and conditions of the stations. Some of these observations were factual. Others were subjective. But the subjective evaluations were based on definite guide points on which each observer was very carefully instructed. Later, the investigators returned to the stations observed and interviewed the managers. From the managers they received some pertinent factual information on the personnel employed at each station.

Now the research is done, and you have the summary tabulations before you. Your next step is to put these data into some meaningful order. Then you will analyze them in the light of your problem. From these analyses you hope to be able to draw some conclusions as to why some stations are successful and others are not. Of course, you will present all of this work in a report befitting the formality of your professional relationship with Mufti. (Your instructor may specify these requirements.)

Your summary tables are presented below. Should you require other information, you may use your good, logical imagination. For example, in describing your research procedure in the introduction section, you will need to fill in with steps that are consistent with good research methodology.

	S	*U*
Courtesy of attendants:		
Unusually courteous	18	3
Above average	44	23
Average	32	42
Below average	4	20
Discourteous	2	12
Customer services:		
Muffler	100	100
Wash and lube	7	23
Brakes	74	37
Carburetor	54	32
Ignition, tune-up	61	33
Wheels and shocks	81	34
Heavy repairs	2	21
Condition of stations:		
Overall appearance:		
Clean and neat	82	10
Fair, but could be improved	18	62
Dirty	0	28
Rest rooms		
Clean and neat	92	22
Fair	8	47
Dirty	0	31
Condition of stations:		
Age of building		
Less than 5 years	31	33
5–10 years	41	38
Over 10 years	38	29
Overall appearance of stock		
Neatly arranged	68	11
Fair	30	63
Poorly arranged	2	26

	S	U
Qualifications of managers:		
Education		
Grade school or less	2	12
Some high school	28	44
High school graduate	56	42
Some college	14	2
Experience		
Less than 1 year	0	11
1 to 5 years	52	41
6 to 10 years	36	38
Over 10 years	12	20
Marital status		
Married	6	24
Single	6	24
Age		
Under 21	—	3
21–25	4	12
26–30	10	19
31–40	51	36
41–50	19	20
Over 50	16	10
Grades on Mufti's Manager's Aptitude Test		
Below 40 (not qualified)	0	9
40–79 (acceptable)	17	43
60–79 (good)	42	30
80–100 (outstanding	41	18
Attended Mufti Manager's School (two weeks' duration)	43	21
Qualifications of service workers:		
Education:		
Grade school or less	18	27
Some high school	43	57
High school graduate	39	16
Experience (similar work):		
Less than 1 year	9	19
1 to 5 years	36	44
6 to 10 years	27	22
Over 10 years	28	15
Grade on Mufti's Aptitude Test:		
Below 40 (not qualified)	10	34
40–59 (acceptable)	47	57
60–79 (good)	36	7
80–100 (outstanding)	7	2
Marital status:		
Married	62	65
Single	38	35
Age		
Under 21	13	14
21–30	66	33
31–40	17	31
41–50	4	20
Over 50	—	2
Attended Mufti's Service School (one week's duration)	59	27
Pricing policy in area:		
Higher than standard	9	23
Equal to standard	74	47
Lower than standard	17	30

	S	U
Promotion efforts:		
Trading stamps	32	14
Discounts (quantity purchase, special group, etc.)	11	10
Participated in recent company-sponsored contest	93	61
Average hourly wages paid relative to local average:		
$0.76 or more below	0	6
$0.26 to $0.75 below	19	41
$0.25 below to $0.25 above	27	33
$0.26 above to $0.75 above	45	17
$0.76 or more above	9	3
Promotion efforts:		
Participate in Mufti's special quarterly promotions	94	51
Participate in Mufti-sponsored contest	93	54
Conducted own special promotion in past year	19	3
Fringe benefits paid service workers:		
Group life insurance	31	9
Group hospitalization insurance	68	42
Paid vacations	88	52
Bonus, incentive pay, profit sharing, etc.	19	4
Accessories handled:		
Antifreeze	100	100
Oil additives	100	100
Radiator chemicals	100	99
Seat covers	84	21
Tires and tubes	100	100
Floor mats	84	22
Waxes, polishes	96	82
Wiper blades	99	81
Valves and caps	90	78
Car radios	6	0
Car heaters	21	1
Jacks	37	9
Tire chains	84	11
Touch-up paint	18	2
Mirrors	97	30
Spot lights	34	4
Batteries	100	100

	None		$1–$600		$601–$1,200		Over $1,200	
	S	U	S	U	S	U	S	U
Advertising expenditures:								
Annual, by media:								
Newspaper	0	13	7	45	32	31	61	11
Handbills	76	70	14	10	10	19	0	1
Radio–TV	98	89	2	0	0	5	0	6
Novelty (calendars, pens, etc.)	36	47	28	34	29	14	7	5
Direct mail	32	52	28	27	31	19	9	2

	Under $600	$601–$1,200	$1,201–$1,800	$1,801–$2,400	$2,401–$3,000	Over $3,000
Annual, total amount:						
Successful stations	12	14	21	25	18	10
Unsuccessful stations	31	36	22	3	5	3

Unless otherwise specified, the numbers are percentages. S—Successful stations; U—Unsuccessful stations.

36. A search for the permanent grocery clerk. At first you were somewhat disappointed in your new job as an assistant to Hans A. Kuhl, industrial relations director, Thrifty Food Stores, Inc. You didn't know just why. Thrifty is a good company to work for. Completion of its tremendous expansion program affords proof that there is opportunity for advancement. Maybe your disappointment was a result of Mr. Kuhl's choosing Johnny Rollins, an Oklahoma graduate and your rival for promotion, to help him conduct a survey of working conditions in the stores.

You wanted to get your teeth into that survey. You were interested in learning just what is behind the chain's number one personnel problem—the alarmingly fast turnover of grocery clerks. In fact, you were even a little happy when Kuhl came back from the survey with the report that he had found no disturbing conditions that could account for the turnover.

The job really got interesting, though, when Mr. Kuhl called Johnny and you into his office and assigned each of you an important part of his next step toward solving the turnover problem. The boss hurriedly explained his theory to you. He believes that since working conditions and wages in Thrifty stores are comparable to those of competitors, the large turnover is a result of the stores' hiring the wrong type of employees—the type least likely to become permanent.

So Mr. Kuhl asked you to survey the personnel records with an eye out for any facts that are significant to the turnover problem. Specifically, he wants to know whether there are any factors (such as age, education, and marital status) that point to the grocery clerks most likely to stay on. Since the problem differs for men and women employees, Mr. Kuhl divided the assignment—the women for Johnny and the men for you.

So your first job was to go through the inactive files and pull out all records of men who have worked in the stores since September of 19X5. Because many of their newest employees have not had a chance to prove their permanence, you eliminated from the active files all records of employees who have been with the company for less than one year. Then you reasoned that the sample's validity would not be changed if you used only every third card from each of the two groups.

Now, with all the preliminary work done and the records before you in two neat stacks (Tables 47 and 48), you are ready to begin tabulating and organizing. A logical comparison of the data from each group, with conclusions and recommendations, should be just what Mr. Kuhl wants, and, of course, you will present your findings to him in a clear and meaningful report.

You want to impress the boss with your superiority over Johnny; so you have decided to write the report from an impersonal viewpoint and to support your conclusions with some good graphic aids. Also, you plan to dress up the report by including the following parts: a cover (with report title); a title fly; a title page; your letter of transmittal to Mr. Kuhl; a table of contents; a table of illustrations; an epitome; and, of course, the report proper.

TABLE 47.   A random sample of personnel records of present Thrifty Food Stores' employees

	A	B	C	D	E	F
Abram, Joe T.	29	12	M	1	7	87
Adams, Henry A.	18	8	S	1	0	18
Allen, J. J.	42	11	S	6	4	28
Anderson, A. A.	33	12	M	2	0	20
Antonio, Bernard	34	8	M	5	6	223
Applin, W. R.	20	12	S	1	0	85
Aycock, M. O.	32	12	S	4	0	31
Barker, James D.	45	8	M	5	26	19
Barnett, Anthony	23	12	M	1	5	118
Barr, Burl A.	43	9	M	5	12	17
Bastian, Earl	34	9	M	6	3	13
Baylor, Dan F.	24	7	M	3	2	15
Beaver, Tom W.	26	8	M	2	4	22
Beck, Herbert A.	41	12	M	2	15	43
Bell, Robert E.	19	12	M	1	1	83
Bell, Wm. A.	20	9	S	2	2	26
Broad, E. D.	25	12	S	3	0	78
Buckley, R. V.	19	12	S	1	0	91
Cabanis, Nelson	39	12	M	4	16	40
Cedar, Rex	30	12	M	3	0	25
Champ, Will D.	27	12	S	3	2	18
Clark, Boyce	40	12	M	3	0	45
Cluck, Travis	23	12	S	2	1	98
Coffey, C. E.	36	12	M	3	0	49
Connally, R. P.	29	12	M	2	5	17
Crump, Hal	18	10	S	0	0	95
Darby, T. E.	30	12	S	5	11	31
Davis, Samuel	42	12	M	3	0	13
Deirman, Geo. D.	19	9	M	2	2	17
DePew, Peter T.	32	12	M	4	7	29
Dickerson, Wm. T.	37	12	M	2	0	69
Dixon, Stanley	20	10	S	3	2	24
Eckhardt, B. E.	23	11	S	1	0	30
Ellis, Chas. T.	31	12	M	1	0	68
Erzkus, Ralph	40	12	M	4	0	35
Fischer, Thomas	28	10	M	2	3	21
Fogle, Richard E.	44	9	S	7	6	20
Fredrickson, Von E.	30	12	M	3	4	29
Garner, James T.	24	12	M	2	5	109
Gault, Raleigh Lee	35	9	M	4	11	33
Glaser, Conrad	33	12	M	4	6	27
Gustafson, V. A.	18	10	S	1	2	15
Guyger, Lorenzo M.	29	12	M	3	5	107
Hargrave, Edison E.	25	12	S	2	0	84
Hartkopf, Archie D.	38	10	M	7	4	38
Hess, Nathan D.	29	12	M	2	3	99
Hipple, Buddy	17	12	S	0	0	111
Hooper, Berkeley	36	12	S	6	9	38
Hubener, Chas. T.	21	12	S	3	1	25
Hutchinson, Elwood	34	8	M	3	7	18
Hyltin, Joe Bill	32	12	M	2	0	71
Innes, Bobby I.	18	12	S	1	0	22
Isbell, Floyd M.	41	9	M	4	18	20
Jackson, Michael	19	12	S	2	0	47
Jackson, T. J.	26	12	M	1	0	93

TABLE 47.   *(continued)*

	A	B	C	D	E	F
Johnson, Richard A.	21	12	M	1	3	77
Jordan, Bernard M.	43	12	M	4	9	35
Joslin, Murray V.	33	12	M	2	0	95
Junkin, Humphry T.	20	12	S	1	0	74
Juul, Dalton Lee	36	12	M	3	2	12
Kavanaugh, James J.	31	12	S	4	0	59
Kendall, Morris E.	35	10	M	3	6	31
King, Dexter W.	23	12	S	2	4	73
Koenig, Harold H.	34	12	M	3	4	73
Lawrence, Vincent	32	12	M	2	0	25
Leath, T. Allen	26	11	M	4	6	13
Legge, Woodrow	31	12	M	3	5	30
Lewis, John A.	27	12	M	1	0	109
Lowther, Lester L.	38	10	M	5	5	39
Lundberg, Raymond	27	12	M	2	0	31
Lyons, Eugene W.	45	12	M	4	13	43
Madison, R. R., Jr.	18	12	S	0	0	19
Mancili, Tony T.	46	11	M	4	9	14
McCarty, Casey	37	12	M	4	12	57
McDonald, Albert A.	21	12	S	2	1	67
McMillan, Chester	39	9	M	3	22	36
Miller, Lloyd B.	30	12	M	2	0	13
Motsenbocker, Hugh	20	12	S	1	0	90
Murphy, Grady D.	18	12	S	0	0	79
Mussett, C. E.	35	10	M	3	8	21
Myers, Cecil H.	29	11	M	2	4	70
Myler, Stuart L.	23	11	M	4	3	19
Nason, Hubert G.	32	12	M	4	6	116
Nicholson, Bob E.	19	12	S	1	2	33
Nordlander, Wm. A.	34	12	M	3	0	12
Nunley, Benjaman T.	24	10	M	3	2	17
Nusom, Oscar A.	22	13	S	1	0	89
O'Connel, David	18	12	S	0	0	58
Owens, P. W.	48	10	M	3	21	14
Page, Owen S.	26	12	S	1	0	29
Patton, Kenny T.	32	12	M	4	6	51
Perrenolt, George A.	19	12	S	1	1	30
Powell, Maurice	30	13	M	2	7	91
Purnell, Clarence E.	37	12	M	6	16	38
Quist, Parker G.	25	11	S	4	7	27
Ratchford, E. G.	44	12	S	7	0	23
Reilly, Seth P.	22	12	S	2	3	16
Richardson, William	40	12	M	2	0	46
Richter, H. Lee	33	12	S	4	2	39
Ritter, Roger B.	27	11	M	2	4	83
Robinson, Hatton C.	45	9	M	5	7	22
Rylander, Bennett	31	12	M	2	3	29
Sachs, Jordan E.	25	12	M	1	0	82
Sandall, Othal	27	12	M	2	0	81
Schell, Aaron B.	19	10	M	1	2	25
Schmidt, David	36	8	M	3	10	35
Schreiber, Richard	40	12	M	3	18	33
Seaholm, Anthony C.	20	12	S	1	0	101
Shafer, Roland	35	13	S	3	0	28
Shaw, Andrew V.	44	11	M	3	12	61
Shelton, Russell	25	12	M	2	3	30

TABLE 47. *(concluded)*

	A	B	C	D	E	F
Smith, Odis Lee	21	12	M	2	0	118
Tanner, Pau. W.	31	12	M	3	0	20
Taylor, Herbert G.	43	12	M	3	7	12
Thompson, Ernest E.	23	9	S	3	1	19
Todd, Waverly	33	11	M	3	0	24
Tuttle, Claude P.	46	10	M	4	5	17
Underwood, Owen S.	19	12	S	1	2	92
Urbanke, Mack	30	12	M	2	5	77
Varnell, Lester C.	28	12	S	3	2	103
Vinson, T. E.	41	12	M	2	0	39
Vosburg, Amos A.	39	9	M	3	14	26
Ward, Dan C.	20	12	S	1	0	100
Weir, James	35	10	M	3	7	14
Whitten, Lloyd D.	19	11	S	2	1	17
Williams, Oxsheer	43	11	M	4	9	15
Wilson, Walter S.	22	12	M	2	0	96
Wruble, James D.	51	10	M	4	27	24
Wynn, Horace W.	32	10	M	3	9	22
Yarrington, Alden	30	12	M	3	0	24
York, Thomas M.	19	10	M	3	2	22
Young, Leonard	24	12	S	2	0	82
Young, Patrick W.	43	12	M	3	13	37
Zauskey, Kenneth P.	24	10	S	4	2	18
Zietz, Horatio A.	37	9	M	5	4	38
Zissman, Robert Lee	25	12	M	2	4	15

Note: Explanation of column heads:
    A.   Age at time of employment.
    B.   Education in years.
    C.   Marital status (Divorced counted as single).
    D.   Number of jobs held before.
    E.   Years of related experience.
    F.   Months of employment with Thrifty Food Stores.

37. Selecting the right magazine for Moroccan Craft. For this assignment assume that you are director of research for Wycliff-Briggs Advertising Agency. Wycliff-Briggs is a comparatively small but rapidly expanding agency which is just now moving up into the big-account class. The new account responsible for the agency's latest move up the success ladder is that of Moroccan Crafts, Inc., manufacturers of a line of quality luggage.

Moroccan Craft's current advertising plan calls for more than the usual dealer cooperative campaigns used in the past. This time, a nationwide campaign is to be run in a major periodical. Which periodical will carry the Moroccan Craft story to the people hasn't as yet been determined, but here is where you come in.

At the oral request of Ms. Wanda Dodd, account executive for the Moroccan Craft account, you are to make the analysis which will point the way to the decision. Your analyis is limited to two periodicals—*Newsweek* and *People*—the others having been eliminated by Ms. Dodd for one reason or other. More specifically stated, it is your assignment to get a picture of the advertising characteristics of the two magazines which will show where the Moroccan Craft advertising would be most at home.

TABLE 48. A random sample of personnel records of Thrifty Food Stores' former employees

	A	B	C	D	E	F	G
Abney, J. B.	27	6	M	6	0	2	D–g
Acock, Thomas	35	8	M	5	0	1	D–g
Adams, William E.	33	12	S	7	1	7	Q–j
Aderholdt, E. D.	37	12	S	7	1	7	Q–e
Agnew, Harold	19	6	M	3	2	2	D–g
Akinson, Wayne E.	30	10	M	4	0	7	D–g
Albright, F. E.	40	8	S	7	0	2	D–g
Alexander, Geo. F.	31	12	M	4	9	10	Q–j
Allen, Tom M.	29	11	M	4	4	7	Q–j
Allman, John D.	38	12	M	3	0	14	Q–m
Amsley, David	46	9	M	3	2	17	D–h
Amundson, Chas. W.	27	10	M	2	3	19	Q–k
Anderson, Paul A.	36	7	M	5	6	6	Q–d
Andrewerka, R. H.	42	8	M	4	3	20	Q–j
Ansohn, Eric W.	30	9	M	5	0	1	D–g
Ashworth, P. T.	44	10	S	5	0	5	D–g
Austin, James T.	31	12	M	4	0	4	D–h
Babcock, R. L.	26	7	S	5	0	3	D–c
Badger, L. E.	41	9	M	3	0	9	D–g
Baggett, Mike	33	10	M	7	0	3	D–i
Bailey, Andrew A.	45	4	M	5	0	4	D–g
Baker, K. T.	35	8	S	5	4	17	Q–d
Balagia, Chas. E.	18	9	S	3	1	9	D–i
Bantel, Fred S.	40	12	M	3	0	2	D–h
Barona, August E.	21	7	S	2	0	5	D–g
Bartholomew, T. E.	38	12	M	4	0	11	Q–e
Baugh, Jeff T.	26	10	S	3	2	47	Q–k
Bedighaus, C. E.	25	9	S	7	1	3	D–h
Bennett, H. A.	38	8	M	4	0	1	D–g
Biggs, Theo. E.	35	9	M	4	0	1	D–g
Boone, David D.	31	10	M	5	0	5	Q–j
Bowden, Arthur M.	40	8	M	5	0	3	D–g
Briscoe, Clyde C.	44	7	S	7	0	1	D–g
Brown, Ed W.	19	8	S	4	0	4	D–g
Bryant, Joe M.	22	8	S	3	0	4	D–g
Bryson, Frank, Jr.	41	4	S	9	0	2	D–g
Bytendorp, Chester	19	8	S	2	1	10	Q–e
Byrd, John Milton	45	8	M	6	2	17	Q–m
Cadwallader, E. A.	38	12	M	3	0	14	Q–m
Caffey, Courtney	46	9	M	3	2	17	D–h
Calhoun, James B.	27	10	M	2	3	19	Q–k
Cameron, Arthur M.	36	9	M	5	6	6	Q–d
Calvert, Morgan	42	8	M	4	3	22	Q–j
Canion, Ralph E.	30	9	M	5	0	1	D–g
Cantwell, Paul D.	35	10	S	5	4	17	Q–d
Cesar, Rudolph	18	9	S	3	1	9	D–i
Chandler, Orville	40	12	M	3	0	2	D–h
Chappell, Wm. O.	21	7	S	2	0	5	D–g
Cheaves, LeRoy, Jr.	44	6	M	8	1	10	D–i
Christianson, W. D.	36	7	M	3	14	9	Q–l
Cloud, Ross S.	25	12	S	4	1	7	Q–e
Conkle, Scott M.	43	7	M	6	0	14	Q–e
Crenshaw, Dennis W.	27	9	M	4	0	15	Q–j
Crews, Adrian	47	11	M	3	4	19	Q–m
Curry, Norman E.	34	9	S	6	0	12	Q–j

TABLE 48. *(continued)*

A		B	C	D	E	F	G
Cyrus, Richard E.	45	8	M	4	0	12	Q–j
Darnell, G. G.	19	9	S	3	0	1	D–f
DeLong, Geo. G.	41	6	M	6	0	6	D–g
Dismukes, Ray H.	32	11	M	4	6	16	Q–j
Distler, Tony	21	10	M	1	0	11	Q–e
Douglas, Will L.	44	12	M	5	0	13	Q–m
Drishka, Marvin	37	11	M	3	4	8	Q–e
Dubois, Wm. A.	43	9	M	4	7	4	D–c
Duffy, Floyd D.	34	10	S	8	5	21	D–b
Duval, Harold E.	22	9	S	3	0	4	D–g
Dyer, Neil E.	30	12	M	3	3	6	Q–j
Dykes, H. B.	48	7	M	6	0	1	D–i
Echols, Leland M.	36	8	S	8	0	7	D–a
Edmiston, Matt W.	37	7	M	4	12	11	Q–j
Eichelberger, F. A.	43	11	M	5	6	13	Q–m
Ekstrom, Bruce I.	39	6	S	8	0	5	D–a
Elmore, Alfred E.	36	9	M	5	0	23	Q–m
Engbloom, Hans E.	32	8	S	8	0	1	D–g
Edwin, Geo. T.	19	12	S	1	0	14	Q–j
Estes, Peter T.	34	9	M	5	6	47	Q–k
Ettlinger, Melvin	28	8	S	5	0	9	D–h
Evans, Allan D.	35	6	M	4	0	4	D–g
Evans, Robert E.	28	8	S	5	0	9	D–h
Ezelle, Guy D.	32	10	M	3	0	51	Q–j
Fahrenkamp, G. F.	43	12	M	4	9	17	Q–m
Faris, W. Frank	20	9	M	2	1	10	Q–j
Feurbacher, R. S.	43	11	M	5	12	25	Q–i
Floyd, Pat M.	24	11	M	2	0	17	Q–e
Francis, Victor A.	34	12	S	6	0	5	D–g
Franklin, Aubrey	43	10	S	8	3	7	D–a
Frazetti, Antonio	20	12	S	1	0	2	D–b
Friedrich, Chester	32	12	M	5	0	11	D–b
Frost, Edgar E.	38	10	S	7	0	7	D–f
Frymire, Raymond A.	31	11	M	3	0	12	Q–j
Fulbright, E. D.	40	5	M	6	0	5	D–g
Fulcock, Edward	50	4	M	8	1	3	D–g
Fusser, Rodney	35	8	M	6	0	2	D–g
Garner, C. G.	24	9	M	5	1	8	D–g
Goode, Thomas	37	11	M	5	0	10	D–b
Gregory, A. V.	45	8	M	6	2	17	Q–m
Grimes, Carl	31	12	M	3	0	9	Q–e
Gunn, Lloyd, Jr.	38	7	M	6	15	23	Q–j
Hakins, Raymond	49	8	S	9	0	4	D–g
Hancock, Paul V.	28	12	S	5	0	4	D–b
Harrison, Edwin	54	7	M	7	24	18	D–c
Hause, Milton	35	8	M	4	3	9	D–c
Herwig, A. H.	20	8	S	3	0	14	D–a
Hinton, Will D.	19	12	S	2	0	13	Q–e
Hruska, Emil	31	8	M	3	9	5	D–b
Hyltin, Alvin	29	5	M	4	3	17	Q–d
Ischy, Mac	18	12	S	0	0	4	Q–e
Jabour, Clifford	27	9	S	4	0	4	Q–e
Johnson, Arthur	30	10	M	5	0	14	Q–j
Johnson, W. H.	37	6	M	4	0	2	D–g
Jones, Wilfred	41	6	M	4	0	4	D–g
Jordan, Milam B.	19	9	M	2	2	5	D–b

TABLE 48. *(continued)*

	A	B	C	D	E	F	G
Joslin, A. L.	43	8	M	5	12	25	Q–m
Junkin, Ralph W.	20	10	S	1	0	2	D–h
Jurecka, Leo J.	32	12	M	5	0	11	D–b
Kelly, Patrick	38	5	M	4	2	3	D–g
Key, Theodore	35	12	S	7	7	9	D–h
Kunze, August M.	50	10	M	5	0	11	D–b
Kyle, Sidney	33	9	M	3	0	20	Q–e
Lawrence, W. W.	42	8	M	5	0	5	D–c
Lee, Vernon A.	25	9	S	3	0	10	D–g
Lewis, Fred M.	44	4	M	6	0	3	D–g
Liesman, Wm. A.	31	11	M	5	0	13	Q–e
Lincoln, Walter A.	36	8	M	4	0	8	Q–e
Lloyd, Roy, Jr.	30	8	M	5	4	2	D–i
Lockhart, Marvin	38	10	S	6	0	7	D–g
Lunceford, T. R.	31	11	M	3	0	12	Q–j
Lund, Wm. B.	32	8	S	8	0	1	D–g
Lupton, A. J.	19	12	S	1	0	14	Q–j
Lyckman, Philip	28	9	S	5	0	9	D–g
Lyckman, Tom G.	34	9	M	5	6	27	Q–x
Lyle, Lanier M	35	6	M	4	0	4	D–g
Lynch, Everett	40	6	M	4	0	3	D–g
Lytton, Earl, Jr.	20	12	S	1	0	41	Q–j
MacDonald, Wm. R.	26	9	S	4	3	11	D–c
Mackey, M. T.	46	12	M	3	0	11	Q–m
Maddox, Calvin C.	33	9	S	6	5	19	D–b
Magoon, Wilson	47	10	M	3	0	8	D–c
Mallett, August	35	8	M	5	0	3	D–i
Marcum, H. H.	41	7	S	7	11	29	Q–j
Martin, Edgar B.	19	6	S	3	0	7	D–g
Martin, Ellis	27	11	M	3	0	9	Q–e
McAngus, Howard	32	8	S	8	0	1	D–g
McCaleb, Clarence	19	12	S	1	0	14	Q–j
McClellan, J. T.	34	9	M	5	6	37	Q–x
McKown, Jack	28	8	S	5	0	9	D–h
McRill, Sam S.	35	6	M	4	0	4	D–g
Mears, I. D.	40	6	M	4	0	3	D–g
Middlebrook, S. S.	20	12	S	1	0	21	Q–j
Miller, Adrian	26	9	S	4	3	11	D–c
Mosley, Willis T.	46	12	M	3	0	11	Q–m
Mosteller, Curtis	33	9	S	6	5	19	D–b
Mueller, Kenneth	47	10	M	3	0	8	D–c
Murphy, Pat J.	35	8	M	5	0	3	D–i
Muston, M. R.	41	7	S	7	11	29	Q–j
Nafcieger, P. T.	27	11	M	3	0	9	Q–e
Nalle, Walter, Jr.	19	6	S	3	0	7	D–g
Nance, Audry	40	9	M	4	0	4	D–g
Nauert, W. H.	30	12	M	4	0	11	Q–x
Nevens, Robert T.	39	4	M	9	0	4	D–g
Newman, Hugh W.	44	12	S	3	0	7	D–b
Nicholas, Alvin A.	29	12	S	5	0	14	D–h
Nichols, Calvin	32	10	M	3	0	57	Q–j
Nicholson, W. W.	43	8	S	4	9	17	Q–m
Norman, Chas. T.	20	11	M	2	1	10	Q–j
Nusom, Burt L.	18	8	S	1	0	5	Q–e
Oates, D. D.	34	12	M	4	11	6	D–c
O'Dea, Dean	33	9	S	6	0	4	D–g

TABLE 48. *(continued)*

	A	B	C	D	E	F	G
Odell, Francis	34	8	M	5	0	4	D–g
Oertli, Frank	19	8	S	2	0	3	D–g
Olle, E. D.	30	9	M	4	0	11	Q–d
Olson, Olaf, Jr.	22	12	S	2	0	7	Q–j
Owens, Thornton	45	8	S	8	9	15	D–a
Pafenbach, Fritz	31	9	S	6	8	13	D–h
Pafford, Wm. J.	22	12	S	2	0	7	Q–j
Page, Ellis T.	22	10	S	3	0	4	D–g
Page, Morris W.	30	9	M	3	3	6	Q–j
Pannell, G. T., Jr.	48	7	S	6	0	1	D–i
Paralta, Amos	36	9	S	8	0	7	D–a
Park, Gene E.	37	9	M	4	12	11	Q*
Peirce, Preston	43	11	M	5	6	13	Q–m
Peschka, Bernard	28	12	M	2	2	16	Q–j
Porter, Wm. A.	49	9	M	4	0	2	D–g
Prince, A. T.	26	11	M	4	1	8	D–b
Purdy, Donald T.	21	8	S	5	2	4	D–g
Pyles, John L.	39	5	S	8	0	5	D–a
Quaker, P. A.	36	9	M	5	0	23	Q–m
Quante, R. M., Jr.	45	7	S	7	0	6	D–g
Querro, Hortence	24	6	M	6	1	2	D–g
Quick, Dan T.	17	8	M	2	0	4	D–g
Quick, Sam A.	44	12	M	3	0	16	Q–g
Raatz, Frank	42	11	S	5	4	21	D–c
Ragsdale, Buford	31	9	M	4	3	13	Q–d
Railer, W. T.	48	8	M	5	17	12	D–h
Rainbolt, Carrol	35	7	S	9	0	2	D–i
Raisch, Milton D.	36	11	S	3	0	16	Q–j
Ramirez, Joe A.	38	5	M	5	0	9	D–g
Ramsay, Rufe	19	12	S	1	0	29	Q–j
Rawlings, G. G.	19	9	S	3	0	1	D–g
Reed, James T.	41	6	M	6	0	6	D–g
Reed, Maxie	32	11	M	4	6	16	D–c
Reeves, Buck	21	10	M	1	0	11	Q–e
Reilly, L. O.	39	8	S	6	0	7	D–c
Renz, C. K.	40	7	M	5	5	14	Q–j
Richardson, Gus	18	11	S	1	1	11	Q–j
Rike, Barney	46	9	M	6	3	31	Q–m
Rucker, Harry	36	9	S	5	0	5	D–b
Sandel, Leonard	39	10	M	3	0	17	Q–m
Sanders, Eugene	27	10	M	3	0	12	Q–e
Saxon, Sam B.	38	6	M	4	0	2	D–g
Scales, T. G.	42	12	M	5	0	13	Q–m
Schaefer, Chas. E.	27	9	S	6	0	2	D–i
Scherbarth, Ben R.	44	12	M	5	0	13	Q–m
Schleuter, Karl H.	37	11	M	4	4	8	Q–e
Schmidt, Richard A.	43	9	M	4	7	4	D–c
Scoffield, Lewis	34	10	S	8	5	21	D–f
Scott, Noel B.	47	5	M	5	0	1	D–g
Sellers, T. M., Jr.	43	12	M	4	0	19	Q–m
Shamrock, Wm. P.	35	8	M	6	0	2	D–g
Sheet, I. A.	48	9	M	6	16	36	Q–j
Sherron, Grover C.	29	9	M	3	1	5	D–g
Shuberg, Geo. T.	25	8	S	3	0	2	D–g
Siek, Mavin T.	21	8	S	1	0	3	D–g
Sifuenties, Fred	34	10	M	3	0	1	D–g

TABLE 48.   *(concluded)*

	A	B	C	D	E	F	G
Smith, Geo. A.	18	9	S	2	0	7	D–b
Smith, Leroy	19	11	S	2	0	19	Q–e
Smith, Steve, Jr.	23	12	S	2	1	13	D–b
Stanley, L. V.	30	9	M	3	0	7	Q–e
Sullivan, Pat	44	6	M	8	1	10	D–i
Swenson, Ollie, Jr.	33	9	S	7	0	5	D–h
Swift, Weldon E.	30	11	M	2	7	11	Q–j
Taber, A. H.	47	11	M	4	5	19	Q–m
Tannehill, Geo. H.	34	8	M	4	0	2	D–g
Taylor, Bob A.	31	9	S	5	0	1	D–g
Taylor, O. L.	45	8	M	5	0	12	Q–j
Teaguri, Vincent	19	11	S	1	0	6	Q–e
Terby, Alton	31	10	M	3	0	1	D–g
Thompson, Joe J.	32	9	M	7	2	19	D–h
Thrasher, Wallace	40	7	S	8	0	9	D–i
Travis, John E.	25	10	S	2	0	4	D–a
Tyler, Stanton	33	8	M	4	0	5	Q–e
Ulit, Amos B.	54	5	M	7	24	18	D–c
Umscheld, B. V.	37	11	M	2	0	14	Q–e
Underwood, Tom A.	19	6	M	3	2	2	D–g
Urban, Elmer	26	7	S	5	0	3	D–g
Uzzell, Marshall	41	10	M	3	0	9	D–g
Van Cleave, Homer	34	9	M	3	0	1	D–g
Veteto, Manuel	18	8	S	2	0	7	D–b
Wade, Dennis E.	50	7	S	8	0	9	D–i
Walberg, Eugene	25	11	S	2	0	4	D–a
Walker, Chas. T.	18	11	S	1	1	11	Q–j
Walters, Leo R.	46	10	M	6	3	31	Q–m
Webb, Roy A.	35	12	M	6	0	2	D–g
Weide, James T.	48	8	M	6	16	36	Q–j
Wendlandt, R. M.	34	10	S	5	0	4	D–g
Wheatley, Gordon	19	8	S	2	0	3	D–g
Whisenant, L. D.	42	12	M	5	4	21	Q–j
Wilson, Oscar	31	9	M	4	3	13	Q–d
Yager, Wm. E.	46	12	M	3	0	11	Q–m
Yeates, John J.	33	10	S	6	5	19	D–b
Young, Melvin	47	11	M	3	0	8	D–c
Zapalac, Ted E.	35	8	M	5	0	3	D–i
Zilker, John R.	33	10	M	3	0	20	Q–e
Zuehel, Gilbert	42	8	M	5	0	5	D–c
Zwiener, A. M.	25	8	S	3	0	10	D–g

Note: Explanation of column heads:
  A. Age at time of employment.
  B. Schooling in years.
  C. Marital status (Divorced counted as single).
  D. Number of jobs previously held.
  E. Years of related experience.
  F. Months of employment with Thrifty Food Stores.
  G. Nature and reason for termination of employment:

D—Discharged	e—Dislike of work	k—No promotion
Q—Quit	f—Drinking on job	l—No salary increase
a—Absenteeism	g—Incapacity	m—Poor health
b—Discourtesy	h—Insubordination	x—No reason
c—Dishonest	i—Laziness	
d—Dislike of manager	j—More pay elsewhere	

* Purchase of own store.

Normally, such studies involve extensive survey-type investigations. At the moment, however, Wycliff-Briggs cannot afford a costly study; so you set out to do the next best thing. Working on the assumption that the bigger agencies have long ago made similar studies, you conclude that analysis of the advertisements they place in a magazine reveals their findings concerning that magazine. Thus your objective is to obtain a summary picture of the advertisements in *People* and *Newsweek*. Your study will get all of the facts which will help make the decision— such information as classes and price levels of goods and services, the buying motives the advertisements appeal to, and the techniques used to present these appeals. These facts can be made to portray the readers they are written for. That is, they'll have a good indication of such things as the typical reader's age, sex, family status, and economic and intellectual status.

You begin your investigation by getting two copies of each of the two magazines in question. Then, based on what you believe to be the major points which reveal the magazines' readers, you construct a tally sheet. Next, you make an ad-by-ad check of the magazines, summarizing your findings after all ads have been checked. Now you are ready for the analysis which will point the way to the best decision. This analysis and the data upon which it is based will be written up in an easy-to-read and eye-pleasing report.

When you are at last ready to write up your report, you face the decision as to scope, tone, and form. You decide to use the impersonal tone (no *I, we,* or *you,* but consistent third person), to include enough identification to make the report readily understandable to somebody up the line from Ms. Dodd and to set up the report with adequate prefatory parts. Although you will break up your data into smaller units and present lots of graphic illustrations, you will nevertheless translate the whole story into words and not shift the burden to your tables and charts. In so doing, you will seek out the concrete word and the specific instance to keep away from statistical jargon and big generalities of talk. You will, in short, work to make the report a readable thing in an eye-attracting setup.

Specifically, the formal report you plan to write will include these parts: a binding cover, a title fly, a title page, your personal letter of transmittal to Ms. Dodd, a table of contents (in organized-outline form), a table of illustrations, an epitome (in direct style, beginning with a distilled digest of your main findings and then shifting back to its real job of compressing each part in order and in proportion), the report body (arranged in logical order), supporting illustrations, and possibly an appendix.

38. Finding the problems at Midway's Aton store. For the past four years the home office advertising department of Midway Department Stores, Inc., has planned and prepared advertising for all major promotions (January white sales, mid-summer clearances, harvest sales, and the like) for the chain's 27 branch stores. Only the day-to-day advertising and a few of the less important promotions were handled by each store's own advertising managers. In general, the success of this plan has been quite plain to the company.

Particularly was the Midway management pleased when they reviewed the store-by-store sales summaries for the major promotions. For the past few years sales from promotions have been exceeding quotas at the individual stores—with only limited exception. One of these exceptions, the store at Aton, is your concern at the moment.

You, a marketing research specialist of some repute, have been retained by Ms. Rita A. Conn, president of Midway, to make a special study of the problem store. Specifically, Ms. Conn wants to know why the Aton store has failed to keep up with other Midway outlets. If possible, she'd like you to pinpoint the sources of difficulty.

She and others of the Midway hierarchy feel that the trouble lies in a general failure of the Aton store to coordinate its display and personal selling efforts with the promotional advertising which comes from the central office. It's your job to test their theory and to shed whatever light you can on the company's problem.

So you plan your research efforts to test management's thinking. During the following weeks you and a crew of assistants shop extensively in all departments of the problem store and of three of the company's more successful outlets, observing and recording all information which you believe might shed light on the problem. If, you reason, the Aton store summaries show less coordination between advertising on the one hand and the display of advertised material and personal sales efforts on the other, then management's theory is substantiated. But, if the opposite, or no relation is apparent, then other causes need to be investigated. Should management's theory be correct, a department-by-department analysis would be needed to pinpoint the sources of difficulty.

Today, after long weeks of careful record keeping, you have the data which should point to the answer. You have but to pore over them, weigh them carefully, and then proceed to the obvious conclusions. In keeping with the formality of the situation and the size of the problem, you will do well to present your analysis in formal-report form.

Your summary data are in Tables 49–65. (Note that the data are expressed in percentages.)

TABLE 49. Displayed advertised merchandise in street window

	Aton	Bell	Cody	Delta
Sporting goods	0	8	8	8
Automotive	4	2	3	6
Hardware	2	2	4	6
Household furnishings	3	6	5	0
Ready-to-wear:				
Men's	1	8	7	2
Women's	0	12	9	0
Children's	0	8	6	9
Appliances	0	4	0	2

TABLE 50. Displayed advertised merchandise in other departments

	Aton	Bell	Cody	Delta
Sporting goods	2	12	15	5
Automotive	0	7	8	6
Hardware	0	7	2	4
Household furnishings	0	8	6	2
Ready-to-wear:				
Men's	4	6	2	0
Women's	0	6	9	0
Children's	2	5	8	0
Appliances	0	0	0	0

TABLE 51. Displayed advertised merchandise in department where sold

	Aton	Bell	Cody	Delta
Sporting goods	82	100	100	100
Automotive	99	96	96	100
Hardware	92	98	94	100
Household furnishings	100	100	100	91
Ready-to-wear:				
Men's	89	100	100	94
Women's	91	100	100	95
Children's	86	100	100	99
Appliances	93	100	99	100

TABLE 52. Advertised items displayed in selling department carried informative signs

	Aton	Bell	Cody	Delta
Sporting goods	33	100	100	100
Automotive	92	98	97	100
Hardware	79	89	94	98
Household furnishings	95	100	100	86
Ready-to-wear:				
Men's	62	97	100	90
Women's	69	99	100	89
Children's	66	100	98	100
Appliances	77	100	89	100

TABLE 53. Informative signs included prices of advertised items

	Aton	Bell	Cody	Delta
Sporting goods	100	100	94	100
Automotive	100	98	92	98
Hardware	96	94	100	96
Household furnishings	98	92	100	100
Ready-to-wear:				
Men's	94	100	98	96
Women's	92	96	90	94
Children's	100	94	100	90
Appliances	100	100	100	100

TABLE 54. Failed to back advertised items with adequate merchandise offerings

	Aton				Bell				Cody				Delta			
	(1)	(2)	(3)	(4)	(1)	(2)	(3)	(4)	(1)	(2)	(3)	(4)	(1)	(2)	(3)	(4)
Sporting goods	24	16	19	41	4	4	6	86	0	3	5	92	3	5	6	86
Automotive	4	6	9	81	6	6	9	79	5	7	8	80	1	5	2	92
Hardware	20	13	20	47	6	7	10	77	8	11	5	76	1	3	3	93
Household furnishings	2	6	4	88	4	2	2	92	2	2	3	93	9	11	9	71
Ready-to-wear:																
Men's	16	14	12	58	6	4	9	81	3	5	8	84	12	10	12	66
Women's	33	13	18	36	9	7	4	80	7	6	6	81	13	13	16	58
Children's	8	2	19	71	3	5	4	88	4	4	3	89	3	5	5	87
Appliances	18	12	17	53	1	3	5	91	6	2	12	80	2	7	2	89

1. Sold out first day.
2. Sold out second day.
3. Sold out third day.
4. Adequate stock for sale.

TABLE 55. Instances in which available salespersons waited on customers immediately

	Aton	Bell	Cody	Delta
Sporting goods	65	94	93	95
Automotive	94	90	91	94
Hardware	85	85	84	93
Household furnishings	92	91	92	85
Ready-to-wear:				
Men's	74	88	86	80
Women's	67	89	88	81
Children's	79	90	91	93
Appliances	70	89	96	94

TABLE 56. Greeting extended customer by salesperson

	Aton					Bell					Cody					Delta				
	(1)	(2)	(3)	(4)	(5)	(1)	(2)	(3)	(4)	(5)	(1)	(2)	(3)	(4)	(5)	(1)	(2)	(3)	(4)	(5)
Sporting goods	44	16	6	28	6	6	78	3	2	11	4	60	19	9	8	3	71	7	17	2
Automotive	4	68	14	4	10	12	60	3	3	22	11	54	16	12	7	3	73	16	7	1
Hardware	15	54	5	0	26	13	59	7	1	20	10	66	6	9	9	2	61	17	8	12
Household furnishings	12	70	0	0	18	4	81	6	1	8	3	68	9	1	19	14	57	19	0	10
Ready-to-wear:																				
Men's	30	44	6	12	18	7	70	18	0	5	5	54	11	10	20	12	60	9	14	5
Women's	10	67	19	0	4	4	56	20	11	9	3	69	19	0	9	16	49	21	0	14
Children's	24	53	3	0	20	3	62	14	0	21	3	61	23	0	13	4	58	23	0	15
Appliances	40	36	4	4	16	6	66	6	9	13	12	49	20	3	16	2	71	19	2	6

1. No greeting.
2. "May I help you?"
3. "Are you being waited on?"
4. "Yes, sir?"
5. Other.

TABLE 57.   Courtesy of salespersons

	Aton				Bell				Cody				Delta			
	(1)	(2)	(3)	(4)	(1)	(2)	(3)	(4)	(1)	(2)	(3)	(4)	(1)	(2)	(3)	(4)
Sporting goods	0	36	58	6	39	58	3	0	44	54	2	0	64	32	4	0
Automotive	16	78	6	0	12	79	9	0	10	81	9	0	33	61	6	0
Hardware	6	76	16	0	6	87	7	0	12	79	9	0	44	52	4	0
Household furnishings	68	22	10	0	41	57	2	0	51	47	2	0	7	84	9	0
Ready-to-wear:																
Men's	2	71	27	0	36	58	6	0	28	69	3	0	2	80	16	2
Women's	16	68	13	0	44	49	7	0	36	62	2	0	2	80	18	0
Children's	8	66	26	0	31	65	4	0	19	77	4	0	33	62	5	0
Appliances	0	51	42	7	60	40	0	0	4	87	9	0	21	76	3	0

1. Very courteous.
2. Courteous.
3. Slightly discourteous or indifferent.
4. Discourteous.

TABLE 58.   Instances when salespersons were informed about advertised merchandise

	Aton	Bell	Cody	Delta
Sporting goods	86	100	100	100
Automotive	100	99	90	100
Hardware	96	98	98	100
Household furnishings	100	100	100	92
Ready-to-wear:				
Men's	74	100	100	89
Women's	91	100	100	94
Children's	90	99	100	100
Appliances	100	100	97	100

TABLE 59.   Instances when salespersons knew location of advertised merchandise

	Aton	Bell	Cody	Delta
Sporting goods	90	100	100	100
Automotive	98	98	93	100
Hardware	92	94	95	99
Household furnishings	99	100	100	93
Ready-to-wear:				
Men's	89	99	99	92
Women's	91	99	98	90
Children's	91	99	94	97
Appliances	96	100	94	100

TABLE 60.   Instances when salespersons encouraged customers to handle merchandise

	Aton	Bell	Cody	Delta
Sporting goods	12	67	61	72
Automotive	33	19	21	34
Hardware	17	23	26	33
Household furnishings	11	44	46	19
Ready-to-wear:				
Men's	21	41	71	29
Women's	23	64	57	41
Children's	9	33	37	38
Appliances	16	37	24	34

TABLE 61.   Knowledge of merchandise displayed by salesperson's presentation

	Aton				Bell				Cody				Delta			
	(1)	(2)	(3)	(4)	(1)	(2)	(3)	(4)	(1)	(2)	(3)	(4)	(1)	(2)	(3)	(4)
Sporting goods	6	20	71	3	32	66	2	0	31	60	9	0	27	71	2	0
Automotive	31	63	6	0	17	61	22	0	13	70	15	2	30	69	1	0
Hardware	22	59	17	2	16	55	21	8	14	61	21	4	29	66	3	2
Household furnishings	28	69	3	0	37	63	0	0	33	67	0	0	17	69	12	2
Ready-to-wear:																
Men's	7	66	20	7	14	81	5	0	20	79	1	0	6	69	25	0
Women's	9	60	24	7	21	78	1	0	31	69	0	0	11	66	21	2
Children's	8	54	21	17	31	67	2	0	23	76	1	0	19	80	1	0
Appliances	2	46	50	2	51	49	0	0	17	69	14	0	47	49	4	0

1. Knew merchandise very well.
2. Knew merchandise adequately.
3. Insufficient knowledge of merchandise.
4. Little or no knowledge of merchandise.

TABLE 62.   Salesperson suggested additional merchandise

	Aton	Bell	Cody	Delta
Sporting goods	2	37	41	41
Automotive	31	19	22	30
Hardware	11	21	24	36
Household furnishings	27	26	29	17
Ready-to-wear:				
Men's	19	46	51	33
Women's	18	56	52	35
Children's	13	31	36	34
Appliances	4	13	13	16

TABLE 63.   Salesperson attempted to trade up

	Aton	Bell	Cody	Delta
Sporting goods	0	16	19	21
Automotive	17	14	13	20
Hardware	9	11	13	21
Household furnishings	21	23	19	13
Ready-to-wear:				
Men's	23	39	37	26
Women's	11	33	30	22
Children's	9	16	18	19
Appliances	67	33	22	36

TABLE 64.   Salesperson's closing remark

	Aton			Bell			Cody			Delta		
	(1)	(2)	(3)	(1)	(2)	(3)	(1)	(2)	(3)	(1)	(2)	(3)
Sporting goods	61	33	6	88	0	12	91	0	9	84	1	15
Automotive	87	2	11	81	5	14	79	6	15	89	0	11
Hardware	67	9	24	74	6	20	76	3	21	93	0	7
Household furnishings	91	0	9	88	0	12	87	2	11	81	14	5
Ready-to-wear:												
Men's	86	6	8	91	1	8	92	0	8	87	5	8
Women's	83	7	10	90	0	10	93	0	7	84	6	10
Children's	81	9	10	91	0	9	87	1	12	82	0	18
Appliances	62	29	9	94	0	6	89	2	9	93	0	7

1. "Thank you."
2. None.
3. Other.

TABLE 65.   Average percent of promotion sales quotas* achieved during past three years

	Aton	Bell	Cody	Delta
Sporting goods	61	114	119	111
Automotive	107	88	91	109
Hardware	81	87	94	113
Household furnishings	103	116	118	84
Ready-to-wear:				
Men's	69	107	113	87
Women's	74	111	108	91
Children's	72	119	103	116
Appliances	59	122	92	103
Store average	79	108	105	103

* Quotas are based on Midway's own formula, which takes into account such factors as population, past sales records, and competition.

39.   Which of three magazines should carry McSwain Pipes' advertising?   As director of research for the Malcolm, Thames and Wardlowe Advertising Agency you are working on an assignment for Edward Karnes, account executive for McSwain pipes. As you understand them, the facts of your problem are as follows.

The McSwain Pipe Company, Ltd., of Edinburgh, Scotland, is just now introducing its century-old line of pipes to the U.S. market. The McSwain people can truly say that their pipes are among the world's finest. Made of only top-grade briar, McSwain pipes are built to exacting specifications. And every one of the company's 11 basic models is handsomely designed. Because McSwain pipes are high in quality they must sell for more than most pipes; but they are not out of the reach of discerning pipe fanciers of moderate means. Retail prices in the United States will start at $20 and will range upward to $75.

In spite of the good qualities of McSwain pipes, they are not known in the United States. If they are to sell, they must be promoted. And it is in this regard that Malcolm, Thames, and Wardlowe came on the scene. They were awarded the McSwain account, and now they are planning their initial campaign with Mr. Karnes serving as account executive.

Mr. Karnes plans to publicize McSwain pipes in full-page color advertisements which will be seen in one of the nation's leading magazines for men. Determining which magazine should carry the message, however, is no small problem for Mr. Karnes. It is on this matter that you, the agency's director of research, have been asked to help. Mr. Karnes has narrowed his selection to three men's magazines—*Sportsman, Male,* and *Mechanix Illustrated. Sportsman* is a magazine for those who like hunting, fishing, and the out-of-doors. *Male,* with its nude photographs and risqué writing, caters to swingers. *Mechanix Illustrated* is just what its name suggests—a magazine for those interested in mechanics. Mr. Karnes cannot decide on the best of the three. So he asks you for help. Specifically, he wants you to compare all pertinent information on the three magazines and to recommend the one that should carry the McSwain message.

The magazine you choose should be the one whose readers are most likely to be potential users of McSwain pipes. As Mr. Karnes points out, they should be the kind who appreciate quality and who can afford to pay for it. Although men of all ages buy McSwain pipes, they are especially appealing to the young sophisticate. In addition, older men of means and those with less responsibility are likely purchasers of fine pipes.

As you have done many times before in similar problems, you consult the latest consumer magazines reports for information on readership characteristics. Then you consult the latest *Standard Rate and Data Service* for cost information. From these two sources you find the information which will point the way to your conclusion (see Tables 66–67).

As usual, you will write up the information in a concise yet thorough report. As it may well be reviewed by the McSwain management personnel, you will present your material in the form of a formal, long report. You will use graphic aids wherever they will be helpful in supplementing your words.

TABLE. 66. Readership characteristics

	Sportsman	Male	Mechanix Illustrated
Primary readers:			
10 years and older:			
Number per copy of circulation			
Males	1.39	1.18	1.31
Females	.38	.61	.32
Total	1.77	1.79	1.63
Projected circulation, numbers			
Males	1,668,000	1,574,000	1,640,000
Females	456,000	814,000	401,000
Total	2,124,000	2,388,000	2,041,000
Ages of male readers:			
10–17 yrs.	21.6%	5.9%	22.2%
18–24 yrs.	12.9	27.1	12.6
25–34 yrs.	15.1	40.7	14.8
35–44 yrs.	19.4	11.0	19.3
45–54 yrs.	18.0	11.9	17.0
55 & older	12.9	3.4	14.1
Median age	35.4 years	29.3 years	35.4 years
Education of male adult readers			
(last school attended by adults):			
Grade school or less	14.3%	4.6%	12.6%
High school	55.1	45.6	62.1
College	30.6	49.8	25.3
Married readers 18 years and older:			
Percent married:			
Men	81.7%	70.3%	81.4
Women	90.9	90.7	96.3
Percent men by age-groups			
18–24 yrs.	5.6%	16.7%	6.0%
25–34 yrs.	20.2	48.7	25.3
35–44 yrs.	29.2	12.8	30.1
45–54 yrs.	27.0	16.7	22.9
55 and older	18.0	5.1	15.7
Occupation of adult male readers			
by percentage			
Professional and technical workers	12.9%	19.9%	14.3%
Officials	8.4	9.8	5.2
Business owners	6.2	6.1	10.1
Farmers and farm laborers	7.2	—	4.7
Clerical	7.9	5.9	5.5
Sales	4.9	7.1	3.1
Craftsmen	21.9	10.0	24.7
Operatives	16.1	11.8	15.6
Service workers	2.9	2.7	3.6
All others	11.6	26.7	13.2
Total family income of readers,			
percent of total:			
Under 5,000	1.4%	0.7%	1.3%
5,000– 9,999	1.4	2.4	2.4
10,000–14,999	3.8	3.1	3.4
15,000–19,999	7.1	9.3	6.3
20,000–24,999	20.7	17.4	28.1
25,000–29,999	28.4	28.3	29.8

TABLE 66   (*continued*)

	Sportsman	Male	Mechanix Illustrated
30,000–34,999	20.2	19.9	15.7
35,000 and over	17.0	18.7	12.9
Stage of life, male head of household, percentage of total:			
Single, under 45	1.8%	12.2%	1.9%
Married, under 45, no children under 18	7.1	15.8	7.7
Married, under 45, youngest child under 6	27.4	36.5	30.0
Married, under 45, youngest child over 6	17.6	9.5	16.1
Married, over 45, children under 18	17.6	8.2	16.4
Married, over 45, no children under 18	23.2	11.7	22.2
Single, over 45	4.0	3.4	3.5
Other	1.3	2.7	2.1

TABLE 67.   **Selected information on advertising rates**

Sportsman:

Rates

1 page (429 lines)	$ 9,375.00
2 columns (286 lines)	6,250.00
½ page (107 lines on 2 columns)	4,700.00
1 column (143 lines or 2 cols. × 71 lines)	3,125.00
1 inch (single column)	311.50
Agate line	22.25

Colors (Two-color—black and 1 color):

1 page	$10,375.00
2 columns	7,175.00
½ page	5,450.00
1 column	3,750.00

4-color page (3 process colors and black):

1 page	13,125.00

Bleed

Full pages, extra	10%
⅔, ½ and ⅓ page, extra	15%

No bleed accepted on back cover.
Either 2nd or 3rd cover bleed but not both.

Male:

Rates   Standard Units

1 page	$11,500.00
⅔ page..	8,250.00
½ page	6,500.00
⅓ page	4,125.00
⅙ page	2,050.00
1 inch	425.00

Colors

2 colors:

1 page	$14,500.00
⅔ page	10,375.00

TABLE 67 (*continued*)

Male	
½ page (horizontal)	8,185.00
⅓ page	5,175.00
4 colors:	
1 page	17,250.00
⅔ page	12,375.00
½ page (horizontal)	9,750.00
Bleed	
Extra	10%

Mechanix Illustrated:

Rates

1 page	$ 7,500.00
½ page	3,750.00
¼ page	1,875.00
⅛ page	925.00
1 inch	468.50
Agate line	33.50

    Line rate applies to that portion of ad in excess of standard unit, but less than next larger unit.

Colors

1 page (black and 1 color), extra	$ 675.00
½ page (black and 1 color), extra	437.50
¼ page (black and 1 color), extra	325.00

¼ page minimum space unit. Check availabilities on ¼ page units.

Bleed

Available in page and ½ page units, extra	15%

No extra charge for bleed into gutter only, or for bleed on 4-color covers, pages or inserts.

---

40. Advising the Downtown Merchants Association how to compete with shopping centers (Requires additional research). Members of the Downtown Merchants Association of ——— (your city or some other city selected by your instructor) are alarmed about the sales they are losing to suburban shopping centers. For the past few years the merchants have watched the shopping centers develop around them. At first they were only annoyed at their new competition. Then, as the centers grew and a trend away from downtown shopping developed, the merchants' annoyance changed to concern. As the trend continued, their concern changed to alarm. Their alarm led them to form a Downtown Merchants Association. They had one objective in mind when they formed the association—to fight back against the inroads made by the shopping centers.

The merchants' plight is understandable. Most have heavy investments in buildings or long-term leases. In fact, most of those who were not heavily invested have already pulled out—many moving to the shopping centers. Thus, those who remain are locked in. Their only chance for survival is to fight back.

At their initial meeting some of the merchants reported what they had heard other towns were doing, and a few made suggestions as to what the group might do. It soon became obvious, however, that a group such as theirs could not develop a coordinated plan of action. They agreed that they needed outside help. Thus it was that you, a marketing consultant, were called in.

As you understand it, your assignment is first to study all aspects of the shopping situation in the city. Then you will search the literature to find out what has been done in other cities or what the experts say can be done. From this analysis you will develop a plausible plan for the merchants to follow. In drawing up your plan, keep in mind that the merchants are willing and expect to pay something. But they must be convinced that what they pay for is likely to produce profits.

Of course, you will present your work in formal report form.

41. Are your store's prices in line with its competitors'? Assume that you, an independent research specialist, are employed by one of your local grocery stores (you choose one) to compare the store's prices with the prices of its two main competitors. For some time now the management has been hearing comments about how much lower the prices of this and that product are at other stores in town. Much of this talk, of course, could be the result of advertised loss leaders —that is, goods advertised at low prices merely to attract customers. But one can't be too sure. Anyway, the fact that sales have dropped recently makes the manager want to investigate the question. And he wants you to make this investigation for him.

To get the information you need, you plan to construct a diversified shopping basket of grocery items and then to check the prices of each item at each of the three stores. Specifically, you will first select a group of items from each department (meats, canned goods, vegetables, etc.). You will take care to select items which can be checked easily—that is, your selections will be carefully specified by grade, quantity, and/or brand. Too, the items you select will adequately represent the goods in each department. Once you have selected the items, you will visit each of the stores and record the prices of each item. As you are concerned primarily with normal prices, you will take care to note any prices that are "specials." Also, you will want to note any possible price effects of trading stamps.

With these data collected, your next chore will be to evaluate them and then to write your results in good report form (as specified by your instructor). Because the management wants to be able to pinpoint the departments and commodities that may be in or out of line, your report will present your findings in some detail.

SUBJECTS FOR LIBRARY RESEARCH REPORTS

The following topic suggestions may be used for library research reports. With most of the topics the specific facts of the case must be created through the student's (or perhaps the instructor's) imagination before a business-type problem exists.

Accounting

1. Report on the need for an availability of accounting graduates in the years ahead.
2. Design an inventory control system for X Company (your choice).
3. How should X Company (lessee) treat lease transactions on its books?
4. Evaluate the alternative accounting methods available to X Company, which is committed to a policy of tax allocation.

5. Evaluate the use of statistical sampling to determine whether a company's internal control system prevents material errors from finding their way into financial statements. Make a recommendation to Company X.

6. As accountant for X Company, justify your treatment of the assets acquired by the takeover of Y Company.

7. Advise X Company management on the question of uniformity of accounting procedures between X Company and its nearest competitor.

8. Recommend to X Company a policy on the translation of foreign currency in the consolidation of overseas subsidiaries.

9. Advise the chief accountant of X Company on the maintenance of capital in company accounts.

10. Advise X Company management on the accounting problems that will come about if it begins overseas operations.

11. Advise X Company management on the problems of departmentalization of factory overhead.

12. Develop a policy for X Company on the costing of joint products and by-products.

13. Advise the management of X Manufacturing Company on the question of whether to use process costing or job costing procedures.

14. Analyze break-even analysis as a deicsion-making tool for X Company.

15. Evaluate for X Company management the validity of the traditional matching process in determining corporate net income.

16. Analyze the relative effects upon income of the Fifo and Lifo methods of inventory valuation during a prolonged period of inflation.

17. Write a report for the American Accounting Association on the effects of computers on the demand for accountants.

18. Evaluate the utility of traditional variance analysis as a means of cost control.

19. Develop a proposal for the accounting treatment of the costs of a research program in X Oil Company.

20. Justify your progressive accounting treatment of revenues received under a four-year construction contract.

21. Establish a bad-debts policy and design a collection system for X Company.

22. Determine the feasibility of a consolidated delivery service for City Y.

23. How should X Company handle the state sales tax on its books?

24. Design an inventory control plan for X Company.

25. Advise X Company management on the validity of return on investment as a measure of performance.

26. What are the methods X Company can use in handling errors which affected net income in prior years?

27. How should X Company handle its patents and copyrights on its books?

28. Report on the status of the use of operations research as a decision-making tool for accountants and managers.

29. How should X Company use cash-flow analysis as a guide in and for profit planning?

30. Evaluate alternative methods of measuring return on investments for X Company.

31. Report to X Company management on the trends in content and design of corporate annual reports.
32. Report to the American Accounting Association on the status of professional ethics in public accounting.
33. Summarize for the accounting department of X Company the most recent trends and developments in accounting theory.
34. Advise partners X and Y of the XY Company how priorities should be determined for cash distribution in the liquidation of their partnership.
35. Advise X Company management on income tax considerations in the selection of a form of business organization.
36. Report to X Company management on the advantages and disadvantages of the uniform cost accounting system.
37. Should X Company use an accelerated method of depreciation?
38. Recommend to X Company the proper disclosure of long-term leases in its financial statements.
39. Recommend to X Company management how it can make better use of the accounting department and accounting information.
40. How should X Company account for pension costs?
41. Develop for Company X a procedure for human resource accounting.
42. Review the pros and cons of installing a time-sharing computer system for Company X.
43. Prepare a report for Company X management on the diversity of factors and practices in transfer pricing.
44. Report on the need and value of a social audit for Company X.

Business education

1. Evaluate the effectiveness of closed-circuit television instruction.
2. How effective is programmed instruction in business education?
3. What should be the content of the business communication (or other subject) course?
4. How should teaching ability be measured?
5. What should be the role of the student in course and curriculum planning?
6. What should be the role of the business leaders in developing courses and curricula for business education?
7. Should business teachers be unionized?
8. Examine the present status of business education teaching as a true profession.
9. Outline historical developments in business education.
10. Recommend an ideal certification program for business teachers.
11. Assess placement responsibilities of business education in secondary schools.
12. How effective is career guidance in business education?
13. What is the ideal education for careers in business?
14. Evaluate the use of student evaluations of teachers.
15. Are programs for exceptional youths desirable in business education?

16. Describe the emerging role of the junior college in business education.
17. How should the standards of achievement in the business education curriculum be set?
18. What is the role of economics education at the secondary level?
19. How should student achievement be measured?
20. What are the proper uses of audiovisual aids in teaching business subjects?
21. What are the relations of theories of learning to the teaching of business subjects?
22. What is the place of student opinions and evaluations in curriculum revisions?
23. Develop a plan for work measurements in the office.
24. Develop an ideal testing procedure for business subjects.
25. What is the place of business education in the public secondary school? (or in technical vocational schools?)
26. Should the business curriculum be specialized or should it provide a generalized, well-rounded education?
27. Evaluate the development of federal aid to business education.

Labor

1. For X Union investigate the impact technological evolution has had on unionism in the past decade.
2. Develop a new compensation plan for X Company that will best motivate employees.
3. Design a plan of employee discipline for X Company.
4. Evaluate the potential labor problems of X Company in _____ (country) where it is planning a new factory.
5. Advise X Company management on the use of the lockout as a means of dealing with its union.
6. For a specific national union make an objective report on union leadership in the nation during the past decade.
7. Evaluate the effects of a particular strike (your choice) on the union, the company, the stockholder, and the public. Write the report for a federal investigating committee.
8. Advise management of X Company on how to deal with Y Union, which is attempting to organize X's employees.
9. For a national union write a report on the trend of corruption in unions over the past 25 years.
10. How have union contracts limited the area of decision making?
11. Explore the relationships of the union and the white-collar worker.
12. Show trends and implications of teacher organizing.
13. Examine recent trends relative to the older worker and the stand taken by unions in this area.
14. Analyze the problem of automation and the unions' reactions to it.
15. Study the status and effects of the "right-to-work" laws.
16. Is it proper for unions to be in business for themselves?
17. Set up plans for unionizing Company X.

18. Recommend a grievance system for Company X.
19. Should antitrust laws apply to unions?
20. Examine and report on discrimination in unions.
21. Should government employees be unionized?
22. Outline the power structure of unions and its implications.
23. Evaluate the future of process unionism.
24. Discuss unionism in retail stores and its effects on prices.
25. What is the status of labor regulations in your state?
26. Are unions monopolistic?
27. How should Company X prepare for upcoming contract negotiations with the union?
28. What are the causes of industrial war and peace?
29. Report on what personnel executives look for in application letters and data sheets.

Finance

1.   Advise overcapitalized X Company on the possibility of repurchasing shares.
2.   Justify the use of ratio analysis to a major client of your brokerage firm.
3.   Evaluate the advantages and disadvantages of issuing "no par" stock for X Company.
4.   Advise the medical doctors at X Clinic as to whether they should incorporate their operation.
5.   Should X Company lease or buy capital equipment?
6.   Advise rapidly growing X Manufacturing Company on the form of organization it should take.
7.   Advise faltering X Company as to whether it would be more valuable as a going concern than it would be in liquidation.
8.   Should X Company establish a holding company in its corporate organizational structure?
9.   Should X Company amend its policy of paying dividends at a constant proportion of earnings to one of paying on a constant per share basis?
10. Examine the possibilities of factoring accounts receivable for X Company, which is experiencing a liquidity crisis.
11. Advise X Company as to whether it should seek to get its stock listed on a major stock exchange.
12. Develop a fundamental inventory control model for X Company.
13. Advise X Company on the policy it should follow in determining dividend payments.
14. Evaluate the utility of the payback method of investment analysis.
15. Recommend and justify a plan for financing expansion of X Company.
16. How will the present state of the market affect the success of the proposed rights offering of X Company?
17. Advise X Company as to whether it should select a capital structure that will serve to minimize the cost of capital and so promote maximum share prices.

18. Advise X Company management on how the prevailing condition of capital rationing in the company should affect its investment decision analysis.

19. What should be the role of the controllership function in cost control at X Company?

20. What is the most feasible way to finance newly formed X Company?

21. Recommend for Company X some compensations and proprietary mechanisms that may serve as an alternative to stock options.

22. Should Investment Group X invest in mutual funds?

23. Should Investment Group X invest in gold?

24. Examine the merits of proposed legislation to regulate the price of consumer credit.

25. Should Company X join an employers' association?

26. Recommend a formal salary scale for X Company.

27. For a national union evaluate the effectiveness of the Occupational Safety and Health Act (OSHA) on workers' health and safety. Recommend union action based on your findings.

28. For a special committee of Congress, review the question of "fairness" in labor contracts with management. Make recommendations for correcting through legislation.

29. What should be the role of National Union X in helping to reduce inflation?

30. Evaluate the prospects for labor-management relations in the year ahead for the National Association of Manufacturers.

31. What should be the role of Labor Union X (or Company X) in politics?

32. Layoffs based on seniority is causing a disproportionate reduction in women and minority workers at Company X. Investigate alternatives which the company can present to the union.

33. What should be the role of Union X in the matter of environmental protection?

Management

1. Advise Company X management on what it should do to overcome resistance to _____ (some basic change, such as a change in compensation plan).

2. Design an employee-selection procedure for X Company.

3. Recommend and justify to the board of directors of X Company a plan for exercising the firm's social responsibility.

4. Design a control system for preventing individual espionage at X Company.

5. Evaluate for X Oil Company the application of statistical decision theory in overcoming the problems of uncertainty in oil exploration.

6. Evaluate for X Company the possibility of using brainstorming sessions in strategic policy making.

7. Evaluate for X Manufacturing Company the use of the informal grapevine as a means of improving communication within the organization.

8. Using the best authoritative ideas available, design a management information system for X Company.

9. Design a public relations campaign for X Company.

10. Recommend an executive evaluation plan for X Company.

11. Develop for X Company a guide to ethics in its highly competitive business situation.

12. Analyze break-even analysis as a decision-making tool for X Company.

13. Evaluate the various methods of determining corporate performance and select the one most appropriate for Company X.

14. Design a program for evaluating a business, taking account of nonprofit measures of performance as well as profitability.

15. Determine the business outlook for the _____ industry.

16. Determine the effects of recent labor-management court rulings on X Company.

17. Recommend a suggestion system for X Company.

18. Recommend to X Company the feasibility of using a community computer center.

19. Report on the civil and criminal liabilities of corporate executives.

20. Advise X Company on the procedures for incorporating in _____ (state).

21. Recommend a profit sharing plan for X Company personnel.

22. Can X Company profitably use a computer?

23. Would hiring handicapped workers be charity or good business for X Company?

24. Can creativity be taught to X Company executives?

25. Design a program for achieving optimum discipline in X Company.

26. Determine for X Company its policy toward aid to education.

27. Assess the extent of pollution control in _____ industry for an association of firms in the industry.

28. Determine the extent of minority recruiting, hiring, and training in the _____ industry for a legislative committee.

29. Determine the extent of discrimination against women in business for an association of businesspeople.

30. For a national association of professional people (your choice) report on the effects of government efforts and plans to regulate professional behavior (minimum fee schedules, ban on advertising, and so on).

31. Evaluate the value of union-management consultation (getting the views of union leadership on employee matters prior to taking action on these matters).

32. Advise Company X on what is the systems approach to planning and how the company can use it.

33. Recommend a plan for using management by objectives at Company X.

34. Review the information available on job stresses related to the social and physical environment. Recommend to Company X what it should do concerning this matter.

35. What should be the role of social responsibility in Company's X's operations?

36. Evaluate and determine the effectiveness of the organization design of a company of your choice.

37. Company X is organized by region (or by product or process technology). Evaluate the possibilities of organizing by its major markets.

38. Company X is in the process of becoming a multinational organization. Evaluate the effects this development will have on its internal and external communications.

39. Working for an organization advancing women's rights in business, develop a plan for educating the public to accept the organization's objective.
40. Advise a manager on how to deal with the informal cliques that develop in his organization.

Personnel administration

1. Interpret for X Company the effects of court decisions on testing and hiring employees.
2. Develop and justify a program of fringe benefits for a large industrial company.
3. Recommend an equitable compensation program for the sales personnel for X Company.
4. Design a program for breaking down line-staff barriers in X Company.
5. Analyze for X Company the problems of hiring under- and overqualified staff.
6. Recommend a retirement plan for X Company.
7. Devise an operational safety program for X Company.
8. Design a workable program for controlling activities of scientific and professional employees of X Company.
9. Survey the literature to find meaningful guides for selecting executives for foreign service for X Company.
10. Design a safety training program for X Company.
11. Develop a method to test morale in X Company.
12. Should X Company use the lie detector test to screen prospective employees?
13. Set up a secretary (or other position) selection plan for X Company.
14. Report to a major labor union the progress of women in the job market.
15. Evaluate the use of teaching machines (or some other innovative teaching technique) for the training programs of X Company.
16. Report to the management of X Company what information the employees need to know about the company and its operation.
17. Report to the safety director of X Company on the validity of the accident-proneness concept.
18. Report to the safety director of X Company on the effect of age and experience on accidents.
19. Develop a personnel testing program for X Company.
20. Report to X Company management on recent trends and developments in employee remuneration.
21. Advise X Company management on the merits and demerits of the guaranteed annual wage.
22. Evaluate the use of sensitivity training for X company.
23. Evaluate transactional analysis for the training of X Company executives.
24. Evaluate the effects of an early retirement plan and recommend what Company X should do about the matter.
25. Evaluate the effectiveness of telephone information programs for Company X (these are programs in which employees can get current, pertinent information on company affairs by dialing a number).

Marketing

1. Determine the major opportunities in the environment for the marketing strategy of X National Bank.

2. Develop a plan for measuring the effectiveness of Company X advertising.

3. Design a PERT/CPM network for the marketing aspect of product management in Company X.

4. Develop a compensation plan for the salespeople of X Company.

5. Assuming a budget of $_____, develop an advertising plan for X Company.

6. For a major shopping center in your area, construct a plan for setting the advertising budget.

7. Develop a global advertising policy for the X Company, a multinational retail organization.

8. Determine the future for trading stamps for X Company, a major chain of department stores.

9. What problems will Company X encounter in trading with countries behind the iron curtain?

10. Set up and defend a multistage approach to pricing decisions for X Company.

11. Determine the problems X Company will encounter in introducing a new product to its line.

12. What is the importance of fixed ratios in setting pricing strategy for X Company?

13. Select the optimal channel of distribution for new product Y in your area and justify your choice.

14. Design a marketing strategy for your professional cleaning service.

15. Develop a segmented profile of the target market for product Y and analyze the utility of this information in Company X's marketing management.

16. Explore the possibilities of trade with _____ (a foreign country) for X Company.

17. Determine changes in successful sales techniques for X Sales Company.

18. Report on the future of drive-in grocery stores for X Investment Company.

19. Determine the value of a college education in marketing work.

20. Should X Department Stores use credit cards?

21. Will pallet warehousing reduce costs for X Company?

22. Determine for Company X the social and ethical aspects of pricing for the market.

23. Determine for the American Consumer League whether advertising should be regulated.

24. Design a promotion campaign for the opening of Bank X.

25. Explore the possibilities of door-to-door selling for X Company.

26. Determine the best method to sell a new issue of common stock for well-established Company X.

27. Should X Company use contests to increase efforts of its salespeople?

28. Determine for a national department store chain the changing trends in service offered in the field.

29. Answer for the X Manufacturing Company the question of whether it should engage in "lease" sales.

30. Should Company X, a regional automotive supply chain, use centralized or decentralized warehousing?

31. Should Company X rent or lease trucks for distribution of its products?

32. How should X Company determine the amount of its advertising budget?

33. Should X Company use its own advertising department or an agency?

34. Design a promotional program for introducing new product Y.

35. Where should X Company locate its next supermarket (or drugstore, service station, and so on) in your area?

36. Determine the influences on fashion in the _____ industry.

37. How can downtown merchants in _____ (city) cope with the trend toward suburban shopping centers?

38. Determine the trends in packaging in the _____ industry.

39. Make a market study of _____ (a city) to determine whether it is a suitable location for _____ (a type of business).

40. Should X Company establish its own sales force, use manufacturers' agents (manufacturers' representatives), or use selling agents?

41. Should X Petroleum Company attempt to increase its share of the market by engaging in active price competition?

42. Determine for X Company the best channel of distribution for _____ product line.

43. How should X Company evaluate the performance of its sales personnel?

44. Should X Company enter the _____ market?

45. What price policy should X Company use on entering the _____ market?

46. How should Company X evaluate the performance of its salespeople?

47. Determine for Company X the best procedure for evaluating the effectiveness of its advertising.

48. Should Company X, a canner of citrus and vegetable products, change from its policy of brand marketing to product-line marketing?

ORAL REPORT PROBLEMS

1. Look through current newspapers, magazines, and so on, and get the best available information on the job outlook for this year's college graduates. You will want to look at each major field separately. You may also want to show variations by geographic area, by degree, and by schools. Present your findings in a well-organized and illustrated oral report.

2. Present a plan for improving some phase of operation on your campus (registration, scholastic honesty, housing, grade appeals, library, cafeteria, traffic, curricula, athletic events, and such).

3. Present an objective report on some legislation of importance to business (right-to-work laws, environmental controls, taxes, and the like). Take care to present evidence and reasoning from all major viewpoints. Support your presentation with facts, figures, and so on whenever they will help.

4. Assume that you are being considered by a company of your choice for a job of your choice. Your prospective employer has asked you to make a _____- minute (your instructor will specify) report on your qualifications. You may project your education to the date you will be in the job market and may make assumptions that are consistent with your record to date.

5. Prepare and present an informative report on how individuals may reduce their income tax payments (federal or state). Probably you will want to emphasize the most likely sources of tax savings—such as tax sheltering and avoiding common errors.

6. Make a presentation to a hypothetical group of investors which will get you the investment money you need for a purpose of your choice. Your purpose could be to begin a new business, to construct a building, to develop land—whatever interests you. Make your presentation as real (or realistic) as you can. And support your appeal with visual aids.

7. The company you work for (your choice) has asked you to study the problem of its relations with the community and to make specific recommendations of what it can do to improve relations. Present your report to the company's board of directors. Use real (or realistic) information.

8. As chairman of the site selection committee for the National Federation of Business Executives present a report on your committee's recommendation. The committee has selected a city and a convention hotel (you may choose each). Your report will give your recommendation as well as the reason supporting your choice. For class purposes, you may make up whatever facts you may need about the organization and its convention requirements and about the hotel. But use real facts about the city.

9. The top administrators of your company have asked you to look into the question of whether the company should own automobiles, rent automobiles, or pay mileage costs on employee-owned automobiles. (Autos are used by sales personnel) Gather the best available information on the matter and report it to the group. You may make up any company facts you may need; but make them realistic.

10. A national chain of sandwich shops is considering locating an outlet near your campus. They have asked you to investigate the matter for them (competition, site possibilities, and so on). Report your finding to the board of directors.

11. As a buyer of men's (or women's, boy's, and such) clothing, report to the sales personnel of your store on the fashions for the coming season. (You may get the necessary information from publications in the field.)

12. You have been appointed chairperson of a money-raising campaign for your favorite philanthropic organization (you choose it). Develop a plan for canvasing the households and businesses in your city. Present your plan to a meeting of the organization's directors.

Illustrations of types of reports

The illustrations which appear on the following pages typify the various types of reports. Although they are competently constructed and well illustrate the traditional forms, they are not submitted as models in all respects. Because of the need to disguise the names of the branded products involved, perhaps the reports have lost some of their realism. Nevertheless, they represent orderly, thorough, and objective solutions to somewhat complex problems.

APPENDIX D–1.   Illustration of a long, formal report

RECOMMENDATIONS FOR 19— REPLACEMENTS

IN ALLIED DISTRIBUTORS, INC., SALES FLEET

BASED ON A COMPARISON OF FOUR SUBCOMPACT AUTOMOBILES

APPENDIX D–1 (*continued*)

RECOMMENDATIONS FOR 19— REPLACEMENTS

IN ALLIED DISTRIBUTORS, INC., SALES FLEET

BASED ON A COMPARISON OF FOUR SUBCOMPACT AUTOMOBILES

Prepared for

Mr. Norman W. Bigbee, Vice President
Allied Distributors, Inc.
3131 Speedall Street, Akron, Ohio 44302

Prepared by

George W. Franklin, Associate Director
Midwestern Research, Inc.
1732 Midday Avenue, Chicago, Illinois 60607

April 13, 19—

APPENDIX D-1 (*continued*)

MIDWESTERN RESEARCH, INC.
1732 Midday Avenue
Chicago, Illinois
60607

April 13, 19—

Mr. Norman W. Bigbee
Vice President in Charge of Sales
Allied Distributors, Inc.
3131 Speedall Street
Akron, Ohio 44302

Dear Mr. Bigbee:

Here is the report on the four makes of subcompact automobiles you asked me to compare last January 3.

To aid you in deciding which of the four makes you should buy
as replacements for your fleet, I gathered what I believe to be
the most complete information available. Much of the operating information comes from your own records. The remaining
data are the findings of both consumer research engineers and
professional automotive analysts. Only my analyses of these
data are subjective.

I sincerely hope, Mr. Bigbee, that my analyses will aid you in
making the correct decision. I truly appreciate this assignment.
And should you need any assistance in interpreting my analyses,
please call on me.

Sincerely,

George W. Franklin

George W. Franklin
Associate Director

APPENDIX D–1 (*continued*)

APPENDIX D–1 (*continued*)

APPENDIX D–1 (*continued*)

Synopsis

The recommendation of this study is that Gamma is the best
buy for Allied Distributors, Inc., Authorized by Mr. Norman
W. Bigbee, Vice President, on January 3, 19—, this report is
submitted on April 13, 19—. This study gives Allied Distributors an insight into the problem of replacing the approximately 50 two-year-old subcompact cars in its present sales
fleet. The basis for this recommendation is an analysis of
cost, safety, and construction factors of four models of subcompact cars (Alpha, Beta, Gamma, and Delta).

The four cars do not show a great deal of difference in ownership cost (initial cost less trade-in allowance after two
years). On a per-car basis, Beta costs least for a two-year
period--$1,608. Compared with costs for the other cars,
Beta is $185 under Gamma, $294 under Alpha, and $317 un-
der Delta. For the entire sales fleet, these differences become more significant. A purchase of 50 Betas would save
$9,250 over Gamma, $14,700 over Alpha, and $15,850 over
Delta. Operation costs favor Gamma. Cost per mile for
this car is $0.06985, as compared with $0.07279 for Alpha,
$0.07393 for Delta, and $0.07592 for Beta. The totals of all
costs for the 50-car fleet over the two-year period shows
Gamma to be least costly at $192,547. In second place is
Alpha, with a cost of $200,104. Third is Delta with $203,280,
and fourth is Beta with a cost of $208,766.

On the qualities that pertain to driving safety, Gamma is
again superior to the other cars. It has the best brakes and
is tied with Alpha for the best weight distribution. It is second in acceleration and is again tied with Alpha for the number of standard safety devices. Alpha is second over-all in
this category, having the second best brakes of the group.
Beta is last because of its poor acceleration and poor brakes.

Construction features and handling abilities place Gamma all
by itself. It scores higher than any of the other cars in every
category. Alpha and Delta are tied for second place. Again
Beta is last, having poor steering and handling qualities.

APPENDIX D–1 (*continued*)

RECOMMENDATIONS FOR 19— REPLACEMENTS

IN ALLIED DISTRIBUTORS, INC., SALES FLEET

BASED ON A COMPARISON OF FOUR SUBCOMPACT AUTOMOBILES

I.   ORIENTATION TO THE PROBLEM

A.   The Authorization Facts

This comparison of the qualities of four brands of subcompact automobiles is submitted April 13, 19—, to Mr. Norman
W. Bigbee, Vice President, Allied Distributors, Inc. At a
meeting in his office January 3, 19—, Mr. Bigbee orally
authorized Midwestern Research, Inc., to conduct this investigation. Mr. George W. Franklin, Research Director
for Midwestern Research served as director of the project.

B.   Problem of Selecting Fleet Replacements

The objective of this study is to determine which model of
subcompact automobile Allied Distributors, Inc., should select for replacements in its sales fleet. The firm's policy
is to replace all two-year-old models. It replaces approximately 50 automobiles each year.

The replacements involve a major capital outlay, and the
sales fleet expense constitutes a major sales cost. Thus,
the proper selection of a new model presents an important
problem. The model selection must be economical, dependable, and safe. Allied is considering four subcompact automobiles as replacement possibilities. As instructed by Mr.
Bigbee, for reasons of information security, the cars are
identified in this report only as Alpha, Beta, Gamma, and
Delta.

1

APPENDIX D–1 (*continued*)

2

C. Reports and Records as Sources of Data

The selection of the replacement brand is based on a comparative analysis of the merits of the four makes. Data for the comparisons were obtained from both company records and statistical reports. Operating records of ten representative cars of each make provide information on operating costs. These reports are summaries compiled by salesperson-drivers and represent actual performance of company cars under daily selling conditions. Additional material enumerating safety features, overall driving quality, and dependability comes from the reports of the Consumers Union of United States, Inc., Automotive Industries, and Bond Publishing Company's periodical, Road and Track. Mr. Bigbee furnished the trade-in allowances granted on the old models. From this material extensive comparisons of the four makes are presented.

D. A Preview to the Presentation

In the following pages of the report, the four cars are compared on the basis of three factors: operating costs, safety features, and total performance. Operating costs receive primary attention. In this part the individual cost items for each car are analyzed. This analysis leads to the determination of the most economical of the four cars.

Safety features make up the second factor of comparison. In this part the analysis centers on the presence or absence of safety features in each car and the quality of the features that are present. From this analysis comes a safety ranking of the cars. The third factor for comparison is total performance and durability. As in preceding parts, here the analysis produces a ranking of the cars.

The report ends with a summary of the strengths and weaknesses of each car. Then a comparison of the strengths and weaknesses leads to a final conclusion and a recommendation.

II.· THE MAJOR FACTOR OF COST

As cost is an obvious and generally accepted requirement of any major purchase, it is a logical first point of concern in selecting a car to buy. Here the first concern is the original cost--that is, the

APPENDIX D–1 (*continued*)

3

fleet discount price. Of second interest in a logical
thinking process are the cash differences after trade-
in allowances for the old cars. These figures clearly
indicate the cash outlay for the new fleet.

A.   Initial Costs Favor Beta

From Table I it is evident that Beta has the lowest
window sticker price before and after trade-in allowances. It has a $181 margin which must be considered
in the light of what features are standard on Beta in
comparison with those standard on the other cars.
That is, the Beta may have fewer standard features
included in its original cost and, therefore, not to be
worth as much as the Alpha, Gamma, or Delta.

TABLE I ORIGINAL COST OF FOUR BRANDS OF SUBCOMPACT CARS IN 19—			
Make	Window Sticker Prices	Trade-In Value for Two-Year-Old Makes*	Cash Costs After Trade-in Allowance
Alpha	3,659	1,757	1,902
Beta	3,358	1,750	1,608
Gamma	3,570	1,776	1,794
Delta	3,850	1,925	1,925

*Trade-in value for Alpha and Beta are estimates
Sources: Primary and Road and Track, 19—

It is clear that where features are listed as standard
they do not add to original cost, but where listed as options they do. As will be shown in a later table, the
Delta has many more standard features than do the
other makes. In addition to a study of standard features, a close look at trade-in values and operating
costs will also be necessary to properly evaluate
original cost.

APPENDIX D–1 (*continued*)

4

Further discussion of standard features of the cars appears in following discussions of safety and per-mile operating costs.

B. Trade-in Values Show Uniformity

Original costs alone do not tell the complete purchase-cost story. The values of the cars at the ends of their useful lives (trade-in values) are a vital part of cost. In this case, the trade-in value is $1,925 for Delta, and the lowest is $1,750 for Beta (see Table 1). Only $175 separates the field.

Although fairly uniform, these figures appear to be more significant when converted to total amounts involved in the fleet purchases. A fleet of 50 Betas would cost $80,413. The same fleet of Gammas, Alphas, and Deltas would cost $89,688, $95,111, and $95,250, respectively. Thus, Allied's total cost of purchasing Betas would be $9,275 lower than Gammas, $14,608 lower than Alphas, and $15,838 lower than Deltas.

C. Operating Costs Are Lowest for Gamma

Gamma has the lowest maintenance cost of the four, .985 cents per mile. But Delta is close behind with 1.0325 cents. Both of these are well below the Beta and Alpha figures of 1.3668 and 1.3808, respectively. As shown in Table II, these costs are based on estimates of repairs, resulting loss of working time, tire replacements, and miscellaneous items.

It should be stressed here how greatly repair expense influences the estimates. Actually, two expenses are involved, for to the cost of repairs the expense of time lost by salespeople must be added. Obviously, a salesperson without a car is unproductive. Each hour lost by car repairs adds to the cost of the car's operation.

The time lost per repair is the same for each car--five hours. Thus, the important consideration is the number of repairs and the costs of these repairs. On this basis, the Gamma has the lowest total cost burden at $543 (see Table II). Delta ranks second with $569. Beta is third with $753, and Alpha is last with $760.

APPENDIX D–1 (*continued*)

5

TABLE II
COMPARISON OF REPAIRS AND RELATED
LOST WORKING TIME FOR FOUR MAKES
OF CARS FOR TWO YEARS

Make	Number of Repairs	Repair Expense	Working Hours Lost*	Total Burden
Alpha	8	$410	40	$760
Beta	8	403	40	753
Gamma	6	280	30	543
Delta	6	306	30	569

*Based on hourly wage of $8.75
Source: Allied Distributors, Inc., Operating Records

Alpha has the best record for oil and gas economy with a per-mile cost of 3.114 cents (see Table III). Second is Gamma with a cost of 3.327 cents. In third and fourth positions are Beta, 3.455 cents, and Delta, 3.668 cents. Figured on the basis of the 55,000 miles Allied cars average over two years, Alpha's margin appears more significant. Its total margin over Delta is $305.11 per car--or $15,256 for the fleet of

TABLE III
COST-PER-MILE ESTIMATE OF OPERATION

	Alpha	Beta	Gamma	Delta
Depreciation	$.02783	$.02770	$.02672	$.02692
Gas	.02900	.03241	.02900	.03241
Oil	.00214	.00214	.00427	.00427
Tires	.00226	.00163	.00084	.00061
Repairs	.00725	.00723	.00527	.00639
Miscellaneous	.00431	.00481	.00375	.00333
Total	$.07279	$.07592	$.06985	$.07393

Source: Allied Distributors, Inc., Operating Records

APPENDIX D–1 (*continued*)

6

50 cars. Compared with Gamma, Alpha's margin is $117.45 per car and $5,871 for the fleet total. Alpha's per-car margin over Beta is $178.06, and its fleet margin is $8,903.

D. Cost Composite Favors Gamma

Gamma is the most economical of all the cars when all cost figures are considered (see Table III). Its total cost per mile is 6.985 cents, as compared with 7.279 cents for Alpha, 7.393 cents for Delta, and 7.596 cents for Beta. These figures take on more meaning when converted to total fleet cost over the two-year period the cars will be owned. As shown in Chart 1,

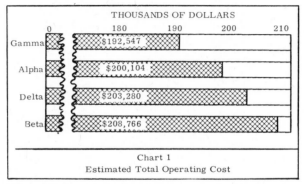

THOUSANDS OF DOLLARS

	180	190	200	210
Gamma	$192,547			
Alpha	$200,104			
Delta	$203,280			
Beta	$208,766			

Chart 1
Estimated Total Operating Cost

a fleet of 50 Gammas would cost Allied a total of $192,547. This figure is under all the other car totals. It is $7,557 below Alpha's $200,104, $10,733 below Delta's 203,280, and $16,219 under Beta's $208,766.

III. EVALUATION OF SAFETY FEATURES

Even though cost receives major emphasis in this analysis, safety of the cars also is important. How much importance safety should receive, however, is a matter for Allied management to decide. Allied salespeople spend a large part of their

APPENDIX D–1 (*continued*)

7

working time driving. And unquestionably driving is a hazardous assignment. Certainly Allied management wishes to minimize these hazards. Thus, it may be willing to sacrifice some
cost in order to get safer vehicles.

A.   Delta Is Best Equipped with Safety Devices

Only Delta has as standard equipment all five of the extra safety
devices considered desirable by The Consumers Safety Council.
The Delta is fully equipped with front disc brakes, vacuum brake
assist, adjustable seatbacks, flow-through ventilation, and anti-
glare mirrors, as shown in Table IV. The Delta's braking system

TABLE IV
LIST OF STANDARD
SAFETY FEATURES

FEATURE	Alpha	Beta	Gamma	Delta
Front Disc Brakes	Yes	No	Yes	Yes
Vacuum Brake Assist	No	No	No	Yes
Adjustable Seatback	No	No	No	Yes
Flow-through Ventilation	Yes	No	Yes	Yes
Anti-glare Mirror	No	No	No	Yes

Source: Road and Track

differs from that of the Alpha and Gamma in that it provides
vacuum assistance. The Beta does not equip its cars with
either disc brakes or vacuum assistance.

Alpha and Gamma are tied in the field of safety features with
two out of the possible five shown in Table IV. The Beta, although offering three of these features as options, does not provide any of the possible five.

Now that the Federal Government has legislated the basic
safety requirements, such as, seat belts, padded dashboards,
collapsible steering column, and shatter-proof windshields,
the extra safety features of the Delta are even more welcome.

354

8

B.   <u>Acceleration</u> <u>Adds</u> <u>Extra</u> <u>Safety</u> <u>to</u> <u>Delta</u>

A life-saving factor that differs greatly among the four makes
is acceleration. It is important as a safety "on-the-spot"
need--something to have when in a pinch. Especially is it important in low-powered subcompact automobiles. When needed,
acceleration should be available in the safest car. It should
never be depended on by a driver to the extent of his taking
chances because he knows that it is available. But acceleration must be included in any brand comparison.

While Gamma's acceleration time from 0 to 30 miles per
hour is the fastest in the group, the Delta leads in both 0 to
60 mph times and in the 1/4 mile acceleration runs. As
shown in Chart 2, Gamma reached 30 mph .3 seconds sooner

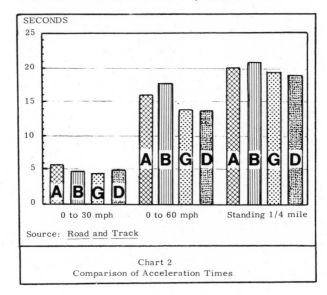

Chart 2
Comparison of Acceleration Times

APPENDIX D–1 (*continued*)

9

than Beta, and .5 and 1.5 seconds sooner than Delta and Alpha, respectively. Delta reached 60 mph .4 seconds sooner than Gamma, which is not a very significant length of time. The Delta, however, achieved this same speed a full 3 seconds faster than Alpha, and 4.5 seconds sooner than Beta.

C.   Weight Distribution Is Best in Alpha and Gamma

Weight distribution affects not only the acceleration of an automobile, but also the effectiveness of its brakes and its handling abilities. The correct proportion of weight on the rear wheels balances the car. In doing so it controls body movements in cornering and braking. The problem is generally caused by the placement of the engine in the front of the automobile. The arrangement of the other essential heavy items at the best places on the chassis results in the best distribution.

As shown in Table V, Alpha and Gamma are tied in this cate-

TABLE V
COMPARATIVE WEIGHT DISTRIBUTIONS,
BRAKING DISTANCES, AND CORNERING ABILITIES

	Alpha	Beta	Gamma	Delta
Distribution, rear, %	47	45	47	43
Braking, 80-0 mph, ft.	330	331	321	390
Brake fade, % increase in pedal effort	30	33	14	43
Control, panic stop	good	fair	excel	fair
Lateral acceleration, in g units	0.680	0.685	0.611	0.614
speed achieved, mph	32.0	32.1	30.2	30.3

Source: Road and Track

gory. Their 47 percent is near the 50 percent automotive experts consider best. In contrast, Delta carries a relatively low proportion (43 percent) of its weight on the rear wheels. This low proportion of weight is not good from the standpoint of traction on slippery roads that seem to be common throughout the Allied sales territory. The Beta is between the two extremes with 45 percent of its weight on its rear wheels.

356

D.   Gamma Has Best Braking Quality

At speeds of 80 miles per hour, Gamma stops in the shortest distance (321 feet); but Alpha (330 feet) and Beta (331 feet) are not
far behind. Delta is well back (390 feet). In tests simulating
panic-stop situations, Gamma's brakes also prove superior to the
others, rank "excellent" by test standards. On the same test
scale, Alpha's brakes rank "good" and Beta's and Delta's brakes
rank "fair." Gamma's brakes also are more resistant to fade
than are the other three. In stops from 80 miles per hour, all
makes exhibit good braking control except Beta. Its stops are
far less consistent than the others.

An overall review of safety features shows Gamma to have a very
slight advantage over the other cars. Its brakes, weight distribution, and stopping distance lead to this conclusion. Alpha is second, scoring high in all categories except acceleration and standard safety features. Delta is third with the best acceleration but
poor braking action. Beta is last, having only scored highly in
cornering ability.

IV.   RIDING COMFORT AND OVERALL CONSTRUCTION

Few things affect the day's work of a traveling salesperson more
than the ride in the car. Thus, the factors of handling ease and
general riding quality should be considered in selecting a car.
Somewhat related to these factors are the overall qualities of construction of the cars in question.

A.   Gamma Ranks First in Handling

The Gamma, with near perfect steering, is overall best handling
car of the group. As shown in Table VI, Gamma exceeds all of
the other makes when values are assigned to each category. Alpha
which is second in this area, is quick and predictable in handling.
During emergency situation tests, however, it jarred and rocked
severely around bumpy corners. Delta, while exhibiting normal
handling characteristics during routine driving, performed misera-
bly when subjected to emergency handling tests. Beta suffered
from being knocked off course by almost any small bump. When
smoother roads were encountered, Beta's handling was judged
somewhat below average.

APPENDIX D–1 (*continued*)

11

	Front Seating	Rear Seating	Ride Light Load	Ride Full Load	Hand-ling	Steering Effort
Excellent						
Good					Gamma	
Fair-to-good	Gamma Alpha Delta	Gamma	Alpha		Delta Alpha	
Fair	Beta		Gamma		Beta	
Fair-to-poor		Delta	Delta	Gamma Delta		
Poor		Alpha Beta	Beta	Beta Alpha		
Low						
Low-to-moderate						Beta Alpha Gamma
Moderate						Delta

TABLE VI
COMPARATIVE COMFORT AND RIDE

Source: Consumers Union of United States, Inc.

B.   Gamma Gives Best Ride

While it is true that Alpha's ride has been judged superior to Gamma's when loaded lightly, Gamma comes out first overall because of the quickly deteriorating ride Alpha exhibits when its load is increased. Gamma's superior ride and directional stability are the best in the group primarily because of its fully independent suspension. A rarity in any front engined car, much less a car in this price field, Gamma's front bucket seats are judged fair-to-good in comfort--relatively high rating in economy car circles. As shown in Table VI, Gamma's rear seating comfort is the best in the group.

C.   Gamma Is Judged Most Durable

The Gamma is assembled with better-than-average care. In fact, Consumer Research engineers have found only 16 minor defects in the car. In addition, the Gamma has a better-than-average record for frequency of repairs.

APPENDIX D–1 (*concluded*)

Delta, second in this category, has only 20 problems. Some
of these problems are judged to be serious, however. For instance, in the tests run the starter refused to disengage after
a few hundred miles had accumulated on the car. The car's
ignition timing, idle mixture, and idle speed were incorrectly
set. An optically distorted windshield and inside mirror were
discovered. In spite of all these defects, the Delta ranks
above Alpha and Beta on durability.

Clearly, Gamma leads in all categories of riding comfort and
overall construction. It handles best. It gives the best ride.
And it has some definite construction advantages over the
other three.

V.   RECOMMENDATION OF GAMMA

Normally, this simulation cannot be merely a count of rank-
ings on the evaluations made, for the qualities carry different
weights. Cost, for example, is the major factor in most such
decisions. In this instance, however, weighting is not necessary for one automobile is the clear leader on all three of the
bases used for evaluation. Thus, it would lead in any arrangement of weights.

From the data presented, Gamma is the best buy when all
costs are considered. The total difference on a purchase of
50 automobiles is a significant $7,557 over the second-place
brand. Gamma has a slight edge when safety features are considered. And it is the superior car in handling ease, ride quality, and construction. These facts point clearly to the recommendation that Allied buy Gammas this year.

APPENDIX D–2.   Illustration of a short report

RECOMMENDATIONS FOR DEPRECIATING DELIVERY TRUCKS

BASED ON AN ANALYSIS OF THREE PLANS

PROPOSED FOR THE BAGGET LAUNDRY COMPANY

Submitted to

Mr. Ralph P. Bagget, President
Bagget Laundry Company
312 Dauphine Street
New Orleans, Louisiana 70102

Prepared by

Charles W. Brewington, C.P.A.
Brewington and Karnes, Certified Public Accountants
743 Beaux Avenue, New Orleans, Louisiana 70118

April 16, 19--

* In the following pages appears a short report written in the direct order (recommendation and summary first). As its introduction reviews the background facts of the problem, most of which are known to the immediate reader, the report apparently is designed for future reference. For reasons of convention in the accounting field, the writing style of the report is somewhat reserved and formal.

APPENDIX D–2 (*continued*)

<u>RECOMMENDATIONS</u> <u>FOR</u> <u>DEPRECIATING</u> <u>DELIVERY</u> <u>TRUCKS</u>

<u>BASED</u> <u>ON</u> <u>AN</u> <u>ANALYSIS</u> <u>OF</u> <u>THREE</u> <u>PLANS</u>

<u>PROPOSED</u> <u>FOR</u> <u>THE</u> <u>BAGGET</u> <u>LAUNDRY</u> <u>COMPANY</u>

I. <u>Recommendations</u> <u>and</u> <u>Summary</u> <u>of</u> <u>Analysis</u>

The Reducing Charge method appears to be the best method to depreciate Bagget Laundry Company delivery trucks. The relative equality of cost allocation for depreciation and maintenance over the useful life of the trucks is the prime advantage under this method. Computation of depreciation charges is relatively simple by the Reducing Charge plan but not quite so simple as computation under the second best method considered.

The second best method considered is the Straight-Line depreciation plan. It is the simplest to compute of the plans considered, and it results in yearly charges equal to those under the Reducing Charge method. The unequal cost allocation resulting from increasing maintenance costs in successive years, however, is a disadvantage that far outweighs the method's ease of computation.

Third among the plans considered is the Service Hours method. This plan is not satisfactory for depreciating delivery trucks primarily because it combines a number of undesirable features. Prime among these is the complexity and cost of computing yearly charges under the plan. Also significant is the likelihood of poor cost allocation under this plan. An additional drawback is the possibility of variations in the estimates of the service life of company trucks.

II. <u>Background</u> <u>of</u> <u>the</u> <u>Problem</u>

<u>Authorization of the Study.</u> This report on depreciation methods for delivery trucks of the Bagget Laundry Company is submitted on April 16, 19-- to Mr. Ralph P. Bagget, President of the Company. Mr. Bagget orally authorized Brewington and Karnes, Certified Public Accountants, to conduct the study on March 15, 19--.

<u>Statement of the Problem.</u> Having decided to establish branch agencies, the Bagget Laundry Company has purchased delivery trucks to transport laundry back and forth from the central cleaning plant in downtown New Orleans. The Company's problem is to select from three alternatives the most advantageous method to depreciate the trucks. The three methods concerned are Reducing Change, Straight-Line, and Service-Hours. The trucks have an original cost of $7,500, a five-year life, and trade-in value of $1,500.

<u>Method of Solving the Problem.</u> In seeking an optimum solution to the Company's problem, we studied Company records and reviewed authoritative literature on the subject. We also applied our best judgment and our experience in analyzing the alternative methods. We based all conclusions on the generally accepted business principles in the field. Clearly, studies such as this involve subjective judgment, and this one is no exception.

APPENDIX D–2 (*continued*)

2

Steps in Analyzing the Problem. In the following analysis, our evaluations of the three depreciation methods appear in the order in which we rank the methods. Since each method involves different factors, direct comparisons by factors is meaningless. Thus our plan is that we evaluate each method in the light of our best judgment.

III. Marked Advantages of the Reducing Charge Method

Sometimes called Sum–of–the–Digits, the Reducing charge method consists of applying a series of decreasing fractions over the life of the property. To determine the fraction, first compute the sum of years of use for the property. This number becomes the de-nominator. Then determine the position number (first, second, etc.) of the year. This number is the numerator. Then apply the resulting fractions to the depreciable values for the life of the property. In the case of the trucks, the depreciable value is $6,000 ($7,500 – $1,5000).

As shown in Table I, this method results in large depreciation costs for the early years and decreasing costs in later years. But since maintenance and repair costs for trucks are higher in the later years, this method provides a relatively stable charge over the life of the property. In actual practice, however, the sums will not be as stable as illustrated for maintenance and repair costs will vary from those used in the computation.

Table I
DEPRECIATION AND MAINTENANCE COSTS FOR DELIVERY TRUCKS OF BAGGET LAUNDRY FOR 19X0-19X4 USING REDUCING CHARGE DEPRECIATION

End of Year	Depreciation		Maintenance	Sum
1	5/15 ($6,000) =	$2,000	$ 100	$ 2,100
2	4/15 ($6,000) =	1,600	500	2,100
3	3/15 ($6,000) =	1,200	900	2,100
4	2/15 ($6,000) =	800	1,300	2,100
5	1/15 ($6,000) =	400	1,700	2,100
	Total	$6,000	$4,500	$10,500

In summary, the Reducing Charge method uses the most desirable combination of factors to depreciate trucks. It equalizes periodic charges, and it is easy to compute. It is our first choice for Bagget Laundry Company.

APPENDIX D–2 (*continued*)

IV. Runner-up Position of Straight-Line Method

The Straight-Line depreciation method is easiest of all to compute. It involves merely taking the depreciable value of the trucks ($6,000) and dividing it by the life of the trucks (5 years). The depreciation in this case is $1,200 for each year.

As shown in Table II, however, the increase in maintenance costs in later years results in much greater periodic charges in later years. The method is not usually recommended in cases such as this.

Table II			
DEPRECIATION AND MAINTENANCE COSTS FOR DELIVERY TRUCKS OF BAGGET LAUNDRY FOR 19X0-19X4 USING STRAIGHT-LINE DEPRECIATION			
End of Year	Depreciation	Maintenance	Sum
1	1/15 ($ 000) = $1,200	$ 100	$ 1,300
2	1/15 ($ 000) = 1,200	500	1,700
3	1/15 ($ 000) = 1,200	800	2,100
4	1/15 ($ 000) = 1,200	1300	2,500
5	1/15 ($ 000) = 1,200	1700	2,900
	Totals $6,000	$4,500	$10,500

In addition, the Straight-Line method generally is best when the properties involved are accumulated over a period of years. When this is done, the total of depreciation and maintenance costs will be about even. But Bagget Company has not purchased its trucks over a period of years. Nor is it likely to do so in the years ahead. Thus, Straight-Line depreciation will not result in equal periodic charges for maintenance and depreciation over the long run.

APPENDIX D–2 (*concluded*)

4

V. Poor Rank of Service-Hours Depreciation

The Service-Hours method of depreciation combines the major disadvantages of the other ways discussed. It is based on the principle that a truck is bought for the direct hours of service that it will give. The estimated number of hours that a delivery truck can be used efficiently according to automotive engineers is one-hundred thousand miles. The depreciable cost ($3000) for each truck is allocated pro rata according to the number of service hours used.

The difficulty and expense of maintaining additional records of service hours is a major disadvantage of this method. The depreciation cost for the delivery trucks under this method will fluctuate widely between first and last years. It is reasonable to assume that as the trucks get older more time will be spent on maintenance. Consequently, the larger depreciation costs will occur in the initial years. As can be seen by Table III, the periodic charges for depreciation and maintenance hover between the two previously discussed methods.

The periodic charge for depreciation and maintenance increases in the later years of ownership. Another difficulty encountered is the possibility of a variance between estimated service hours and the actual service hours. The wide fluctuations possible make it impractical to use this method for depreciating the delivery trucks.

The difficulty of maintaining adequate records and increasing costs in the later years are the major disadvantages of this method. Since it combines the major disadvantages of both the Reducing Charge and Straight-Line methods, it is not satisfactory for depreciating the delivery trucks.

Table III

DEPRECIATION AND MAINTENANCE COSTS FOR
DELIVERY TRUCKS OF BAGGET LAUNDRY FOR 19X6-19X0
USING SERVICE-HOURS DEPRECIATION

End of Year	Estimated Service-Miles	Depreciation	Maintenance	Sum
1	30,000	$1,800	$ 100	$1,900
2	25,000	1,500	500	2,000
3	20,000	1,200	900	2,100
4	15,000	900	1,300	2,200
5	10,000	600	1,700	2,300
	100,000	$6,000	$4,500	$10,500

APPENDIX D–3.   Illustration of a memorandum report

MEMORANDUM   THE **M**URCHISON **C**O. **I**NC.

July 21, 19 –

TO: William T. Chrysler
             Director of Sales

FROM: James C. Colvin, Manager
             Millville Sales District

SUBJECT: Quarterly Report for Millville Sales District

SUMMARY HIGHLIGHTS

After three months of operation I have secured office facilities, hired and developed
three salesmen, and cultivated about half the customers available in the Millville Sales
District. Although the district is not yet showing a profit, at the current rate of development it will do so this month. Prospects for the district are unusually bright.

OFFICE OPERATION

In April I opened the Millville Sales District as authorized by action of the Board of
Directors last February 7th. Initially I set up office in the Three Coins Inn, a motel
on the outskirts of town, and remained there three weeks while looking for permanent
quarters. These I found in the Wingate Building, a downtown office structure. The office
suite selected rents for $340 per month. It has four executive offices, each opening into
a single secretarial office, which is large enough for two secretaries. Although this
arrangement is adequate for the staff now anticipated, additional space is available in
the building if needed.

PERSONNEL

In the first week of operations, I hired an office secretary, Ms. Catherine Kruch.
Ms. Kruch has good experience and has excellent credentials. She has proved to
be very effective. In early April I hired two salespersons-- Mr. Charles E. Clark and
Ms. Alice E. Knapper. Both were experienced in sales, although neither had worked in apparel sales. Three weeks later I hired Mr. Otto Strelski, a proven salesman
who I managed to attract from the Hammond Company. I still am searching for someone for the fourth subdistrict. Currently I am investigating two good prospects and
hope to hire one of them within the next week.

PERFORMANCE

After brief training sessions, which I conducted personally, the sales people were assigned the territories previously marked. And they were instructed to call on the accounts
listed on the sheets supplied by Mr. Henderson's office. During the first month

APPENDIX D–3 (*continued*)

Memorandum   -2-   July 21, 19–

Knapper's sales totaled $17,431 and Clark's reached $13,490, for a total of $30,921. With three sales people working the next month, total sales reached $121,605. Of the total, Knapper accounted for $37,345, Clark $31,690, and Strelski $52,570. Although these monthly totals are below the $145,000 break-even point for the three subdistricts, current progress indicates that we will exceed this volume this month. As we have made contact with only about one half of the prospects in the area, the potential for the district appears to be unusually good.

366

APPENDIX D–4. Illustration of a letter report

International Commmunications Association
3141 Girard Street · Washington, D.C.

January 28, 19--

Board of Directors
International Communications Association

Gentlemen:

Subject: Recommendation of Convention Hotel for the 1978 Meeting

RECOMMENDATION OF THE LAMONT

The Lamont Hotel is my recommendation for the International Communications Association meeting next January. My decision is based on the following summary of the evidence I collected. First, the Lamont has a definite downtown location advantage, and this is important to convention goers and their spouses. Second, accommodations, including meeting rooms are adequate in both places, although the Blackwell's rooms are more modern. Third, Lamont room costs are approximately 20% lower than those at the Blackwell. The Lamont, however, would charge $200 for a room for the assembly meeting. Although both hotels are adequate, because of location and cost advantages the Lamont appears to be the better choice from the members' viewpoint.

ORIGIN AND PLAN OF THE INVESTIGATION

In investigating these two hotels, as was my charge from you at our January 7th meeting, I collected information on what I believed to be the three major factors of consideration in the problem. First is location. Second is adequacy of accommodations. And third is cost. The following findings and evaluations form the basis of my recommendation.

THE LAMONT'S FAVORABLE DOWNTOWN LOCATION

The older of the two hotels, the Lamont is located in the heart of the downtown business district. Thus it is convenient to the area's two major department stores as well as the other downtown shops. The Blackwell, on the other hand, is approximately nine blocks from the major shopping area. Located in the periphery of the business and residential area, it provides little location advantage for those wanting to shop. It does, however, have shops within its walls which provide virtually all of the guest's normal needs. Because many members will bring spouses, however, the downtown location does give the Lamont an advantage.

APPENDIX D–4 (*continued*)

Board of Directors   -2-   January 28, 198-

ADEQUATE ACCOMMODATIONS AT BOTH HOTELS

Both hotels can guarantee the 600 rooms we will require. As the Blackwell is new (since 1977), however, its rooms are more modern and therefore more appealing. The 69-year-old Lamont, however, is well preserved and comfortable. Its rooms are all in good repair, and the equipment is modern.

The Blackwell has 11 small meeting rooms and the Lamont has 13. All are adequate for our purposes. Both hotels can provide the 10 we need. For our general assembly meeting, the Lamont would make available its Capri Ballroom, which can easily seat our membership. It would also serve as the site of our inaugural dinner. The assembly facilities at the Blackwell appear to be somewhat crowded, although the management assures me that it can hold 600. Pillars in the room, however, would make some seats undesirable. In spite of the limitations mentioned, both hotels appear to have adequate facilities for our meeting.

LOWER COSTS AT THE LAMONT

Both the Lamont and the Blackwell would provide nine rooms for meetings on a complimentary basis. Both would provide complimentary suites for our president and our secretary. The Lamont, however, would charge $200 for use of the room for the assembly meeting. The Blackwell would provide this room without charge.

Convention rates at the Lamont are $13–$15 for singles, $15–$19 for double-bedded rooms, and $16–$20 for twin-bedded rooms. Comparable rates at the Blackwell are $15–$18, $18–$23, and $19–$25. Thus the savings at the Lamont would be approximately 20% per member.

Cost of the dinner selected would be $9.00 per person, including gratuities, at the Lamont. The Blackwell would meet this price if we would guarantee 600 plates. Otherwise, they would charge $10. Considering all of these figures, the total cost picture at the Lamont is the more favorable one.

Respectfully,

Willard K Mitchell

Willard K. Mitchell
Executive Secretary

APPENDIX D–5. Illustration of a long-form audit report

To: William A. Karnes   Date: May 3, 19--

From: Auditing Department

Subject: Annual Audit, Spring Street Branch

Introduction

Following is the report on the annual audit of the Spring Street branch. Reflecting conditions existing at the close of business May 1, 19--, this review covers all accounts other than Loans and Discounts. Specifically, these accounts were proofed:

Accounts Receivable	Savings
Cash Collateral	Suspense
Cash in Office	Series "E" Bonds
Collections	Tax Withheld
Christmas Club	Travelers Checks
Deferred Charges	

Condition of Accounts

All listing totals agreed with General Ledger and/or Branch Controls except for these:

Cash in Office	$1.17 short
Tax Withheld	.21 short
Travelers Checks	.97 short

Exceptions Noted

During the course of the examination the following exceptions were found:

Analysis. The branch had 163 unprofitable accounts at the time of the audit. Losses on these accounts, as revealed by inspection of the Depositors Analysis Cards, ranged from $7.31 to $176.36 for the year. The average loss per account was $17.21.

Proper deductions of service charges were not made in 73 instances in which the accounts dropped below the minimum.

Bookkeeping. From a review of the regular checking accounts names were recorded of customers who habitually write checks without sufficient covering funds. A list of 39 of the worst offenders was submitted to Mr. Clement Ferguson.

APPENDIX D–5 (*continued*)

A check of deposit tickets to the third and fourth regular checking ledgers revealed six accounts on which transit delays recorded on the deposit tickets were not correctly transferred to the ledger sheets.

During the preceding month on 17 different accounts the bookkeepers paid items against uncollected funds without getting proper approval.

Statements. Five statements were held by the branch in excess of three months:

Account	Statement Dates
Curtis A. Hogan	Sept. through April
Carlton I. Breeding	Dec. through April
Alice Crezan	Nov. through April
Jarvis H. Hudson	Jan. through April
W.T. Petersen	Dec. through April

Paying and Receiving. During the week of April 21–27, tellers failed to itemize currency denominations on large (over $100) cash deposits 23 times. Deposits were figured in error 32 times.

Savings. Contrary to instructions given after the last audit, the control clerk has not maintained a record of errors made in savings passbooks.

The savings tellers have easy access to the inactive ledger cards and may record transactions on the cards while alone. When this condition was noted in the last report, the recommendation was made to set up a system of dual controls. This recommendation has not been followed.

Safe Deposit Rentals. Rentals on 165 safe deposit boxes were in arrears. Although it was pointed out in the last report, this condition has grown worse during the past year. Numbers of boxes by years in arrears are as follows:

2 to 3 years	87
3 to 4 years	32
4 to 5 years	29
over 5 years	17
Total	165

Stop payments. Signed stop payment orders were not received on three checks on which payment was stopped:

Account	Amount	Date of Stop Payment
Whelon Electric Company	$317.45	Feb. 7, 19–
George A. Bullock	37.50	April 1, 19–
Amos H. Kritzel	737.60	Dec. 3, 19–

APPENDIX D–5 (*concluded*)

Over and Short Account. A $23.72 difference between Tellers and Rack Department was recorded for April 22. On May 1 this difference remained uncorrected.

William P. Bunting
Head, Auditing Department

Copies to:

W. F. Robertson
Cecil Ruston
W. W. Merrett

APPENDIX D–6.   Illustration of a technical memorandum report

MEMORANDUM

the **CROWELL COMPANY,** inc.

To: Charles E. Groom   June 3, 197X

From: Edmund S. Posner

Subject: Graff Lining Company's use of Kynar pipe lining

Following is the report you requested January 9 on the Graff
Lining Company's process of using Kynar for lining pipe. My
comments are based on my inspection of the facilities at the
Graff plant and my conversations with their engineers.

Dimension limitations

Graff's ability to line the smaller pipe sizes appears to be
limited. To date, the smallest diameter pipe they have lined
in 10-foot spool lengths is 2 inches. They believe they can
handle 1½-inch pipe in 10-foot spools, but they have not
attempted this size. They question their ability to handle
smaller pipe in 10-foot lengths.

This limitation, however, does not apply to fittings. They can
line 1½-inch and 1-inch fittings easily. Although they can
handle smaller sizes than these, they prefer to limit minimum
nipple size to 1 inch by 4 inches long.

Maximum spool dimensions for the coating process are best
explained by illustration:

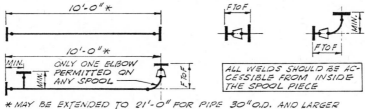

APPENDIX D–6 (*continued*)

Graff corrects defects found. If the defect is small, they correct by retouching with sprayer or brush. If the defect is major, they remove all the coating by turning and reline the pipe.

<u>Recommendations for piping</u>

Should we be interested in using their services, Graff engineers made the following recommendations. First, they recommend that we use forged steel fittings rather than cast fittings. Cast fittings, they point out, have excessive porosity. They noted, though, that cast fittings can be used and are less expensive. For large jobs, this factor could be significant.

Second, they suggest that we make all small connections, such as those required for instruments, in a prescribed manner. This manner is best described by diagram:

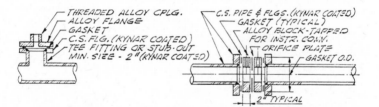

Graff engineers emphasized this point further by illustrating a common form of small connections that will not work. Such connections are most difficult to coat. Pinhole breaks are likely to occur on them, and a pinhole break can cause the entire coating to disbond. A typical unacceptable connection is the following:

APPENDIX D–6 (*continued*)

<u>Preparation of pipe for lining</u>

Graff requires that all pipe to be lined be ready for the coating
process. Specifically, they require that all welds be ground
smooth (to avoid pitting and assure penetration). Because welds
are inaccessible in small pipe, they require forged tees in all
piping smaller than 4 inches. In addition, they require that all
attachments to the pipe (clips, base ells, etc.) be welded to the
pipe prior to coating.

<u>The lining procedure</u>

The procedure Graff uses in lining the pipe begins with cleaning
the pipe and inspecting it for cracked fittings, bad welds, etc.
When necessary, they do minor retouching and grinding of welds.
Then they apply the Kynar in three forms: primer, building,
sealer. They apply the building coat in as many layers as is
necessary to obtain a finished thickness of 25 mils. They oven
bake each coat at a temperature and for a time determined by the
phase of the coating and the piping material.

<u>Inspection technique</u>

Following the coating, Graff inspectors use a spark testing
method to detect possible pin holes or other defects. This
method is best explained by illustration:

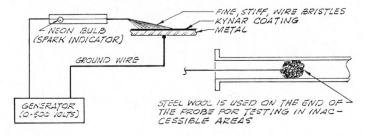

APPENDIX D–6 (*concluded*)

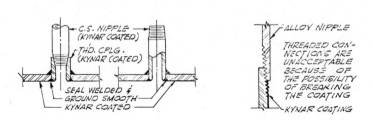

A third recommendation is that we establish handling procedures
to protect the coated pipe. As the Kynar coating will chip,
we would need to make certain that we protect all flange spaces.
Also, we would need to be careful in shipping, handling, storing,
and erecting the pipe.

Corrections for the diagnostic test

Following are the corrected sentences for the diagnostic test at the end of Chapter 16. The corrections are underscored, and the symbols for the standards explaining the correction follow the sentences.

1. An important fact about this typewriter is, that it has the patented "feather touch".
   An important fact about this typewriter is that it has the patented "feather touch." *Cma 6.1, OM 3*

2. Goods received on Invoice 2741 are as follows; three dozen white shirts, size 15–33, four mens felt hats, brown, size 7, and five dozen assorted ties.
   Goods received on Invoice 2741 are as follows: three dozen white shirts, size 15–33; four men's felt hats, brown, size 7; and five dozen assorted ties. *Cln 1, Apos 1, SC 3*

3. James Silver__president of the new union__started the campaign for the retirement fund.
   James Silver, president of the new union, started the campaign for the retirement fund. *Cma 4.2*

4. We do not expect to act on this matter__however__until we hear from you.
   We do not expect to act on this matter, however, until we hear from you. *Cma 4.3*

5. Shipments through September 20, 1976__totaled 69,485 pounds__an increase of 17 percent over the year__ago total.
   Shipments through September 20, 1976, totaled 69,485 pounds, an increase of 17 percent over the year-ago total. *Cma 4.4, Cma 4.1, Hpn 2*

6. Brick is recommended as the building material__but the board is giving serious consideration to a substitute.
   Brick is recommended as the building material, but the board is giving serious consideration to a substitute. *Cma 1*

7. Markdowns for the sale total $34,000, never before has the company done anything like this.

Markdowns for the sale total $34,000; never before has the company done anything like this. *SC 1*

8. After long experimentation a wear__resistant__run__proof__and beautiful stocking has been perfected.
   After long experimentation a wear-resistant, run-proof, and beautiful stocking has been perfected. *Hpn 2, Cma 2.2*

9. Available in white__green__and blue__ this paint is sold by dealers all over the country.
   Available in white, green, and blue, this paint is sold by dealers all over the country. *Cma 2.1, Cma 3*

10. George Steele__who won the trip__is our most energetic salesperson.
    George Steele, who won the trip, is our most energetic salesperson. *Cma 3*

11. Good__ he replied__sales are sure to increase.
    "Good," he replied. "Sales are sure to increase." *QM 1*

12. Hogan's article__Retirement? Never!, printed in the current issue of Management Review, is really a part of his book A Report on Worker Security.
    Hogan's article, "Retirement? Never!," printed in the current issue of *Management Review,* is really a part of his book, *A Report on Worker Security. Cma 4.2, QM 4, Ital 1*

13. Formal announcement of our pre__Easter sale will be made in 32 days.
    Formal announcement of our pre-Easter sale will be made in 32 days. *No 1*

14. Each day we encounter new problems.__Although they are solved easily.
    Each day we encounter new problems, although they are solved easily. *Cma 5.1, Frag*

15. A list of models, sizes, and prices of both competing lines are being sent you.
    A list of models, sizes, and prices of both competing lines is being sent you. *Agmt SV*

16. The manager could not tolerate any employee's failing to do their best.
    The manager could not tolerate any employee's failing to do his best. *Pn 2*

17. A series of tests were completed only yesterday.
    A series of tests was completed only yesterday. *Agmt SV*

18. There should be no misunderstanding between you and I.
    There should be no misunderstanding between you and me. *Pn 3*

19. He run the accounting department for five years.
    He ran the accounting department for five years. *Tns 2*

20. The report is considerable long.
    The report is considerably long. *AA*

21. Who did you interview for the position?
    Whom did you interview for the position? *Pn 3*

22. The report concluded that the natural resources of the Southwest was ideal for the chemical industry.
    The report concluded that the natural resources of the Southwest are ideal for the chemical industry. *Agmt SV, Tns 1*

23. This applicant is six feet in height,__twenty-eight years old, weighs 165 pounds, and has had eight years' experience.

This applicant is six feet in height, is twenty-eight years old, weighs 165 pounds, and has had eight years' experience. *Prl*

24. While__reading the report, a gust of wind came through the window blowing papers all over the room.

    While she was reading the report, a gust of wind came through the window blowing papers all over the room. *Dng*

25. The sprinkler system has been checked on July 1 and September 3.

    The sprinkler system was checked on July 1 and September 3. *Tns 3*

Appendix F

The gunning fog index

Products of the readability studies discussed in Chapter 2 are formulas for measuring readability. Perhaps the easiest to use and the most popular is the Gunning Fog Index.

Steps in applying the index

The ease with which the Gunning Fog Index is used is obvious from a review of the simple steps listed below. Its ease of interpretation is also obvious in that the index computed from these simple steps is in grade level of education. For example, an index of seven means that the material tested is easy reading for one at the seventh-grade level. An index of 12 indicates high school graduate level of readability. And an index of 16 indicates the level of the college graduate.

The simple steps for computing the index are as follows.

1. *Select a sample.* For long pieces of writing use at least 100 words. As in all sampling procedure, the larger the sample, the more reliable the results will be. So, in measuring readability for a long manuscript one would be wise to select a number of samples at random throughout the work.
2. *Determine the average number of words per sentence.* First count words and sentences in a sample selected. Then divide the total number of words by the total of sentences.
3. *Determine the percentage of hard words in the sample.* Words of three syllables or longer are considered to be hard words. But do not count as hard words (1) words that are capitalized, (2) combinations of short, easy words (*grasshopper, businessperson, bookkeeper*), or (3) verb forms made into three-syllable words by adding *ed* or *es* (*repeated, caresses*).

4. *Add the two factors computed above and multiply by 0.4*. The product is the minimum grade level at which the writing is easily read.

Application of the Gunning Fog Index is illustrated with the following paragraph.

In *general, construction* of *pictograms* follows the *general procedure* used in *constructing* bar charts. But two special rules should be followed. First, all of the picture units used must be of equal size. The *comparisons* must be made wholly on the basis of the number of *illustrations* used and never by *varying* the *areas* of the *individual* pictures used. The reason for this rule is *obvious*. The human eye is grossly *inadequate* in *comparing areas* of *geometric* designs. Second, the pictures or symbols used must *appropriately* depict the *quantity* to be *illustrated*. A *comparison* of the navies of the world, for *example,* might make use of *miniature* ship drawings. Cotton *production* might be shown by bales of cotton. *Obviously* the drawings used must be *immediately interpreted* by the reader.

Inspection of the paragraph reveals these facts. It has 10 sentences and 129 words for an average sentence length of 13. Of the total of 129 words, 26 are considered to be hard words. Thus, the percentage of hard words is 20. From these data, the Gunning Fog Index is computed as follows.

Average sentence length	13
Percentage of hard words	20
Total	33
Multiply by	0.4
Grade level of readership	13.2

Critical appraisal of the formulas

Readability formulas are widely used in business today. Perhaps the reason for their popularity is the glitter of their apparent mathematical exactness. Or perhaps they are popular because they reduce to simple and workable formulas the most complex work of writing. Whatever the reason, the wise writer will look at the formulas objectively.

Unquestionably these formulas have been a boon to improving clarity in business writing. They emphasize the main causes of failure in written communication. And they provide a convenient check and measure of the level of one's writing. But they also have some limitations.

The most serious limitation of the formulas is the primer style of writing that can result from a slavish use of them. Overly simple words and a monotonous succession of short sentences make dull reading. Dull reading doesn't hold the reader's attention. And without the reader's attention, there can be little communication.

Perhaps the formulas are most useful to the unskilled writers. By intelligent use of the formulas, they may at least be able to improve the communication quality of their work. Their writing styles, which were poor to begin with, do not suffer. Skilled writers, on the other hand, can violate the formulas and still communicate.

Charles Dickens, for example, was a master in communicating in clear yet long sentences. So was Pope. And so are some business writers. Because most business writers fall somewhere between these extremes of writing ability, the wisest course for them is to use the formulas as general guides. But never will a formula replace the clear and logical thinking that is the underpinning of all clear writing.

Index

This book has been set linotype, in 10 and 9 point Times Roman, leaded 2 points. Chapter numbers are 48 point Torino and chapter titles are 36 point Torino. The size of the type page is 29 by 47 picas.